Praise for *Behind the Bears E...*

"R. E. Burrillo is an archaeolog[...] archaeologist—not stuffy and te[...] enquiring. His deeply personal [...] sand-year arc of human occupatio[...] [...], contentious place we call Bears Ears. Drawing from his explorations and field-work of the region's plateaus and canyons, where past and present coexist, Burrillo's love and hope for Bears Ears binds these pages with honest glue."

—GREG CHILD, author of *Over the Edge*

"The desert archaeology of R. E. Burillo is alchemical. He con-jures empathy for ethnography, transforms soil strata into living stories. It's the trick of poets and magicians, the way the man vanishes colonialist, arms-length fetishizing and categorizing of ancient artifacts. Fierce yet playful, admonishing and ambitious, *Behind the Bears Ears* is as vast and consuming as the landscape itself, a read in which white America learns what it has failed to grasp by both excavation and exploration. Come to it now, on bended knees with eyes wide open to this nation's erasure of all things Indigenous."

—AMY IRVINE, author of *Air Mail* and *Desert Cabal*

"An engagingly personal, well-informed, wide-ranging account of Bears Ears and its archaeology, its ongoing importance to Native peoples, and its future."

—STEPHEN H. LEKSON, author of *A Study of Southwestern Archaeology*

"*Behind the Bears Ears* conveys a deep respect for the place and the people who have lived closest to it. A fine primer for newcom-ers to the region and an entertaining refresher course for those already embedded in the landscape."

—SCOTT THYBONY, author of *The Disappearances*

BEHIND THE BEARS EARS

BEHIND THE BEARS EARS

Exploring the Cultural and Natural Histories of a
Sacred Landscape

by R. E. Burrillo

TORREY HOUSE PRESS

Salt Lake City • Torrey

First Torrey House Press Edition, October 2020
Copyright © 2020 by R. E. Burrillo

Published by Torrey House Press
Salt Lake City, Utah
www.torreyhouse.org

International Standard Book Number: 978-1-948814-30-0
E-book ISBN: 978-1-948814-31-7
Library of Congress Control Number: 2019955067

Cover art by Jonathan Bailey
Cover design by Kathleen Metcalf
Interior design by Gray Buck-Cockayne
Distributed to the trade by Consortium Book Sales and Distribution

Torrey House Press offices in Salt Lake City sit on the homelands of Ute, Goshute, Shoshone, and Paiute nations. Offices in Torrey are in homelands of Paiute, Ute, and Navajo nations.

Acknowledgments

The author thanks Dr. Bill Lipe, for carefully reviewing the entire manuscript and offering tons of invaluable edits; Drs. Steve Lekson and Marc Toso, for also reviewing the entire manuscript and offering their own suggestions and impressions; and Donna "Rex" Baker for additional edits and suggestions. Lyle Balenquah, Eric Descheenie, Alastair Bitsói, Ajani Yepa, Honor Keeler, and Angelo Baca provided an immensity of Indigenous perspectives, insights, quotes, and media sensitivity training. Thanks are also due to Tim Peterson and Dr. John Ruple for providing information and guidance about the recent history of the conservation struggle; Rosemary Sucec, for her ethnographic input and review; Dr. Kevin Jones, for his help with the book and for everything else that he does; and Dr. Thomas King, for providing useful guidance and edits vis-à-vis the cultural resource regulations and practices referenced throughout the book. Jonathan Bailey provided the cover, and was especially helpful in crafting Chapter One. David Roberts and Morgan Sjogren were immensely helpful in crafting Chapters Eleven and Twelve. Thanks also to Aaron, Connie, Greg, Ben, Josh, Amanda and Zak, and Eran for enough shared adventure and wisdom to keep me thoroughly lost for centuries; and to Molly, Chelsea, Shayne, Ryno, Mark and Virginia, Emily, Sasha, and one or two other Flagstaff freaks for keeping the home fires burning.

Timeline (Pecos Sequence)

PERIOD YEARS BEFORE PRESENT (BP) OR BC/AD	GENERAL DIAGNOSTIC FEATURES AND ARTIFACTS
Paleoindian > 13,000-10,000 BP	Exact timing and method of arrival still hotly debated. Small groups of people foraged over very large territories, large (now extinct) mammals were hunted. Clovis is the oldest identifiable formal material culture, followed by Folsom.
Archaic 10,000-2,000 BP	Subsistence lifestyle based on wild foods. High mobility, especially during the middle portion, with generally low population density. Diet breadth increased over time.
Basketmaker II 1500 BC-AD 500	Includes what some researchers call the Early Agricultural period (2000–500 BC), semi-sedentary habitation in shallow pit houses, no pottery, maize and squash. Cedar Mesa appears to have been the focal point of settlement in southeast Utah during this period.
Basketmaker III AD 500-750	Habitation in deeper pit houses and first appearance of communal architecture. Beans are added to farming. Appearance of bow-and-arrow and first formal pottery. Turkeys are raised for companionship and to make feather blankets.
Pueblo I AD 750-900	Large villages and kivas appear, deep pit houses still in use, red ware ceramics produced in Bears Ears become incredibly popular throughout the region. Settlements shift toward high uplands and the Bluff area, with most of Cedar Mesa depopulated.
Pueblo II AD 900-1150	Most of southeast Utah depopulated, followed by rapid growth and expansion of vast social system centered on Chaco Canyon. Great houses and Chacoan roads appear throughout the region. Corrugated and elaborate black-on-white

(cont.) ceramics proliferate, while red ware production in Bears Ears comes to a halt.

Pueblo III

AD 1150-1300

Post-Chaco diaspora, large pueblos and towers appear near canyon heads and water sources, and people begin living in cliff dwellings. Turkeys are still raised, but now they've become a food item. Curious influx of people from Kayenta region.

Pueblo IV

AD 1300-1500

Colorado Plateau depopulated by Ancestral Pueblo groups by about AD 1290, with most people moving into large plaza-oriented pueblos in the Rio Grande region and the Hopi mesas. Although full-time occupation had halted, archaeology and oral histories both suggest that Pueblo people never stopped visiting and utilizing southeast Utah. Earliest Ute, Paiute, and Diné archaeology dates to this general time period or a little after.

Protohistoric

AD 1500-1850

Spanish arrival, warfare, and influence on Indigenous communities throughout the Southwest. The Pueblo Revolt of 1680 exerts further changes on local communities, especially Pueblo and Diné. Euro-American colonization began after 1848.

Historic

AD 1850-1960s

Mormon settlers arrived in Moab by about 1850, and the present-day town of Bluff by 1880. Mormon and Gentile cowboys jostled with Indigenous residents and each other in sometimes colorful, sometimes brutal ways that still influence cultures in the area. Looting of antiquities became a lucrative local practice following a stock market crash in the late 1800s, and then surged again starting in the 1960s. A uranium boom developed after WWII, and its effects are also still felt in local communities. Tourism started picking up right about the end of this period, and—for better or for worse—has been increasing ever since.

BEARS EARS
NATIONAL MONUMENT

2017 Boundary

2016 Boundary

2015 Boundary

10 miles

Map created by

Vanessa Holz / Designer
vhdesign.graphics

Zach Scribner
GIS Analyst/Archaeologist
streamlinemaps.com

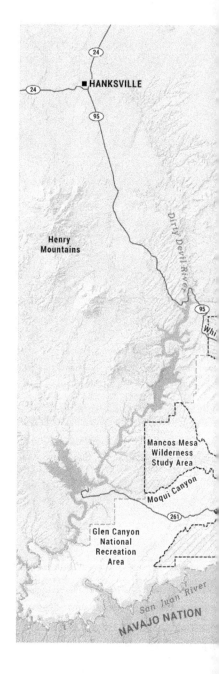

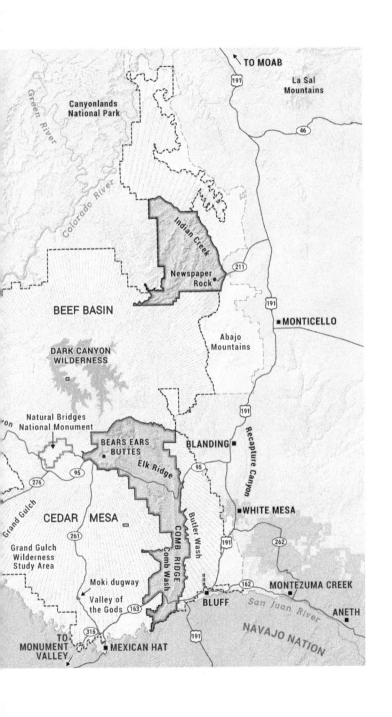

TO MOAB

191

La Sal
Mountains

46

Green River

Canyonlands
National Park

Colorado River

Indian Creek

211

Newspaper
Rock

191

BEEF BASIN

MONTICELLO

Abajo
Mountains

DARK CANYON
WILDERNESS

191

Natural Bridges
National Monument

on

BEARS EARS
BUTTES

BLANDING

Recapture Canyon

Elk Ridge

95

95

276

Grand Gulch

CEDAR MESA

261

WHITE MESA

262

Butler Wash

COMB RIDGE

Grand Gulch
Wilderness
Study Area

191

Moki dugway

Comb Wash

162

MONTEZUMA CREEK

Valley of
the Gods

163

BLUFF

San Juan River

ANETH

NAVAJO NATION

TO
MONUMENT
VALLEY

316

MEXICAN HAT

191

Contents

Foreword   1

Introduction   3

Chapter One: The Mammoth-Killers   13

Chapter Two: The Foragers   35

Chapter Three: The First Farmers   61

Chapter Four: The Bean Farmers   85

Chapter Five: The First Villagers   111

Chapter Six: The Chaco World   131

Chapter Seven: The Cliff Dwellers   167

Chapter Eight: The New Foragers   191

Chapter Nine: The Conquerors   221

Chapter Ten: The Wranglers   247

Chapter Eleven: The Pillagers   307

Chapter Twelve: The Builders   351

Afterword   393

Selected References and
Recommended Reading   399

Foreword: A Healing Movement

Sing your song, write your stories, and paint your pictures of this place we know as home: Bears Ears. Home to the ancestors, plants, animals, elements, and newcomers. As a young girl, I would travel with my family to the small community of White Mesa for community gatherings. White Mesa, Utah, is a part of the Ute Mountain Ute Tribal Reservation. I greet the elders as "my grandparents." Our Mother Earth and father the Creator—we acknowledge their presences with gratitude. In 2015 the southeastern region in Utah grabbed the world's attention and united the Native people who live in and historically occupied the area. Voices from the past speak to each of us with urgency. The flowers, sage, and great cedar trees move in a way that reminds us of our ancestors and their movement. How do we know they were here and alive? The ancient pueblo structures and canyon walls tell the stories of days gone by.

To protect this shared home, a group of Indigenous people came together to be the voice for the land, elements, animals, ancient structures, and cultural ways of life. Five Native nations—Navajo, Ute Mountain Ute, Hopi, Pueblo of Zuni, and Ute Indian Tribe of Utah—became the Bears Ears Inter-Tribal Coalition. My grandparents told me we get nowhere in life alone. Healing became the vehicle to travel the path toward permanent protection and access to the land. Healing relationships between the tribes led to the realization that allies would be necessary—archaeologists, conservation leaders, and recreation visitors who come to love this place, too. As we learned from one another we also understood it didn't matter how and when you and your family arrived, we need each other. Healing relationships from a personal place allowed for the healing to radiate outward, drawing strength, clarity, and understanding from within the circle of life. We all breathe the same air and share space; it is time to inspire each to share their truth.

With courage we ride the lightning bolt to deliver the message: we are standing together. Together, beyond tribal differences, contemporary or historical, ethnicity and religion, we will stand together. As unique as each Indigenous group in this world, our stories weave the beautiful diversity of our space, our region, our Bears Ears.

I became a voice on behalf of my Ute Mountain Ute people, not realizing I would become a leader for the greater campaign for Bears Ears National Monument. Serving as the only woman in the Coalition, my role was an integral piece of the entire movement. My heart shined through as a daughter, mother, and grandmother, as my mother and grandmothers prepared me. With the grace of respect, words, and actions, we showed the world that an exchange of negativity was not the solution. Peaceful actions proved to be the strength of the core healing spirit of the movement.

As citizens of our tribes, counties, states, and nation, we are the public. All our voices are necessary in the process of decision-making. Together we shall sing our songs, paint our pictures, and share our truths. Together we stand with Bears Ears. We stand in sacred places where our grandparents and ancestors once stood, inviting allies to protect and love this beauty, too. The wind blows through the trees singing of the generations of yesterday, the sun warms Mother Earth today. Braiding the knowledge of our ancestors, scientific data, and the process of democracy inspires our continued efforts to protect sacred, open spaces that we share. Our Mother Earth is me, as I am her.

Regina Lopez-Whiteskunk

Introduction

I n January of 2017, just days after Bears Ears National Monument was proclaimed in southeast Utah, I had the immense privilege of being invited to an event celebrating its establishment at Monument Valley in the Navajo Nation.

I was living in Cortez, Colorado, at the time—just about halfway between my two on-again, off-again homes of Flagstaff, Arizona, and Salt Lake City, Utah—and had to make the long, cold drive by myself. My route took me around Canyons of the Ancients National Monument, a Bill Clinton creation from 2000 that was proclaimed in order to protect 175,100 acres of the San Juan region—the vast drainage basin of the San Juan River, centered on the Four Corners, of which Bears Ears is the westernmost natural and cultural province.

It had snowed recently. The final stretch through the northernmost portion of the Navajo Nation was thickly blanketed in white, and my vehicle pirouetted less than gracefully during the dozen or so times that I lost control of it. I wondered how many people were willing to make this perilous journey just to celebrate the recent proclamation of a national monument when they could easily wait until the snow melted and go see the place itself. The answer, when I finally arrived, turned out to be hundreds.

I carried a notebook with me. I often do. The notes I took at the celebration were added to an assemblage of scribblings comprising about thirteen years of thoughts, observations, experiences, and archaeological research focused on southeast Utah.

My first encounter with what would become Bears Ears National Monument was in 2006. I was not yet an archaeologist—merely an aficionado of the old and interesting. I spent a week in November backpacking through the upper third of Grand Gulch, the great defile that cuts through the impressive land mass of Cedar Mesa beneath the gaze of the Bears Ears formations. Much of my time was spent marveling over how scarcely visited such a wondrous and heavenly place could be. In the four days I spent down in the Gulch and three additional days spent atop Cedar Mesa, I saw exactly three other people, including a fellow backpacker to whom I gave a ride between trailheads so he could complete a loop. We hardly said a word to each other.

That was then. Things have changed quite a bit. By the time I got involved in research and conservation efforts in the Bears Ears area, I was paying off a rather sizable karmic debt that I felt I owed the place. And it isn't "scarcely visited," anymore.

Early archaeologists like Alfred "A. V." Kidder—that tendency of going by the first two initials in publication is a venerated one among archaeologists—regarded the entire San Juan region as a single "culture area." The archaeologically recognized Bears Ears Culture Area, or simply the Bears Ears area, is the westernmost portion of the northern hemisphere of the San Juan world, sometimes also known as the Mesa Verde region.

That's important. As archaeology has progressed upward from consideration solely of artifacts, to consideration of sites, to consideration of communities, to consideration of culture areas, and finally to consideration of landscapes and regions,* archaeologists have come to appreciate that no accurate portrayal of human sociocultural *anything* can be fully understood at less than a regional scale. To understand the history and cultures of

---

* At the same time, scientific methods have spiraled ever downward in scale from jars and mummies, to tree rings and pollen, to phytoliths and other microscopic crystalline things, to trace elements, to atomic isotopes.

the Bears Ears area, especially during the ancient and slightly more recent precontact time periods, it has to be seen in the context of the San Juan region as a whole.

This is a running theme in the developing world of American archaeology, and a major subtheme of this book is the role that Bears Ears has played—and continues to play—in the story of that development.

The other two subthemes are the cultural history of the place itself and the story of my own unlikely involvement there, which interdigitate and converge in a number of intriguing ways. It makes for long chapters, as these three subthemes and the narrative arcs they describe are explored in a gradually tightening weave, but there's a reason. My hope is that telling the human story of the place in such a way will lead the reader into a deeper understanding of why it is so important to so many people.

Despite its foundation and reliance on research of a decidedly technical nature, the format and style of this book are more like mainstream wilderness writing than niche academic composition. This, too, is a stylistic departure—or so it might appear. Whether writing for a general audience or for the academy, archaeologists all too often comprise their work of dry, technical authorship dripping with citations and stuffed with incomprehensible jargon that acts as a gauntlet against intruders.

Meanwhile, here is Frederick H. Chapin—early American polymath with a penchant for business, mountaineering, photography, and what passed for archaeology in his days—writing about the archaeology of the San Juan region in his book *The Land of the Cliff-Dwellers* back in 1892:

> The light of noonday floods the walls of the ramparts, and penetrates into the deep recesses of the cave; but, as the sun sinks westward, a dark shadow creeps across the front of the cavern, and the interior is in deep gloom. It is then that the explorer, standing among the crumbled walls and gazing up

at the loop-holes above, or following with his eye the course of the cañon down to its end where it joins the greater gorge, wonders what events happened to cause this strong fortress to be deserted or overthrown.

Effective public scholarship includes generous scoops of both the entertaining and the humanistic. The only thing that appears to be in short supply in the sciences these days is public scholarship itself.

That's especially problematic for archaeology. To my knowledge, no other science has to contend in the public realm with monsters as formidable as *Indiana Jones*, *Ancient Aliens*, and religious and ideological "interpretations" that span the gamut from annoyingly appropriative to awesomely racist. Compound that with the equally terrifying threat of inadvertently hastening the destruction of archaeological sites by romanticizing and advertising them, and we've got quite a challenge on our hands.

Southeastern Utah practically overflows with archaeological relics, including "photogenic" ones like cliff dwellings. I first read about Cedar Mesa, heartland and crown jewel of the Bears Ears area in terms of archaeology, in David Roberts' *In Search of the Old Ones* while working as a seasonal restaurant manager at the North Rim of the Grand Canyon. As they did (and still do) with Edward Abbey and the book he wrote about Arches, a lot of people have criticized Roberts for writing a little too lovingly about the place he loved so much—thereby exacerbating the subsequent tourist crush. Evidently, what they both should have written was: *This place sucks, just a bunch of rocks, too many goddamn cedar gnats, go to Disney World instead!* Maybe some places are just too wonderful to write about...?

Maybe. Although, I don't see throngs of tourists stampeding all over Jack London's Yukon trying to make friends with wolves. Nor have the copious and impassioned writings of Jacques Cousteau inspired vast hordes of poor swimmers to drown trying to follow in his flipper wake.

But inspiration can't be entirely discounted, either. I first learned about Grand Gulch from a book, after all—and then got even more excited about the place when I read Ann Zwinger wax sweetly about it in her own book *Wind in the Rock*. According to a handful of sources, *A Walk in the Woods* and *Wild* brought unprecedented numbers to the Appalachian and Pacific Crest Trails, respectively. Not surprisingly, about half of those sources included cheers and much rejoicing over how the United States still has so much wilderness for people to enjoy, while the other half included foaming snarls and teeth-gnashing over the grim specter of overcrowding.

I can see both arguments. On the one hand, the great undeveloped outdoors in North America is—and, hopefully, shall remain—so vast and copious that the notion of its ever getting too dense with visitors borders on derangement. On the other hand, overcrowding is a *big* problem in bottleneck areas where people tend to throng like storybook lemmings after they've been pointed out. You can walk the entirety of the Grand Canyon's inner gorge without seeing much more than a handful of other people, for example, but you can't walk fifty yards from the gift shop to the South Rim without seeing much fewer than a gazillion of them.

Unfortunately, there's not a whole lot that anyone can do about that. Amazing places invariably attract visitors, and most of them share their experiences with others through one means or another, and so it goes whether we laud or lament. This is especially true in what was supposed to be the Space Age but has, in fact, turned out to be the Information Age. A time in which secrets aren't really an option, anymore—at least not when those secrets are, in a very real sense, just sitting there waiting for the next person to find them.

The death of place comes for everywhere, eventually. You can whine about it, or you can take steps to mitigate its impacts, but the one thing you can't do is stop it.

Moreover, the archaeological splendors of the Bears Ears area have attracted a lot more than just tourists. They attracted some of the earliest of what are very generously called "archaeologists" back in the late 1800s, followed by a lot of what are more matter-of-factly called "looters." The varied natural splendors of the area have also attracted uranium speculators, oil and gas developers, herders of both cattle and sheep, miners, loggers, and—for one brief but lively moment in the late 1990s—armed revolutionary wackos.

Long before all that, however, the Bears Ears area attracted people for different reasons. Very different reasons, from one era to the next, although whatever that attracting power was, it never wavered. Still hasn't.

That attractive element both underscores and precipitates what I consider the most intriguing aspect of the place: a borderlands phenomenon, so beautifully expressed there. At almost every given instance in its spectacular prehistory, history, and modernity, the Bears Ears area is the interdigitating limit where different peoples meet, articulate, and assume entirely new and novel sociocultural expressions within what is operatively a cultural crucible that never cools.

Let me say a few more words about prehistory.

Like most modern, progressive types in the field of anthropology (archaeology being a subfield of anthropology in the US), I dislike the term because that prefix *pre-* implies that the people in question have no real history. Which is patently ridiculous, since literally everything is a result of the history that came before it.

The term is arguably racist to boot, depending upon who's using it in reference to whom. In professional usage, it refers to the time period before *written* history, which in North America means all the stuff that happened before Europeans arrived with parchment and quill. But there's a caveat to even that simple explanation: the Spanish and Spanish-speaking Mexicans aren't often included in it, despite their often-copious written accounts, so in the American Southwest "history" officially begins after the end of the Mexican-American War in about 1850. All of which seems silly to me, given the astounding temporal stretches chronicled by Indigenous oral histories. But, alas, it's what I've got to work with.

On a related note: throughout this book you will see non-Western cultures, beliefs, and histories described almost entirely in Western terms. Which sucks because, as with nutrient energy, you invariably lose a lot of quality when it gets metabolized through alien systems. It simply isn't possible to talk or read about other cultures in terms of your own language and concepts with anything even close to total accuracy. Imagine trying to describe the process of baking bread entirely in terms of boiling soup, and you'll have some idea what I mean.

In fact, as Diné politician, scholar, and activist Eric Descheenie once pointed out to me, the very concept conveyed by the term "culture" is itself completely foreign to Indigenous North American knowledge systems—let alone that of more loaded terms like *nation*, *tribe*, or *sacred*.

Unfortunately, there's only one set of tools in our collective toolbox at present, so it's the one I'm forced to use. But that dejected pronouncement comes with its own caveat: for the reasons just described, knowledge of non-Western peoples that comes wrapped in Western packaging should always be treated as starting points to understanding rather than end points. A foundation, in other words, on which a multiplicity of perspectives might be *built*, as opposed to a concrete and dogmatic edifice to be venerated on its own.

When writing about the place in 1946, Wallace Stegner described southeastern Utah as the heart of our last great wilderness. "This is not real tourist country," he went on to say, and at the time he wasn't wrong. The first automobile had reached the vicinity of Mexican Hat, at its southernmost extent, in 1921—and in the two decades between that historic event and when Stegner penned his words, very few had followed it.

Edward Abbey, always eager to see what his hero Stegner had seen, penetrated into the area in a rattletrap beast in the 1950s, and then immediately began howling about how nobody should ever build a highway into it (the road he took was less than a

decade old). Ann Zwinger followed soon after, and although she
was never as fierce and ribald as her friend and fellow author
Cactus Ed, she also lamented what she knew was coming.

The road Abbey took into the area in some of his earliest
essays was built in the 1950s to accommodate uranium exploration. The road Ann took a little later to reach Grand Gulch was
built to shorten the distance that same uranium had to be hauled.
And every scientist, hiker, backpacker, photographer, artist, poet,
logger, grazer, weirdo, cop, and grave robber has taken those
same roads ever since.

On that snowy morning in January of 2017, I took the long
but scenic route along one of them to an event celebrating an
arduous and ongoing effort to protect the place.

In attendance were folks from nearly all the Native American
tribes in the region, along with a smattering of white conservationists and other allies like me. Nonprofit groups represented there
included Utah Diné Bikéyah, Friends of Cedar Mesa, Archaeology Southwest, and Conservation Lands Foundation, all of whom
would be co-litigants on a lawsuit filed against the Trump administration when it moved to eviscerate the monument a year later.

The speakers were all members of the tribes. Eric Descheenie
talked about his then-current career as a Diné politician in Phoenix living far away from his homeland, as well as about how
Bears Ears National Monument was an especially symbolic win
for women because of the area's feminine healing energy. Navajo
Nation Council delegate Davis Filfred reported being "thankful
from the bottom of [his] boots," commenting later on how he'd
gotten the council to pass legislation supporting the monument.
Shaun Chapoose, chairman of the Ute Indian (Uinta-Ouray)
Tribe Business Committee and one of the most fiery speakers
I know of, delivered an exceptional polemic about the importance of the monument and how he hoped Trump would be too
busy "building his Great Wall" to trifle with it. I never tire of
that man's wit.

The speech that affected me the most, however, was from
Regina Lopez-Whiteskunk, former Ute Mountain Ute council-
member and co-chairwoman of the Bears Ears Inter-Tribal

Coalition. We're pals at this point, appearing alongside each other in a number of publications, but I'd never met her before the celebratory gathering in Monument Valley. She recalled being horribly disrespected and ridiculed by the Utah congressional delegation when she and other tribal members testified on Capitol Hill about the urgent need to create elevated protections for the Bears Ears area. As it turned out, she was the first coalition member called when the new monument was designated, and she'd had one hell of a time trying not to blurt the news out to everyone in the world before it was officially announced. It was a touching—and, given her treatment by Utah's finest, vindicating—story.

Regina also emphasized that everyone who knows that place is deeply and invariably moved by it; that we all have our "Bears Ears stories" as a result; and how she wants to hear each and every one of them. I pondered that as I drove back through the wondrous and towering monoliths of Monument Valley and southeastern Utah, now a shimmering blue from moonlight on snow and ice. It was the honor of a lifetime to be invited to the coalition's event in the first place. To eat the food they served (made with herbs and such that were presciently gathered at Bears Ears the previous fall) and watch them laugh at the "coyote pups" playing in front of the speakers. This was about the midway point in my own involvement in the conservation battle, and it was about to ramp up in a pretty big way—but that event was, and remains, the most instructive part.

This book is my response to Regina's request.

Chapter One: The Mammoth-Killers

The human story of the Bears Ears area begins rather far away from the place itself. So does the story of Bears Ears archaeology. And so, for that matter, does my own.

As far as scientists can tell, humans first arrived in the American Southwest no later than about fourteen thousand years ago and quite possibly a lot earlier than that. Hypotheses about their methods of arrival vary considerably, although it's clear that people didn't evolve here from our last common ancestor with the other primates. Biological studies point instead to northeastern Asia, and a great many Indigenous narratives also include migration from someplace to the north. Exactly how and when have been subjects of ongoing debate for decades, and this has a lot to do with how archaeologists operate.

Because it's usually impossible to discern cultures or societies from the purely material record, particularly in cases where all that remain are bones and stone tools, archaeologists typically give typologies or groupings of styles umbrella titles called *material cultures*, and sometimes *artifact complexes* or *traditions*. This approach is useful for building chronologies, but becomes a bit more troublesome when one tries to move from describing things to understanding people.

The earliest known artifact tradition in the Americas is the Nenana Complex, so-called because of a site found in the Nenana Valley in Alaska, and the people who created it appear to have thrived sometime before and up to about 11,500 years ago. Overlapping this in mainland North America are the Clovis and Western Stemmed traditions—the latter restricted to the

Great Basin region of Nevada and western Utah, and the former being found throughout the entirety of North America. This by itself is enough to convince most researchers that the first people to arrive in North America stepped off the boat, or dog-sled, or whatever it was up in modern-day Alaska, and then worked their way downward. The keyword being "most."

These artifact traditions fall into what most American archaeologists call the Paleoindian period, which represents adaptations to terminal Pleistocene environments and is charac-terized by small groups of relatively mobile foragers who used most sites only briefly or infrequently. The Paleoindian tool-kit typically included large *lanceolate* (long and thin) projectile points, spurred-end scrapers, gravers, and borers or awls—and, in the case of the Western Stemmed tradition, mysterious little crescents that look like fake moustaches. The primary differ-ence among these artifact traditions themselves is the slight variability exhibited in projectile point form, which likely resulted from changing environments and subsistence strategies but may just as likely have been components of group identity.

The Clovis complex takes its name from the site where it was first discovered, when a road crew in eastern New Mexico stum-bled upon an assemblage of very large and very old bones, mixed into which were a number of slender, delicate-looking projectile points about as long as an adult finger. Clovis points are beauti-ful, intricate, and above all *delicate* things. Some researchers have looked good and hard at their design, and concluded that they're about as useful against a charging beast the size of a U-Haul as a pocket knife would be against a bulldozer. Which means they were either intended as very pretty trade items, or as very pretty knives for carving up animals that were already dead. Or both. But almost certainly not for spearing live ones.

When scientists began using modern radiocarbon dating on Clovis-associated materials, starting with the dead animals with which Clovis points were associated and moving on to excavated perishable organics, they were delighted to discover that they coincide perfectly with the retreat of the great ice sheets that covered the landmass between mainland North America and northeastern Eurasia roughly fourteen thousand years ago. The retreat of those glaciers created an ice-free corridor along the Rocky Mountains that channeled the wandering Pleistocene hunter-gatherers into the heart of the continent. Once there, they migrated outward, reaching every nook and cranny in both North and South America within about five hundred years—or roughly 1/200th the amount of time it took anatomically modern humans to cross the same distance between our collective homeland in Africa and northwestern Eurasia in the first place. As crazy and unlikely as that sounds, current evidence suggests that it's true. One can only assume the Clovis people were full-time sprinters.

Researchers have found and documented something like ten thousand Clovis artifacts, which means there may be as many as ten thousand more lurking in the closets of sticky-fingered ne'er-do-wells. Clovis is known best as the material culture associated with the "first" people to arrive in mainland North America some thirteen thousand years ago, the operative word being in quotations because it gets challenged more or less constantly.

Mounting evidence shows that people were in the Americas at least a few thousand years before Clovis, further underscoring the unlikelihood of what I call the Continental Sprinter Hypothesis. Confidently dated pre-Clovis sites appear on an almost yearly basis. Most researchers now consider the "Clovis First" model dead and buried, with many having felt that way for well over a decade at this point, much to the satisfaction of Native American scholars who've doubted/hated it all along. Although this never stops journalists from trotting out the "rewrite history" meme every time a new one is found. In following with Betteridge's Law,* anytime you see the clickbait-y headline "[blank] could rewrite history," put your money on "but probably not."

The scientific, historic, and cultural importance of Clovis itself—and the growing number of sites that predate it—cannot

---

* "Any headline that ends in a question mark can be answered by the word 'no.'" It's named for British tech journalist Ian Betteridge, although the observation that egregious editorializing should not be taken at face value is about as old as journalism itself.

be understated. However, apart from one site (and possibly a second), the role that Clovis plays in the Bears Ears area is a small one. So far. Ongoing research hints that there may be more to that story.

Following Clovis, the Folsom tradition is also associated with distinctive spear points. They had grooves or *flutes* that extended from the concave base almost to the very tip, not entirely unlike the blood grooves in some medieval swords, but nearly as wide as the blade itself.

The Folsom complex was discovered just over twenty years before the discovery of Clovis, and it also took place in New Mexico. In 1908, a cowboy named George McJunkin, investigating damages to his ranch after a devastating flood that killed eighteen people, stumbled across the rib bones of a gigantic bison in an arroyo bed into which the flood had deeply cut. In among the bones were a number of stone tools, including fluted projectile points that look to us now like miniaturized versions of Clovis points with flared tangs that make them look a bit like Pac-Man ghosts. McJunkin, being no fool, recognized that he was looking at something that might be of interest to archaeologists, and— being as careful as possible not to disturb the integrity of the deposits—removed a few sample bones and one of the projectile points and sent them to the Denver Museum of Natural History.

It turned out that the bones were those of *Bison antiquus*, a species of giant bison that had followed woolly mammoths into extinction by ten-thousand years ago at the latest. The undeniable temporal connection between those bones and the Native American stone tools jumbled in with them established human antiquity of North America as being at least nine thousand years older than anyone had previously conjectured. The discovery of Clovis a few years later would push it back even further, but Folsom was the game changer.

The thing about McJunkin that warrants additional discussion is his ethnicity. He was one of the numerous but largely unsung Black cowboys in American western history. Born into slavery in Texas, he was nine years old when the Civil War came to an end, and he made his way thence into the world of cowpunching. He was far from alone in this. When freedom for Africans in America (finally) came about with the Thirteenth Amendment, a large number of them headed west to work as cowhands because the east was [a] full of racists and bad memories, and anyway [b] distinctly lacking in jobs for them outside of porter or elevator operator.

Other Black people who helped shape the American West during the historic period include Bass Reeves, Mary Fields, Nat Love, and Bill "Bulldog" Pickett, all of whom are worth at least an afternoon of reading and probably a Hollywood film of their own.

Paleoindian archaeology is sparse throughout the Colorado Plateau, Bears Ears being no exception, and one of the biggest reasons for this is something researchers call *taphonomy*. This is the process by which an organism is fossilized and the study of what happens to it between its death and subsequent discovery. It's a term coined and used by paleontologists, who actually study fossils, but it's been successfully hijacked by other studiers of natural history—including archaeologists—for their own purposes. Generally speaking, it's the study of site formation with regard to organic physical remains, and in most cases that means what happens to your bones and belongings after you come a cropper.

Taphonomy and its study can best be understood by envisioning a Thanksgiving dinner. These are typically attended by ten to twenty people of varying ages, and about half as many different food items from which to take slices and gobs; there are several dozen ceramic plates and bowls, and numerous metal utensils; there are glass drinking cups, and paper napkins, and so on. There's also a big table, candles on the table, seats around the table, music playing in the background, and sometimes dogs, which will turn out to be important later on because dogs always are.

The feast commences. The feast ends.

The things that wind up in the trash are the bones, the soft or gooey items that got scraped off plates because of eyes bigger than stomachs, the napkins, and whatever plates, bowls, and glasses happened to break. And then the dogs get into the trash, so most of the organic morsels—and, given what I know about dogs, a lot of the napkins and maybe some of the glass—disappears. What remains goes into the outdoor trash can, at which point a raccoon makes off with the shiny things and whatever bones the dogs couldn't choke down. Come then the birds, and insects, and grubs, and bacteria... By the time the detritus of our hypothesized Thanksgiving feast arrives at its final resting place, it consists of a few turkey leg bones that were too big for any scavengers to handle and a small pile of broken dishes. And from *that*, archaeologists are expected to recreate the feast, the family, the setting, the music, and so on.

This is the problem of taphonomy. If the feast occurred yesterday, archaeologists could just ask people about it. Testimony would be hazier if it occurred a year or two ago, but photos might exist. Ten years ago, and at least the table and chairs and most of the people themselves are still around, albeit with a dusty sheen on all. But one hundred years ago? The furniture has probably been replaced more than once, and most likely the house and the people as well. How about one thousand years ago? Or ten thousand?

So, part of the reason that Paleoindian archaeological materials are so sparse is because Paleoindian people were squishy bipeds who didn't drive cars or build skyscrapers, instead relying on animal skins and ephemeral huts and whatever food they managed to collect or clobber with simple tools. Precious little of that is going to endure in open settings for over a hundred centuries. And, owing to the process of taphonomy, what does remain is often little more than what you get at the end of our hypothesized Turkey Day trash narrative: a few broken tools and the really big bones.

Archaeological literature on Paleoindian lifeways has traditionally emphasized big-game hunting for this very reason, to the extent of postulating that over-exploitation of Pleistocene megafauna that hadn't yet learned to fear humans led directly to the extinction of those animals throughout the continent. This so-called "Overkill Hypothesis" has been challenged in more recent literature, and I personally think it's a case of correlation not equaling causation. People were inspired to move great distances into uncharted and potentially very scary places at the same time that these huge and hard-to-feed animals began to die off, after all, so it's much more likely that a lurking variable like climatic pandemonium was the primary impetus of both.

The other main reason folks like the ones who left Clovis and Folsom artifacts behind are so often characterized as obligate big-game hunters is because Paleoindian-associated artifacts most often occur in lower elevations along major river valleys, where Pleistocene megafauna liked to congregate. This includes the original Clovis site itself in Blackwater Draw, New Mexico. But water is a pretty good place to congregate. I would be more surprised to find that the artifacts of a hunting-and-gathering people most often occur, say, on the tops of mountains. And, as of this writing, only about a dozen kill sites are known from the entire Clovis assemblage continent-wide. So, I'd hardly say they were leaning on hunted megafauna as the sole meat component of their respective meat and potatoes.

Behavioral ecologists (i.e., people who study the ways in which environment and behavior have shaped one another in human and other animal species) have pretty well demolished the idea that Clovis people were obligate megafauna hunters. A diet consisting primarily of meat is a hard sell for the human body right out of the gate, although humans are amazingly adaptive and our diets can be highly variable depending on our local environments—the Inuit people, for example, really do eat a diet of almost nothing but fatty animal bits. But look where they live. Besides which, they always target and savor the half-digested vegetables in those animals' stomachs, and narwhal skin has been found to contain more vitamin C than citrus fruit. So, yeah, it's possible for people to subsist on a diet consisting primarily of meat, but only after many generations of adaptation to rather extreme circumstances, and in any event, that doesn't typically include the meat of trumpeting goliaths.

Not that scavenging or hunting of megafauna never happened, of course. Confirmed mammoth kills by Paleoindian people are less common than one might think but that's still a lot more than zero. It's the *obligate* part that's problematic.

The one confirmed Clovis site in the entire Bears Ears area is a hunting camp located not far to the west of Bluff, a colorful community situated on the San Juan River that only recently—after nearly 240 years—became incorporated as a town. The site is located near the San Juan River, which is indeed where you would expect to find Pleistocene megafauna—but also where you'd find plants, fish, ducks, and, oh yes, *water*. It's basically an assemblage of stone tools and the abundant little chips of stone residue from making them—what archaeologists call a *lithic scatter*.

Most archaeological sites in the United State *in toto* are lithic scatters. This is primarily because they don't erode or decay, like perishable organic things, and because sticky-fingered visitors are unlikely to collect pocketfuls of the archaeological equivalent of what a colleague of mine once described as "pencil-sharpening shavings." Although it's also because stone tools were a fantastic idea when human beings first invented them, and remained so for a very, very long time. As retired university professor James O'Connell once explained it to me, "A good, sharp edge is ideal for two purposes: opening animals, and closing arguments."

That's it for confirmed Clovis sites in the Bears Ears area. There aren't any Folsom sites until you get nearer to the town of Moab well to the northeast, most likely because there weren't any bison. Bison were to Folsom-complex foragers what gold is to Tolkien dwarfs—there's effectively no finding the latter unless there's a lot of the former.

But *confirmed* is a tricky word, in this case. Also to the west of Bluff is a rock art panel that supposedly contains at least one and possibly two mammoths, although if you look at the "mammoth" from almost any angle other than the one prescribed by its recorders it looks more like a dog, or an aardvark, or an antelope with a snout, or a kangaroo, or a unicorn, or a 2004 Chevy Silverado, or almost anything else your mind can imagine. You'll find that's a common problem with the study of rock art. Sometime between its creation and eventual discovery an errant boulder strikes a petroglyph panel *just so*, and subsequent hordes of experts spill bounteous ink and bile over the question of whether or not the people who carved it were involved in a cult that worshipped flying mushrooms.

Having said all that, I spend a lot of time looking at rock art, or rock *writing* as my Hopi friends prefer to call it, and that supposed mammoth really does look awfully mammoth-like to me. So, who knows? At any rate, the controversy over whether or not it's genuine is a fun one.

It was discovered by genial and popular local artist Joe Pachak, who was often hired and/or volunteered to apply his considerable artistic skills to recording local archaeological petroglyph (pecked-in) and pictograph (painted-on) panels. Whilst so engaged in 2011, he spotted what he believed to be a petroglyph depicting a Columbian mammoth, one of two species of woolly mammoth formerly endemic to North America and arguably the older of the two, superimposed with what also appeared to be a Pleistocene bison.

Joe knew he'd found something big, and quickly got on the horn to professional archaeologists so they could come and have a look. Their conclusion: the panel does indeed depict a Pleistocene mammoth and bison, dating about thirteen thousand to eleven thousand years ago. In the community of Bluff, there was much rejoicing. Briefly.

Voices of dissent in the archaeological and paleontological communities popped up almost immediately. The most reliably dated mammoths in North America all date to before about eleven thousand years ago. Although the Huntington Mammoth— so-called for its discovery near Huntington, Utah, a rural community two hundred or so miles north of Bears Ears—is presumed to have died no more than 10,500 years ago. It has been called the last holdout of the mammoth extinction by its discoverer, paleontologist David Gillette. But it also lived and died near a boggy and densely vegetated lakeshore, where chewy greens were plentiful. There is zero evidence of mammoths and people living together in the much more xeric Bears Ears area, although if the folks at the Clovis site west of Bluff had migrated south through Huntington, there was at least one they might have spotted along the way.

Dating petroglyphs is also notoriously difficult. They are often just lines scratched and hammered into rock, after all—there's nothing *to* date.

Researchers have weighed in on the subject in a variety of public forums. A particularly intriguing hypothesis has been advanced by noted local archaeologist Winston Hurst, who remains agnostic but hopeful, which suggests that maybe the timing isn't all that important because people talk about, think about, and depict things out of time all the time. This is part of the reason that storytelling was invented, after all. The associated notion of "cultural memory" is one in which important or sacred images, stories, and songs are so vividly passed along that recipients can interpret them with considerable accuracy many generations later.

We aren't very good at this, these days, because our technophilic culture has done to our attention spans what a belt sander does to a crayon. I can't even remember phone numbers, anymore, now that I've got a device in my pocket that does it for me. But if it was a matter of "retain complicated information with precision or you'll stumble to a very unpleasant death," I'm betting we could still do it.

Furthermore, there is plentiful evidence to suggest that people living in the Bears Ears area during ancient times were well aware of how things went down in more-ancient times—and here, too, Clovis comes into the picture. In the spring of 2017, a schoolteacher was ambling around on top of Cedar Mesa when she stumbled upon a beautiful and seemingly flawless Clovis point.

That's crazier than you might imagine. I know people who've devoted entire careers to studying the Paleoindian era that haven't seen a Clovis point in the wild, let alone one that's in pristine condition. My current employers as of this writing have a standing offer of a keg of good beer or a bottle of decent wine for the first person who finds a complete Clovis point on the job, and there's little-to-no chance it will ever be claimed.

Thankfully, she did the right thing: after presumably freaking out with joy, she left it exactly where it was and informed Bureau of Land Management (BLM) archaeologist Don Simonis. It turns out the point was probably curated by an Ancestral Pueblo (ca. 1500 BC to AD 1492) individual or family, and was made from the beautiful tiger-striped Alibates chert that occurs in Texas and Oklahoma. Clovis points made from Alibates chert are found all over the country. They were the Toledo steel or Fabergé eggs of their time, in that they were highly distinctive of the place where they were made and essentially impossible to fake with local materials.

And ancient people were, after all, people. They liked to collect and marvel over cool old stuff the same as people do today—more so, in fact, because it was *their* history. This is why a small but steadily increasing number of archaeologists in the United States are, themselves, Indigenous people. And archaeology doesn't work when there's nothing left to look at.

This is what makes the tale of the Clovis point from Cedar Mesa so heartwarming. It's fair to say that a fair number of individuals who stumbled across a stunning Clovis point during a hike would now have a sweet souvenir in their sock drawer. Plus, amoral thieving swine aside, even moving the thing twenty feet from where it was found in order to hide it safely under a rock would have destroyed its invaluable contextual integrity. The fact that it was found in an Ancestral Pueblo artifact scatter tells the story of how and why it got there. Move it just a few yards this way or that, and the factual storyline is broken.

Fittingly enough, it is during this earliest of material-culture chronology that we get our first glimpse of what I consider to be the most incredible and noteworthy aspect of the human history of the Bears Ears area. Called various things by various authors, what I prefer to call the *borderlands phenomenon* in social science, is the textured and fluctuating patterns of collision, conflict, and coalescence of different cultural groups in the places where the fringes of their respective territories overlap or interdigitate. These are the forges of culture, often the birthing places of new and unique ones that spring forth from all that elbow-rubbing.

Because these are the peripheral or "backwoods" portions of their total occupational footprints, far away from what social scientists call the *cultural core*, it's where you'll most often get a unique blend of both overt self-identification and fierce, sometimes zealous group loyalty.

And it makes a lot of sense to me, too. I grew up in a mobile home community, which I'm told is the *nouveau*-PC term for trailer park, which was just far enough outside of suburbia to be considered "rural." Roughly half of my friends were independent-minded to the point that they regularly denounced their US citizenship—often very loudly, and usually at keg parties—just as often as they denounced loyalty to our school district, and they were the ones who routinely dated students from other ones. The other half, the ones you more often see on television these days, were some of the most frenetically patriotic human beings I've ever seen. Patriotic in terms of our school district, with concomitant hatred for its rivals; but also in terms of our country as a whole. What this suggests is that the farther a community is from its cultural core, the deeper it is in the hinterlands where people from *other* groups might be encountered, the more often people fracture into those who cling as desperately as possible to their respective group identity and those who readily jettison it in order to explore what those others might have to offer.

Jesse Tune, one of my fellow newer-generation archaeologists and now an assistant professor at Fort Lewis College in Durango, has studied the Paleoindian period in the greater Bears Ears area for several years. Based on determining the geographic sources of much of the isolated lithic tools found in Paleo sites across the region, using both stylistic cues and fancy microscopic science, he's found that people came to the area from at least three different origination points: the Great Basin, the desert South-west, and the Rockies. Once there, subtle but distinctly local patterns and styles began to emerge that Tune is only just beginning to tease out of the material record.

What drew them to the Bears Ears area in the first place is uncertain, given its signal paucity of mammoths—although, again, the idea that they were *only* subsisting on hunted mega-fauna has been scientifically challenged on the grounds of being moronic. If you ask members of the Indigenous community, especially the tribes most closely associated with Bears Ears, they'll almost always report that it makes a lot of sense to them because it's The Place. *Axis mundi* and *ultima thule* in a single, spectacular package. I can't exactly argue with that. It drew me across an entire continent before I'd even seen it on a map.

Although one of the major threads of this book is the develop-ment of Southwest archaeology vis-à-vis the Bears Ears area, it's useful to lay out the earliest iterations of archaeology as a whole—which, like the area's human story, begins rather far away.

American archaeology differs most significantly from that practiced across the pond in that it's a branch of anthropology instead of history. Functionally speaking, history deals with figuring out what happened in the past, where, and by whom, in order to reconstruct it into a timeline or narrative. Anthropology is a branch of science concerned with figuring out the nuts and bolts of human behavior, the reasons that we look and act how we do. In other words, history is the Who, What, Where, and When of the past; anthropology is the How and the Why.

In the American Southwest, the act of suturing the two together commenced about as soon as archaeology itself did, with the earliest archaeologists not only making trait lists and chronologies but also investigating the extant Indigenous community to try to make sense of past versions of those same things. The torch was enlarged in the 1950s by researchers who complained that archaeological historians were too dry and boring, and became a blaze with the New Archaeology of the 1960s and '70s and its emphasis on archaeology as Science.

Elsewhere on the spectrum of anthropology, the practice of observing the behaviors and characteristics of human beings that haven't died yet is called *ethnography*, from the root words *ethno* (relating to race or culture) and *graph* (to write). It is the cataloging of cultural traits, in other words; the investigation and interpretation of which is called *ethnology*. This is where American archaeology does have an advantage, if pressed in the right way, over methods and practices of archaeology that aren't anthropologically informed. Understanding the human past can only be accomplished with any sort of intellectual integrity by understanding the human present—and, to a certain extent, the opposite is also true.

The most important thing to remember about ancient people is that they were *people*. Curiosity about the human past appears to be a human universal, as evidenced by the Clovis point found in an Ancestral Pueblo site atop Cedar Mesa. One of the earliest acts of what could tentatively be called proto-archaeology took place in New Kingdom Egypt (roughly 1150-1070 BC, or right around three thousand years ago), when one of the pharaohs ordered the excavation and reconstruction of the Sphinx—its having been originally constructed about one thousand years earlier and devoured by the desert in the interim.

This tying of present cultures to past ones in order to reclaim some proud earlier glory, underscore local rights and affiliations, or otherwise associate a current society with a past one pops up all over the temporal and geographic human world. Take the Aztecs. The great city-state of Teotihuacan rose and fell in the Valley of Mexico between about AD 300 and 1150, and in its prime it was the largest city in the pre-colonized Americas, with an estimated population of two hundred thousand. Its influence can be seen in areas as far as one thousand miles away. Then a revolution took place, following what the material evidence indicates was a vicious famine as a result of climate change in the early AD 500s, and most of the place was burned to the ground—particularly religious centers and homes of the fat and wealthy, as often occurs in revolutions—before being abandoned.

Almost one thousand years later, the Aztecs decided that the crumbling ruins were a sacred place where the world was created, and gave it its name (*Teotihuacan* means "City of the Gods" in Nahuatl, the language of the Aztecs; we have no idea what it was called by its actual occupants).* The Aztecs modeled much of their architecture, artwork, and other civic accoutrements after those of the Teotihuacanos, in much the same way that the United States models a lot of its own public architecture and other civic characteristics after those of Imperial Rome. And, not entirely unlike the ancient city-state they came to worship, the Aztecs' own imperialistic majesty eventually nose-dived into a whole lot of public butchery and other heinousness not long before the Spanish showed up to make things even worse. The Romans fared little better. But I'm sure we'll be fine.

Skipping forward a bit, professional interest in the prehistory of the Southwest commenced not long after the end of the Mexican-American War of 1846 to 1848, and for the ostensive purpose of refuting the idea that the Southwest was the ancestral home of the Aztecs. Pioneering early archaeologists thereby provided data supporting the contention that *our* Southwest was not significantly related to *their* Mexican past, although this doffs its own hat to the thorny issue of how both countries felt about their respective Indigenous peoples. This is why you'll find a Montezuma Creek in Utah, an Aztec Ruin in northern New Mexico, and a Montezuma Castle and Well in central Arizona.

American archaeology really begins with what is generally—and generously—called *antiquarianism*, a social movement among the European wealthy that swirled around an obsession

---

* For that matter, the word *Aztec* is actually a shortening of the Nahuatl phrase *aztēcatl*, meaning "person from Aztlan," their cultural place of origin.

with ancient sites, manuscripts, and artifacts. Its roots are hazy, but it was a recognizable thing by the 1500s. These were hobbyists rather than scholars, who amassed collections of historic curios for display in their homes in much the same way as modern hunters with their taxidermy menageries, and today we wouldn't call them *antiquarians* so much as *goddamn thieves*. But they had this going for them: the antiquarian movement made much of the importance of human material history as a subset of natural history.

In the 1500s, the importance of secular study of the past ramped up considerably, including the creation of king's antiquary as an official role played by scholars starting in 1533. As with the Aztecs and the New Kingdom pharaohs, the principal component of their task was to gather materials and investigate genealogies and other evidences about the history of their respective kingdom in order to add some polish to their boisterous historical claims.

None of the antiquarians were interested in *pre*history, of course. The Bible told them everything they might want to know about history going all the way back to the beginning of the universe, calculated by theologian and logician Archbishop Ussher in 1650 as having taken place on October 23 of 4004 BC (presumably at just the right time in the morning that the sudden appearance of a sun wouldn't freak anybody out). They were entirely focused on more recent history.

During the Enlightenment, or roughly the entire 1700s, the intrigue of the past as a means for rich people to gather baubles and royally appointed scholars to piece together fun facts about everything leading up to the great and glorious present began losing ground to the larval form of modern science. The discovery of deep time—that is: geologic time—by James Hutton in the latter portion of the century got other intellectuals into a tizzy about what might be lurking in the suddenly *enormous* stretch of pre-recent history. The deeply religious continued to insist that the entire universe was created in October of 4004 BC, with those of slightly shallower zeal having doubts about this but still maintaining that millions of years was simply out of the question.

But the Age of Enlightenment isn't called what it is for no reason, and the secular contention spread like wildfire. By the time the United States split from Europe and began Manifesting its Destiny across the continent, most people were fairly certain that world history extended considerably further back in time than 4004 BC.

Enlightenment thinkers, particularly the French, also armed some of the earliest archaeologists with a concept of social change and progress more firmly rooted in naturalistic, rather than overtly religious, convictions. Where before everyone just assumed that they were God's chosen people—and, naturally, also assumed that everyone else was lying when they said the exact same thing—scholars and philosophers began studying processes of gradual change that seemed more likely to have developed into the status quo over time. The assumption of progress itself was still a given, of course. No European intellectuals would dare presume that the brutes who preceded them were on anything like the same level of development as they were. And that presumption, that "evolution" is synonymous with "progress," is a meme that results in many headaches in academic circles to this day. But it was a start, at least.

Meanwhile, the juxtaposed philosophies of progress and gradual, naturalistic change had undergone their own symbiotic evolution in the study of the human condition, especially following publication of Darwin's *On the Origin of Species* and *The Descent of Man*. Lewis Henry Morgan, considered by many to be the father of American anthropology, espoused in the late 1800s a theory of social evolution that postulated three stages in human sociocultural development: savagery, barbarism, and civilization. These were further subdivided and delineated by technological innovations, such as the discovery of fire, the development of agriculture and writing, domestication of animals, and so on.

This unilineal or teleological—they both mean "proceeding in only one direction," like a train on a set of tracks—model is another example of the problem of conflating evolution with progress, and it came with its own set of headaches that bedevil professors of anthropology even now. Moreover, such rigidly unilineal thinking begets an associated rigidity of thinking itself, such that Morgan was absolutely convinced that no politically complex systems had ever occurred in the Americas. How could they? You can get Civilized people acting like Barbarians, sometimes, but you won't find Barbarians doing things that only Civilized people can do.

The underlying scenario that still fertilizes that sort of sectarian misconception is an endogamous dilemma that doesn't often dog our European counterparts: the majority of archaeologists and anthropologists in the United States are white, and most of the people—past or present—that they study are very definitely not. This, too, is starting to shift—I'd need two or three extra sets of hands to count all the non-Anglo archaeologists with whom I've worked in recent years. But they're still far fewer in number, by at least an order of magnitude. And the harshest perception engendered by this disparity is that archaeology is simply a fancy scientific form of colonialism: the relegation of America's Indigenous past into books and museum displays while Native Americans themselves are relegated to skid row.

Although it is worth pointing out that some of the earliest anthropologists in general, including a few archaeologists in particular, had their hearts in the right places and were simply trying to mitigate the widespread cultural and physical genocide of Indigenous cultures by seeking to at least preserve their memory. The combined forces of progress and evil are driving these people into extinction, they reasoned, so we'd better at least do them the honor of giving them and their cultures functionally permanent remembrance before both are snuffed out. Adolph Bandelier, although a keen student of Morgan, was arguably a member of this club.

Where he is known at all, Bandelier is known best for two things: the national monument due south of Bears Ears in New Mexico that bears his name, and his Ancestral Pueblo historical fiction called *The Delight Makers*. But he was also instrumental in the intellectual battle against the ignoble forces that insisted the architectural splendors of places like Mesa Verde and Chaco (neither of which he ever got a chance to visit) were made by the

Aztecs just before they fled south into Mexico. He openly balked at any specious pie-in-the-sky hypotheses about the archaeology of the Southwest that involved lost Phoenicians, Israeli tribesmen, and the like. If Bandelier had heard the *Ancient Aliens* crowd, who hypothesize *literal* saucers in the sky, he would've choked on his tea.

Bandelier was no romantic. In fact, he seemed to despise romantics. But he was eager to give readers a thorough glance at what Pueblo history supposedly looked like before its modern iterations vanished for good.

The rest of the time, however, anthropologists were busily collecting data in order to scientifically demarcate social categories that functionally justified larger-scale efforts to eradicate Indigenous peoples from lands that would be better utilized by better peoples (which is to say: themselves). For all that he deserves credit as an explorer and early conservationist *par excellence*, John Wesley Powell serves as a useful example of this. Like Bandelier, he was also an avid student of the teachings of Lewis Henry Morgan and his unilineal model of cultural evolution—sometimes called Social Darwinism, to my annoyance.* Powell's extensive and rather impressive ethnographic investigations nonetheless add up to a massive effort to catalogue and examine all the features that set Native Americans above the level of Morganian savages but still firmly below that of civilized Europeans.

---

* Darwin's hand-drawn schematics look like bushes rather than ladders for a reason: evolutionary adaptation does not progress in a single direction according to some predetermined design. It bounces around at random like a ball in a tumble dryer, getting stuck into a pattern whenever a particular design confers benefits in a particular environment. Change the environment, and the design becomes a flaw. That's the limiting factor of nature. The only place where the law of the jungle is *actually* lawless is in our flimsy and corruptible legal systems.

My own "Bears Ears story" starts a little closer to the place itself than do those of its human history and role in Southwest archaeology, but it's still a schlep.

I was born and raised in upstate New York, which I often consider to be part of greater New England owing to a distinct contiguity of gray skies, cows, and Dunkin' Donuts. We lived in the borderlands between what was firmly Suburbia and what was firmly The Sticks.

Outside of reading way too much H. P. Lovecraft and Edgar Allan Poe than any normal child should, my pastime activities as a youth included riding four-wheelers through the woods with my best friend, drinking illegally acquired beer and blasting guns at absolutely everything; helping said friend and his father fix cars and chop wood; and ferociously hating any and all self-righteous blowhard liberals. The fact that I grew up to be what I am today underscores the fact that origin is not always tantamount to destiny.

Growing up with little else to distract me, the old moss-enshrouded cemeteries and numerous abandoned buildings of the New England region became just as much a fixture as ATVs and woodpiles. My best friend in those days was a country-boy comrade named Dann who had the good luck to live on the rural side of the border that delineated our respective school districts. My family resided just over the suburban side, which meant I got to deal with *that* during grade school while he was surrounded by kids a lot more like us—which, in retrospect, created its own set of problems. He was, in his own words, "an ignorant redneck and damn proud of it," but in private he loved nothing so much as a good book. He introduced me to J. R. R. Tolkien when I was about fourteen, which is not a discovery one expects to make in the hayloft of a cobwebby barn.

Serendipitous happenstance of that sort isn't altogether uncommon in my life, and I suspect that's true of a lot of people's lives if they'd just take a moment to notice it. To give one other example of this: if you're at all familiar with the syndicated comics *B.C.* or *The Wizard of Id*, you'll know they were created over half a century ago by Johnny Hart. His grandson, Mason Mastroianni, was a couple years ahead of me in high school, and he remains the most incredibly gifted artist I have ever met. Mason and I were among the small cadre of social outcasts who could often be found sitting in the art room drawing while the other kids were off playing sports or pawing at each other. I ended up being better at writing, as it turns out—but, to quote Aesop Rock, I "used to draw."

Bigger than his talents, however, is Mason's heart. His family bought him several cars while he was a student, and he was remarkably generous when it came to their use, especially toward poor kids like me. After attending the country's premiere art schools and landing a gig in the new world of Hollywood CGI, Mason's big-heartedness became known to the world when he quit what was probably a very lucrative Tinseltown career (this was before CGI techs started getting mightily screwed over by big production firms, or so I'm given to understand) for the much humbler one of newspaper cartoonist after his grandfather passed away in 2007. Mason has been drawing *B.C.* ever since. He assumed the controls to *The Wizard of Id* in 2015.

Mutual friends occasionally crack jokes about how Mason grew up to draw fake people from antiquity and I grew up to study real ones. Given some of my childhood pastimes, it's a little less surprising to me.

Exploring all things derelict and decrepit climbed steadily up the list for my rural bestie and I, as we searched further and further afield for fun distractions from the everyday and mundane. Dann's family owned a few three-wheelers that helped with these explorations, on occasion, but mostly we crept around on foot. I guess that's probably how I got into hiking.

There's a lot of physical history in the greater New England region, if one knows where to look, although a lot of it is notably decadent in nature. Take cemeteries. While early Euro-American settlers in the Northeast built most of their homes out of trees— while clear-cutting the entire Eastern Seaboard—the wet and verdant climate rotted most of those away within a generation or two. Stone walls endure, as do a few stone structures, but they're rare outside of major settlements that are still occupied. This is our old friend taphonomy at work, again.

But cemeteries were fairly common, given how eponymously religious the Puritans were. And gravestones are called grave*stones* for a reason. Thus, if you wander around in the northeastern woods long enough, you're going to stumble across one or two of them.

This did little to assuage the already formidable association between "the Northeast" and "gloom" that I'd developed thanks to Lovecraft and Poe, but it also gave my fellow country lad and I something to look for. Finding an abandoned house or farmstead was always cool, but they tended not to be very old and, anyway, there was always the chance of disturbing the sort of squatters you really don't want to disturb. But graveyards, including old ones with antiquated designs like winged skulls on the stones— those were always fun to find. They occupied a lot of our wandering attentions in those earliest days.

Sex, drugs, and Dungeons and Dragons would eventually usurp a lot of that flailing adventurousness, as they often do for people in their later teens (given some variability on that third component). But exploring "abandoned" places remained a fixture for me and for him, right up until his untimely death in 2016. I think we were always searching for our real homes, and the *idée fixe* for both of us was a paradoxical place where sunlight and shadows both abound.

I would find mine in the deep, winding, wondrous canyons of the northern Southwest. Some never do.

Chapter Two: The Foragers

While the earliest archaeologists are little distinguishable from treasure hunters, the development of archaeology as a science began in the form of history reconstruction. In broad strokes, history is the sequence of events that took place in the past within a given area. Thus, reconstructing local history from the material residue left behind by past peoples is just a matter of determining what happened, by whom, and in what order. Easy, right?

In the developing world of Southwest archaeology, folks seeking to make sense of the archaeological record often sought to do so in the creation of various sequential schema or occupation histories that could fit neatly along a linear timeline. These were the *culture-history* archaeologists, as we refer to them, although I've always thought "material culture" archaeologists would be a better title. They looked at trends in the material residue, decided upon what they saw as significant patterns (e.g., "These people ate a lot of pork"), and then affixed to these nebulous groupings a cultural title befitting that observation ("We'll call them the Pig-Eaters").

Thus, in the Southwest, the people who made baskets but not ceramics became known as Basket Makers (later condensed into Basketmakers); and the ones who lived in what the Spanish called *pueblos* became known as Pueblo people, their predecessors now called Ancestral Pueblo for this reason—although for a long time before that they were all called Cliff Dwellers because some of them did, indeed, dwell in cliffs. Long before them roamed the supposed big-game specialists during the Paleoindian—literally "very old Indian"—period. I shall have much more to say about these classificatory pigeonholes as this story unfolds, but for now it's enough to have that as a basis.

The progenitors of that basis, represented principally by A. V. Kidder at the first-ever Pecos Archaeological Conference in 1927, recognized that there must be some transitional phase between the spear-hurling Paleoindians and the crop-growing Ancestral Pueblo peoples. Richard Wetherill provided one of the missing links in the form of the Basketmaker farmers he investigated in the Bears Ears area, but even that seemed a far leap from mammoth gristle. Kidder in particular insisted that there must have been a culture phase that was "pre-agricultural, yet adumbrating later developments" (*adumbrate* means "outline," by the way). This postulated culture phase was dubbed Basketmaker I, with the subsequent phase thereby getting the title Basketmaker II, and all was over bar the finding of actual evidence of its existence.

Nobody ever did.

There were contenders, though, and when researchers began to recognize material components during the 1940s and '50s that fit these criteria—pre-ceramic, pre-agricultural, non-Paleoindian—for some reason the title of Basketmaker I wasn't applied to them. This is most likely because they didn't find any baskets. I'm not kidding about that. Instead, these sites that consisted of older-than-Basketmaker but smaller-than-Paleo stone artifacts were corralled into local "cultures" or "complexes" with names like San Jose, Cochise, Picosa, and, because the late Jesse Jennings was nothing if not a pragmatist, Desert Culture. The term *Archaic*, which usually means "outdated" in popular usage, was introduced as an umbrella name in a foundational 1958 paper, and that's the one that stuck.

The Archaic period spans approximately 10,000 to 2,500 years Before Present, or BP—which actually means "before 1950" rather than "before today," because nuclear weapons testing and similar shenanigans have mucked up the background radio-carbon signal in our environment since about that time. Most researchers further divide the Archaic into four subperiods: Early (approximately 10,000 to 8,000 BP), Middle (8,000 to 5,000

BP), Late (5,000 to 3,000 BP), and Terminal (3,000 to 2,500 BP), although most Southwest researchers lump the Terminal Archaic into the earliest Formative period on account of the appearance of farming.

The Early Archaic encompasses most of the early and middle Holocene, the geologic epoch in which we currently dwell, during the Altithermal climatic period—a stretch of about 4,000 years when the summer temperature throughout western North America was considerably warmer than today. For basically the entire Intermountain West, including the Colorado Plateau, environmental changes during this period have been particularly well-documented in some of the dry caves of the Great Basin, where relative abundances of plant and animal remains can be read like a census.

Piñon pine approached its modern distribution during this period, or started to anyway, which is fun to think about because most people seldom realize that trees can and do migrate. It happens so slowly that it escapes our notice. When glaciers expanded across the northern portions of the Americas and Eurasia during the last ice age, a lot of plants fled south. Many of them were crushed against the Alps in Europe, being plants and having no ability to fly over or tunnel beneath them; but in North America there were no such impediments, so they just kept marching south.

When the glaciers retreated, the trees turned around and started the ponderous journey home, although in some cases it wasn't ponderous as much as explosive. The coincidentally named ponderosa pine experienced one of the most extensive and least ponderous post-glacial expansions of any tree community in the world, which is why you can now walk under a virtually unbroken canopy of pondie boughs from Flagstaff around the Grand Canyon, across the Colorado Plateau, and then upward along the Rockies into Canada. Meanwhile, the arid Altithermal period effectively dried all the major lake systems of Nevada and Utah, leaving a conspicuous "bathtub ring" on the geology surrounding the shores of once-mighty Pleistocene lakes like Bonneville. By about eight thousand years ago, piñon pines expanded into newly xeric environmental niches to occupy most of the places they still occupy—like Cedar Mesa.

With changing climates came the expansion and modification of artifact assemblages as people adapted to a wider, more dispersed plant and animal resource base. That expansion was, at least in part, a product of adjusting to Altithermal dryness and the death toll it wreaked on producer-consumer communities in the West. Drought spirals upward, after all, taking its biggest toll on those species with the biggest appetites. When there isn't enough grass to feed big animals, like deer and other ungulates, they get replaced by smaller, fleeter ones that require fewer leaves to power them along. Like rabbits. This is confirmed in the archaeological record by low abundances of ungulate remains during the early and middle Holocene, suggesting that large terrestrial mammals were rare during this time. If the woolly mammoths and other *huge* mammals of the North American ice age hadn't died out long before, the Altithermal would've gotten them.

Continuing the trend that began during the later Paleoindian period, higher-elevation settings were used even more frequently during the Early Archaic, probably representing further generalization of subsistence strategies. Which makes sense—you wouldn't catch me straddling some perilous crag in search of suspect comestibles if turkey sandwiches are still plentiful in the valley below. This was the dawning of the age of *broad-spectrum foraging*, which is fancy talk for "hunting and gathering for increasingly diverse stuff."

The Middle Archaic period spans the remainder of the mid-Holocene, during which the climate continued to be generally warm and dry. People used more or less the same projectile points as they did in the Early Archaic, which is annoying because distinctive styles of projectile points (meaning spear- or arrowheads) are almost the only artifacts to which field-workers can ascribe any temporality before ceramics come along.

Decades of research into why projectile point typology

looks the way it does has added up to a big "beats us" in terms of functionality beyond the simple and obvious, like how arrowheads are smaller than spearheads because arrows are smaller than spears. Otherwise, the variability of their shapes neither adds nor deletes any significant advantages. The best we can surmise is that they were probably cultural markers, although this, too, is problematic. The Elko side- or corner-notched projectile point, for example, first appears in the Early Archaic, dominates artifact assemblages during the Middle Archaic, and then holds steady at a low rumble right up until about the year AD 1000. That's over seven thousand years. That makes the notion of an Elko "culture" a bit hard to swallow.

In addition to Elko series projectile points being all the rage, a slight increase in the frequency of grinding stones during the Middle Archaic seems to indicate a stronger reliance on plant resources than in previous periods. But the big word in the Middle Archaic is *mobility*. Middle Holocene environmental changes reconfigured the spatial and temporal distribution of resources that were important to earlier occupants of the region, as in the shifting and shuffling of plant communities.

I was on top of Cedar Mesa with legendary local hiking guide and Friends of Cedar Mesa board president Vaughn Hadenfeldt a few years ago, when he spotted a gorgeous Middle Archaic projectile point. That was it—just the point. The only sites we know from this period appear in a highly obscure 1959 report in *El Palacio*, magazine of the Museum of New Mexico. A team of archaeologists working on a salvage project found a total of five sites on a low mesa just north of the San Juan River near the town of Aneth, and all of them were artifact scatters with no domestic components.

So, people were definitely in the vicinity of Bears Ears during the Middle Archaic, although probably not in festival-size crowds.

The beginning of the Late Archaic coincides roughly with the time when the climate began to approach what we think of as modern conditions. With the cooler and generally more hospitable climate of the late Holocene, the density of large mammal populations rebounded significantly, and large mammal bits become a lot more common in archaeological assemblages. Archaeological evidence indicates that nearly every available resource in nearly every available place was in use.

Serendipitously, at least for archaeologists, Late Archaic peoples more often lived in rock shelters than did more mobile earlier groups, where the dry atmosphere preserved an array of perishable items like baskets, mats, and sandals. The Late Archaic was also a time of trade in exotic or hard-to-find items like obsidian, turquoise, and marine shells, the first two of which can be sourced back to their locations of manufacture using high-tech analysis while the last can be sourced to the ocean because that's where marine shells are from.

Finally, throughout much of the Colorado Plateau the archaeology dating to the tail end of the Late Archaic is one of increasing sedentism, as people started settling down for a bit of farming. The question of whether Late Archaic foragers learned and adopted farming *in situ* or were replaced by incoming farmers from elsewhere—i.e., whether it was cultural transmission of knowledge or migration of actual people—is ongoing, but the Bears Ears area offers a tantalizing clue.

Old Man Cave is a dry shelter located on the northeastern edge of Cedar Mesa, where early agricultural materials were discovered in the late 1800s. Subsequent reexamination of the site revealed that it was looted in recent years, because of course it was, but Archaic cultural materials were nonetheless evident in the churned-up deposits underlying the agricultural ones. An open-twined sandal characteristic of earlier Archaic varieties returned a radiocarbon age of 7,440 ± 100 years ago, setting a presumed baseline for initial occupation, and additional subsurface testing yielded six more dates from charcoal, grass chaff, and rodent feces. Based on all these data, it appears that the cave was steadily occupied for a whopping one thousand years before going unused for another six thousand or so, after which it was reoccupied for an indeterminate spell. That big hiatus suggests that it wasn't knowledge about farming that moved into the area, but farmers themselves.

Dating Archaic period sites can be just as challenging as dating Paleoindian sites, owing to their general paucity of organic materials. In the Moab area to the north, Squaw Park Cave has been dated to the Archaic period in general, and several sites in Ten Mile Wash have been dated to the Middle Archaic period in particular. In the Bears Ears area, the current frontrunner for studying and understanding Archaic period lifeways on a landscape level is Dark Canyon.

Dark Canyon is the most appropriately named place in all of Bears Ears. Deep, dark, and all but inaccessible for about half the year, it was originally called Vega Canyon, for reasons I've never been able to ascertain. Dark Canyon and its major tributaries comprise a 76.3-square-mile Wilderness Area. The environmental character of the place is such that conducting extensive archaeological studies there is a grim affair. Water abounds, but the springs themselves are widely spaced, and the complex terrain makes it impossible to access the canyon bottoms in all but the Peavine Canyon Corridor using anything but feet or hooves. Food, camping and cooking gear, and all scientific and safety implements must be hauled around on human- or horseback.

Every year since 2005, a team of ten to twelve volunteers from the nonprofit Wilderness Volunteers has accompanied district archaeologist Don Irwin and a rotating cast of seasonal employees (like me) on a weeklong effort to conduct survey, monitoring, and site recordation in the Dark Canyon Wilderness. After twelve years of three or four small teams working diligently on systematic pedestrian surveys for a week at a time, they've managed to inventory about four percent of the main and tributary canyon systems. It's a big place.

Based on these data, we now know that the Dark Canyon Wilderness was at least lightly or moderately utilized during every phase of local occupation from Early Archaic through to this morning. However, the overwhelming bulk of occupation there appears to be bimodally distributed between Archaic and late Pueblo sites, with appreciably more of the former.

And then there's the ubiquitous (to me, anyway) topic of Bears Ears as a cauldron of cultural coalescence. In an article he wrote for *Archaeology Southwest Magazine*, Irwin reports that the Archaic artifact assemblages in Dark Canyon include projectile points from the Southern Colorado Plateau or Oshara tradition, and the Northern Colorado Plateau tradition.

This distinction between northern and southern variants in the Archaic material cultures of the Colorado Plateau also occurs with sandals, so it's more than a vagary of stone tool styles. Phil Geib contends in a few other publications that during the Archaic period the Northern Colorado Plateau tradition was centered on the Colorado, Green, and Lower San Juan River drainages, or approximately what is now Glen Canyon National Recreation Area; and the Southern Colorado Plateau tradition was centered on the Little Colorado River drainage not far from Flagstaff. Which makes Bears Ears the periphery or "backwoods" of both, where, as in all peripheral settings, attachment to respective cultural heartlands was thin and at least some of the locals commingled to create diverse new variants.

I had the pleasure of acting as a crew chief on three of those Wilderness Volunteers excursions in the Dark Canyon Wilderness, and the most exciting of them was the second year.

Irwin had decided to situate base camp near a spring known to be fairly reliable, and we approached it from two angles. He and I, along with the other seasonal archaeologist, hauled all the heavy equipment about halfway along the canyon bottom by ATV until we reached the non-motorized zone, then hauled it the rest of the way on horseback with help from a couple more Forest Service folks. We would meet everyone else at the appointed rendezvous spot.

I rode a horse part of the way, a wily equestrian oaf named Tazz—short, I'm fairly certain, for Tasmanian Dickhead.* Thanks to him, I learned more than I ever thought necessary about trees and the tensile resilience of their lowermost branches relative to the consistent metric of my face.

I respect horses, but I stop far short of loving or even liking them overmuch. Tazz had a lot to do with this.

The volunteers and trip leaders came down via a connecting trail, hauling all their personal goods on their backs, and we met and set up base camp in a spot as close to the spring as possible that would also accommodate such a large group of people. Which is to say: we set up base camp about half a mile from the spring. The dirty, muddy spring.

By the end of the second day, we were already sick to death of using hand-pump water filters to purify gallons upon gallons of water and haul them back to camp in bottles and cooking pots. By the third day, mud and silt had infiltrated our filters to a point far beyond the recommended specifications, and most of them failed. Then one of the volunteers got the brilliant idea that, since people in movies and television shows always dug down for water (as did people digging a well for their house), digging down into the compacted clay at the bottom of the spring pool would undoubtedly yield more water. What occurred instead was a poignant lesson in geohydrology: by removing the impenetrable layer of clay, he exposed the deep layer of sand underneath, which is famously *not* impenetrable. Our horrid but precious water percolated downward into the sand and disappeared.

Not long after this, some impressive rainwater pools were found in the deep defiles of a nearby side canyon where the sun hadn't yet been able to dry them up since the last of the monsoons over a month before. The water tasted like tree sap, and we had to skim a variety of floating things off the top of the pools before filtering, but that didn't stop us from being really giddy about it.

For a total of five days, I led a crew of four—including the two trip leaders (one of whom is in his sixties, the other in his

---

*Razzmatazz, as it turned out.

seventies, and both of whom made me look weak and flabby by comparison)—up slopes and across benches and down cliffs and around pour-offs and through tangled stands of scrub oak and manzanita until we no longer looked like archaeologists so much as wolverine tamers. It was a blast. I've never seen people so thoroughly cut, gouged, and scratched to pieces look so thoroughly pleased with themselves.

On a related side note, it was also in Dark Canyon where I learned one of the most interesting facts that had thus far eluded me: canyons breathe. During a clear day in any season, the ground absorbs a sizable fraction of solar radiation and heats up, heating the air around it. This causes the air to rise, which can create a steady breeze up and out of the canyon during the day depending on factors like topography and air pressure. At night, the process reverses. Cold air is denser than warm air, because the molecules are more tightly packed (think of steel "shrinking" when it's cold), so when the sun goes away all the colder air from higher elevations sinks down into the canyon floor.

This process of air inversion is why the air in Salt Lake City is so reminiscent of Beijing during the winter. And the process is emphatically pronounced in places where you've got mountains right next to canyons, as with Dark Canyon and the Abajos, because mountaintops are where you get the *really* cold air. In certain places, if you stick around long enough, you can feel the wind blowing uphill toward the canyon head during the day and back downhill toward the canyon mouth at night.

Or you can learn about it the way I did, along with acclaimed climber and fellow author Greg Child and our mutual friend Aaron. We made the fun mistake of backpacking the Dark Canyon Wilderness in late autumn of 2019, and compounded that by sleeping on the canyon floor at an intersection between major tributaries. The little REI keychain thermometer I've got on my backpack was just above zero degrees Fahrenheit the last time I could poke my head outside my sleeping bag for more than a few seconds. Every liquid we had with us froze solid all the way through. We were beyond miserable.

A fourth companion, backpacking toward us from another

section the canyon, slept on a bench no more than twenty or thirty feet above the canyon floor. In a T-shirt.

And that's Dark Canyon. A high-elevation bowl that's too cold to farm because it acts like a giant convection refrigerator. For that reason, it's comprised of mostly Archaic archaeology, with an alluring but miniscule smatter of late Pueblo stuff here and there; followed later by historic Ute families who, like folks of the Archaic period, were broad-spectrum foragers. It's a neat place to visit, although if you're reading this book in order to get some hints about where you might go to find highly photogenic archaeology for your social media feeds: Dark Canyon isn't it. Archaic peoples left behind precious little in the way of material culture, being semi- to fully mobile foragers who never built homes out of stone.

One of the coolest sagas from the Archaic period is also the one that pins it into the lifeways of descendent Indigenous communities living in the greater Bears Ears region today: the tale of *Solanum jamesii*, or the little wild or Four Corners potato.

Back in 2017, near the town of Escalante, a team of researchers from the University of Utah discovered potato starch residues in the tiny crevices of a ground-stone tool. Similar analyses by researchers at the University of Utah had already challenged the long-standing notion that ground-stone tools—manos and metates, for the most part; think mortars and pestles, but a lot bigger—came into widespread usage in the mid to late Archaic period because of increased broadening of diets to include things like seeds. Nobody mashes tubers like potatoes in a big grinding apparatus, after all; do they?

As it turns out: yes, they do. While the increasing appearance of grinding technology in the Great Basin and the Southwest during this time period most certainly means they were *also* processing nuts and seeds and so forth, it turns out they were also mashing tubers. Big deal, right? But this opened the door to refinements in the analytical process, as well as collaborative efforts between the scientists and Indigenous peoples of the region to see what else might be lurking in the figurative and literal crevices of this story.

This comes up a lot throughout this book, so I'll just state it bluntly here: scientific archaeologists and traditionalist Native Americans haven't had what you'd call a comfortable relationship. They still don't, as a matter of fact, although that's finally changing. Respectful dialogue, collaboration as equals, and acknowledgment that traditional cultural knowledge is just as important as scientific data in puzzling out the human past accomplishes a handful of goals at once—starting with people being *happy* about it, and ending with a more complete picture of history.

Enter the Four Corners potato. Spearheaded by Lisbeth Louderback, an assistant professor at the U and curator of archaeology at the Natural History Museum of Utah, the research team investigated numerous artifacts and consulted with numerous Indigenous farmers, chefs, and botanists to rebuild its story. And it's a good one. It turns out that about a dozen Native American tribes report sustained or sporadic consumption of the little wild tuber, including the Southern Paiute, Hopi, Diné, and Zuñi tribes—i.e., most of the cast of Bears Ears. So, it wasn't exactly news to them that their ancestors were also eating the things.

What *was* surprising is data suggesting that the plant was either manipulated or outright domesticated as early as eleven thousand years ago (or about 9000 BC). All varieties of the common potato, including the ones sprouting ambitious green shoots in your kitchen because you've forgotten about them until just this moment, are different forms of *Solanum tuberosum*. It was domesticated in the Andes right around seven thousand years ago, and subsequently sent all over the world as a result of colonization—alongside maize,* chocolate, peppers, tomatoes,

---

* Literally *Zea mays*, and called "maize" by archaeologists in a lot of the more recent literature, which is why I use the term myself—the word "corn" is a generalized British term for "grain."

and tobacco. Accordingly, it has long been assumed by scientists that all domesticated plant and animal species in the Americas got that way in Meso- or South America and then moved north. That might not be true.

Four Corners potato plants are pretty rare in the wild, requiring a specific set of growing conditions. And the way to make them palatable is to boil them in a certain type of white clay—called "potato clay" by the Hopi for this very reason—to leach out the toxins that make it taste awful on its own, according to a Hopi botanist quoted in the researchers' press release. This underscores the ecological knowledge that must have been employed and passed along for millennia in order for these impressive little spuds to be substantial enough dietary components to still be detectable on a bunch of very old rocks.

From there, the still-unfolding story shifts over to the ballooning world of Native American food revitalization. The central figure is an Oglala Lakota fellow named Sean Sherman, author of an incredible cookbook titled *The Sioux Chef's Indigenous Kitchen*. In a nutshell, widespread ideas about organic, holistic, grass-fed, and other buzzwords for non-industrialized foods have opened a niche into which Indigenous peoples stepped with a hearty, "Hey, looking for us?" Efforts to stamp Native cultures out of existence to achieve the goal of assimilation didn't stop with shoving kids into Indian schools and hitting them if they spoke anything other than English—they also included discouraging or outright banning long-established dietary traditions. Indigenous groups and their allies throughout the country have been pushing for an ancestral food revival ever since, and the movement has gained considerable momentum in recent years.

Thanks to all this, humble little *S. jamesii* is at the center of a micro-revolution in and around the Bears Ears area. Utah Diné Bikéyah, a nonprofit group at the center of the Bears Ears National Monument effort, reported in a recent newsletter how Indigenous farmers throughout the region have begun planting it in their gardens. This wasn't really possible before the collaborative effort noted above—even if it was indeed domesticated so long ago, knowledge of the tricky process of cultivating it was subsequently stamped out. But, as UDB notes, local Indigenous farmers are now "re-learning the physiology of this crop." That's something worth celebrating, given how knowledge about a species of edible potato that's endemic to arid conditions might be of some use to all of us if, oh I don't know, maybe something happens with the climate…

The potatoes themselves are about the size of a marble. They taste a bit like store-bought reds with a hint of peanut and a tougher skin that gives a satisfying *crunch* when you eat a handful at once.

The first archaeologists to investigate the Bears Ears area itself were, naturally enough, antiquities collectors—or "antiquarians," harkening back to the European movement of that name—who practiced a form of archaeology we would now more accurately call rapacious looting. They took an interest in the archaeological richness of the Bears Ears area thanks to reports generated through exploration, government surveys, and other formal forays into the area in the mid to late nineteenth century.

This was during the period immediately following the Civil War, when the federal government decided that paying a bit of attention to the western territories was an important component of its domestic policy. To that end, two waves were dispatched from the East. The first wave, starting in 1866, were six all-Black cavalry regiments that were deployed to help deal with the Native uprisings, run down cattle rustlers, and generally police the West for stagecoaches, wagon trains, railroad crews, and the like. They were called "buffalo soldiers" by the Indigenous people they encountered, supposedly because of their kinky black hair, although nobody knows for sure—at any rate, the name stuck.

The second wave, starting the very next year, were the four so-called Great Surveys to explore and map the western United States. Between the years 1867 and 1879, the survey expeditions carried out under Ferdinand V. Hayden, Clarence King, George Wheeler, and John Wesley Powell resulted in maps and notes for thousands of square miles that were so accurate that many of them could still be used today. There was much bickering over funds between them, of course, and no small amount of hijinks and adventure before the sum of their efforts was subsumed into (and, ultimately, dwarfed by) the US Geological Survey in 1879.

William Henry Holmes was an artist, cartographer, and early American anthropologist, who began his lengthy and complex career sketching fossils at the Smithsonian. In 1872, Holmes caught the attention of Hayden, and was hired on to his survey team as artist and topographer. Carefully sketching plants, animals, rocks, people, and archaeological sites all day, every day, for several years engendered a natural curiosity about the things being sketched, and it wasn't long before Holmes started gaining attention as a pioneering geologist and archaeologist.

William Henry Jackson was also a deft hand at sketching, and some of his sketches of archaeological sites in the Bears Ears area are so expertly crafted that I was able to use them for a condition-assessment project almost a century and a half later—but he's best known for his skills with a camera. After obtaining a camera and moving out west in 1867, the amiable Jackson befriended and photographed scores of Indigenous individuals living in the Omaha region. This attracted the attention of the Union Pacific railroad company, who hired him to take scenic photographs along their routes for advertising purposes. And *that* attracted the attention of Hayden.

The Hayden Survey, including both William Henries, arrived in the greater Bears Ears area in the mid-1870s, reaching Mesa Verde by 1874. What they encountered halted Hayden in his tracks. The last "official" investigation of that area had taken place under the direction of Major John Macomb in 1859, but when people started blowing great holes in each other over the little matter of whether or not it was okay to own other human beings as property, Macomb became too distracted to publish a report in time for Hayden to read it. Because of this, he and his men were slightly taken aback by what they suddenly saw before them.

Realizing that sketching, photographing, and describing archaeological sites was going to be a major part of inventorying

the Four Corners area whether he liked it or not, Hayden assigned
Holmes and Jackson as leaders of two archaeological exploring
parties in the Dolores, La Plata, Mancos, and McElmo areas on
the Colorado Territory side of the northern San Juan in 1875.
Later that same year, Jackson pushed his exploring party into
Bears Ears country proper as far as Comb Wash, where he took
what are probably the first photographs of archaeological sites in
that area.

In 1876, the Great or Centennial Exposition—the first
official world's fair to be convened in the United States—took
place in Philadelphia to mark the one hundredth anniversary
of the signing of the Declaration of Independence there. It was
officially named the International Exhibition of Arts, Manufac-
tures, and Products of the Soil and Mine, and the "international"
part is why it's now called the first world's fair: thirty-seven
different nations participated in the event. Some ten million
people came to see the multitudinous displays and wonders on
exhibit in the small city within a city that was the Centennial
Exposition between May and November. Among its highlights
was an exhibition of photographs and clay models of Mesa Verde's
cliff dwellings by William Henry Jackson.

That was the first of two fuses that ignited nationwide
interest in the archaeology of the Four Corners area. The second
and slightly larger one would take place at the World's Columbian
Exposition, a slightly larger follow-up party that took place in 1893.

The first person to make a noteworthy archaeological
collection in Grand Gulch was Charles Lange in or around 1880.
He came to Bluff as a member of the 1879 San Juan or Hole-in-
the-Rock Expedition, although he was already an adult when he
arrived. Rumor has it that Lange took abundant photos of the
area and his amassed wealth of pilfered prehistory, and that the
photos still exist somewhere. I know people who check eBay
at least once a week to see if they've serendipitously surfaced
anyplace as an inheritance or something, but no luck yet.

Not including those commissioned from elsewhere, Albert R.
Lyman, who arrived in Bluff in 1881—his mother was pregnant
with him in Fillmore, Utah, when she set off with the Hole-in-

the-Rock expedition—was one of the earliest locals to not only explore the Bears Ears area but also take careful notes about his explorations. Unlike Lange's purported photographs, Lyman's writings never disappeared. Moreover, in an oral history recorded in 1970, Lyman discusses excavations made at the Bluff Great House in the early 1890s, as well as two prehistoric roads that he recognized around the turn of the century—one just to the north of Bluff, and the other nearer to Cedar Mesa.

Starting in 1890, Colorado entrepreneurs Charles McLoyd and Charles Cary Graham made use of trails cut by Mormon pioneers in 1879 to launch their own explorations of the area. That trend continues today, incidentally, with looters sometimes taking advantage of newly blazed logging and development-exploration roads before local law enforcement even realizes they've been created.

McLoyd and Graham scrambled through Grand Gulch all the way to Shangri-La Canyon, excavated what is now called Perfect Kiva in what was then called Graham (now Bullet) Canyon, and conducted a number of additional investigations in upper Grand Gulch between Graham/Bullet Canyon and Kane Gulch. Theirs was also the first team to excavate Turkey Pen Ruin, an iconic site that continues to yield a bounty of information to this very day.

Most of their collected and excavated materials were bought by Reverend Charles H. Green of Durango in 1891. Green was a well-to-do pastor affiliated with the Art Institute of Chicago, and that last element might explain his exuberant fixation with archaeological relics, although they were becoming pretty popular by that time in any case. According to a number of sources, Green paid for an additional expedition of his own to add to his collection, and then purchased even more collections just for good measure.

Fastidious in nature, he not only catalogued his collection but published the catalog. It bears the bemusing title *Catalogue of a Unique Collection of Cliff Dweller Relics Taken from the Lately Discovered Ruins of Southwestern Colorado and Adjacent Parts of Utah, New Mexico and Arizona: Scientifically Estimated to be the Oldest Relics in the World: A Short History of the Strange*

Race, Region and Ruins. Don't ask me what sort of scientific estimation the good reverend used to conclude that his looted goods were the "oldest relics in the world" or the material residue of a "strange race," because I couldn't begin to guess. After a thorough description of his collection, Green's publication wanders into an exhaustive screed that includes speculation that the Cliff Dwellers were "driven out" of the northern Southwest and moved south to become, in succession, the Aztecs, Toltecs, Mayans, and Inca. Not a bad guess, given the evidence at the time, although every single bit of it turned out to be wrong.

Of more consequence for the Bears Ears area than Green's speculation on the origin and fate of those whom we now call the Ancestral Pueblo was the fact of his being so public-minded in the first place. As a public scholar myself, I can certainly empathize. Keeping scientific information locked away from the public behind literal gates in laboratories and/or figurative gates in jargon-drenched technical literature is a good way to make the public dislike you, especially when (as now) that science is publicly funded and takes place on public lands.

But the flipside of public scholarship is popularity, as Bears Ears conservationists are learning more and more by the day. In addition to cranking out a publication about his own collection and associated historical fantasies, Green also took his treasures around the country in a variety of public display venues and magazines before finally dumping them into Chicago's Field Museum. This had some repercussions, including invigorated interest in the area and subsequent efforts by McLoyd and Graham to ramp up their own collection efforts.

Reverend Green's public operations also inspired Frederic Putnam of the Peabody Museum. The World's Columbian Exposition, follow-up to the Centennial one, was scheduled to occur in Chicago in 1893,* and Putnam decided that his ineluctable

---

* It was supposed to be the quadricentennial celebration of Columbus landing in the Americas in 1492, the "92" part being therefore of some importance. The fact that they had 400 years to prepare and still got the date wrong speaks volumes.

destiny included displaying the single most impressive collection of artifacts and images from the mysterious cultures of
the ancient Southwest. All that stood in his way was the minor
obstacle of not having one.

To that end, he hired Hopewell archaeologist Warren K.
Moorehead to lead an expedition throughout the northern San
Juan region from Durango to Comb Ridge, a distance of some
two hundred miles; and to explore, sketch, map, photograph,
and—most importantly—dig archaeological sites along the way.
The expedition was planned and directed by the magazine *The
Illustrated American*, a general-audience publication not unlike
Harper's that was moderately popular at the time. Part of the deal
was that they would publish a series of exciting reports of the
expedition as it unfolded.

Their field reports would run under the series title In Search
of a Lost Race, hearkening back to Green's assertions about the
ancient Southwesterners being a unique species of human. These
were the days of widespread Darwinian misinterpretation, after
all—when educated white people in America and Europe saw
different ethnic groups as varying types of dead ends on evolutionary branches that hadn't been able to reach quite as high as
their own. Nowadays, it's the *un*educated ones who occupy that
position.

The real-time publication of field reports is worthy of some
comment. It was a fairly common practice at the time, believe
it or not, but still a remarkably dumb one. What happens if your
six-month journey gets suddenly and inexorably curtailed by
total tragedy on day forty-two? Or if one or several of the dispatches get lost in the mail? Or if any of incalculable numbers
of other calamities were to occur? The annals of Instagram
include numerous examples of users posting the first six breathtaking days of a planned three-month Appalachian Trail hike,
followed abruptly by a post about how it's hard getting around the
house on crutches. Others, somewhat more ominously, just stop
altogether.

Of course, calamities are exactly what producers are hoping
for when they post supposedly real-time content in the form of

so-called "reality television" shows—they'll go out of their way to manufacture them, if necessary. In a weird and amusing way, the *Illustrated American* Exploring Expedition preceded them in this regard.

It was, almost by design, a shitshow. Equipment and funds often arrived late, and in some cases never arrived at all. Same with personnel—the trip doctor, for example, never appeared, which meant the team was comprised entirely of eastern dandies with no clue how to splint a broken leg. Permits to cross the Ute and Navajo Reservations also never showed, so they had to slip around them as inconspicuously as possible (while dispatching real-time field reports about their movements for publication in a popular magazine). All of this put them further and further outside their collective comfort zones, and deeper and deeper into harm's way. No small amount of expedition material was lost or stolen as a result.

My favorite part of their epic journey is the one where they tried to boat the Animas River down to its confluence with the San Juan in a poorly constructed wooden boat. This was a publicity stunt that would put both PETA and Putin to shame: a group of hand-wringing gentlemen from the big cities of the East Coast—with, again, no physician in attendance—attempting to run the maritime equivalent of a jalopy down an unmapped and hardly known stretch of river through an area literally famous for its rocks.

It went about how you'd expect.

The boat itself was wrecked and abandoned at Farmington, just above the Animas-San Juan confluence, but not before a considerable amount of expensive equipment and scientifically invaluable materials were lost over the side. Afterward, the bedraggled but somehow undrowned expedition members dutifully dispatched their report of the undertaking from a permanent camp in Bluff. Moorehead himself reported the feat thusly: "The most dangerous feat of river navigation attempted since Major Powell and his party floated down the Colorado River has been accomplished by the *Illustrated American* Exploring Expedition." If you know anything about Powell's expeditions, this is like equating the Indy 500 to a back-alley drag race that ended in flames.

All told, they visited something like one hundred archaeological sites between Durango and Comb Ridge, the majority of which had never been described or excavated before. Although the trip was a disaster, it did result in an astonishing array of photographs, drawings, field notes, maps, and excavated artifacts. And all of it was totally destroyed when the *Illustrated American*'s New York office burned down a few years later. Moorehead would comment that the fire was "a fitting end" to the enterprise.

Luckily, the fourteen short installments of In Search of a Lost Race still remain. They're the only extant relics from this singularly loony episode in the history of Southwest archaeology.

My own journey into Southwest archaeology commenced the year after my last season living and working at the North Rim of the Grand Canyon. I had attempted (and failed gloriously) to obtain a degree in English lit from the University of New Orleans right after escaping high school, and wound up as a professional vagabond in the seasonal resort circuit instead. That lifestyle took me all over most of the North American continent, including occupational residency in eight different states. It's a lot of fun, if you can pull it off and don't mind never having a permanent address.

While living and working at the North Rim, I fell in with what is variously called the "recreational archaeology" or "site bagger" scene, those devotees of authors like David Roberts and Craig Childs whose idea of a fun weekend is to hoist a backpack and go looking for some ancient artifact, structure, or rock art they'd heard about someplace. I often liken the relationship between that scene and professional archaeology to the one between birdwatchers and ornithologists: the former aren't scientists, by any stretch, but nor are they collectors or despoilers. They've simply got an obsession with finding and ogling over a certain type of thing.

I first dipped my toe into this particular pastime when my roommate Dave Rock took me to visit an alcove in the backcountry of Zion National Park. We spent half a day scrambling around in pockets of sand, tripping over manzanita branches, and doing that special type of ambulation that's often a point of pride among red rock connoisseurs: ascending and descending near-vertical sandstone inclines like two-legged spiders with *way* too much confidence in our boot soles. That was the first time I'd tried friction-climbing bedrock slopes, having only recently arrived in sandstone country, and I somehow managed to slip and go for a merry tumble only two or three times.

It turned out to be what I would nowadays consider a very ho-hum archaeological site: a shallow alcove, a handful of faded pictographs, and some lithic and ceramic residue. Back in those days, however, it was the first time in my life that I'd ever visited such a thing. It was the first time that I realized doing so was *possible*. Growing up in the only-slightly-post-Puritan culture of the rural Northeast, I'd been taught that everything worth finding has been found, every place worth exploring has been mapped and developed, and daydreaming about adventure is no way to earn a paycheck (that being, of course, what life is all about).

It was in rebellion against that ethos that my childhood bestie and I spent so much time poking about the forests of upstate New York, a more tactile escape than our books would allow. Like Chris McCandless in *Into the Wild*, we would create adventures by turning the known into the unknown through the simple act of pretending maps didn't exist.

Thus, being taken to a genuine archaeological site that Rock had only recently discovered himself—unmapped, as far as we could tell—was mind-blowing. It didn't matter to me that it was such a meager site, and it frankly still doesn't. It was life-altering.

I oohed and aahed until it started to get dark. I almost fainted when I found a ceramic sherd that had a design painted onto it. I didn't take it with me—even back then I understood that doing so was naughty—so, instead, I borrowed the design itself and developed it into a tattoo to commemorate that infatuating first encounter. A couple years later, that tattoo would spark a conversation with an Indigenous archaeologist and alter my perceptions yet again.

The decision to become a professional archaeologist grew out of that first encounter, snowballing in size and strength with every grueling weekend excursion my friends and I took to the Southwest backcountry looking for stuff to gawp at. It was—and remains—a fun way to spend a few days off, albeit a selfish one. The recreational archaeology scene isn't notably destructive, or at least it wasn't before the invention of heinous maladies like automated geotagging; nor does it tend to contribute toward research or preservation efforts.

This is one of the ways that karmic debt is incurred, in my estimation. I would end up owing quite a lot of it to Bears Ears.

I kept working in the service industry through my undergraduate courses, of course—both because college is exorbitantly expensive and because tending bar is loads of fun—but I was able to devote myself to my studies, nonetheless. Unlike the English program at the University of New Orleans, here was a field of study I cared about in a place that felt like home (Northern Arizona University in Flagstaff). I had dropped out of UNO with a grade point average that was considerably south of unsatisfactory. I would graduate from NAU number one in my class.

The real journey began outside of the classroom, as it often does. In this case it was in Walnut Canyon, near the outskirts of Flagstaff, where the National Park Service had taken to employing anthropology students at relatively low wages to work on archaeological projects, thereby providing both cheaper labor for themselves and valuable field experience for the students.

And what, besides a paltry nine dollars per hour, did I get out of working for them?

Scene: it is just before dawn, still dark but edging toward bluish gray. A sky the color of rifle barrels. Thin layers of crunchy snow cover the ground; a light breeze blows the odd drift of scintillating crystals from the boughs of stately ponderosa pines arching overhead, twisting wistfully as they fall. We stamp our feet, blow great clouds from our mouths and noses, slurp steaming coffee and mutter with weary cheerfulness about how it'll be getting warmer soon. Gear gets stowed in packs, brief chat from the crew chief about safety, and we descend. We scramble and slide to the canyon bottom, walk over icy rocks and tumbledown scree, and start the slow clamber up the other side toward a series of alcoves. By now the sun is up, peeking through the trees on the opposite rim, casting strange shadows in the alcoves where half a dozen young men and women unsling their packs with shivering grins. All around are standing rock walls, pottery sherds, corn cobs, glassy rock fragments, bits of ancient plaster and mortar, and uncountable numbers of loose and scattered stones. Clipboards, pencils, rulers, scales, line levels, and compasses come out, and the team sets to work drawing, by hand, detailed and precise maps of every single object. Every detail in every wall segment, every artifact, every loose rock; all of it. Tiny stones take whole minutes to map in. Walls take hours, sometimes days. It probably took less time to *build* the structures we're recording than it takes to make such detailed maps of their crumbling remains, and yet nobody complains. The coffee is long gone; tea and hot chocolate are shared. Stories are told between sandwich bites. And then we pack up and trudge back as the sky edges toward darkness once again.

And that's archaeology, or one aspect of it: careful, precise, tedious, and often employing outdated means of execution. I couldn't get enough of it. I would soon learn that most of modern archaeology consists more accurately of walking and walking and walking—and then writing very long reports about what, if anything, you found along the way (the technical term for this is *pedestrian survey*). The days of digging up graves and shipping whatever they contain back east to museums are long gone, thankfully.

It was the deeper plunge into academia somewhat later that prompted me to start questioning the ethics of modern American archaeology all over again, as I had when I was just a wily pilgrim with a sturdy backpack and open weekends.

My exodus following graduation was a weird one, fittingly enough. I was homeless. On purpose.

It was an idea that an old friend and I had kicked around for a number of years, and he'd taken the plunge and tried it a few years earlier when he was in graduate school for engineering. He lived for about half a year in a tent in the New Hampshire woods, commuting to the UNH campus where he used the fitness center for all things hygienic and his tiny office for pretty much everything else. This same friend would later face a traumatizing ailment and equally traumatizing mistreatment by the American medical industry at about the same time that I did (undiagnosed celiac disease in his case; Lyme disease in mine), but for those blissful months he lived out a fantasy we had both talked about for years. I was sick with envy, so to speak, and set about evening the score.

I found a place on the edge of town, equidistant to the gym where I had a membership and a place where I could rent a four-by-eight-foot storage unit for forty dollars a month. I stacked everything but my clothes neatly into the back two-thirds of the space. In the front I placed a hamper, a small shelf for laundry soap and similar necessaries, and a wheeled steel vanity with two wire shelves for pants, socks, underwear, shoes, and a bar overtop for hanging shirts and jackets.

In addition to fitness equipage, membership at the gym provided me with clean showers, bulk soap and shaving cream in pump-top dispensers, ample sinks, mirrors, and fresh towels. For all that, plus hot tub and dry sauna and pool, I paid thirty-five dollars a month. That's seventy-five dollars total monthly outlay for nearly everything a modern home can provide in terms of necessity—a closet for clothing, safe storage for valuables and necessities, and a place to groom that also encouraged exercise. Everything but a kitchen and a place to relax and sleep in privacy. I addressed those needs in other ways.

Into the forest I brought a set of nesting steel pots, a plastic bowl and a few utensils, a two-burner stove, a cooler, a chair, a folding aluminum table, tent, sleeping pad, blanket, pillow, water jug, and plastic basins for washing. I also brought a bucket, shovel, and handsaw for campfires. Headlamp and lantern. Extra batteries. Car charger for the phone. Matches. Notebook. And…not much else.

It was that easy.

Granted, I had the advantage of living someplace that's surrounded by public lands, where they ask only that you move your camp at least every two weeks. There was also no fire ban that summer, so I sat beside—and occasionally cooked over—a cheery little blaze most nights. And it was summer, after all; I didn't need a dogsled team to get around. And, of course, my gender and palefacedness bequeathed the privilege of feeling safe while camping alone in the wilderness without benefit of proximity alarms or a moat. But still.

My neighbors were coyotes. My lawn was a paradise of stout little scrub oaks and tall, stately ponderosas. My nightlight was the moon and stars. All this for a monthly "rent" about equal to the cost of two tanks of gas. My clientele at the country club where I mixed drinks had no idea their head bartender was slumming it among the pines right outside their stately second or third homes.

I wouldn't know it for another year, but that was also when I got sick.

Chapter Three: The First Farmers

Researchers of the ancient Southwest often refer to the stretch of time following the Archaic as the Formative, in deference to the outdated idea of unilineal cultural evolution that postulated a steady upward march in social progress to which all human societies are invariably compelled. It's the time in which peoples of the Southwest adopted maize agriculture, learned how to make ceramic vessels, replaced the atlatl with the bow and arrow, and began constructing increasingly large and impressive masonry structures. Because of this, application of the umbrella term *Formative* was—and, in some people's eyes, still is—tantamount to saying they had moved forward from Hobbes' "nasty, brutish, and short" life of Stone Age savages and were on their way toward civilization. How nice for them!

Under the Formative umbrella, the Pecos classification—or local variants of it—is most commonly used by archaeologists to assign ancient sites in the northern Southwest to one or more of a series of culture phases, starting with Basketmaker II and running through Pueblo IV. It's an impressive effort, compartmentalizing the entire sweep of about two thousand years of prehistoric cultural and behavioral adaptation into a set of six discrete pigeonholes, but it's also inherently flawed. It is still loosely rooted in unilineal evolution, for one thing, such that the gradual creation and proliferation of ever-greater architectural splendors should proceed in a nice, gradual, forward march. For the enormous freestanding superstructures of Chaco Canyon to be built in the Pueblo II period and not be outdone—or even matched—in the subsequent PIII or PIV periods makes as much sense in this particular rubric as the Mayans building the mighty temples of Tikal before going back to living in wood huts in the jungle. Both of these really did happen, and both of them carry the same basic message: "progress" is relative, not inherent.

For this reason, most researchers employ research strategies based on local phenomena rather than structured by culture-history stage units, which are problematic for their tendency to pigeonhole entire *actual* cultures into blanket classes based on trends in the material record. That way, they can detect and explore more subtle differences in the material and behavioral record. Nonetheless, there is definite region-wide patterning in architecture, occupation and abandonment sequences, and tree-cutting booms and busts that articulate with climate data in a manner that broadly agrees with the Pecos classification.

So, to keep things simple, I'm choosing to retain the Pecos classification as a generalized outline of the prehistory of the Bears Ears area. But I'm also choosing to jettison the term *Formative*, because to me it smells problematic. I always tell people that the Formative years of my own adulthood were spent in New Orleans, between the ages of approximately eighteen and twenty-three, because during the preceding years I was a total putz and afterward I was less of one. There was actual progress, of a sort. Indigenous cultures, on the other hand, were fine just as they were before, during, and after the so-called Formative era, or between approximately 1500 BC and AD 1492.

Nobody is quite certain how maize made its way to and then throughout the Southwest when it did, although it definitely came from Mesoamerica. The classic dichotomy when it comes to questions about how cultural or behavioral components move between different regions is diffusion versus migration, the first being the movement of ideas or behaviors across a given landscape via local adoption while the second is the movement of people themselves. The difference is like that between the British Invasion of the 1960s, in which British culture *figuratively* penetrated into America when hip young Americans decided British music and television shows were cool; and the British invasion of the 1600s, in which British culture *literally* penetrated into America when British people arrived on boats and started killing everyone.

As for how maize came to be, that's a fascinating story in its own right. One that we're just now beginning to understand. Maize as we know it today, in particular the "feed corn" variety that dominates the Midwest and "sweet corn" variety that dominates almost everything we eat, is relatively new and does not occur naturally in the wild. Its ancestral form is a rough, tough grass called *teosinte* with ears of hard little kernels that are effectively inedible. It can still be found in Mexico's Central Balsas River Valley, or a variant of it can at any rate, and it looks like cornstalks would look if they were branching shrubs instead of stalks.

Starting some nine thousand years ago, people began the dual process of suppressing the branches so that they produced lower numbers of larger ears, and then selecting and replanting the ones whose ears had kernels that were the least like gravel. Nobody is entirely certain why they picked teosinte, and it's altogether possible that they were experimenting with all sorts of different plant species. But it's the one that worked. Kernels became a tiny bit larger every year, with increasing rows of kernels per ear and higher nutrient content over time.

By about 6,500 hundred years ago, now fully recognizable as maize, it had spread downward into South America. By 4,000 years ago, it was in the American Southwest. It moved into all sorts of different areas with different growing conditions, and accumulated a vast array of variations in the process. It was a slow explosion, but the maize family exploded nonetheless, with six primary types—flint, flour, dent, pop, sweet, and waxy—and hundreds of varieties.

Then, with modern industrialization, the process reversed. Within-crop diversity of all commercially grown and sold cultivars has reduced dramatically in the last one hundred years, as agribusiness interests zero-in on factors like yield predictability and pest resistance. The total number of known varieties in 1903 was right around three hundred, with commercial seed houses offering handfuls of different ones in different places. By 1983, we were down to twelve.

This is a result of *monoculture*, the practice of growing a single species in a given growth environment (a field, say) in order to ensure predictable harvests and, while you're at it, increased nutrient depletion in the soil and risk of epidemic pathogens in the food-supply chain. This isn't a hypothetical risk; it really can happen, especially in the plant world. In or just before 1905, a species of tree parasite called *Cryphonectria parasitica* made its way to the United States from Southeast Asia, where the local trees had largely grown immune to its evils, and discovered that it and the mighty American chestnut trees were seemingly made for each other. The parasite infested the trees like a key in a long-lost lock, and by 1940 almost every single mature American chestnut in North America was dead.

Diversity is a safety strategy. That's why nature invented it in the first place. It buffers against unexpected impacts with devastating effects on narrow targets, what biologists sometimes call *stochastic shocks*, by variegating the targets. A chestnut blight in a diverse forest is crappy for the chestnuts, but the forest itself endures. A chestnut blight in a forest full of nothing but chestnuts is an arboreal apocalypse. And the same is true of social, cultural, psychological, linguistic, and sexual diversity.

According to Hopi archaeologists, traditional notions of the creation and spread of maize agriculture are a little different—albeit not *entirely* different—and have much to say about diversity. The Hopi are among the direct descendants of the Ancestral Pueblo communities of the Bears Ears area, and their cultural history is one of migrations, with groups from various places gradually coming together over time. When you add those two components together, the emergent story is one of the Hopi and their ancestors moving and adapting to conditions all over the

Southwest and beyond—and their sacred principal crop doing exactly the same thing. The results of these overlapping patterns of migration and diversity are the Hopi people themselves, and maize.

In the Bears Ears area, the BMII or Early Basketmaker period is usually pinned to between 400 BC and AD 450, although the time from about 2000 BC up to then—called by many researchers the Early Agricultural period—was one of significant, crucial, and largely undetectable experimentation. We do know that people living on and around Cedar Mesa were fully dependent on maize (it made up seventy-eighty percent of their dietary protein) by 400 BC.

That doesn't happen automatically except in rare circumstances of top-down forcing, like when Native Americans were suddenly consuming a lot of sugar on reservations because they were cut off from their ancestral food sources—or when, in the span of less than a century, the historic Irish became almost totally dependent on a tuber that's originally from the Andes. What fascinating trials and errors led from the introduction of maize to its near-total dominance over local subsistence practices during that 1,600-year gap is one of tremendous interest in the realms of both scientific literature and Indigenous traditional cultural knowledge.

Then there's the question of why they—or, for that matter, anyone—adopted agriculture in the first place. The popular answer among behavioral ecologists is that the adoption of agriculture in general was precipitated by resource depression, which is what you get when people and/or climatic shifts shove all the choice comestibles off the table. It's the next step in the sequence of expanding diet breadth that began with commencement of the Archaic period: first the giant animals go, and then the big animals, and then the small animals, and then the fruits and berries that are highly dependent on good weather to grow, and so you're left eating—and defecating—grasses and their seeds. Which handily explains why maize, rice, wheat, oats, barley, rye, and nearly all the rest of the world's principal carbohydrate domesticates are grasses. You wouldn't choose to eat grass unless richer vegetal foods and nutrient condensers* have become awfully sparse relative to the consumer population.

Nearly every study conducted on the subject has found a downward spiral of low-cost/high-yield food items does precipitate adoption of cultivated foods. Foraging is preferable where possible, because it typically includes a greater variety of fare and is almost always easier. Farming, as any farmer knows, is not an action so much as a process. Preparing the field, planting, watering and/or weeding, scaring away birds and other interlopers, harvesting and processing… Having a garden patch is like having a child that stays in one place while it grows. You can't even order it to hide under its desk when a hoard of locusts appears. It just *stands there.*

So: farming is a huge pain compared with foraging, and it only really makes sense when foraging ceases to be an option. Simple, universal answers like that are satisfying, but the situation gets a bit more complicated the deeper one dives into it.

In terms of relative yield, for example, maize provides more dietary calories than the majority of popular Southwestern plants that foragers were eating. Only pine nuts and black walnuts decisively win on this account, and that's because they're fatty nuts. And maize offers a lot more than just calories. Although famously deficient in lysine and tryptophan, both of which can be found in beans but can also just as easily be found in wild items like amaranth, maize is remarkably nutritious. And it can be dried to rock-hard and then stored almost indefinitely. And you can ferment it into maize beer (called *chicha* in Peru and other far-south places). And you can roast fish and tamale fixings wrapped inside its husks. And you can make it into bread. And it comes in a variety of pretty colors, or anyway it used to. And you can pop it.

---

* *Nutrient condensers* are prey species, in that they do carnivores the blessed favor of condensing entire hillsides of bitter roughage into ambulating barbecue fare. Think of it this way: imagine one person spends days, months, or years collecting seashells; and then another, more enterprising person clunks that one over the head and takes the shells all in one go. That, in a nutshell, is how meat-eating evolved.

And you can get sugar from its stalks, like you can with its near relative sugarcane. And tea brewed from its silk has medicinal properties. And you can make pipes out of the cobs...

In sum, there's a lot more reasons to take an interest in maize than the simple calorie-modeling concept of "hunting and bad weather killed off all the deer—so, grass it is."

Because of this early and stolid relationship with maize, habitations in and around the Bears Ears area during the Early Basketmaker period focused first on rock shelter habitations in canyon areas where floodwater could be utilized for runoff irrigation. Unlike the so-called Cliff Dwellers of later eras, who preferred south-facing alcoves with maximal winter sun and summer shade, Early Basketmaker alcove-dwellers didn't much care what direction they faced. By about 100 BC, however, open-air sites with relatively substantial pit houses began to appear in higher upland areas, indicating that the locals had figured out the precarious practice of dry farming.

Dry farming in places like Cedar Mesa is tricky as hell, and the fact that preindustrial people figured out how to do so with such success is beyond impressive. Trust me on this. Midway between my earliest introduction to archaeology and my involvement in the Bears Ears conservation battle, when I was battling the dual enemies of Lyme disease and academia, my typically slapdash approach to research would focus quite narrowly on Ancestral Pueblo farming strategies in southeastern Utah.

It all began when I was helping my friend and research partner Michael Lewis collect plant samples for his doctoral dissertation on dietary reconstruction. Despite being wobbly of both body and mind at the time, I still retained enough knowledge of the area to serve as a local guide (if a clumsy one) for a fellow grad student from the Pacific Northwest who'd never really spent any time in the Bears Ears area. He paid for food and gas out of his grant money, for which I was incalculably grateful, and we spent a week ambling around doing science. Evenings involved campfires, fatty steaks seared over the flames, a lot of cheap red wine, and the sort of meandering conversations that would be impossible to map in a mere three dimensions.

During one of these dialogues, Michael told me about an exciting paper coauthored by our mutual advisor, Joan Brenner-Coltrain, in 2005. The subject of the paper was how stable oxygen isotope ratios in the cellulose of archaeological maize cobs could, when compared to stable oxygen isotopes in local water sources, be used to infer how they were watered. The original research was conducted under controlled laboratory conditions, and Joan and some other mutual colleagues had been running analyses of a similar sort on modern maize cobs from experimental plots in Range Creek for several years, but to our knowledge the method had never been functionally applied in an archaeological context. We both pondered this as we chewed the fat (literally).

From that sprang the Cedar Mesa Water Project, later renamed the Bears Ears Water Project after a stint with the Manti-La Sal National Forest and subsequent realizations about the cultural interconnectedness of all the major landforms of the area. It really was like a mosaic, or a quilt, with people living *here* during this period and *there* during that period, depending upon variables like climate, local conditions, resource depression, and whatever people were into at the time. It is impossible to study the archaeology of any one portion of the Bears Ears area and get the whole story. You've got to look at the entire area, holistically, to even start to get a clue.

The project itself involved collecting samples from snow, streams, springs, and rainfall on and around Cedar Mesa to determine background water-chemistry levels; analyzing archaeological maize cobs for oxygen isotope ratios in their cellulose; and then comparing the two in accordance with the original study. We designed the project to include both mesa-top and canyon-bottom settings in as far-flung corners as we could, ostensibly to broaden our data set but *maybe* also to give ourselves an excuse to make the trips as lengthy as possible. I was still pretty sick at the time, having only just tipped over from fighting off disease to beginning the lengthy process of recovering from its damages—or so my physician explained. Being on and around Cedar Mesa helped me feel immensely better, and I was determined to milk my newest academic pursuit for all the field time it would yield.

What followed was a series of memorable trips with a series of memorable friends over the next five years, until my relationship with the University of Utah became complicated. I dragged my dear friend Eran all over the sweet sandstone backcountry so much that she became addicted, and now works full-time for the National Park Service in Canyonlands' iconic Maze.

Collecting water samples was great fun. Collecting snow samples was great fun. After we were permitted to collect archaeological maize samples for analysis, that was great fun as well.

Science, it turns out, can be great fun. Spread the word.

The most memorable trip of all was in October of 2013, during one of our federal government's occasional experiments with showing voters that bullies really can get what they want if they bully hard enough—a seventeen-day shutdown. These occur when Congress fails to pass all the individual spending bills that comprise an annual federal budget, and/or if the president doesn't sign or outright vetoes any of those spending bills, and they'll sometimes happen for pretty childish reasons. The one in 2013 occurred because President Obama wanted American citizens to have easier access to healthcare. Because of that unholy trespass, most nonessential services were halted, which meant a lot of federal employees were furloughed and a lot of federal buildings were closed.

But not federal lands. Not all of them, anyway. People just *assumed* they were, because ranger stations and visitor centers were all shuttered. Those of us who knew better had the places all to ourselves.

So, there we were—camping and scrambling around the Cedar Mesa area during what is universally regarded as the greatest month of the year to be there, and there was hardly another soul in sight. Golden cottonwoods, singing birds, choirs of coyotes at night, and not a single unleashed poodle, screeching ATV, or lumbering rental RV with families screaming at each other inside. I imagined that this was how earlier authors and locals alike must have experienced the place back in the day, or at least a closer approximation than is usually possible. You don't often get to step into a time machine like that.

And all because our president wanted people to stop going bankrupt as a result of getting sick, an experience that was all too real for me at the time.

My research team would grow to include a few other names, and several publications boiled out of it during the past seven years, but I wouldn't say the project is finished. Ever. The upshot is that we were able to test and support a hypothesis first proposed by Bill Lipe and R. G. Matson when I was a mere stripling, that relied—and relies still—on ethnographic information provided by Hopi farmers. Briefly: they planted in deep, sandy soils with good moisture retention, and relied on water from melted snow in the soil to germinate the maize and sustain it until (hopefully, in a good year) late-summer rainwater during the annual monsoon, or rainy season, allowed it to fill out its ears.

Timing was crucial. It takes a lot of water to fill maize kernels, and the plant's water demand therefore skyrockets at that stage of its development, so the crop has to be hitting that stage just as the rains start to fall (usually on the Fourth of July, just in time to ruin picnics throughout the Four Corners). If the maize seed went into the ground too early, the plant would hit the tassel/kernel stage too early and die of dehydration. If it went in too late, the plant would still have high water demands after the rains had stopped and you'd end up with the same problem. Figuring out how and when to plant in order to hit that bull's-eye would be hard enough with a climatic database and a calculator, and the Ancestral Pueblo of Bears Ears had neither. But figure it out they did.

This practice is still part of the assemblage of methods used by traditional Hopi farmers today. It is one of several strategies they employ depending upon the terrain, and that appears to have been true in ancient southeastern Utah as well. In the case of dry farming, sandy slopes with good moisture retention are preferred—even more so ones that face north, since they undergo less bare-soil evaporation—just as they were with the Ancestral Pueblo. Hopi traditionalists sometimes employ tractors and other modern gadgetry to clear the fields, but for the most part they still do it all by hand. Maize seeds are planted between six and eighteen inches beneath the surface, depending on how far down the stored soil moisture is in a given location that year, and spaced three to five paces apart. They still use a stick to dig the hole, for the simple reason that it disturbs less of the soil and thus exposes less of it to additional evaporation.

Agriculture figures massively in Hopi culture and traditions. According to Leigh Kuwanwisiwma of the Hopi Cultural Preservation Office, agricultural activities "serve to reinforce traditions in each new generation." The Hopi calendar is entirely structured around the maize-farming cycle.

Circumstances are a little different at the Pueblo of Zuñi, but not terribly so. Direct-precipitation farming isn't really an option there either, since the water demands of maize and other crops far exceed what falls from the sky during the growing season, but they traditionally had the advantage of a small tributary of the Little Colorado called the Zuñi River running nearby—until it was dammed by the Bureau of Indian Affairs in 1908 to create Black Rock Reservoir.

This is one of the most blatantly ridiculous cases of American bureaucracy versus Indigenous cultural knowledge. The dam was constructed as a component of the Black Rock Irrigation Project, one of the largest public works projects at the time, in order to make the downstream area more livable for white homesteaders. The dam and associated series of irrigation canals were constructed between 1904 and 1908, and suffered a catastrophic failure the very next year due to unexpectedly high rainfall. The reservoir also began to fill with silt almost immediately, thanks to logging and overgrazing upstream. But the worst part was that the dam and its irrigation channels shifted the loci of farming away from the areas the Zuñi had traditionally farmed and toward ones where the primary sediment context was tightly compacted clay, arguably the worst type of deposition for growing crops outside of bare rock. Nonetheless, the US government forced the Zuñi to relocate themselves and their farms to these areas. Compounding all this was the forced enrollment of Zuñi children in the much-maligned Indian school system, where they were viciously punished for speaking their own language or doing anything else that seemed more Native than American, starting in 1903.

Between these efforts and the encroachment of mainstream American accoutrements like grocery stores, farming at Zuñi largely fell out of practice by World War II. However, as with the topic of Native foodways, interest in traditional gardening at Zuñi has revivified in the past couple of decades. And the centerpiece of that focus is the traditional Zuñi practice of "waffle farming." This is a tenuous strategy that involves building up little walls of dirt about half a foot high, which describe a grid of squares about one foot by one foot in size. The result looks like the surface of a waffle. This simple tactic causes water to pool into the squares, reduces bare-soil evaporation, and offers a few other advantages that are frankly disproportional to the amount of labor they require. It's an ingenious strategy, and one that's making a comeback thanks to tradition-reclamation and sovereignty efforts.

In the Bears Ears area, at least so far as we can tell, there wasn't any waffling going on. But the data from my team's research all point toward a modified version of what the Hopi dry farmers do to this day, underscoring the ongoing cultural connectedness between them and their ancestors.

By the AD 300s, the Early Basketmaker occupation in the Bears Ears area was mostly clustered into neighborhoods of pit houses in open-upland settings like the top of Cedar Mesa. These things warrant some discussion. It's one of those areas where potentially uncomfortable misunderstandings can occur, epitomized by one student's comment during a lecture on the topic a few years ago: "They lived in *holes in the ground*? Eww!"

The answer is a concise "sort of," with the addendum "for very good reasons."

A pit house is just a structure whose floor is lower than the surrounding ground level. You start by excavating a pit, either square or circular, about three to five feet deep. The walls are shored-up with stacked rocks or side-by-side sandstone slabs, or by stabilizing the dirt itself through wetting and pounding at it the way you would an adobe brick and then letting it dry before construction continues. The roof is generally constructed from a combination of larger and smaller poles, starting with four stout uprights holding a square assemblage of almost-as-stout primary beams just above head height. Smaller poles are then leaned from the outer rim up to these primaries in a tight wall all the way around, except for the door opening, with brush and thatch covering that, over which a last layer of earth or plaster is sometimes added.

They're simple to make, although they aren't *easy* to make, in much the same way that Bob Ross can make painting look both simple and easy until you try it. But with practice, you can build one yourself. I've done it.

So, if you're in a pit house, you aren't really living in a *pit* so much as a house that's sunken into the ground. Why? At about thirty feet below the ground virtually any place on the planet, the temperature is constant year-round. This is the *mean Earth temperature* and, in the northern San Juan region, it's right around fifty degrees Fahrenheit. It's what happens when you reach the point where insulation from outside sources meets radiant heat from the center of our big blue marble. There's more and more seasonal variation in temperature as you move toward the ground surface, having less and less deposition to act as an insulator, but even just five or so feet beneath the present ground surface there's a surprisingly dramatic reduction in temperature seasonality. The earliest pit houses in the Bears Ears area, ones that were in use during the Early Basketmaker period, were relatively shallow— usually set just a foot or so into the ground. As time went on, they got deeper and deeper.

Nor was it a teleological savagery-to-civilization development that propelled people out of pit houses into the non-pit type. For one thing, folks in the Southwest never really stopped using them. Why would they? For another, they weren't—and aren't—

unknown to Euro-American cultures either. This was eloquently explained by Forest Service archaeologist Peter Pilles in a lecture he gave at the Verde Valley Archaeological Center in Arizona, from which comes the following:

> If you read your basic textbooks on Southwest archaeology, you're fed one of a number of fairytales. And one of them is that there is a *pit house to pueblo transition*. At April third, five o'clock in the afternoon, every single person jumped out of their pit houses, tore them down, and began building pueblos—and began becoming civilized. Well, every culture that we've looked at in the Southwest, we do find that there are pit houses that extend late into time. In fact, our own culture lived in pit houses. Ever hear of the dugouts in the Plains? The sod houses? Those are pit houses!

This is the thinking behind "root cellars." Back in the days before refrigerators and sodium benzoate, farmers who wanted to store items like root vegetables—potatoes, beets; really anything that can't be dried into a rock like beans or maize kernels, and that won't immediately rot like un-jerked meat—did so in a semi-subterranean room. Hence the name.

My grandparents built their house just after my grandfather returned from World War II (minus part of his right hand from a sniper round and his entire left arm from a mortar explosion, which somehow didn't stop him from driving a truck for a living or, for that matter, *building a house*). Along with a couple of gardens and an apple orchard on the property, their house also included a traditional root cellar. I loved the place. When the weather was sweltering, with a relative humidity of Towels Have No Power Here, I could usually be found with a flashlight or a handful of candles reading books in the crypt-like root cellar. Getting really into Tool was the next logical step.

The relevance of Early Basketmaker archaeology to the Bears Ears area is voluminous, and for one reason in particular: it was first discovered there.

The terminal 1800s was a turning point in the developing story of Southwest archaeology. The era of the independently funded pseudoscientific looter whose primary goal was to gather materials for museums was drawing to a close, although the avowed goal of amassing the greatest collection of archaeological materials would soon enough shift from museums to institutions of higher learning—which had its own consequences. Late-1800s archaeologists were beginning to understand that information about the past was also valuable, if perhaps not *quite* as valuable as what the past offered in terms of tangible goodies, and this was reflected in developments like careful notes about *provenience* (location relative to other stuff) and *stratigraphy* (location in terms of depth).

The most colorful and illustrative figures during this era in Bears Ears area archaeology are undoubtedly the Wetherill family. They were originally cattle ranchers from the Mancos Valley area in southwestern Colorado, who made a name for themselves as antiquarians from their own diggings in the great cliff dwellings in nearby Mesa Verde. Richard Wetherill and his friend Charlie Mason "discovered" Cliff Palace while searching for stray cattle in 1888, although apparently Richard's younger brother had spotted the place once before, setting in motion a chain of events that resulted in a tremendous amount of interest in the archaeology of Mesa Verde among scientists and the public. Riding this wave, Richard and his brothers extended their explorations in an ever-widening circle that would gradually encompass both southeastern Utah and northern New Mexico.

Among the visitors who arrived at the Wetherills' ranch in those days to marvel over the archaeology of Mesa Verde was Gustaf Nordenskiöld, a young Swedish scientist who was so enthralled by what he saw that he decided to stick around and do some graverobbing of his own. Trained as a geologist, Nordenskiöld's 1893 report, *The Cliff Dwellers of the Mesa Verde*, is arguably the first publication in all of Southwest archaeology to deal with it in a scientific manner. He includes detailed site descriptions, accurate and precise maps, and discussions of the principal of stratigraphy in the excavation descriptions. In doing so, Nordenskiöld set an early standard for prompt and thorough description of archaeological investigations that went well beyond the "we found the skulls and pottery in a cave five miles north of that place where Billy lost his mule" type of field notes that preceded it.

None of this was lost on Richard Wetherill. It would take some time before the type of systematic excavation espoused by Nordenskiöld caught on in the Southwest, coming to full flower with A. V. Kidder and Earl Morris in the early 1900s, but its earliest student was Richard.

Nordenskiöld set another, somewhat less auspicious early standard when he was arrested late one evening in 1891 at the famous Strater Hotel in Durango for the crime of looting—despite there being no laws against doing so at the time. The basis of the arrest was most likely plain old xenophobia. By the time Nordenskiöld had amassed a large collection of Mesa Verde artifacts for a European museum, local and regional residents were starting to think foreigners shouldn't be removing artifacts from what they considered *their* turf. Nordenskiöld was exonerated, of course, because—again—at the time there were no laws against the removal of archaeological materials without a permit. The arrest seems a symbolic action of the "we don't like your kind around here, boy" sort.

The Wetherill brothers first became interested in southeastern Utah in 1893 at the World's Columbian Exposition in Chicago, where the efforts of the profoundly misguided and circus-like *Illustrated American* Exploring Expedition were prominently displayed—along with the Grand Gulch materials Reverend Green had purchased from McLoyd and Graham. Richard was invited to attend the expo in order to accompany the Mesa Verde materials that were also on display.

It was there that Richard met the Hyde brothers, Talbot and Fred, heirs to the Bab-O Soap Company fortune who'd also fallen in love with the displays of pots, baskets, sandals, and—of special relevance to Mrs. Wetherill—mummies from the mysterious and enchanting Southwest. The resulting Hyde Exploring Expeditions into southeastern Utah between 1893 and 1903 amounted to a limited but intensive investigation of some of the most archaeologically significant portions of the Bears Ears area, particularly in and around Grand Gulch.

The tale attached to Mrs. Wetherill and mummies is a riotous one. Richard and his new wife, Marrietta, were camped within the Gulch for about a month during his first expedition, working alongside his team out of a series of camps and relying on melted snow as their chief source of water. The expedition was, in effect, their honeymoon. One evening, the snow fell so heavily that Richard became concerned about all the mummies he'd amassed from his diggings. He didn't want them to get wet. Tossing and turning for a while, he finally rumbled out of bed and hastily dressed. Marietta, blearily roused, yanked the covers up and went back to sleep. She was roused a few more times by her husband coming and going until, sounding pleased with himself, he announced at last: "They're all here. Where would you like them—at the head of the bed or at the foot?"

You can well imagine Marietta's response. She sat bolt upright, sleep running away from her like frightened rabbits, and beheld her husband cradling a crowd of withered and long-dead houseguests. She managed to croak, "At the foot, Mr. Wetherill. At the foot of the bed."

Some honeymoon.

Probably the greatest discovery Wetherill made in the Bears Ears area was a cave containing about one hundred wholly or partially articulated bodies, most of them bearing evidence of a violent slaughter and all buried well beneath the overlying Ancestral Pueblo materials. Nobody knows precisely why Richard kept digging once he'd reached the sterile soils beneath the Pueblo deposits. I don't even think *he* knew why he kept digging—his notes are famously vague on this point, aside from a minor observation about the ground looking weird in one place.

Wetherill couldn't have been happier. "Our success has surpassed all expectation," he wrote in a letter to the Hydes that is currently curated at the American Museum of Natural History. "In a cave we are working we have taken 28 skeletons and two more in sight and curious to tell and a thing that will surprise the archaeologists of the country is the fact of our finding them at a depth of 5 and 6 feet in a cave in which there are cliff dwellings and we find the bodies under the ruins..." His grasp of basic grammar was a marvel. In a follow-up letter to Nordenskiöld he reported, in a slightly calmer manner, "We have now taken 90 skeletons from one cave. The heads are different from the cliff dweller. We find them two feet (2) below the lowest sign of the Cliff Dweller," after which he provided a sketch.

What Richard and his team had found was an earlier, non- or pre-ceramic culture that predated the overlying Pueblo materials by an indeterminate but probably considerable stretch of time. This would be the first official documentation of the "Basket People" (later revised to Basket Maker, and then revised again into Basketmaker) culture-period, popularized by Wetherill's friend Dr. T. Mitchell Prudden in an 1897 publication called *An Elder Brother to the Cliff Dwellers*. Prudden was a regular at the Wetherill ranch, and although a pathologist by trade, he, like Nordenskiöld before him, would become enamored of Four Corners archaeology.

Speaking of Prudden: in a somewhat popular 1903 publication, he became quite probably the first author to publicly lament the destruction of archaeological sites in the Bears Ears area by looters (Bandelier had already raged about it elsewhere in the greater Southwest). In the mere fifteen years that had passed since the discovery of Cliff Palace, an alarming number—if not the majority—of sites in the northern San Juan drainage were hit by pothunters, according to Prudden. This was the first of two peaks in the illicit antiquities trade in the Bears Ears area, the second of which commenced in the 1960s and rumbles along still.

But the 1893 discovery of the Basketmaker complex by Wetherill, and Prudden's subsequent publication, failed to arouse the interest of most of the academic world at the time. So, there were older, more "primitive" people who lived before the Cliff Dwellers and didn't make pottery—so what? Some even accused

Wetherill of perpetrating a hoax. Popularizing Basketmaker archaeology would fall instead to the later team of A. V. Kidder and Samuel Guernsey, and almost totally by accident.

Kidder, like Edward Abbey and Joseph Wood Krutch (and me), was a born and bred easterner who came to the Southwest and fell madly in love with it. He brought with him a generalized conviction—picked up at Harvard—that all the world's civilized cultures had emerged from the struggle of making agriculture work in the desert. Mesopotamia and Egypt were obvious examples, and modern scholars would probably throw Peru into the mix as well, although modern scholars would also hasten to add that "great cultures" was relativistic and unfashionable.

But there was something else lurking behind Kidder's fascination with the American Southwest. Whereas in Mesopotamia and Egypt the long historical sequences were overlaid with later civilizations, wars, floods, and so on, the comparably shorter occupational history and excellent preservation conditions of the Southwest suggested that here could be found answers about the development of human nations that weren't as convoluted or marred. To that end, Kidder and Guernsey set off from Harvard to see what the American Southwest had to offer.

Working in northeastern Arizona in 1913 and 1914, the team of Kidder and Guernsey—and then just Guernsey, as Kidder busied himself with investigation of Pecos Pueblo in New Mexico—investigated at least one seemingly nondescript cave that turned out to contain material elements nearly identical to those found in Wetherill's Basketmaker sites in southeastern Utah. Only this time, they'd been found by Harvard Men.

And with that, the Basketmaker material culture first discovered by Wetherill some two decades prior was officially on the board.

Wetherill's diggings in this and other "caves" (alcoves) in the Bears Ears area skirt the line between scientific excavation and pothunting, but he is nonetheless owed some credit for at least attempting to be scientific about it—and for reporting his finds as diligently as he could. In addition to the many letters he wrote about his discoveries, he also provided an abundance of notes and data to others so that they could publish research articles about his finds. That's how this particular site became the focus of a number of publications.

Here again, as with the fire at the *Illustrated American*'s office, we encounter the confounding element of data loss that was such a serious problem prior to digitization: the location of this momentous find was lost for nearly one hundred years. Then, in the late 1980s, the site fell into what local historian Fred Blackburn called his "reverse archaeology" project, subsequently dubbed the Wetherill-Grand Gulch Project. Painstaking investigations of Wetherill's notes and the materials themselves helped Blackburn and his colleagues to finally relocate the place.

I went to visit this landmark of archaeological history a handful of summers ago. There's no outstanding architecture, no rock art, or even any loose artifacts at this point. It's been stripped clean—first by Wetherill and his shovels, and then by thoughtless visitors, many of them guided by maps they purchased from equally thoughtless swine that are nonetheless operating within the law. Given the extreme cultural importance of the place, that last fact is almost unconscionable.

Whether it was the scene of an ancient massacre or a long-term ancient graveyard (different teams of researchers disagree on this point), the nature of the place underscores how significant it is to the tribes whose ancestors were interred there. It's an alcove, with a spring nearby, and what's looking like well over one hundred burials in it. Think the battlefield at Gettysburg, or the sunken battleships at Pearl Harbor that still have seventy-eight-year-old skeletons entombed within them. With all that in mind, the place should probably be closed to visitation.

But there's a problem with that, too. I learned about that problem at Glen Canyon National Recreation Area, known to most people simply as Lake Powell—although the "lake" (reservoir) occupies only about fifteen percent of the total area. I took a job there as a seasonal archaeologist after graduating from NAU and moving out of my tent in the woods outside of Flagstaff. A good enough antibody test would probably have detected Lyme in me at the time, but I wasn't symptomatic so of course I didn't seek one. I was on top of the world.

Anyway, the generalized problem of protective barriers was explained to me by world-renowned backcountry vandalism expert Johannes Loubser, in his thick South African patois: "A fence, a wall…these things just make people want to climb over them." This was his way of admonishing the NPS for recommending that they erect a barrier around a recently vandalized archaeological site, although it's a lesson that extends somewhat beyond that particular case.

The only way to completely prevent this is when the barrier covers the entire access route. That tactic works fairly well in the case of literal caves, where the opening is relatively small compared with the rest of the thing, but it doesn't work so well when the "cave" is actually an alcove with a great gaping maw of an opening.

The site where I worked with Loubser is called Descending Sheep Panel. Its own story bears some relevance, here.

The stretch of river below Glen Canyon Dam and above the boundary of Grand Canyon National Park is known as Marble Gorge. Because of security risks—thanks partly to 9/11 and partly to *The Monkey Wrench Gang*—nobody is allowed within a certain distance of the dam itself without earning a lot of sudden and well-armed attention. For this reason, there is only one professional concessionaire that's permitted to take trips of boaters all the way down Marble, starting at the very base of the dam. The guides working for that concessionaire know about many of the archaeological sites along the river, especially the more popular ones, so they're instructed to give little talks about respectful visitation while also standing guard until their clients are back aboard the boat. Knowing that might have saved a twenty-eight-year-old North Carolina man named Trenton Ganey a lot of headaches.

One sunny morning in June of 2011, a small group on a guided fishing trip through Marble Gorge (fishing guides can

motor upriver from the boat launch, so their permitting proce-
dures aren't nearly so draconian) stopped by an archaeological
site called the Descending Sheep Panel to gaze and marvel and
then use the pit toilets. While there, Ganey scratched *TRENT* into
the sandstone wall next to the petroglyphs for which the site is
named.

The site is called the Descending Sheep Panel because of a
set of mountain sheep depicted marching at a downward angle
toward the ground. They're etched into the rock surface with
almost laser-like precision. Nearby, another, rather more abstract
petroglyph depicts what Hopi elders have interpreted as the
creation or emergence of the Antelope Clan, one of their
oldest.

Because of its immense cultural significance, NPS personnel
swing by to monitor the site fairly regularly, and one of them had
done so that very morning. She also took photos of the site while
she was there. This became somewhat crucial when, later on that
day, a bunch of gleeful boaters came down the river in a concessionaire craft and their mindful guide immediately radioed the
NPS about the graffiti. This was relayed to the law enforcement
officer on the river—along with the fact that it definitely wasn't
there in the morning. That meant the perpetrator had done it
sometime within the last couple of hours, and was probably still
someplace on the river.

The interpretive ranger who visited the site in the morning
had also noticed people on a fishing trip hanging out at the beach
nearby. When their description reached the law enforcement
folks, they tracked down the fishing guide and asked if anyone on
his trip was named Trent.

"That's me," announced a guy in his late twenties, stepping
into the limelight of local history with a puzzled grin on his face.

Except in circumstances where people are stupid enough to
air their crimes on social media (an occurrence baffling for its
increasing popularity), catching a wilderness vandal red-handed
is about as easy and commonplace as hitting a needle in a hay-
stack with a blowgun. The vastness of the wilderness we've still
got in this country, which is obviously not a bad thing, means

that there's no realistic way to accurately predict where vandals are going to strike and lay traps for them.

Thus, the Trent case was one of a kind. Its elements all converged in a weirdly perfect way, including the suspect having carved his own name into the panel. He even told the arresting officer that he "thought it would be cool," rather than the slightly less prosaic "I don't know what you're talking about" that commonly accompanies such events. And they had before and after photos from the very same day, purely by chance.

After admitting to the deed, Ganey was told by the arresting NPS personnel about the history and extreme cultural importance of the site. He didn't have to respond with an outburst of sincere regret but, to his credit, he did anyway. Ganey later agreed to be interviewed for an article in the *Arizona Daily Sun* in order to plead with others not to follow in his footsteps.

In the end, Ganey plead guilty in exchange for a ten-thousand-dollar fine, sixty months of supervised probation, and one hundred hours of community service. Part of his fine went toward hiring Loubser.

The law under which he was charged—the Archaeological Resources Protection Act of 1979, or ARPA—carries a fine of up to two years imprisonment and/or twenty thousand dollars for the first offense. If that sounds steep, it's also worth noting that ARPA cases are notoriously difficult to convict. According to a report by the National Park Service, a total of 1,720 incidents of archaeological looting were reported by federal agencies between 1985 and 1987, the year before ARPA was amended. These resulted in 134 citations, 49 arrests, 57 criminal misdemeanor charges, 16 felony convictions, and 17 civil penalties, the last three categories falling under ARPA. That's about five percent of reported incidents. The conviction rate increased roughly twenty percent following the 1988 amendment to include more legally useful language, but that's a twenty percent increase of five percent, not an increase *to* twenty percent.

There are four elements of proof required for an ARPA case to lead to conviction, and it's often the second of them that monkey-wrenches the works: "that said [archaeological] resource was located on public or Indian lands, or obtained illegally and transported across State lines." In other words, the burden is on the prosecution to prove that the garbage bag full of pottery in the defendants' pickup truck was removed from public or reservation land rather than, say, Uncle Jack's garden.

Obtaining that proof can be quite challenging—and, as people in the Bears Ears area would learn in 2009, occasionally deadly.

Chapter Four: The Bean Farmers

While the "Early" and "Late" Basketmaker designations are favored by researchers more inclined toward intellectual propriety than culture-history traditionalism, the latter portion of the Basketmaker era is still most often called Basketmaker III in the literature. Kidder would be proud to know that the saddle he fashioned for the bipedal pack animals that bear the burden of Southwest archaeology lumber under it still, or at least I hope he would. I still prefer Late Basketmaker because it sounds more like practical history and less like the third installment of a 1980s Hollywood action franchise.

In general terms, the ratios of known Early to Late Basketmaker sites throughout the Southwest indicate that a large population increase occurred during the latter period. This evident population boom has led researchers to suggest that what they're most likely seeing are groups of homesteaders moving into previously unoccupied frontier or borderland areas. In the Bears Ears area, researchers initially noted a hiatus in the Late Basketmaker period on Cedar Mesa, interpreting it as supporting evidence that just such a migration episode had occurred—from the heart of Bears Ears to someplace else. Subsequent investigations, however, indicated that the earlier supposition of a hiatus was based primarily on sampling error.

Sampling error happens all the time in the social sciences, and is one of the reasons we employ statistics to interpret our data rather than simply saying "look; see?" The classic analogy is that of the blind fellows and the elephant, supposedly derived from ancient India. Each person feels a bit of the elephant's exterior and comes to a different conclusion about it. The one investigating its nose thinks it's some sort of very thick snake, the one investigating its ear thinks it's a giant fan or possibly land-walking stingray, etc. The larger the sample size, in other words, the more of the picture you'll see—and the closer you'll get to a confident interpretation of the whole.

In archaeology, being among the harder of the so-called "soft sciences," it usually just means that the sample area was plotted along a project corridor where nobody happened to settle in the distant past because they preferred the higher ground just beside it—something like that, anyway. The lake contained plenty of fish; they just weren't hanging out where Dad parked the boat. Sampling strategies are designed to avoid these types of errors, with greater degrees of efficacy as time goes on.

Nominally speaking, the gap between Late Basketmaker and Pueblo I is often taken to represent the greatest leap in terms of material-culture developments. They're entirely different terms, after all. On the contrary, the vastest suite of observable differences occurs between Early and Late Basketmaker. The latter period—which runs between about AD 450 and 750, with subtle regional variations—can be distinguished from the former by the introduction of at least three new cultural traits. These include shifting from the atlatl-fired "dart" or spear to the bow and arrow, the adoption of ceramics, and adding beans to the maize-squash medley, as well as construction of the first definite appearance of public architecture. Although they appeared rather suddenly as a suite of seemingly linked traits, each one deserves some consideration.

First on the list of traits that seem to materialize whole cloth during the Late Basketmaker period is the bow and arrow, which presents its own set of interesting questions.

It is often, if not always, assumed that the bow is a superior product to the spear launcher or *atlatl*, and it does confer the advantages of being easier to load and way easier to fire in tight quarters. It's also easier to fire a bow while standing atop a dugout canoe or astride a horse, although neither of those help explain its rise to dominance in the prehistoric Southwest for what I hope are obvious reasons. But the disadvantages are about equal in number. Bows are more complicated and difficult to manufacture than atlatls, for a start, with more parts that are likely to fail—including a high-tension string that can inflict serious damage if it snaps near a sensitive body part.

The biggest disadvantage of bows versus atlatls, however, is one that surprises most people when they first encounter it: bows, at least the early ones, are far less powerful. The explosive thrust that a strong and seasoned atlatl user can transfer into the projectile is just ungodly, and the weight of the projectile itself—tens of times larger than an arrow—contributed greatly to its force. Until you get those high-tech modern compound things, there wasn't a bow in North America that could beat an atlatl for oomph. I've seen modern enthusiasts propel atlatl darts deep into tree trunks.

On the other hand: while someone who's practiced with an atlatl for thousands of hours can practically use one to thread a needle, the learning curve is imposingly steep compared with that of a bow. Being an expert at anything always requires a lot of time and practice, but the distance between Dreadful and Good Enough is much shorter with a bow than with an atlatl. And, again, you can fire one of them from a narrow space. All you need is enough room to draw your arm back to full draw, or about one full arm's length in front of you, which means you can even do it while leaning over a wall. It's not so easy to spring from cover and fire an atlatl, let alone do it while running.

Next up is ceramics. There are places in the Bears Ears area where you can't walk for stepping on ceramics, like seashells on a beach after a hurricane, although such places are steadily dwindling in number and size thanks to increasing hordes with sticky fingers.

In general, though, potsherds* are all but ubiquitously assocated with archaeological sites in the minds of most enthusiasts, to the point where students of archaeology often treat lithic scatters with something bordering on disgust. Exactly how and why people discovered ceramic technology in the first place is still up for debate—and is, furthermore, way beyond the scope of a short book focused on southeast Utah. But its production warrants a glance.

Clays occur as fairly common natural deposits, although specific types and qualities vary considerably. What we call clay often contains several different types of clay minerals, most commonly comprised predominantly of hydrous aluminum silicates, with varying amounts of metal oxides and organic material mixed in as a result of its formation in the presence of water. This gives it a trait called *plasticity*, which means that when you mix it with the right amount of water you can mold it into shapes that stay that way after it dries. If you then subject it to intense heat, the clay also partially melts—or *vitrifies*, which literally means "becomes like glass"—resulting in a rock-hard material after it cools. Basically, ceramics are what you get when you make mud pies out of a certain type of mud and then manage to actually bake the things.

The adding of temper, or *tempering*, is an important component of the process when mixing up the clay. It's a simple but crucial way to respond to a nearly universal physical problem: nearly everything shrinks as it dries or loses moisture through cooking or firing, and when there's a volume of it in one place, that shrinkage creates voids or cracks. The addition of temper—tiny bits of something that can survive the intense heat—keeps the vessel from cracking and potentially exploding during the firing process, because the vitrifying clay clings to it. Something highly textured is best, because you want the clay to have as much to grip as possible, which is why local potters didn't take long to figure

---

* Shards are what you get when glass breaks. If you refer to pottery fragments as "shards" rather than "sherds," any nearby archaeologists will barrage you with hurtful words.

out that ground-up pieces of previously fired ceramics make for the best tempers. But that would come later.

There's a lot more to it, of course, but that's the gist of ceramic production. And some of the clay that's available in the Bears Ears area is primo stuff. The characteristics—particle size, organic content, cohesiveness, and so on—that make certain clays singularly sticky are legion in the geology of southeastern Utah. You can investigate these properties yourself by driving there during a rainstorm.

Archaeologists differentiate ceramic groupings by *wares* (that is: technological tradition, like firing method) and *styles*. Ceramics at the earliest Late Basketmaker sites throughout the San Juan River Basin are typically *brown wares*, or ceramic types that are brown in color and constructed from self-tempered alluvial clays.

The widespread adoption of ceramic technology during the Late Basketmaker period also marks the appearance of ceramic production in the local archaeology, including ceramic firing pits or "kilns." They don't look like what you probably think they look like. They were dug into the ground, and their typical dimensions were approximately those of a bathtub (although the earliest ones in the Bears Ears area were more often circular than rectilinear). They were covered with a crib-style wood pile not unlike a well-laid Boy Scout bonfire heap, which was completely burned down and buried over a period of up to several days. Vessels were then dug out of the kilns after they had cooled, and the kilns themselves were not often reused, so what remains are circular or square-shaped arrangements of upright slabs that can—and, on occasion, do—fool the most ignorant amongst looters into thinking they're burial cists.

Kilns make for an interesting and greatly underappreciated topic in the study of Southwest prehistory for one principal reason: the Southwest is an arid place, and prehistoric kilns required a *lot* of wood. I've attended a number of prehistoric-style pottery firings done by experimental archaeologists, survivalists, and people like my friend Kelly Magleby who is a specialist at so-called "primitive" or reconstructionist skills, and I never fail to comment on how serious a fire one is required to build for just a few ceramic vessels. Little surprise, then, that kilns were located farther and farther away from domestic habitation sites as time passed and available firewood dwindled, which undoubtedly presented its own problems.

Hopi people would later pioneer the process of using coal to fire their pots. They figured out how to mine coal by hand, using it to fire clay vessels at such high temperatures that the resulting ceramics turned a brilliant golden-yellow. This information would eventually come in very handy for Peabody Coal and the wretched lawyer they hired to fleece the Hopi and Diné communities out of their land, water, and health.

And then there's the issue of beans. Nowadays, they tend so often to be lumped into the maize-beans-squash trifecta, sometimes called the Three Sisters or Holy Trinity of Native American farming, that it's natural to assume they were always a package deal. In fact, no—the earliest evidence of maize on the Colorado Plateau dates to around 2000 BC (or about 4,000 years ago), with roughly 500 years between that and squash, and then beans don't appear until commencement of the Late Basketmaker period. That's a temporal gap of nearly 2,500 years.

As the bartender famously asked the bear, "Why the big pause?"

The most common and threadbare explanation hinges on something called *ethnographic analogy*, or the assumption that because we do things a certain way, that must be the way everyone does it. In this case, modern beans take forever to soak and then a further forever to cook. I learned how to make red beans and rice, a favorite local dish, when I lived in New Orleans, and the way to prepare the beans was to soak them overnight and then plan for at least three hours of simmering on the stove. Banks have been robbed with less prep time.

So, naturally, modern archaeologists surmised that ancient beans were no different, and therefore required the sort of cooking technology that would allow for overnight soaking and considerable stretches of simmering atop a fire. The self-evident solution to the question, then, is that beans and ceramics appear in the archaeological record at the same time because you can't cook the former without the necessary technological advantage conferred by the latter. Mystery solved; drinks all around; moving on.

But there's a problem with that hypothesis, and I had the honor of being the first to officially explore it while I was a graduate student. Long-term boiling in baskets was always assumed to be impossible because if you put a basket—made, as it is, of vegetal matter—on top of a fire, it burns. But that isn't the only way to boil water inside a vessel. The oldest way is to heat rocks in a fire and then drop the rocks into the vessel, and we now know Early Basketmaker people were using limestone to do this with maize and, advertently or inadvertently, upping its nutrient availability as a result. And you definitely *can* do that in a watertight basket, provided you keep the rock in motion so that it doesn't rest against any one part of the vessel wall for too long. Members of the Pomo Tribe in California stone-boil acorn mush in baskets to this very day.

With that in mind, I found an heirloom variety of the beans they were growing. I also bought a few large baskets of a broadly similar style to those of Late Basketmaker baskets in the Bears Ears area, some assorted technological doodads like a scale and a laser thermometer, and then gathered up a handful of rocks. The whole enterprise cost me no more than seventy-five dollars, and it took about two hours using the electric range in my apartment to heat up the rocks (which means it would take considerably less time if I'd used a real campfire, as they can get nearly three times as hot). The beans tasted a bit like nontoxic epoxy resin, which I'd used to waterproof the baskets in the absence of that much pine pitch. And a bit like rocks. But that was nothing a little Tony Chachere's Original Creole Seasoning couldn't assuage.

The reason for beans' late arrival probably wasn't due to technological limitations so much as to the migration of people *with* beans, ceramics, and the bow and arrow into the area. I presented my results on a poster at the 2014 meeting of the Society for

American Archaeology in Austin, which is how and where I met Bill Lipe—friend, mentor, and Bears Ears area archaeologist par excellence.

Although a lot of archaeologists have played—and continue to play—major roles in the Bears Ears area, I would credit Bill Lipe with playing the biggest. Like Theodore Roosevelt, Bill was sick a lot when he was a kid in the 1940s, and he spent a lot of time at home reading. My own childhood included me *pretending* to be sick so that I could stay home from school and read.

Formative experiences in Bill's early life included camping trips to archaeological sites in the Southwest courtesy of a professor at the University of Oklahoma. He was introduced to places like Bandelier and Chaco that way, and a lifelong devotion took root. He would end up running the Cedar Mesa Project, arguably the most important archaeological investigation in the region, and serve as president of the Society for American Archaeology—among much else. He's one of very few people that aren't rock stars or politicians to have a book written about him during his lifetime.*

He also has one of the most impressive speaking voices I've ever heard, which undoubtedly served him well in the field. It's a combination of kindly and booming. Despite being in his early eighties at this point, Bill rarely wants or needs a microphone when giving a public talk in even the largest of chambers. He sounds like a wolf in a canyon.

I, on the other hand—having grown up shy and bullied—sound more like a mouse in a tissue box.

Site types and architecture during this time period also demonstrate a suite of characteristic variability. The most common type

---

* *Tracking Ancient Footsteps: William D. Lipe's Contributions to Southwestern Prehistory and Public Archaeology*, by R. G. Matson and Timothy A. Kohler. It was published in 2006, the year of my first-ever visit to Bears Ears.

of Late Basketmaker site is the hamlet, or communal residential site, which accounts for the overwhelming majority of the known Late Basketmaker sites in the region. I've recorded about a dozen of these things in the last few years, and they give the sensation of almost-but-not-quite villages. This appears to be the beginning of communal living patterns that would evolve into the massive stone and adobe apartment complexes that typify the archaeology of Chaco Canyon, as well as the still-occupied Pueblo villages of Hopi, Zuñi, and others.

Ramadas, or brush-covered shelters in the "plaza" areas between these larger features, served to protect outdoor work areas from the sun—where hearths, racks for drying hides, and work areas for grinding maize and drying food for long-term storage could be found. By about the late AD 600s, although probably starting a bit earlier, community organization of these residential structures began to exhibit what Bill Lipe calls the "San Juan pattern" of settlement layout: surface architecture to the north, domestic pit structure, and *midden*, or trash-disposal area, to the south.

I've also discovered at least a few cases of what I'm pretty sure were later-Pueblo people returning to the abandoned pit houses of their Late Basketmaker ancestors to use old pottery sherds as ceramic temper. Recycling has a deep history in the Bears Ears area.

Some of these Late Basketmaker hamlets in the central and eastern reaches of the Mesa Verde region were fully or partially enclosed in stockades or palisades that may have served either defensive or social functions. Such elements used to occur in the Old World, where the now-defunct word *pale* referred to a stake or pointed piece of wood that was typically installed in the ground to form a perimeter around a house or settlement—and from which derive the words *paling* (as in a paling fence) and *impale* (as in that thing Dracula was so keen on). The phrase "beyond the pale," usually translated as "outside the boundaries of decency," derives from this.

Pit houses continued to be used, but they took on a curious bi-lobed appearance with what appears to be a domestic chamber and attached antechamber. They look like Venn diagrams from above. The architectural construction of these new pit houses also changed from simple basin-shaped depressions or informal pits covered with a mud-and-wood superstructure to more substantial structures erected over more substantial pits. A typical pit house contained a shelf around the rear section of the main room, an antechamber connected to the main chamber by a short passageway, and a ladder that enabled entry into the house via a hole in the roof (which also allowed smoke to get out).

It was also during the Late Basketmaker period when proto- or early *great kivas* first appear in the archaeological record. These take some unpacking, but the short version is that while the pit house of the Early Basketmaker period never fell out of use until very late in the Pueblo era, a communal version started to appear throughout the Mesa Verde region in the 700s. The earliest of these were circular pit structures about twenty to thirty feet in diameter, relatively shallow, without an antechamber. You could fit a fair number of people around the inside of a structure like that, and researchers think that's exactly what they were intended for.

This interpretation is based on numerous lines of evidence, the strongest one being simple observation of similar practices by descendent groups. In the modern Pueblos, kivas (from the Hopi *kíva*) are large, square or circular structures with an opening in the roof. They're often the locations of communal practices and ceremonies, and access to them is strictly controlled. Because of their importance, early anthropologists interpreted them as a—if not *the*—distinguishing feature of Pueblo culture. This was a crucial point in cementing the continuity between the modern Pueblo peoples and their ancestors, something that we largely take for granted today. But it also grew into a troublesome meme in the realm of Southwest archaeology, where every circular structure became a "kiva" virtually overnight.

They aren't. They're houses. They were often the primary domestic household for a single family, and continued to be so well into the Pueblo II or Chaco period.

The exception to this generality is great kivas, which were much larger by comparison and did indeed seem to serve communal purposes. This is the first definitive appearance of public architecture in the Pueblo world as a whole. In the Bears Ears area in particular, there's an enormous rock art panel that depicts extensive caravans of people converging in one of these structures—that being, of course, another good line of evidence for their function.

The shift from expedient to more substantial architecture during the Basketmaker-Pueblo transition used to be explained as a result of greater and greater reliance on farmed maize for sustenance. People became more and more dependent on their crops and, thus, more and more inclined to stay put. However, there are at least two problems with that simple model. The first is that mounting evidence—especially from the Bears Ears area itself—indicates little, if any, significant variation in levels of maize consumption from Early Basketmaker all the way through to the appearance of the Spanish. The second comes as an instructive tale from another Southwestern tribe.

The seasonal round of Diné farmers—beautifully depicted in the straightforwardly titled 1983 film *Seasons of a Navajo*—involved planting their maize in the spring and then heading uphill with their sheep to live in their higher-altitude summer home. An autumnal return to their lower-elevation winter home would then include harvesting the maize that had grown all year in their absence. Anticipating varmints, they would drop a handful of kernels into each hole during planting, which included "one for the deer and one for the rabbits" as it was once explained to me. Deer and rabbits are indeed pestilential opportunists when it comes to crops, as my grandfather always warned, but rabbits only nibble the youngest sprouts before the leaves get tough and deer don't often mess with it until the ears are formed. Between those two constraints and a few others, each tiny hill of three to five seedlings planted in the spring would typically yield an average of one robust, unmolested cob-bearing stalk in the fall.

But that's when farming *only* maize, which has fearsome leaves—try running through a mature cornfield in a sleeveless shirt and you'll find this out, too—and a woody stem that repels most herbivores between the sprout stage and when the kernels are ripe. Bean plants, on the other hand, are green and leafy all season long. They require almost constant attention.

It was also during what archaeologists call the Late Basketmaker period that the Fremont, the Ancestral Puebloans' cousins in the Great Basin, first began to make the monumental shift from foraging to agriculture—when, in other words, the Archaic precursors of the Fremont actually became the Fremont—although the greatest lurches of that shift most likely took place during the later Pueblo II period as a result of Chaco's practically immeasurable radius of influence. The border between the two culture areas, essentially the Escalante River area and the northeastern portion of the Bears Ears area, was wide open until about midway through the Late Basketmaker period.

Maize agriculture jumped the gap, becoming a central aspect of what defined Fremont in general terms throughout the Great Basin; but so did beans, ceramics, and the bow and arrow. These elements trickled through the borderlands at various intervals rather than all in one go, with the Fremont adopting and adapting their own distinctive versions. A hard territorial boundary between the two groups seems to have solidified by about AD 500, only to break down again roughly half a millennium later.

The term *Fremont* is broadly applied to the Formative material culture that dominated the Great Basin between about AD 400 and 1450. They were named in 1931 by Noel Morss for the river where their archaeology was first investigated, itself named after explorer John C. Fremont. In truth, it's a lousy moniker for the tremendous breadth of cultural and behavioral variety it encompasses, and was only used by Morss to distinguish the farmers in his little riverine project area from the better-known Ancestral Pueblo farmers to the southeast. Unfortunately, there doesn't seem to be a better one on offer. No two tribes can agree on what to call them, and Ancestral Great Basin (like Ancestral Sonoran or Ancestral Mississippian) is far too broad to be at all meaningful.

The Fremont remained contemporaneous with the Ancestral Pueblo right up until both of them abdicated the Colorado Plateau (hence their being often characterized as cousins, along with what I'm told is intriguing DNA evidence). They shared a few things in common besides farming, but there are hard distinctions between them. Rock art and other decorative styles, for a start—the Fremont made pictographs, petroglyphs, distinctive clay figurines, and an assortment of personal accoutrements that set them apart from every other North American material culture. They also wore moccasins, for the most part, rather than the woven sandals preferred by ancient and historic Pueblo folks. They tempered their ceramics with crushed volcanic rock, like basalt, instead of crushed old ceramics like the later Pueblo potters did. Their projectile points were unique to their culture areas. And they never built any cliff "dwellings," although they were deft hands at high-altitude cliff granaries.

And that's just about all that most Fremont researchers agree upon.

My limited grasp of the Fremont material culture derives principally from being compelled to learn about them at Range Creek. I went there in 2008, just before commencing my career as a full-time archaeologist.

Field schools are a necessary evil in the domain of archaeology. I don't know the exact history of how this practice came about, although the Bears Ears area was the field component of Edgar Lee Hewett's field school in the early 1900s. My own cynical inclination is that it has something to do with how often people with college degrees and no field experience get hired onto crews like fabled albatrosses. An honors thesis on late-Holocene faunal exploitation patterns won't save you from drowning the first (and, as it were, last) time you erect your tent in the bottom of a wash during the rainy season.

Hence, most people who hire professional archaeologists to do fieldwork will not—except in times of dire need—hire ones who haven't attended a field school. It's an added expense on top of the already exorbitant cost of post-secondary education in the United States, but it often makes up for that by being really fun.

Range Creek has a rather remarkable story all its own. It is one of several major tributaries of the Colorado River that cut through the mighty Tavaputs Plateau, including Nine Mile and Desolation Canyons, about one hundred miles north of Bears Ears. That's approximately ten days of walking for an average adult human with a backpack, or closer to five if you really mean it—which explains why rock art panels with Basketmaker (specifically San Juan Anthropomorphic style) components have been found there amid an otherwise dizzying density of Fremont sites.

It was "discovered" by mainstream archaeology in the early 2000s, when Waldo Wilcox—last of a line of ranchers who'd operated there for several generations—sold his 4,200-acre spread to the Trust for Public Lands. Range Creek Canyon itself is conservatively estimated to comprise about 50,000 acres in total, but the Wilcox family had controlled the entire place through a relatively simple stunt that appears with exhausting regularity in the annals of the Intermountain West: they set up shop at the only logical ingress and egress points. No kidding. If your private property extends across the mouth of an enormous canyon, and there are no state- or federal-administered roads extending through it before the property becomes yours, then the entire canyon is effectively yours as well. Dirty pool, that—but there you are. This practice has an interestingly deep history in the Bears Ears area, as well.

Because of the No Trespassing signs posted by the Wilcox clan at the top and bottom of the canyon, combined with the harshness with which they were enforced, what turned out to be an astonishing assemblage of Fremont archaeology remained largely free from looting and vandalism. Waldo did his own collecting, of course—but one person and his pals practicing occasional molestation on hundreds of sites is nothing compared to how hard other places with comparable assemblages got hit. That isn't *protection* in a heroic sense so much as an incidental one, but it is protection nonetheless. The place was leased by the University of Utah a little over half a decade later, and has been a field school and remote research station ever since.

The field school lasts for ten weeks of eight-day stretches with alternating six-day weekends off, which is how private-sector archaeology schedules are usually written because it maximizes travel time. We lived in our personal tents in the horse pasture, which made for at least one lively encounter between skittish horses and even more skittish students, and we had to do a bunch of ranch duties like mending fences. Nights are for socializing and hearing stories from salty old archaeologists when they swing past.

My own stint took place the same year that the awful *Indiana Jones and the Crystal Alien Whatevers* came out, so there was no shortage of jocular references to it while we toiled in the sunshine. In one painfully memorable scene, Indy picks up a chunk of charcoal and assigns it a radiocarbon age (bypassing an elaborate process that involves, at the very least, a mass spectrometer) just by looking at it. Taking his lead, students and teaching assistants alike spent the entire summer doing ocular 14C analysis on everything they saw. Our affable professor, for example, was clearly left over from the Miocene.

Concurrent with discovery of the Basketmaker material culture by Richard Wetherill, and its subsequent popularization by Prudden and others, permanent Euro-American settlements were steadily infiltrating the Bears Ears region in the late 1800s. The Grand Staircase-Escalante region, just to the west, was the last place in the contiguous United States to be formally mapped at about that same time. With these increasing settlements came a switch from exploration of the newly discovered and largely unknown depth of human history to more organized, systematic collection and documentation of archaeological remains. This change was already well underway in European archaeology, and was finally forging a presence over here.

Richard Wetherill was himself an interesting all-in-one springboard, catalyst, and scapegoat during this developmental period. Having learned about stratigraphy and the importance of careful notes from people like Gustaf Nordenskiöld, the Swedish scholar who taught Richard a thing or two about natural science before getting arrested for the crime of being Swedish, he was among the more careful and considerate excavators of archaeological sites in the Southwest at the turn of the century. A good many researchers believe Wetherill was very likely the first person doing archaeological work in the United States to utilize the principles of stratigraphy, laid down (pun unintended) by geologist Charles Lyell in the early 1800s and postulating that—absent any modifying factors—the layers in a sequence of deposits get older as one moves downward.

Still, being unaffiliated with any formal institutions, he was technically an amateur, and many formally trained archaeologists refused to see him as any more than a jumped-up looter. This was especially, and with some consequence, true of Edgar Lee Hewett.

Hewett was a leading figure in the developing world of Southwest archaeology for over forty years, despite getting a late start, at age forty. I made the leap to the uncertain livelihood of professional archaeology from the rather more certain one of being a bartender not long before turning thirty, so I understand the delay.

Hewett helped form the Archaeological Society of New Mexico in 1898, and later established a field school in Santa Fe that would become the School of American Archaeology and later the School of American Research. From 1909 until the 1940s, he directed both the Museum of New Mexico and the School of American Research, and he also helped found the anthropology department at the University of Southern California in 1934.

For all his potency and effectiveness as a builder of institutions, however, it is worthwhile to include a note about his bellicose character. Friends and enemies alike referred to him as "El Toro," often behind his back. In 1980, Rosemary L. Nusbaum compiled and published the letters of her husband, legendary archaeologist and conservationist Jesse Nusbaum—another student of Hewett—in a book called *Tierra Dulce: Reminiscences from the Jesse Nusbaum Papers*, and it includes the following:

There was an old duffer called Hewett
Who was head of the School—and he knew it.
When anyone came,
Who knew naught of his fame
He took out his trumpet, and blew it.

Hewett was a results-driven person who pounded relentlessly on an impetus or design until it became reality, so falling into his disfavor was never a wise move for anyone even tangentially connected to the field of archaeology. Cue Richard Wetherill.

Following his successful expeditions and excavations throughout the greater Mesa Verde region, including his work in the Bears Ears area, Richard moved his nuclear family from the Wetherill ranch in Mancos down into Chaco Canyon to work for George Pepper on behalf of the American Museum of Natural History. Once there, he established a trading post and employed an army of locals—mostly Indigenous ones—to conduct extensive excavations throughout the ruins of that most amazing place.

That caught Hewett's attention. He'd always lamented the loss of ancient sites and materials to despoilers, and saw little difference between socially respected pothunters and socially *disre-spected* ones—relegating Wetherill and his financiers, the Hydes, into one collective and heinous category. He let fly this distaste in a campaign against their operations in Chaco.

Serendipitously, during a visit to Washington, DC, in 1900, Hewett met and befriended John F. Lacey, an Iowa congressman and chairman of the House Committee on Public Lands. From 1904 to 1906, following the loss of his wife to tuberculosis, Hewett devoted himself to the task of drafting antiquities legislation that would make it illegal to excavate archaeological sites on public lands without obtaining a permit from a federally recognized institution. Working closely with Lacey, along with William Henry Holmes (of the Hayden Survey, and now director of the Bureau of American Ethnology after John Wesley Powell) and President Theodore Roosevelt, the culmination of these efforts was 16 USC 431-433, otherwise known as the Antiquities Act. It was signed into law by Roosevelt on June 8, 1906.

The Antiquities Act plays a big role in the saga of the Bears Ears area, particularly in the recent dustup over national monument boundaries. It is, for several reasons, among the most contentious pieces of legislation ever passed.

First and foremost, the Antiquities Act was the first piece of legislation that explicitly and officially made it illegal to dig or collect archaeological materials on public lands without a permit—a thorn in the side of the burgeoning antiquities market in the western United States, albeit a pretty minor one (subsequent legislation would carry stiffer penalties). Of larger overall impact was the fact that it allocated to the president the power to "declare by public proclamation historic landmarks, historic and prehistoric structures, and other objects of historic or scientific interest that are situated upon the lands owned or controlled by the Government of the United States to be national monuments."

In other words: although the Constitution gives control over public lands to the legislative branch of our federal government (aka Congress), the Antiquities Act gives a tiny portion of that power to the executive branch—just enough to draw an invisible line around things or places of historic or scientific interest. It doesn't even say what to do with them afterward; that part is decided in the specific management plan of each individual monument. And it doesn't say how big they should be, beyond a vague stipulation about confining it to "the smallest area compatible with proper care and management of the objects to be protected." Given what we know about ecology and the interrelationship of all things in the natural world, it could be argued that the smallest area compatible with the proper care of a single tree is the entire planet.

Lawyers and politicians will be debating points like these for some time to come. But it's the unstated dependent clause in the phrase "of historic or scientific interest" that I think deserves a little extra attention. Of historic or scientific interest *to whom*?

It is worth noting that Theodore Roosevelt spent much of his life prejudiced against Native Americans. *Big time.* In a January 1886 speech in South Dakota, he famously said: "I don't go so far as to think that 'the only good Indian is a dead Indian,' but

I believe nine out of ten are, and I shouldn't like to inquire too closely into the case of the tenth." That opinion changed, however—and rather dramatically—with the so-called Closing of the West and the end of the Plains Wars later that same century.

When the fighting was officially over, Roosevelt no longer considered Indigenous peoples of North America to be enemies. Now they were citizens, deserving of the same rights as everyone else. In a 1905 speech in Oklahoma, standing alongside Comanche leader Quanah Parker (the two would remain friends the rest of their lives), Roosevelt told the crowd: "Give the red man the same chance as the white." A year later, when the US military attempted to block publication of Apache leader Geronimo's autobiography, Roosevelt personally intervened to make sure the book got published. He even went to live among the Hopi for a short time after he lost his bid for reelection in 1912.

Granted, Roosevelt retained what historians often call a Darwinian—although more accurately a Morganian—attitude toward Indigenous peoples. He continued carving chunks out of Native reservations for disposal into the national forest system right up until he left office. He publicly dedicated a monument to Captain John Underhill, a leader of the horrific Pequot War and one of the most ruthless and genocidal sociopaths in American military history, for having "helped to lay the foundation of the nation that was to be." And so on. So, I wouldn't go as far as to say that Theodore Roosevelt was an ally or champion of Native Americans—far from it. But his attitude toward Indigenous people during his term in the White House had at least evolved to the point of considering them fellow Americans.

From this, we may logically conclude that when President Roosevelt signed legislation containing the phrase "of historic or scientific value," he meant that phrase to mean "of historic or scientific value to American citizens." Including Indigenous ones. That—or something like it—was very likely running through President Obama's mind one hundred and ten years later.

So much for the national monuments portion of the Antiquities Act, which I understand was primarily Lacey's contribution. The other portion, which called for the permitting of archaeological work on public lands and the punishment by fines and/or imprisonment for looting, came from Hewett.

Until then, the chief—and pretty much only—power the federal government had to protect archaeological sites on public lands was to withdraw specific tracts, parcels, or places from purchase or civilian entry for a temporary period. This was devised and employed for use by the General Land Office (or GLO, a precursor to the BLM) as an exigent tool when places of obvious natural or cultural specialness needed immediate protection. Under this policy, the temporarily withdrawn tract was reserved from private land claims until the federal government could decide how best to manage it.

Early examples of this include the withdrawal of the ancient cliff dwellings of the Pajarito Plateau, Hewett's stomping grounds, from entry, sale, settlement, or other forms of disposal pending a determination on a national park proposal. At the insistence of Hewett and others, this tactic was turned toward Chaco in 1901 with a proposal to remove from public ownership and development the bits of land that contained the splendid architectural remains of Pueblo Bonito, Chetro Ketl, and Pueblo del Arroyo— directly countering a homestead claim Wetherill had filed to ensure his continued business and residency.

Word was spreading through Washington that Wetherill's efforts were "the purest vandalism," in the words of S. J. Holsinger of the GLO. In 1902, Holsinger drafted a proposal to turn 746 square miles of the Chaco region into Chaco Canyon National Park, and the following year the Hydes packed up and bounced— leaving Wetherill and his family to their fate. When the Antiquities Act was signed into law, efforts to turn Chaco Canyon into a national park were swept off the table as Roosevelt made it into a national monument instead. One portion of the Pajarito Plateau withdrawal would be made into a national monument named for Adolph Bandelier in 1916 by President Woodrow Wilson.

Although national parks and monuments differ greatly in a number of legislative ways, in this case their intent focused on a common theme: Richard Wetherill had to quit digging and living in the ancient sites of Chaco. Thereafter, any archaeological work conducted on public lands had to be done with oversight and permitting by the federal government itself or a federally recognized institution.

There is still a heady stigma against being an archaeologist who doesn't have an official institutional affiliation. Anyone appearing in a paper, giving a talk, or doing anything else in the realm of professional archaeology without the name of some institution or other tacked onto their own name is thought to be "avocational," a fancy word for "amateur" that is functionally indistinguishable from "scum."

This obsession with affiliation has led to a variety of creative responses among archaeologists, up to and including the creation of their own "institutions" just to have an official-looking affiliation to put after their names. Indeed, when I'm doing neither university-funded research nor cultural resource inventories for private firms like SWCA, my professional affiliation is Desert Dog Archaeology—a humble little firm whose operative address is often Barstool #5 at Flagstaff Brewing Company.

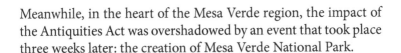

Meanwhile, in the heart of the Mesa Verde region, the impact of the Antiquities Act was overshadowed by an event that took place three weeks later: the creation of Mesa Verde National Park.

Contrary to popular perception, given the *antiquities* nature of the national park, its creation had nothing to do with the act that preceded it by less than a month. Mesa Verde National Park was the result of decades of campaigning by Virginia Donaghe (later McClurg) and Lucy Peabody. Donaghe visited the area in the mid-1880s to write about its archaeological splendors after they were popularized by the Hayden Reports, and she'd fallen instantly in love with them. She spoke on behalf of their protection at the 1893 World's Columbian Exposition, because apparently everybody in the world was there, and followed this with petitions to Congress. After women were given the vote in Colorado in that same momentous year, the Colorado Federation of Women's Clubs felt emboldened to take on just such a task as their next political challenge—with Virginia Donaghe and her new co-leader, Lucy Peabody, at the helm.

Things get a bit weird at that point. Donaghe gradually lost patience with Congress's continued harrumphing and general failure to act, and in 1905 she bailed on the effort and turned her energies toward helping an oily charlatan named Harold Ashenhurst "re-locate" a cliff dwelling from Mesa Verde—reachable in those days only by a very long and bumpy ride—to Manitou Springs, where tourists could more easily appreciate it. The Manitou Cliff Dwellings are still there today, but they are not re-located. They are built to look like Mesa Verde's Spruce Tree House, Cliff Palace, and Balcony House all rolled into one, and the construction materials came from a surface pueblo in the Dolores area that was extensively pilfered to make that happen.

Peabody was appalled, but by that time she'd managed to befriend archaeologists Jesse Walter Fewkes and Edgar Lee Hewett, the latter of whom was busily helping John Lacey write the text that would become the Antiquities Act. They encouraged her to keep waging her campaign to protect Mesa Verde as a national park, so she maintained the lion's share of her focus on that. In 1906, three weeks after the Antiquities Act was passed, Congress finally caved, and Mesa Verde was made into a national park later that same year.

Considered as a result of grassroots legislative pressure, orchestrated by people who don't exactly dominate American politics, and created for the chief purpose of protecting Indigenous material heritage, Mesa Verde National Park was without predecessor or successor—until Bears Ears.

The park's creation included an agreement to lease the land from the Ute Tribe, since it's technically part of their reservation, but that relationship quickly soured when the National Park Service disallowed Ute individuals from continuing to hunt within the park's boundaries. It soured even more in subsequent decades when the NPS extended the park's boundaries without the tribe's permission, and they remain understandably salty about that to this day. The tribe manages its own, somewhat larger portion of Mesa Verde as a tribal park, and I always encourage friends who are heading to the area to visit both parks.

Mesa Verde National Park was managed by political superintendents for its first decade and a half of operation, although *mis*managed would be a better word for it. As a result, the National Park Service director (its first) Stephen Mather decided to move in a different direction, and in 1921 he doffed hat to a request from Hewett and appointed archaeologist Jesse Nusbaum to the position of park superintendent—making him the first-ever National Park Service archaeologist in the process. Jesse lived there for the next two decades, along with his first wife, Aileen, and her son Deric. Among my favorite possessions is an original 1928 copy of *Deric in Mesa Verde*, written by Jesse's twelve-year-old stepson (with help from his mother, of course).

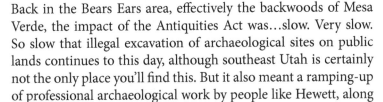

Back in the Bears Ears area, effectively the backwoods of Mesa Verde, the impact of the Antiquities Act was…slow. Very slow. So slow that illegal excavation of archaeological sites on public lands continues to this day, although southeast Utah is certainly not the only place you'll find this. But it also meant a ramping-up of professional archaeological work by people like Hewett, along with his students and affiliates with the Santa Fe School.

In the summer of 1907, a young A. V. Kidder and several companions signed on to Hewett's field school. They met up in modern-day Bluff before setting off for McElmo and Yellowjacket Canyons just over the border in Colorado. According to an account by Kidder that appears in Don Fowler's excellent book *A Laboratory for Anthropology*, after showing them a few sites Hewett "waved an arm, taking in, it seemed, about half the world, [and said] 'I want you boys to make an archaeological survey of this country. I'll be back in three weeks.'" Drain the ocean with a teaspoon while you're at it.

Kidder would go on to publish one of the best accounts to date of archaeological investigations in southeastern Utah in 1910. He and Byron Cummings of the University of Utah were jointly in charge of survey and excavation efforts on Alkali Ridge, to the east of Blanding, with future Utah archaeological icon (and nephew of Cummings) Neil Judd working under the two of them as a student. In his 1910 report, Kidder wrote that "there seems to have been a great centre of population along the whole middle portion of Alkali Ridge," in addition to numerous cliff dwellings and canyon-head pueblo groups throughout the surrounding drainages and tributaries.

In addition to reams of technical literature, some of the most interesting and entertaining writing from the world of American field archaeology derives from the next several decades in and around the Bears Ears area. Something about that place and the study of its deep, rich history seems to attract colorful characters. Included on that roster is the chief creator of the Pecos culture-phase period sequence, A. V. Kidder.

Kidder was by all accounts a jovial fellow, who enjoyed doing things like growing dense beards just to show up the snootier Harvard Men and, like my own deranged friends and I, would often celebrate being finished with fieldwork by taking a cursory shower and then charging back into the field just for fun. There are, I've been told, worse forms of addiction.

When not conducting formal archaeology, Kidder was known to go rushing off on one exploratory lark or another, sacrificing the health and sanctity of several vehicles in the process. He gave his Ford Model Ts names like Old Blue and Pecos Black. I often give my own adventurous vehicles names like You Bastard.* The wreckage of Pecos Black still sits, rotting and rusting, in a field at Pecos Pueblo, with the humble little gravestones of Kidder and his wife nearby.

In a similar vein, fellow student and archaeologist Earl Morris motored all over northern Arizona and northwestern New Mexico in an equally infamous Model T that he called Old Joe. As Neil Judd recounts in his autobiography, Morris was exploring far out in the Lukachukai Mountains one day, when the sand proved too much for Old Joe and he burned out a bearing. Morris spent

---

* Borrowed, with thanks, from Terry Pratchett.

the long night musing over his predicament, and in the morning replaced the bearing with a square of bacon rind that lasted the rest of the season. Judd's deduction: "You don't get bacon rind like that anymore!"

Kidder's 1910 publication also included observations to the effect that many of the area's burials "have been much pillaged by 'pot-hunters,' relic-seekers, and other vandals who, digging carelessly, have broken fully as much as they have recovered, and who have also entirely destroyed the skeletal remains." And although pothunting was and is practiced throughout the region, the area east of Blanding—where Kidder and his colleagues found the most damning evidence of it back in their own day—remains an unfortunately favored hot spot.

Chapter Five: The First Villagers

The word *Pueblo* was applied as a blanket descriptor to the Native American groups living in large, multistory masonry villages in northern Arizona and New Mexico by the Spanish upon their arrival, to differentiate them from the more nomadic tribes in the region. It disseminated into modern American usage when the newly formed United States signed the Adams-Onís Treaty with Spain in 1819, which included the purchase of Florida and settlement of a border dispute that left California, New Mexico, and Texas still in Spanish hands. That sale was a calculated move by the Spanish Crown to raise money for their ailing empire while settling tensions between colonists at the same time, and it worked—for a little under two hundred days.

Thanks largely to the documents that changed hands during the 1819 treaty process, using Pueblo as a catchall for Indigenous North Americans living in masonry villages became official US policy, and it remains so today. Colonialistic implications aside, useful aspects of this happenstance include the continuity it implies between the people living in the modern Pueblos and their masonry-building ancestors—hence *Ancestral Pueblo*. Which is why it still baffles me when people talk about the "mysterious disappearance" of the ancient people of the Colorado Plateau, whose descendants live less than a day's drive away in buildings that don't look a whole lot different.

The best way to think about the Pueblo I period is as a "decisive turning point in Southwest prehistory," as stated in the opening chapter of the delightfully titled *Crucible of Pueblos: The Early Pueblo Period in the Northern Southwest*. Crucible is a terrific heuristic for comprehending what happened during that time period. It was the short temporal stretch—lasting only between about AD 750 and 900, with the usual localized variations—in which major sociocultural changes occurred that greatly affected the resulting history of the Pueblo world in toto. Yet very little research on the Pueblo I period appears in the bulk of technical literature, and almost none at all in the popular and mainstream domains. Even Basketmaker gets more play than that, or at least Early Basketmaker does, although I suspect this is at least partly due to the quaint and curious way in which it was discovered by a controversial figure.

Moreover, archaeologists' longstanding obsession with later "cliff dweller" architecture as the be-all/end-all gives short shrift to the earliest Pueblo period, because all you can really say about that aspect of it is, "It's when they moved from pit structures and *proto*-villages into aboveground masonry affairs and *actual* villages." True enough, as far as it goes, but that statement amounts to as much of the full story as saying, "Beer appeared when people started drinking fermented bread soup." It completely skips over a rich and interesting history.

Research on Pueblo I sites in the Bears Ears area dates back almost to the beginning of formal archaeological work in the Four Corners region as a whole. As early as 1913–14, Kidder's colleague Earl Morris (he of the mighty bacon rind) excavated or tested several Pueblo I sites in the area, recognizing them as representing a potential transitional type between earlier Basketmaker sites and the later cliff dwellings in places like Mesa Verde. Great efforts were subsequently made to describe and standardize Pueblo I as an identifiable stage of cultural development at Kidder's 1927 Pecos Conference, where it was characterized as having a population that practiced cranial deformation and lived in rectangular masonry pueblos. Sites of this stage could also be identified by the presence of gray pottery with neck banding. Beyond that, however, efforts to compile an attribute list that could diagnostically identify Pueblo I in Southwest archaeology were stymied by a recalcitrant trend of nonconformity on the parts of the sites themselves.

On a landscape scale, probably the most fascinating aspect of the Pueblo I period is the staggering amount of population movement. Although Pueblo I period groups were the first to build what can confidently be called villages, former Colorado state archaeologist Richard Wilshusen often characterizes them as more akin to modern trailer parks than to apartment complexes—aggregations of little homes with maybe a communal architectural center, but otherwise not exactly built to last. Major population centers boomed and busted in the Durango, Dolores, central Mesa Verde, and Bears Ears areas in a cyclical wobble until the end of the Pueblo I period when, it seems, everyone packed up and headed to northern New Mexico—and not for the last time.

Beginning with the architectural changes that so fascinate Southwest archaeologists, Pueblo I habitations commonly consisted of an arc of wattle and daub or *jacal* (interwoven sticks with adobe plastered over), straight adobe, and/or stone masonry rooms with one or more pit structures located in an unenclosed plaza or courtyard area situated almost invariably to the south. The shallow, bi-lobed Late Basketmaker pit structure was replaced by a deep—six feet or so—generally sub-rectangular structure with a ventilator shaft. Pueblo I settlement layouts typically demonstrate continuation and refinement of what Lipe called the San Juan pattern, with surface roomblock for storage, domestic pit structure, and trash midden arranged from north/northwest to south/southeast. Except when they weren't. Residential units were often aggregated, with adjacent rooms arranged end to end to form curving or L-shaped composite roomblocks—again, except where they weren't. For every north-south aligned roomblock, pit structure, and midden complex there were just as many "field houses" where individuals or small families lived nearer to farms or other important resource patches, and their look spanned a frustrating gamut.

This is why early Pueblo archaeology gives archaeologists headaches, and it speaks to the general difficulty of shepherding human social behavior into neat little pigeonholes like trait lists and statistical models: it will defy your efforts wherever it can.

The emergence of villages is often touted as *the* hallmark attribute of the Pueblo I period throughout the San Juan Basin, although—and not surprisingly—its expression could be quite variable in form and organization. Where they did occur, these early villages consisted of multiple households with contiguous aboveground storage *and* living rooms, sometimes with an associated oversized pit structure (the great kiva), rock art panels, and even shrines and plaza areas where the landscape allowed. They were vibrant and dynamic civic centers where people congregated from across and outside of a given region, and development of these villages probably has much to do with how they were better than scattered hamlets for bringing diverse and disparate groups into a single community.

Caution, however, is warranted around the word *because*. In the Bears Ears area and surrounding region, the early Pueblo period is marked by some nasty climatic downturns and subsequent aggregation of dispersed populations into relatively smaller pieces of higher-elevation landscape where crops could still grow—and that meant rubbing elbows with folks you may not like who used to live a comfortable distance away. So, at least in part, one reason these villages emerged might not be the proactive one of bringing people together in harmony so much as the reactive one of creating a space where people who'd been smooshed together by default had to learn how to get along. In any case, the result was the same: blending of traits, practices, and families from different corners of the realm.

In broad strokes, the climate took a spiraling nosedive right around AD 700 or so, including several stretches of dry years that would have totally depleted the seven years' worth of dried rations that Hopi informants say is the target range for a typical one-family storage structure. But temperature scales consistently. Ten extra growing-season degrees can tip lower elevations into the Nope Too Hot end of the livability gradient while

simultaneously tipping higher elevations *out* of the Nope Too
Cold end. Or, in more technical language, rising local temperatures can precipitate an upward shift in the elevational
dry-land farming belt as a result of increased numbers of frost-
free days. When rising temperatures make the lower portion of
the landscape too hot and dry for farming, they also make the
higher portions more hospitable. The onset of lower temperatures has the opposite effect. It only makes sense to follow such
movements.

There's an annual version of this in Arizona, in fact—one
with very deep roots. When the onset of summer brings an overall increase of about fifty degrees, high-elevation Flagstaff shifts
from subarctic to temperate and low-elevation Phoenix shifts
from temperate to charbroiled. And, each year, certain privileged
types in Phoenix reenact what the Ancestral Pueblo farmers of
Bears Ears did in the early 700s: they pack their stuff and head
uphill. Indigenous residents of the Grand Canyon did the exact
same thing for millennia, occupying the inner gorge during the
winter and the higher, cooler rims during the summer.

In the Bears Ears area, farmers responding to the sharp climatic spikes during that time period aggregated atop and alongside Cedar Mesa's smaller but taller cousin Elk Ridge,* home
of the Bears Ears formations. It was also during the Pueblo I
period—or the early Pueblo years in general—that another and
slightly more curious phenomenon appears to have emerged in
the Bears Ears area: the association of a number of important
local population centers with twin geological formations. At least
three major early villages are in direct association with big twin
rocks—one near Bluff and two in the higher uplands. And that's
in addition to the Bears Ears themselves.

---

* Most of them did, anyway. As famed Cedar Mesa archaeologist Bill
Lipe once pointed out to me, a smaller portion of the lower-uplands
farmers in places like Cedar Mesa headed instead for Bluff via Comb
Wash. In other words, some folks made their way uphill to Elk Ridge in
search of arable lands and game; and some made their way downhill to
the tempestuous richness of the San Juan River.

When I spoke to some Indigenous folks in the area about this phenomenon, they made reference to the Hero Twins that appear in both Hopi and Diné (and Mayan, and a whole bunch of other) cultural narratives. Maybe the reason the Hero Twins story is told at all is in remembrance of the time the climate went haywire and everyone was saved from starvation by flocking to the feet of a set of literal geological twins? The trouble with this deduction is that the Maya, at the very least, were preaching about their own set of Hero Twins—Hunahpu and Xbalanque—at least a few hundred years before.

But that doesn't mean the Hero Twins correlation is wrong. A prophesy fulfilled is a belief redoubled. If everyone was already talking about a pair of ancestral twins who cleared the world of monsters so that people could inhabit it, and then the rains came to a halt, and approximately seventy-five percent of the collective local population aggregated around a set of twin formations in the hopes that it would save them, and then doing so *did* save them—that would make for quite an impression, wouldn't it? Any population center tethered to some twin-like manifestation or other that emerged thereafter would probably be of considerable clout on that basis alone, and a cursory look at the archaeology of such places bears this out.

In any case, the association with the Bears Ears themselves becomes more prevalent than ever in the archaeological record during this time. In the modern era, that lofty sandstone pair is an important piece of the sacred geography of at least twenty-five—and probably many more—separate Indigenous groups from around the entire region.

Then there's the always-relevant topic of pottery. Pottery is a big deal in North American archaeology for a couple of reasons. First, it tends to carry a lot of cultural importance. Second, and with the process of taphonomy in mind, it lasts.

Pueblo I ceramics are marked by the addition of neck-banded gray ware, arguably the one and only truly diagnostic trait pegging an artifact to that time period. They're bulbous at the base, requiring a small depression in the sand or a woven ring to sit upon so they don't tip over, and they taper to a mouth that's straight-parallel with bands around the neck that look roughly like vinyl siding on a house. Just imagine a gray light bulb without the black tar-and-nipple bit at the top, sitting upright, with walls as thick as your finger and big enough to hold a medium-size helping of movie theater popcorn.

Although ceramics produced in any one place during this time tended to wander all over the region through trade, a distinctive type that's totally unique to southeastern Utah made its appearance during the mid to late 800s and appears never to have been traded out. It's pretty stuff. The lines are very fine and the slip is thick, so the combined result is a glossy gray surface with darker designs that look ghostly, like trees in a dense fog.

This gives rise to a set of speculative musings: that this particular pottery style was considered too *local* to be exchanged, which suggests that it was more closely linked with group identity than other items; or that the time period in which it developed was one in which trade itself was greatly restricted. The late 800s saw the second of two nasty droughts in the Pueblo I period, fixed by most climate reconstructions at about 880, and the available evidence points to a corresponding population aggregation in the higher uplands of southeastern Utah after the one described earlier. People get touchy during times like that.

Something similar seems to have occurred in southwestern Utah, as well, during the later Pueblo II period. I had the pleasure of conducting a bunch of inventory and site-recording in that area over the past few years, and there was plentiful evidence of trade between the Virgin branch of Ancestral Pueblo and their Fremont cousins. Very nearly all this trade was evidenced in the form of distinctive projectile points. The ceramics didn't mix at all. Despite the seeming plenitude of both Fremont and Ancestral Pueblo artifacts of other types, it always seemed that they had Pueblo ceramics—even if they, too, were non-local types. Other archaeologists have reported finding the same thing elsewhere in the broader region.

Pottery, it seems, had cultural importance that extended beyond the realms of both mundane and ritual usage. It said who you were. In recent years, I've spoken with Pueblo and Diné potters who make the same argument—emphatically so when it comes to sale of their work to tourists. There are some styles and designs that are *not* meant to wind up in the homes of people from, so to speak, the other side of the tracks.

All this, in turn, helps to inform an understanding of why looting is such an ugly practice. I've heard a lot of non-Indigenous people grumble and moan about how folks shouldn't get so uppity about a bunch of discarded stuff winding up in a museum or on someone's mantelpiece. It's just trash, when all is said and done—if it wasn't there it would be crumbling apart underground or something. Which is true of some of it, for sure; but do you know the difference? Imagine the same fate for Grandma's blanket that she crocheted all through a long winter to keep her fingers from freezing. Imagine the same fate for Grandpa's medals from the war. Imagine the same fate for their Bible, or their photo albums. Imagine the same fate for their *skulls*.

The point is that some objects have meaning and importance that are firmly anchored in familial or cultural milieus, and therefore shouldn't be bartered at the same swap meet as everything else. Discerning the sacred from the mundane isn't easily quantifiable, which is why reciprocal dialogue between the Indigenous and archaeological communities is of paramount importance for studying the material-historic record of North America.

It was also during this period that an entirely new type of pottery emerged across the greater Mesa Verde region, with its production center focused squarely on Bears Ears: red ware, so-called because it looks red or orange after firing. Intriguingly—and, to students of local archaeology, often confusingly—these gorgeous reddish-hued ceramics aren't the result of using exceptionally red clays, but of firing the usual stuff in an oxidizing atmosphere (i.e., one in which there is plentiful oxygen), whereby the iron content in the clay essentially rusts. The oxygen-free or reducing atmosphere of the classic burn-and-bury method of Pueblo pottery firing wouldn't yield this result, because being buried is not often conducive to healthy breathing. So, in order to fire clay in such a way that its iron content blooms as a rich red-orange color, a steady draft is needed—which means a lot more wood and attention are required to keep the temperature steady.

Modern reconstructionist potters and other primitive-technology wonks are always very eager to point this out, because it means that firing red wares is a lot harder and more involved than firing white or gray wares. Most of them, anyway; my friend Kelly Magleby is convinced that it's *easier* to make red wares, because it takes place aboveground where you can keep an eye on things. In any case, it certainly takes a greater toll on local wood stores.

These gorgeous orange-hued ceramics, called either Abajo or San Juan Red Wares, became all the rage for a while, being traded all over the greater Mesa Verde region and beyond. It appears that they were highly prized and sought-after. Serving food to your guests in a genuine San Juan Red Ware bowl was probably the equivalent of offering to pick your friends up in a Porsche. Its association with large architectural sites and ritual centers, however, suggests that it was more often a ritual item than a flashy domestic one.

They never waned in popularity until well into the Pueblo II period, when their production came to an abrupt and mysterious halt.

Discovery of the Pueblo I material-culture period is a tale in its own right.

Earl Morris is often credited as the first archaeologist to take serious stabs at a region-wide chronology of the ancient Southwest, as well as discoverer of the Pueblo I material complex in the La Plata region in 1913, although the team of Kidder and Guernsey found evidence of the same cultural stage in the Kayenta area during the same field season. Morris was also the son of a pothunter, a fact little-known outside the realms of deepest inquiry into the history of Southwest archaeology. Following popularization of the archaeological riches of Mesa Verde and the concurrent economic slump that preceded the Silver Panic of 1893 (you'll get tired of seeing that year), antiquities trading was seen as just one more potential source of income in dire times—and Scott Morris, Earl's father, took to it with gusto. He taught Earl the practice at a very young age.

After graduating from Farmington High School in 1908, when the school itself was just two years old, Earl Morris enrolled at the University of Colorado in Boulder with a major in psychology. His childhood experiences wouldn't stop nagging him, however, and he gradually shifted his focus toward archaeology. Working and studying on behalf of the university museum, he transformed from a pothunter and antiquities collector to a budding young scientist, and his revised academic curriculum came to include field apprenticeship to a landmark researcher: Nels Nelson.

Nelson, according to archaeological historian Don Fowler, was "a tall, robust Scandinavian with a jovial manner, a salty sense of humor, and one glass eye." The annals of Southwest archaeology are stuffed with colorful characters, and Nelson was no exception. He was affiliated with the American Museum of Natural History, and was conducting investigations in the Rio Grande region at the time Morris was assigned to his tutelage. For several years prior to this occurrence in 1915, Nelson had employed a technique established long before in Europe that involved working from a known level of cultural occupation downward to an unknown one. The idea of superposition in stratigraphy—that earlier things are found deposited beneath later things—was well-known by then, of course, but the idea of building that into a *seriation* or chronological order of past occupations was one that American archaeologists hadn't yet bothered to employ. It made sense in Europe, where the depth of human occupation in some places went back thousands of years and included nearly as many different cultural expressions, but in North America the archaeology was still presumed to be too new and ephemeral to yield anything so complex. This is why the discovery of Folsom was such a game changer.

Nelson, presciently, disagreed. He'd chosen the Rio Grande

region to apply the concept of seriation because he could begin at a confident known point when he found Native materials mixed in with Spanish ones and then work backward/downward from there. Morris worked with him, learning the established tricks of the trade and picking up some new ones as well.

It was in this way that Nelson was the first to notice that pottery at the Pueblos with European-influenced glaze was preceded by unglazed (but often slipped) black-on-white pottery, beneath which it was possible to establish rough trends in different decorative styles that correlated more or less with the same strata in different sites. An approximate chronology of Southwest prehistory began to take shape.

Further refinements were needed, and they continue to this day, but Nelson had essentially proven that it was possible to relatively, if not absolutely,* assign ages to the archaeological sites of the Southwest by cross-referencing the pottery assemblage with sequences confidently established in other localities. Morris carried that torch forward with vigor.

A little over one hundred years later, Jonathan Till at the Edge of the Cedars Museum in Blanding would explain to me how the Bears Ears area has some of the most characteristically "patterned" archaeology in the country, which is why I keep bringing up things like ceramic styles when talking about the material-culture sequences there. Wherever thoughtless oafs haven't jammed all the prettiest sherds into their pockets, a trained observer can often read ceramic assemblages like books. Although caution is advised: those "books" were written by the ancestors of people who've got their own views on how they should be read—and by whom.

As for Pueblo I: what Morris discovered in the La Plata area in 1913, when he was still under Nelson's tutelage, was an

---

* This is an important distinction. *Relative dating* refers to where things fall in a sequence from A to Z, while *absolute dating* pins things to a fixed point in time (like 1985 or 5000 BP). The first is why you can always pick on your little sibling for being younger than you while the second is why you look ridiculous doing so when you're both in your sixties.

unexpected material complex on a high ridge northwest of Mancos Springs. Morris correctly surmised that occupying these mesa tops were the remains of a culture not yet Full Pueblo, as he called it, but definitely post-Basketmaker. Based on the ceramic assemblage and the seriation worked out by he and Nelson, Morris guessed that they were about 1,500 years old—being off by around 500 years, as we now know, which is a considerable gap until you remember that Archbishop Ussher's estimate of the planet's creation was off by about 4,536,977 years—and likely represented the opening salvo in what thereafter developed into what was then called Full Pueblo culture. Thus, the term he used in his notes: Pre Pueblo.

Credit for first describing it in the literature belongs rightly to Byron "Dean" Cummings.

Cummings was a famously, almost notoriously kind and gentle man. It's difficult to find any historic photographs of him where he isn't smiling warmly. He was dean of the College of Arts and Sciences at the University of Utah—hence the nickname—and had taken to exploring the archaeology of southeastern Utah starting in about 1906. A couple years later, accompanied by his nephew Neil Judd, Dean Cummings became one of the first non-Native individuals to set eyes on Rainbow Bridge, becoming embroiled in an eye-rolling controversy because of it. His nephew played a role in that journey and its subsequent controversy, and would himself do some of the earliest work in the Bears Ears area in the 1920s, although he mostly made an early name for himself chasing the Basketmakers and Cliff Dwellers through the canyons nearer to modern-day Kanab.

While he published precious little in all his years of exploring and investigating the Southwest, transcripts of Cummings' field notes are available to researchers at the Natural History Museum of Utah. They are, in a word, revelatory. The following 1908 excerpt is courtesy of Westin Porter at the NHMU:

Have you ever spread your blankets on the warm sands of the southwestern plateau and stretched out your weary body in full relaxation?...Have you ever then filled your lungs with

God's pure mountain ozone and gazed up through that clear atmosphere into the heavens spread out above you where a million dancing, sparkling suns seemed to be nodding assent to your reveries and encouraging your happiness? If you have not, then your time has not yet come. You are not yet fit to die.

Like Hewett and Kidder, Cummings was appalled at the extensive pothunting that was taking place throughout the Four Corners area, and often sought to attract the attention of state and federal officials to intervene. A 1910 article in the *Salt Lake Herald-Republican*, precursor to the *Salt Lake Tribune*, bore the descending headlines of "Robbery of Ruins Has Been Stopped," "DEAN COMES FROM SCENE," "Byron Cummings Tells of the Wonders to Be Seen and Work That Has Been Done Among the Treasures of Utah," "WILL CONSECRATE HIS LIFE TO GREAT STUDY," and "Has Already Succeeded in Interesting State and Government in the Protection of the Vast Historic Wealth," before getting on with the story itself: Dean Cummings had single-handedly made antiquities theft a thing of the past.

Robbery of ruins was, of course, not stopped in 1910—nor, indeed, has it been stopped in the century since. The *Herald-Republican*'s preemptive "Robbery of Ruins Has Been Stopped" was not only wrong but embarrassingly so. Nonetheless, arm-wavy editorializing aside, this and Kidder's earlier-mentioned report from that same year helped make southeastern Utah a high-profile example in efforts to stymie looting for one hundred years and counting.

Interestingly, Cummings was also a dedicated and passionate supporter of athletic programs at the University of Utah, and is often called the father of university athletics. He organized the U's first football team in 1893, according to several biographies, and was involved in the school's Athletic Association from 1894 through the year of the newspaper article mentioned above. The university's football team was named after him until 1927.

Since then, football at the U was played in Ute Stadium, now Rice-Eccles Stadium; and the team itself is known as the Utah Utes, owing to a memorandum of understanding between the university and the tribe. The MOU allows the school to use the name in exchange for devoting human and financial resources to "encourage, inspire, and support tribal youth to lead healthy lives and to pursue post-secondary education." I assume some of that really happens.

Colorful characters abound in the early days of Bears Ears archaeology, but perhaps none more colorful than Charles Bernheimer, who appeared on the scene about a decade after Cummings.

Yet another easterner—from New York, in fact—who stumbled into the Southwest and got instantly, hopelessly addicted to it, Bernheimer joins the Hydes on the list of rich dilettantes who made archaeology possible at the time. His passion for the Southwest developed in his middle age, after attaining considerable wealth as a cotton broker in the Bear Mill Manufacturing Company, and that wealth allowed him both the freedom to take long trips to his newfound playground and the money to finance them. He made a total of fourteen trips during the 1920s and early 1930s, publishing a few mainstream articles and one book about his travels. He also donated to scientific institutions all the artifacts that he found, were given to him, and/or he and his teammates dug up along the way.

Bernheimer's paraphrastic passion often exceeded his grasp of the facts. A 1929 *New York Times* article based on notes from his doings, for example, included the following: "Some five or ten thousand years ago a community of Americans made their homes in caves carved out of the solid rock high above the floors of canyons in the Southwest."

He was off by about five or ten thousand years. I'm also uncertain how their modern descendants would feel about their being called "a community of Americans," although I suspect *not great* would be a start. But the relationship between archaeology and journalism has always been a strained one, even before Indiana Jones was poured all over the topic like water on a grease fire.

In the wake of the Bears Ears National Monument contro-versy—although *wake* isn't the right word, since it rages on today and will probably never completely stop—this became more apparent than ever. Here was a really hot topic that involved, serendipitously, real-life cowboys and Indians! Scores of major media outlets across the country flocked to it like sharks to a strug-gling seal, many of them surmounting considerable distances by simply calling around and asking who the "experts" were. From those experts, recommended by other supposed experts in a strategy that's half cat-and-mouse and half game-of-whispers, they cobbled together reams of suspect copy that includes a lot of pretty pictures, a lot of punctilious phrases, and anywhere from a little to a lot of editorializing fluff and plain old bullshit.

For example: one day, friend and fellow author Morgan Sjogren got the idea to stake a uranium claim within the bound-aries of the original Bears Ears National Monument after Trump (at the behest of the Utah delegation and energy lobbyists) drasti-cally reduced it. She makes her living as a writer and trail runner while living on a shoestring budget out of her Jeep, by the way—hence her trade name, the Running Bum. So, when she staked the claims, she did so looking the way she always looks: wearing filthy running shoes, a raggedy wide-brim hat, scruffy flannel shirt, and feathery hippie earrings. She resembled an energy industry pro-fessional the way a duck resembles a dragon.

It was obviously an act of protest, as well as a way for Sjogren and her former partner to learn how the leasing process works, and the BLM officials with whom she met understood this. They played along, as their jobs required, with barely con-cealed chuckles. They even joked with her about the process after it was concluded. And then, with almost uncanny alacrity, jour-nalists started blowing up her phone asking—and I swear I'm not making this up—what she, as *an expert in uranium mining*, could tell them about the situation in Bears Ears.

Back in Bernheimer's day, things weren't much different. Nobody had high-powered computers stuffed into their pockets with which they could access the greatest assemblage of informa-tion in our species' history in seconds, of course, so fact-checking was a much more arduous process. On the other hand, lack if that same technology meant that journalists and researchers writing public-oriented copy weren't competing with ten thousand other Johnny-come-lately entrants per hour to every available media niche. If you could write well, media outlets just as often came begging to *your* door as you would go begging to theirs for a sweet bite of societal attention—especially if you didn't need their money. And Charles L. Bernheimer most certainly did not.

Having visited Rainbow Bridge in 1921, he arranged to take the exact same trip again the following year but with scientists along to explain all about the ruins of Betatakin and Keet Seel (both are included in Navajo National Monument today) that were included on the itinerary. That's how fabulously well-to-do he was; he could afford to hire experts to accompany him on lengthy adventures just to tell him what, exactly, he was looking at. To that end, he reached out to Clark Wissler at the American Museum of Natural History, who recommended Earl Morris.

The trip was a pleasant success. Bernheimer and Morris—along with a few others, including Richard Wetherill's good-natured and conservation-minded brother "Hosteen" John—took a number of splendid photographs, which would work their magic for decades afterward. It also cemented for Morris his own version of what the Hydes had been to the Wetherills: a wealthy benefactor eager to support his investigations.

This is how Morris and Bernheimer wound up together in the heart of Bears Ears country in 1929, along with storied local guide Ezekiel "Zeke" Johnson. Their itinerary was the wild and woolly canyon-and-mesa country west of Blanding, where the surface had barely been scratched by predecessors like McLoyd, Graham, and the Wetherills. Their adventure through the area described an enormous loop that included Cottonwood Wash, Butler Wash, and Comb Wash; from there into Arch Canyon, and then up over Elk Ridge and back down into Kane Gulch and Grand Gulch; and from the junction of Grand Gulch and the San Juan down to its junction with the Colorado. From there they turned west, journeyed along the corridor of the Colorado to White Canyon, and took that up to Natural Bridges—from which they made their way over Elk Ridge again and back to Blanding.

According to my calculations, the smallest possible linear distance for that undertaking is about 375 miles. Little wonder, then, that their pack train consisted of forty-four animals. Leading forty-four pack animals through Grand Gulch strains the imagination, although admittedly I'm not much of a horse person thanks largely to a character named Tazz.

A report of the archaeological work conducted on that huge journey consists entirely of the following:

Mr. Charles L. Bernheimer, accompanied by... Mr. Earl H. Morris, visited the district at the junction of the San Juan and Colorado Rivers, locating Basket Maker and Cliff Dweller remains.

> Clark Wissler,
> American Museum of Natural History

Wissler's lackluster impression of the archaeological-inventory portion of Bernheimer's expedition reflected Morris's own lackluster impressions from the field. He'd spent the stretch of years between that first trip to Rainbow Bridge and this one exploring and excavating in Canyons de Chelly and del Muerto—thanks entirely to Bernheimer's generous patronage—and thought, for good reason, that the archaeology he encountered in the Bears Ears area was flimsy by comparison. He considered the Late Basketmaker materials he excavated there crude and janky compared with those from his other study areas.

Although he didn't use these exact words, Morris was the first archaeologist to characterize the Bears Ears area as the "backwoods of Mesa Verde," as I have done several times already. But he didn't mean it as a compliment, as I very much do. He meant the place where Verde's weird, less-civilized cousins dwelt. The *boonies*.

Bernheimer, by contrast, was ecstatic and flabbergasted in about equal measure. A textiles man himself, having made his fortune in the cotton industry, the excavated woven goods that

Morris thought so humdrum made his eyes all but burst from his head—at least if his own reporting is anything to go by. Morris is purported to have cringed when, in the aforementioned *New York Times* piece, Bernheimer excitedly recalled how they had discovered Basketmaker burials from as many as ten thousand years ago who wove cotton and used Australian boomerangs.

I've got a copy of that article—it's available for purchase from the *New York Times* online archival vault—and it's an eyebrow-raiser. The subheading reads "The Bernheimer Expedition, Returning from Unexplored Utah Desolation, Brings Evidence of a Strange and Complex Civilization of Early America." About five paragraphs in, Bernheimer muses that the discovery of a mummified elderly woman might suggest that the Basketmakers killed their old people when food was scarce. Seriously. There's also a photograph depicting a pair of gorgeous food-storage structures in White Canyon with the caption "The Ancient Basketmakers Lived in Caves" underneath, despite there being two non-Basketmaker storage structures and *zero* caves in the photo. I'll leave unexplored the question of whether or not they really used Australian boomerangs.

They did weave cotton, though—albeit not until much later (approximately the mid-AD 1000s, or Pueblo II period). So, that part was almost right.

However, lest I paint an unfairly negative picture of Bernheimer, he really was musing to the best of his ability based on what he'd picked up in bits and pieces from Morris and his colleagues. He had no formal training. Furthermore, the man was by all accounts a giant sweetheart. Regional historian Harvey Leake, great-grandson of John Wetherill, refers to him in a *Canyon Country Zephyr* article as "the Gentleman Explorer," and every reliable account of the man concurs heartily. And although Morris was miffed by some of the outlandish claims Bernheimer spewed into the papers, he maintained equanimity about it when he was around his friend and benefactor. People really liked Bernheimer.

Almost overlapping their big Bears Ears trip was one involving good old Nels Nelson. As curator of the American Museum of Natural history, Nelson organized a two-week expedition into Grand Gulch in 1920. It was an extension of a larger field effort by him to organize the various threads of Southwest archaeology into one coherent cord by seeing it for himself. The total range of his expedition included portions of California, Nevada, Utah, Arizona, and New Mexico, although he focused chiefly on Grand Gulch and New Mexico's Mimbres Valley. The Grand Gulch portion was separately and independently funded by the extremely wealthy Cartier family of wristwatch fame.

The expedition's stated goal was to link Richard Wetherill's collections at the museum to their respective homes on the landscape, which included trying to make sense of Richard's esoteric cave-numbering system. Altogether, they cataloged a total of eighty sites, taking dozens of photos and creating a handful of maps, although they had limited success at the specific task of associating what they found with what Richard had scribbled in his notes.

Nelson's report on the Cartier Grand Gulch Expedition is a hoot. He presents his crew in a theater-like roll call, including what he considered their most important attributes. Thus, you find:

John Wetherill, guide, chief cook, pack balancer, etc., etc.
Albert Smith, a happy young man, son of Colorado, who talked in his sleep.
Oliver Rickets, a Harvard medical student, fast learning the ways of the West.
(H)Ataclienaez ("Tall Singer"), a Navajo Indian with a very fine name, though he never sang for us. Was pleasant, courteous and dignified, and always faithful to his work, as well as to the fleshpot [nowadays used to describe a brothel, but in those days it simply meant that he helped with the cooking]. And he didn't smoke.

He even includes a separate roll call of the animals in his outfit, including a mule named Skippety Ann and a horse named Old Reliable (I'd like to have met that one).

Nelson's opinion on the natural splendors of the place itself was, in a word, effusive. For instance: "[Grand Gulch is a] great rift in the earth, tortuous and fantastic, with mushroom or toadstool rocks, monuments of standing, seated, and bust figures, hats atilt, and every conceivable form and shape on which imagination seizes or turns into semblances of life."

That one paragraph comprises what we would now call the environmental context portion of a technical field report. The phrase "tortuous and fantastic" would later be borrowed for the frontispiece of the 2014 issue of *Archaeology Southwest Magazine* about the place, predecessor to an even bigger issue published as a result of the national monument effort.

Nelson also provides the following caveat: "Stiff necks from looking up—not for N.Y.'s." Since Nelson makes no mention of any members of the Cartier family being with him in Grand Gulch, he was probably referring to that oft-loved and just as oft-ridiculed eastern dandy of the early days of Bears Ears archaeology: Charles Bernheimer.

As a fellow transplanted N.Y., my neck often concurs.

Chapter Six: The Chaco World

Although it started a bit earlier in some places, from about the mid-AD 1000s through the 1100s the Bears Ears area and most of the Four Corners bore witness to the rise of an impressive system of community organization that appears to have radiated outward from Chaco Canyon in northern New Mexico. It didn't behave like an empire, or a "country" as we commonly use the term, and whether or not it counts as a "state" is a subject of much debate.

In sum, the region-wide sociocultural phenomenon associated with Chaco shrugs off just about every Western concept that's applied to it. We aren't even sure how it began, although there are some tantalizing ideas about that.

At the end of the Pueblo I period, the entire northern San Juan region—including the Bears Ears portion of it—was, apparently, altogether depopulated.* To some extent, this was an extension of the wholesale migrations that characterized the early Pueblo period, when centers of dense occupation and settlement shuttled all over the map in pursuit of ever-shifting niches of

---

* Archaeologists have taken to using this word instead of *abandoned* for a couple of reasons. One, the connotations of abandonment are dire—it's what you do to a puppy or a child that you don't love anymore, and then only if you're a monster. And two, abandonment implies never looking back, whereas ancient North American populations routinely vacated entire regions only to return a dozen generations later when the soil nutrients were replenished and/or quantities of game were back up to snuff.

environmental suitability. Although stragglers and holdouts are a certainty, between the years of about 900 and 1020, the northern San Juan was steadily emptied. Everyone, it seems, had decided to converge upon the southern San Juan in and around Chaco Canyon.

Chaco is the alpha and omega of the Pueblo II period.

In broader terms, the Pueblo II period spans the interval from about AD 900 to 1150, its beginning marking the time when nearly everyone had fled or started to depopulate places like the Bears Ears area at the end of the Pueblo I period. What likely precipitated that first (of two) major depopulations of the greater Mesa Verde area was a climatic change to cooler conditions starting near the end of the ninth century that made the higher-elevation farming zones of the Pueblo I period a lot less attractive. Early Pueblo II populations dispersed over much wider areas to seek out those ecological niches where farming could still be practiced, resulting in a new settlement pattern characterized by small hamlets, or clusters of unit pueblos. Habitation sites of this period are not common anywhere in or near the Bears Ears area, which is why many researchers are confident that the northern San Juan as a whole was near-totally emptied.

The flip side of depopulation is aggregation. When, for example, lower-upland formations like Cedar Mesa became un-farmable during the erratic climate of the Pueblo I period, people from relatively dispersed occupation areas converged on much smaller higher-upland formations like Elk Ridge—where they now lived cheek to cheek with what used to be distant neighbors. This was presumably the case in Chaco during the early Pueblo II period, where two earlier Late Basketmaker proto-villages—known as *Shabik'eschee* and, creatively, 29SJ423—had grown to unusually large sizes and likely signaled that this was the place to do that. Population growth did indeed occur in the Chaco Canyon area during the subsequent time period, although probably more from the influx of migrants than anything else, but it did so ponderously.

Then came the roaring 1000s, and an era of environmental lushness and plenty not matched before or since in Southwest climate records. This is what's known to scientists and historians as the Medieval Warm Period, Medieval Climate Optimum, or Medieval Climatic Anomaly—it all depends on what sort of spin you're trying to put on your research narrative—and it spanned the North Atlantic region around the globe from about AD 950 to 1250. Scientists speculate that it was caused by a combination of increased solar radiation and decreased volcanic activity, although there is other evidence to suggest that ocean circulation patterns also shifted to bring warmer seawater to the North Atlantic.

Whatever the minutia of its origins, it had enormous impacts on human history around the globe. The Vikings did some of their most expansive exploring and settling (and raping and pillaging, although not nearly as much as their reputation suggests) during this time, founding extensive settlements in Iceland and Greenland just before the commencement of the eleventh century. Archaeological evidence of wheat fields and vineyards dating to this period can still be found in places like northern England and Switzerland—places where wheat fields and vineyards would be unthinkable today.

But climate change is always a two-sided coin, and evidence from the Sierra Nevada Mountains, the Andes, parts of already parched Australia, and much of the Asian steppe indicate extended drought during this same stretch of time. Bread baskets become dead zones, in other words; and vice versa. People who point to the Medieval Climatic Whatever as evidence against human-influenced or *anthropogenic* climate change in the modern era—and there really are a few that do—should do well to remember that.

Climate anomalies of any type are not felt in all places at the same time, and in the American West the wettest years seem to stretch between about 1000 and 1150. Nor were the good times restricted entirely to the Pueblo world. The abundant rains of this time period caused population surges among both the Ancestral Pueblo and their cousins in the Great Basin, the Fremont.

In Chaco Canyon, what appears to have happened was this: a densely aggregated population, made up of dry-land farmers from various regional backgrounds, suddenly had a bonanza on its hands. The result would change the Pueblo world forever after.

The origins of the gargantuan sociocultural network associated with Chaco are fuzzy, and explanations range from pragmatic and behavioral to postmodern and ritual-obsessed. I lean toward the former, being in my heart of hearts a stubborn cultural materialist and behavioral ecologist (albeit a decidedly postmodern one) who believes that practicality usually precedes ritual. We first start doing something because it makes sense to do so, in other words, and then the practice becomes ritualized—sometimes enduring long after it has ceased making sense.

A handy example is the taboo some cultural groups have against eating pork. Through modern eyes, it is purely ritual; there is nothing particularly unhealthy about pork as compared with other animal meats, and nothing about pigs that makes them particularly well- or ill-suited as food providers compared with other animals. But that wasn't always the case. Wild pigs aren't any more prone to infection than most other animals, but living in artificial pens without access to a natural menu turns them into the pathogen equivalent of waterfront property, especially for trichinosis—a vicious and occasionally fatal tissue infection. And pigpens were invented long before sterile kitchens and the concept of the "temperature danger zone" (between 40 and 140 degrees Fahrenheit) that nowadays gets beaten into every restaurant worker. Trichinosis was therefore given a big head start in the historic arms race between productivity and pestilence, with predictable results.* Modern methods of cooking and

---

* This particular lesson from history is one we seem hell-bent on failing to learn. Some of the most virulent of modern outbreaks, including

refrigeration took care of that problem, for the most part, but the taboo endures.

It used to make sense, in other words, and what remains is a vestigial behavior that hasn't been entirely jettisoned because it doesn't really need to be. Not yet. But when famine starts kicking down doors, you'd better believe pork is back on the menu—as has happened in numerous other cases. My favorite example of *that* comes, fittingly enough, from Bears Ears.

One element of the suite of goods either carried or culturally transmitted north from Mexico in the early agricultural periods was *Meleagris gallopavo*, the Linnaean taxonomic name (after Carolus Linnaeus, the man we have to blame for binomial nomenclature in science) for turkey. During the 1970s, Bill Lipe and his longtime colleague R. G. Matson conducted an extensive cultural resource inventory on Cedar Mesa that has since become the stuff of legend, and the site they probably investigated the most thoroughly was one called Turkey Pen Ruin. First mapped by Richard Wetherill and his cohort during the 1893-4 field season in which his wife got to cozy up with some mummies, it's an impressive alcove-and-bench site comprised of at least a dozen structures occupied and reoccupied numerous times throughout Ancestral Pueblo history. These include the partially intact remains of a wattle-and-daub enclosure that's been informally interpreted as a turkey pen, from which the site gets its name. Materials from a test pit dug by Matson showed continuous occupation or reoccupation dating back to about AD 1, and they included abundant human feces (or *coprolites*), maize cobs and stems, feathers, bits of human hair, and cordage, as well as lots and lots of turkey droppings.

Analysis of these materials continues to this day, and probably will for some time. They were dug from the midden rather than from structural rubble or burials, so it's not as ethically dicey, and the wealth of information that has sprung forth from that one test pit is staggering. Archaeologists got their first glimpse of just

---

AIDS and COVID-19, have their roots in woefully cavalier treatment of animals during their journey from feral to feast.

how far back in time maize-farming dependence had established in the Bears Ears area—starting around 400 BC, as it turns out. Along with a few sites from the area immediately surrounding Cedar Mesa, it was also where researchers got a good look at the still-developing story of turkeys in the northern San Juan.

Turkeys, it seems, were domesticated—to the extent that farm turkeys can be considered domesticated, even today—in Mesoamerica sometime before the period between AD 1 and 200; and were an established feature of Early Basketmaker life by at least this stretch of time and maybe as early as 1000 BC. Like the llamas and alpacas husbanded by the Incas in the high Andes, they ate a diet consisting mostly of maize kernels. And, also like the two domesticated *camelids* of the Andes (but unlike Andean guinea pigs), they weren't kept for food. Instead, the earliest turkeys appear to have been raised and lovingly doted upon as providers of feathers for use in rituals and for making blankets. They were even given formal burials, like dogs, which is hard for us to imagine given that we rapaciously rip whole turkey carapaces apart every Thanksgiving and then toss the bones in the trash without so much as a second thought.

Early turkeys in the Southwest were, in other words, kept as feather-bearing friends and lovingly interred the way that we would a beloved pet, right up until the late 800s. And then the weather changed.

The salad days of turkeys in the northern Southwest, which ran for upwards of two thousand years, came to a staggering halt when people started consuming them during the tail-end of the Pueblo I period—and then to a much more decisive halt in the late Pueblo II and Pueblo III periods.

The initial decision to start looking at the family's feathered friend as something that might go well with gravy probably resulted from the nasty drought that occurred right around AD 880, which also seems to have inspired the near-total depopulation of the northern San Juan over the next hundred years. Going from an occasional food item to a staple one after about 1050 likely has more to do with the explosion of populations and aggregated population centers during that time period. Analyses of faunal material from sites dating to that stretch show a massive overall dip in large game, even while the robust rains of the Medieval Climate Anomaly poured on, suggesting that even in times of plenty our voraciousness doesn't keep pace with local carrying capacities so much as run out in front of them and make faces.

That's how turkeys jumped the gap from sources of company and feathers to sources of wishbones and, much later, second-rate bacon. You can almost picture children chasing them around Basketmaker hamlets while their parents scold them not to bother their beloved pet Gobbles too much, and just as easily picture the same scene in the courtyards of Chaco where the parents would be scolding their kids for playing with their food. And food, it seems, was the springboard from which Chaco came to be the mighty regional whatever-it-was that it was.

The center of the San Juan Basin is the least agriculturally productive portion of it. It's too low and dry. Out near the rims, communities can perch themselves at just the right elevation to fit within the upper and lower limits of the dry-land farming belt, and thereby also situate themselves in optimal spots for hunting at higher elevations and seeking riverine resources at lower ones without going far from home. For this reason, it's the prime bowl-rim properties that got snatched up first, and when climatic conditions start getting wobbly—as they always do—you can bet that every arable niche of any worthwhile size was staked and guarded. Chasing these niches around as they boomed and busted helps explain the moving target of population centers in the northern San Juan during the Pueblo I period.

Within the grim interior of the bowl, however, Chaco Canyon was like an oasis. Climatic and geomorphological happenstance made it into a favorable environmental patch (occasionally, anyway) set within an otherwise un-farmable desert. The people who'd settled there during previous periods of population movement, the ones that had built *Shabik'eschee* and 29SJ423, were therefore environmentally circumscribed; and, accordingly, development of hierarchy and food distribution occurred in situ because people couldn't simply migrate elsewhere when stressors accumulated. There was no "elsewhere" to migrate into. The immediate surroundings were too harsh, and the fertile rim lands—like the Mesa Verde region, including Bears Ears—were already occupied.

It looks as though the early Chaco locals figured out how to irrigate and farm a small oasis in a big hurry, with the desert pressing in around them as a firm reminder of the cost of failure. They succeeded.

The earliest defining features of what would come to be widely regarded as the Chaco phenomenon, system, or world date to as early as AD 850, when some of the earliest construction began on its iconic great houses. A great house, simply put, is a large pueblo complex. The focus of archaeological interest in Chaco is centered upon about a dozen of these sandstone behemoths located within Chaco Canyon itself in what is sometimes called Downtown Chaco.

Chaco expert Steve Lekson sees their shape and construction as a combination between the local idea of very large pit house villages, as at *Shabik'eschee*; and architectural ideas from the northern San Juan and places like Bears Ears, where people often built horseshoe-shaped roomblocks around elaborate, oversized pit houses. The result was a monumentally scaled-up version of the classic Pueblo I unit pueblo, and I do mean monumentally scaled up: at its architectural zenith in the early 1100s, Pueblo Bonito—greatest of the Chaco great houses—had about eight hundred total rooms and was larger than the Roman Colosseum.

Although that word *rooms* is a tricky one. Some early speculators, and even a few modern ones, emphasize how the overwhelming majority of Pueblo Bonito's eight hundred or so rooms are tiny square things, with no obvious ventilation. Surely nobody was living in *those*, so the entire structure must have existed solely for ceremonial purposes!

This is like arguing that your own home can't possibly be a functional domestic structure because your pantry would be a lousy place to sleep. If you live in a house, it is probably comprised of somewhere between four and ten rooms—although you might *occupy* only two or three of them. The rest are for gathering as a group, or for cooking things, or cleaning things, or storing things, and at least one of them is for making unpleasant things go away with a satisfying **whoosh** sound. With a few obvious differences, the same was undoubtedly true of the great houses of Chaco.

The earliest great houses were large habitations of between half a dozen and a dozen households arranged around a great kiva, a communal structure first introduced in the Late Basketmaker period. Surrounding these were clusters of other, much smaller residences out to about a mile or so therefrom. We can think of great kivas as roughly analogous to a capital building in a downtown district, although it's wise to be cautious when applying analogies to Chaco. They may have been the homes of elites, set amid but apart from the commoners occupying the swarm of smaller residences that surrounded them. They may also have been ceremonial centers with ritual overseers, like monks at a monastery.

What Chaco appears to have become in those early days was, in effect, a maize-based "food bank" according to an idea championed by Lekson and others. Even in good years, the farming could be very unpredictable in the more farmable rim provinces—like Bears Ears, where my own research on prehistoric farming techniques suggests that dry farming atop Cedar Mesa was successful one out of every three to five years. That sounds like a disastrously fatal success rate until you take into account the fact that storage structures, or granaries, make up a large portion of the architecture there, and a granary of average Cedar Mesa size filled with dried maize could sustain a small family for up to about half a decade. Thus: a drought lasting longer than about seven years would be the one that compelled folks to pack up and skedaddle, and reconstructions of drought severity and population movements seem to bear this out.

Chaco, then, appears to have acted sort of like a gigantic granary complex or redistribution center. This goes a long way toward explaining why large portions of Chaco's great houses look not so much like *house* houses as *ware*houses. Communities from all around this hub of the San Juan Basin could cache their surpluses of maize and other goods there for later use by either themselves or other communities during shortfalls. When weather conditions swung upward in the early to mid-1000s, surplus became opulence. This is probably how the Inca got their start as well, building and relying on local food banks to shore up shortfalls, until the climatic conditions of Chaco Canyon and the Andes effectively swapped places at about AD 1150—after which the Inca gradually rose to imperial dominance, while things up north took a decidedly more dismal turn.

As the centuries ground on and the Chaco core community developed, great houses grew larger and larger through additional construction surges. They came to share distinctive commonalities, like walled-in kivas, core-and-veneer masonry (that is: a wall made up of two stone walls with a rubble-stuffed core in between), and T-shaped doorways. This last one is curious, because in Chaco and in the subsequent period in Mesa Verde, T-shaped doors are almost always associated with rooms adjacent to kivas or towers, or within towers.

So, what about these T-shaped doors? Archaeologists are unsure how they came about, or why, although they appear rather abruptly during the heyday of Chaco and figure prominently in the great houses of Chaco Canyon itself. They later appear at Aztec Ruin, in central Mesa Verde at structures like Spruce Tree House, and elsewhere throughout the northern San Juan region, including the Bears Ears area. They also appear somewhat later pretty far to the south, in the Sierra Madre region of northern Mexico, where dozens of them were built into Paquimé at around AD 1400.

Popular wilderness author Craig Childs made chasing T-shaped doors all over the place a focal point and narrative springboard in his 2006 book *House of Rain*, interviewing Hopi elders who hinted at their cultural importance without giving too much away and tracing them into the archaeological record as early as Nordenskiöld—who associated them with the later-era sites that he found to be constructed "with more care and skill than sites lacking T shapes." This makes sense if they originated at Chaco, because it means they would have arrived in central Mesa Verde with people fleeing Chaco's demise.

Hypotheses for their origination vary considerably. They're not as easy to close as rectangular doors, since you would need a big T-shaped slab to slot into them, so they may have been designed to mean "this door is always open." It has also been suggested that the smaller bottom and wider top are better for air circulation, although this runs into the immediate problem of the *interior* doors not being shaped that way. It's also possible that the larger opening at the top made it easier to carry an armload of goods into a structure from the outside. And, of course, there is the usual cadre of knuckleheads suggesting that T-shaped doors are conduits that connect Chaco, the Maya, the Egyptians, and little green fellows in spaceships.

Whether or not you buy any of the functional explanations for the genesis of T-shaped doors during the early eleventh century in Chaco, they certainly *became* symbolic, a point on which everyone seems to agree. They appear in rock art, on textiles, etched into the plaster on kiva walls, and even carved into mug handles.

One tendril of this phenomenon that I find fascinating is what I playfully think of as Chaco one-room apartments. These are smallish structures, sometimes perfectly square, typically about five feet to a side. They sometimes occur all by themselves, but usually they're located at more complex sites comprised of an array of structures—and yet these things are almost always detached, off by themselves. You might even call their nature "aloof." They have one entrance: a T-shaped door; and often a hearth built into the floor. And that's it. If that's the dwelling place of some exalted elite, it's an awfully paltry one.

The observation by some authors that they are most often associated with kivas holds true for the ones I've seen, such as the one at Perfect Kiva in Bullet Canyon. There's one in a canyon on the west side of Cedar Mesa that sits directly above several kivas that you'd need a wing suit to reach. And I've seen another one in the Natural Bridges area that *is* a kiva, albeit a uniquely remodeled one.

Perhaps they were the official quarters of the local religious leader? If so, their relative paltriness might offer a clue about the station of religious leaders in their respective era's pecking order. They all date to various times after the fall of Chaco. Refugee priests? Were they part of Chaco's expansion, which probably reached the hinterlands last?

They're not saying.

That last question is a pivotal one, by the way. Bears Ears wasn't just the backwoods of Mesa Verde, as Earl Morris implied. It was also, for a relatively short time, the backwoods of Chaco. The might and majesty that was the Chaco social system emerged out of the aggregating of various peoples from all across the region, after all, bringing their beliefs and traditions with them. Those traditions, styles, and ideas moved fluidly throughout the Intermountain West—and, seemingly, beyond—during the heyday of Chaco's social system.

That social system, or super-community or state or proto-empire or whatever it really was, extended over an area that measured about 150 miles in diameter, making it larger than any of the great city-states in Meso- or South America prior to then. And it included a relationship *with* the great city-states of Mesoamerica, as evidenced by exotic items from far to the south.

First and foremost on that list are scarlet macaws. These are large, colorful parrots native to the rainforests of Mesoamerica, although the word scarlet in their name is a bit misleading. Their heads and bodies are indeed a brilliant red, but their wings band from red to yellow to blue, and they've got a big patch of white around their eyes. They figure prominently in the iconography of the Aztecs and the Maya for any number of reasons, including the fact that white, yellow, red, and blue are the most common colors of ancestral, or heirloom, maize.

Those four colors also represent the cardinal directions in traditional Hopi culture: yellow for north, blue or green for west, red for south, and white for east. Nor is that anything new. I know of at least one Early Basketmaker pictograph panel depicting four life-size figures arranged in a row, each of them dressed entirely in one of those colors.

Scarlet macaw feathers are found throughout the Southwest in a variety of settings. One of the most beautiful things I've ever seen is a sash made of scarlet macaw feathers, buckskin, and squirrel pelt, lovingly housed at the Edge of the Cedars State Park Museum in Blanding, Utah, which was found in southern Canyonlands National Park just to the north of Bears Ears. Radiocarbon dating of the squirrel pelt pegged the sash to about AD 1150, putting it a bit after the diaspora that accompanied the downfall of Chaco, although whether it was carried north by Chacoan refugees or happened to arrive way up there by trade is tough to puzzle out.

Still, it's not terribly surprising to find out that people traded something as cool as scarlet macaws or their lovely plumage over such a great distance. They're gorgeous birds, if temperamental and bite-y as pets; and the fact that they come in the exact set of colors already deemed sacred way back in Basketmaker times certainly didn't hurt their appeal. The earliest evidence we have suggests that macaws were imported starting around AD 900, with some researchers eyeballing that as evidence that the germ seed of Chaco's subsequent development into something state-like might have come with them. What's more amazing is that they probably weren't just imported. Painted bowls from the Mimbres region of New Mexico depict juvenile macaws, something you wouldn't expect to see unless they were being bred locally.

And then there's *Theobroma cacao*, Linnaean moniker for the tree that gives us chocolate. The Mayans, Aztecs, Olmecs, and their predecessors made extensive use of cacao beans for at least five thousand years. On the list of items from the Columbian Exchange—the universal term for the transference of plants, animals, and technologies after Columbus invaded the Caribbean—that one ranks nearly as high as maize and tobacco for its overall impact factor.

Cacao was made into a drink for medicinal purposes by the Olmecs, the first large-scale civilization in Mexico, although archaeological evidence of personal use is lacking. The Mayans produced several varieties of cacao drink, often blending the roasted bean paste with cornmeal and peppers before mixing it up into a brothy beverage for a number of uses. The beans themselves were used as currency, a tradition that continued with the Aztecs, where two beans bought you a decent avocado, thirty bought you a rabbit, and three hundred bought you a male turkey. Some people even made counterfeit cacao beans out of avocado pits and wax, because there's always a few.

Cacao made its way north in beverage form. Far north. In 2003, traces of theobromine—the chocolate-derived alkaloid that you should never give your dog—were found on sherds from elongated ceramic vessels from Pueblo Bonito. Moreover, basic eyeball comparison showed that these vessels were similar to the ones used by the Mayans to consume their own cocoa-like concoctions. I don't know how this fact had escaped notice all that time…but there it was. Chaco's reach was indeed far.

How?

As with the question of how Chaco emerged and developed into such a regional powerhouse in the first place, the question of what its enormous social system was—and how it operated—inspires no small amount of debate. Although most researchers converge on one contention: it almost definitely wasn't through warfare. Studies of intergroup and interpersonal violence throughout this area point to a Pax Chaco, as both Steve Lekson and Steven LeBlanc like to call it (after the Pax Romana of 27 BC to AD 180 in the Old World, a period of peace between Octavian's ascension and the death of Marcus Aurelius), between about AD 900 and 1150. A number of studies on archaeo- and osteological materials from this time period point to a near-total lack of interpersonal violence.

Thus, however it was that the Chaco core expanded its sociocultural umbrella to encompass and influence so many local populations over so large an area, it wasn't through invasion. Not invasion by armies from Chaco, anyway. The more likely scenario is that closer-in Chacoan outliers like Chimney Rock were colonies or outposts directly associated with the core, while farther-flung ones in places like Bears Ears represent local participation in the Chaco regional system via envy and emulation—or, to put it another way, invasion of *ideas* from Chaco.

I got to see a version of this as an undergrad, when I helped Northern Arizona University professor Corina Kellner analyze materials from her study area in Cotahuasi, Peru. The location is about 200 kilometers—or right around 150 miles—from where the impressive and bellicose Wari Empire emerged and collapsed between about AD 500 and 1000. What the evidence from Cotahuasi suggested was not imperial control by the Wari so much as local emulation. As Wari rose to prominence in the region, material culture in Cotahuasi became very Wari-like in appearance, but was still manufactured by locals using local goods. When Wari went into decline and eventual collapse, local customs simply reverted back to local tradition. The party was over.

Kellner, in a move that first inspired me to not fear the use of modern analogies to approximate ancient behaviors (Indigenous people are *people*, after all—an assumption that represented a stumbling block for early archaeologists and a few modern politicians), told me to think of all the kids who act like their favorite celebrities. The elites live in castles in faraway lands, like Hollywood, and they don't exert any literal type of coercion. Yet hordes of people endeavor to be just like them, often emulating their behaviors and fashions to so ludicrous a degree that you'd swear they were hypnotized.

Nor does this analogy conflict with the non-local items that flowed into Chaco during its golden age. To argue that they were tributes demanded by tyrannical rulers—even beneficent, surplus-redistributing ones—in the distant capital is a hard sell, given that actual Meso- and South American empires had a tough time keeping that up with the considerable advantages of shorter distances and massive armies. But neither is anyone holding a gun to people's heads when they start fan clubs for musicians whom they'll never actually meet, or buy their spoiled kids a non-native Harry Potter owl before realizing that most owls are basically screeching feathered wolverines. People see something they really, really like, and they want in on it.

So, it's altogether possible that the Chaco system wasn't something to which people were bent, but rather something to which they bended themselves.

The overarching sweep of Chaco's role in the history of Southwest archaeology warrants some attention before delving into its demise.

In the developing world of early Southwest archaeology, Chaco was the first serious fly in the ointment for the culture-historians and their Morganian myth of cultural progress as inherent and one-directional because, according to that model, its mighty architectural splendors and far-reaching social network *should* be the apogee of Southwestern prehistory. In the inaugural Pecos Conference of 1927, Kidder envisioned Pueblo II as one stage in a progressive continuum culminating in the large communities of the Pueblo III or Great Pueblo period, presumably represented in and around Chaco Canyon. That's where all the palatial architecture is located, after all.

In its entirety, the original Pecos definition of Pueblo II is: "The stage marked by widespread geographical extension of life in small villages; [ceramic] corrugation, often of elaborate technique, extended over the whole surface of cooking vessels." In other words, they weren't expecting much. The notion that the Pecos classification sequence represented gradual, progressive change through time was reinforced by concurrent research, although research that's specifically designed to support a given model or idea has an annoying tendency to find plenty of evidence that does so. Confirmation bias is a powerful thing.

Meanwhile, backing up a bit, University of Arizona professor A. E. Douglass began engaging himself in studies of climatic changes and their possible relationships to astronomical phenomena in about 1901. Having noted that trees—*most* trees, that is—produce one series of new cells per year, arranged in concentric circles with the oldest ones at the center, he concluded that the relative width of the rings are therefore a fairly accurate depiction of how much wood the tree produced from year to year. And trees are able to produce more wood in wet growing seasons than in dry ones. Thus, if you compared the relative thicknesses of tree rings, counting backward from the outermost one, you could potentially create a record of wet versus dry years extending as far back in time as that particular tree had lived. What's more, you could match up the patterns with the rings in older timber, and extend the record even further back in time—considerably so, as it would turn out.

Working over several years on living trees to prove his concept, Douglass applied his method in a backward progression from living pines and firs to dead logs, carefully building a climatic chronology ring by millimeters-thick ring. It didn't take long to reach the end of what the forests alone could tell him, and he turned next to Spanish Colonial churches and ancient Native structures to see how much deeper down the rabbit hole he could roll.

Earl Morris was the first archaeologist with whom Douglass worked, providing him with timbers from Aztec Ruin—an enormous site due north of Chaco Canyon, where Morris conducted work during the formative years of his career. Together, they designed a boring tool consisting of a piece of steel tubing with fine saw teeth at one end that could take samples from in situ timbers without their having to be sawn across. Tree-ring specialists in archaeology (dendrochronologists) use a version of their original tool to this day. It was long supposed that the Chaco-like archaeology of Aztec indicated a precursor civilization to that of Chaco Canyon, for no other reason than because the largest structure in Chaco—the mighty Pueblo Bonito—was bigger.

When word came back from Douglass of his findings, they revealed that the timbers in Aztec were cut a good forty to forty-five years *after* those of Pueblo Bonito. Whatever their relationship had been, it was clear that Aztec was a later expression than what had occurred in Chaco. This discovery would end up having some pretty big implications for the Bears Ears area and its own relationship with the Chaco world.

After that, Morris became downright fanatical about collecting tree-ring samples.

Meanwhile, Douglass began sampling timbers from Chaco Canyon itself, as well as a number of other sites in the general region. These advancements showed that the Pueblo II period was much more complex than the developmental model implied. Final construction episodes at stupendous communal structures in downtown Chaco, like Pueblo Bonito and Chetro Ketl, were dated to at least two hundred years *before* the major cliff dwellings at Mesa Verde. The structures at Aztec, or at least the great house complex of Aztec West, were tree-ring dated to just about squarely in-between the two. Whatever the might and majesty of Chaco was, it came and went before the indubitably awesome but comparatively much more prosaic cliff dwellings of the northern San Juan. The teleological model was broken.

By the late 1920s, Douglass had established a floating chronology that placed Pueblo Bonito, Aztec, and the cliff structures of Mesa Verde in a confident sequence, but that sequence remained floating because he hadn't yet been able to anchor it to the historic or modern era. It may all have coalesced and ended fifty, five hundred, or (although unlikely) five thousand years before the Spanish arrived. A grant from the National Geographic Society, directed toward Douglass at the behest of Neil Judd, allowed him to gather enough specimens to finally attach his tree-ring chronology to the Christian calendar. He investigated wood beams from the Hopi villages, with their permission and oversight, and engaged Earl Morris in pursuing other specimens of likely use in the remnants of Kawaikuh, Chacpahu, and Kokopbeama in the vicinity of the Hopi mesas within the Navajo Nation—although they still didn't quite connect.

That gap was finally closed when Lyndon Hargrave and Emil Haury found a log beneath a Mormon farmstead that resembled others known to be associated with the final era of Ancestral Pueblo occupation in the San Juan Basin. The log dated to AD 1237, and overlapped with the outermost rings of the most recent log from Aztec by twenty-six years.

At long last, the occupations—or at least the last known construction periods—of Pueblo Bonito, Aztec West, and the Mesa Verde cliff dwellings could be given calendric dates. Pueblo

Bonito covered a time span of about AD 900 to 1130, or just over two hundred years of occupation and expansion, with the greatest period of growth occurring in the late 1000s (as would also be true of the other great houses of downtown Chaco), followed by a lull and then a final surge. Aztec West correlated with that late surge in Chaco Canyon, and appeared to have been abandoned* in or around 1150, only to be re-occupied by settlers from Mesa Verde in the early 1250s.

Another major Chaco "outlier" called Salmon Pueblo was constructed around 1090, and was seemingly occupied straight through to the 1280s—although not by the same people. Later research would show that it was abandoned by its Chaco builders by about 1120 and then, like Aztec West, reoccupied by locals in the 1200s. The latest dates in Canyon del Muerto and Keet Seel on Navajo Nation lands dated to the 1280s, and the enormous sites Morris had tested elsewhere on the Nation spanned between 1254 and 1495. Lastly, the beams Douglass himself had tested at the Hopi villages swung in during the mid-1300s and continued through to the present.

Douglass's original contention, that the relative narrowness or thickness of tree rings could give clues about the climate at the time, yielded fruit as well. Particularly droughty stretches appeared to happen once every hundred years or so, with the most alarming of them stretching for twenty-three years—from 1276 to 1299. Further investigations and advancements in tree-ring dating and more refined methods of absolute dating, like radiocarbon, would fix the dates that are currently—if sometimes tenuously—attached to the Pecos culture-phase sequence that I've been using throughout this book.

In the end, whatever the Chaco regional system was, tree-ring data going back to the late 1920s also testify that it fell into decline in the early 1100s. That decline co-occurred with a climatic plunge, during which both local and far-flung residents

---

*Archaeologists continue to use the word *abandoned* with regard to specific sites or structures, because that did—and does—indeed happen from time to time.

undoubtedly lost faith in the established sociopolitical system, including the Bears Ears area. And it wasn't pleasant.

When things started shaking apart, a new center or "capital" was either moved to Aztec or emerged there as elites from Chaco Canyon sought to reestablish power. Aztec Ruin is situated closer to the rim of the great bowl that is the San Juan Basin, where we already know that farming was easier. But that isn't the only reason Aztec deserves its own measure of attention.

For one thing, it's enormous. Aztec Ruin is comprised of two Chaco-like great houses, Aztec West and Aztec East, along with a dizzying assortment of spatially associated structures and settlements, the majority of them remaining blessedly unexcavated today. Aztec West alone is larger than all but the largest great houses in downtown Chaco. It is one of a handful of what were formerly lumped in with other Chaco "outliers" that emerged in the middle San Juan starting with Salmon Pueblo, located about midway between Chaco and Aztec, which was built and occupied between about 1090 and 1100. Aztec West, for all its size, virtually erupted out of the ground in the early 1100s at a time coincident with the disintegration of the vast Chaco system. This is why the term *outlier* is in quotes for both Salmon and Aztec. If an outlier is something associated with a cultural core while that core is still thriving, then Salmon and Aztec are more like *successors*.

Salmon was abandoned not long after, with the still poorly understood Aztec East being built at about the same time, leading Chaco scholars like Paul Reed to conclude that Salmon's residents fled north to join their friends at Aztec West. According to Gary Brown in a 2018 volume edited by him and Reed, "the scale of influence tilted from Aztec West to Aztec East as the twelfth century unfolded," suggesting to him that society in Aztec as a whole became more segmented in rather short order. In any case, Aztec hit its stride as twilight fell on Chaco.

While scholars have debated—and will undoubtedly continue to debate—over whether it was migration of Chaco elites or an entirely local manifestation of Chaco-like cultural elements in the middle San Juan, the sheer scale of Aztec Ruin and its associated influence throughout the region suggests that it was where the new capital went up after the old one in Chaco Canyon itself went into decline. All things considered, that explanation makes the most sense, although the moving of capitals isn't something to which most people's minds are altogether well-attuned.

A fair-to-decent comparison would be when the British burned the United States capitol building in Washington during the second year of the War of 1812, after which a new capitol was built to the north in Philadelphia under the direction of a nervously and aggressively galvanized leadership that took a more iron-fisted approach to foreign and domestic policy than its swampy predecessor had. This didn't really happen, of course—although it almost did.

If the genesis of Chaco fulfills the criteria of *ecological*, and its impressive expansion fits the bill for *cultural*, then what happened next—fitting nicely into neither of these pigeonholes—was *political*.

The great houses that went up in Chaco Canyon itself did so gradually, with waves of construction adding and adding to the original structures until they reached their leviathan final sizes. Which is why I get annoyed when cleverly fuzzy thinkers apply all manner of mathematical wizardry to explain the "blueprint" of Pueblo Bonito, as one presenter did at a research conference at Crow Canyon Archaeological Center last year. There *wasn't* a blueprint; it wound up looking like that after a very long series of episodic accretions.

The new capital that went up in Aztec, however—and which rivaled the very largest of the original great houses—did so in about a decade, and only lasted for about three. Getting swept into a popular cultural fad couldn't do that, and responding to environmental phenomena certainly couldn't either, any more than one or the other could explain the pyramids of Egypt. Organizing that sort of labor force required top-down control, which makes the spurious name *Aztec* almost appropriate. The actual

Aztecs were so adept at exerting top-down control that they managed to have complex public education and sanitation systems throughout an enormous city that they built atop an island *that they also built.*

The demise of Aztec Ruin in New Mexico wasn't exactly like that of Teotihuacan, where it appears that an increasingly hungry and angry citizenry erupted into fiery rebellion. Nobody burned the great house of Aztec West down, for a start, and instead we find evidence of lower-status Mesa Verde hinterlanders moving into the abandoned structures within the following century like squatters occupying Trump Tower in a post-apocalyptic novel. But it was similar enough.

Curiously, the closest comparison between the downfall of the Chaco-Aztec system and other events of that nature is probably the Classic Maya. The Mayans built utterly jaw-dropping stone palaces all over the Yucatán Peninsula between about AD 250 and 900, most notably in sites like Tikal, Tulum, and Chichén Itzá. This is considered by many researchers the height of the Mayan civilization, although I think that's a loaded term. The height of civilization in Papua New Guinea was never more than foraging with a side of cultivated yams and pigs, and they were perfectly happy for about forty thousand years until Europeans showed up. Anyway, from the late 800s through the end of the 900s there was a gradual shaking apart of the mighty city-states of the Maya, culminating in a total walkout from all but a handful of them. When Hernán Cortés arrived in 1525 to loot and pillage in the name of God and the Crown, the local Mayans—living contentedly in relatively small agricultural villages—seemed blissfully unaware that the mighty temples of Tikal* were hidden under heaps of vines just a few kilometers away.

They had tried that whole "state-level society" thing, and decided that it sucked.

During the latter half of the Pueblo II period in the northern

---

* Filming location for Yavin 4 in *Star Wars*, where the Rebels plot their assault on the Empire, which becomes more ironic the more you think about it.

Southwest, the so-called Pax Chaco disappeared in a hurry. Archaeological evidence from this period indicates an extreme uptick of interpersonal violence throughout the region that's almost undoubtedly associated with a major breakdown of social influence or control.

Of course, the golden era of the Pax Chaco also meant that everyone was living pretty happily and harmoniously in or near dense community centers when it all went pear-shaped in the early to mid-1100s. One option was to stay put, and either condone or endure the waves of accompanying interpersonal tension in the stubborn hope that it would all prove short-lived. The other option was to vamoose.

As more and more people took that option, ducking hypothesized Chaco enforcers and scattering into the sticks, what they probably found in a lot of cases was what happens when previously over-exploited hunting and farming grounds are given numerous human-free years to recover.

Back in the Bears Ears area, local populations expanded during this time, further underscoring the assumption that Chaco refugees made up a sizable portion of them. Reoccupation of sites initially established prior to the tumultuous Pueblo I population shuffle was fairly common. One site that I had the privilege of recording atop Cedar Mesa was comprised entirely of Basketmaker III and late Pueblo II components, suggesting that these were people moving into areas that were successfully farmed a few hundred years before and taking up residence in the most optimal homestead locations.

What's more, there's also the small but seductive possibility that a lot of what developed in Chaco during its heyday derived from ideas that first nucleated in the Bears Ears area. There is evidence, for example, that people there were constructing smaller versions of great houses during the Pueblo I period before everyone kicked rocks, and the distinctive red ware ceramics that the Chaco system wound up and pitched all over the region certainly had their origins there. Local researcher Owen Severance—for whom one of the handful of Chaco outliers in southeast Utah is named—is convinced that some of the area's prehistoric roads now labeled "Chacoan" actually predate the term's namesake. Although not everyone agrees with this contention.

In any case, all the full-fledged great houses in the Bears Ears area that are Chacoan in nature date pretty firmly to the era of Chaco's decline. By the end of that era, the entire region found itself in the grip of a severe drought, and people throughout the Four Corners ceased construction of big Chaco-style great houses. Which makes sense—communal labor is a lot harder to organize when people are both disillusioned and very hungry. Local families *built* much fewer homes, with a region-wide lull in tree-cutting dates suggesting that people stopped moving around and hunkered down to weather the bad times like Midwest Americans in tornado shelters.

Bears Ears area ceramics during this time period also hint at intriguing tales. Production of the iconic local red wares that were traded so far and wide during the Pueblo I period came to a dead stop during Chaco's expansion. By that period's end, Twilight of the Idols for Chaco, nonlocal red and polychrome (literally "more than one color") ceramics make their way into the Bears Ears area from the eastern portion of the Kayenta area to the south. Whether this was the former red ware producers returning home after their pushy Chaco rivals met their demise or entirely new people entering the area is uncertain, but they definitely brought some distinctly Kayenta practices with them. In addition to multicolored ceramic styles, Kayenta-style square-shaped kivas also started being built in the Bears Ears area.

This interweaving of Mesa Verde and Kayenta cultural elements, which I've tried to call "Mesa-Yenta" to universal disapproval and a few bad words from my colleagues, is yet another iteration of the borderlands phenomenon in southeastern Utah.

Speaking of which: the "boom" farming seasons of the early half of this time period had their own repercussions in the Pueblo/Fremont borderlands far to the north of Chaco. For only the second time—the first having occurred during the Late Basketmaker period—that border effectively broke down. This is well-displayed at Newspaper Rock in Indian Creek, northernmost extent of both the 2016 and 2017 national monument boundaries, where Fremont and Ancestral Pueblo (and Archaic, and Ute, and Diné, and historic Euro-American) images all dance together in an astounding display of multi-ethnicity.

It's also displayed in Beef Basin, in the northwestern periphery of the Bears Ears area, although this wasn't fully appreciated or recognized until fairly recently, when researchers from Brigham Young University began looking intently at the archaeology of the place. What they found, among much else, is Fremont-style metates, clay figurines, rock art, and pit houses—all of it suggesting either Fremont occupation or, at the very least, influence in an area that is otherwise dominated by Ancestral Pueblo archaeology, most of it post-Chaco in age. The relationship that may have existed between the Pueblo and Fremont residents of Beef Basin can only be guessed at. Chances are about equally likely that they lived side by side contemporaneously or variously occupied different spots at different times. A similarly confounding relationship between the two cultural groups can be found atop Fiftymile Mountain in the Grand Staircase-Escalante area, to the west.

Those post-Chaco components, whose dates of occupation center around AD 1169, give the impression not of being part of the outward-expanding waves of Chaco regional influence so much as frontier settlements created by Chaco loyalists fleeing the nastiness that attended its breakdown. Although similar in shape to other sites in the Chaco sociocultural system, those of Beef Basin appear (to archaeologists, anyway) a lot more expedient or hastily constructed. And towers are abundant—architecturally distinct from those of the central Mesa Verde and Hovenweep traditions, which often give the impression of being ritual or symbolic in nature. Beef Basin towers look more like defensive lookouts.

In a sense, the northern periphery of Bears Ears may well have been Chaco's last stand.

And the sum of all *that* is called Pueblo II.

This is why many scholars—including all the Indigenous ones with whom I've spoken—don't think much of the culture-history approach in archaeology. It's troublesome primarily for its tendency to convey a perception of discontinuity.

Perceived discontinuity can become especially troublesome when it falls into the hands of people with an agenda. At an open forum on public lands that took place in Bluff in 2016, one of the attendees testified that modern Native American perspectives on the landscape of Bears Ears shouldn't count because the ones who'd built all the pretty cliff dwellings and rock art that people come to see are long gone. I've encountered that same sentiment in op-eds and the ravings of individuals innumerable times through the years, and it always follows the same pattern. And with the same purpose in mind.

Noted conservationist and dear friend Jonathan Bailey did a great job of outlining this problem in a conversation we had while I was writing this book. "What archaeologists are providing aren't 'cultures' in the traditional sense," he averred via text message. "They are archaeological designations based upon similarities in lifeways and expressions of said lifeways." I can always count on him to help me simplify my ravings.

In other words, when archaeologists talk about *material cultures* like Pueblo II, they mean consistent assortments comprised of similar-seeming stuff—period. The ones who left those assortments weren't different people, at least not necessarily; that's the "pots = people" fallacy that makes a lot of archaeologists and Indigenous individuals alike very grumpy. They were just making different things during different time periods, the same as mainstream Americans used to play gramophones and now use streaming music services beamed directly into their pockets. We wouldn't say Gramophoners and Smartphoners represent different cultures—or, heaven help me, *races*—of people, either.

But a lot of people who visit places like Chaco and Aztec still retain that perception of discontinuity. It's the same one that compelled Warren Moorehead, Joseph Smith, and the geniuses at the

History Channel to conclude that they were built by "a lost race," white people from the Middle East (a double fallacy), or beings from outer space, respectively. They think "Native American" and they see a teepee on the plains, or a mounted warrior with no shirt and a lot of feathers, or Hollywood actor "Iron Eyes" Cody—who was one-hundred percent Sicilian, by the way—shedding a tear over roadside littering. They don't think buildings the size of the Roman Colosseum and intricate social networks that spanned half a continent.

Anyway, getting back to my friend: I've mentioned how the history of Bears Ears archaeology is full of characters. Its modernity is no exception, and Jonathan Bailey is well deserving of the descriptor. Like Greta Thunberg, his being on the autism spectrum accompanied a youthful expression of genius. He was published in a technical journal by fourteen years old, and by his mid-teens he was a celebrated photographer and conservationist. By his late teens, he'd also come out of the closet—in a tiny rural town in Utah, it is worth noting—and partnered with a young Native American lad. You can imagine how well that went over in the local community.

By the age of seventeen, the resulting harassment and death threats had compelled him to drop out of high school. No matter—within the next half-dozen years, his work appeared in scores of periodicals, and he currently has two books on shelves countrywide. And his conservation work (mostly volunteer, and in some cases with him paying *all* the costs out of pocket) was instrumental in efforts aimed at forcing federal agencies to do a better job looking after irreplaceable archaeology in the Uinta Basin, the San Rafael Desert, the Price River, Molen Reef, Mussentuchit Badlands, and, of course, Bears Ears.

Not that he ever receives credit, or at least anything like the credit he deserves.

Because of all this, I value Jonathan's perspective considerably. We met when he was twenty-one, during the early stages of my involvement with the Bears Ears conservation effort, and in one of the weirdest ways imaginable: we happened to glance over and spot each other on the same trail, at the exact same time, headed toward the exact same target, on Cedar Mesa—in the backwoods of Chaco.

The archaeology of Chaco Canyon itself continues to be a focus of much research, for better or for worse. In early 2017, a team of researchers conducted and published a groundbreaking study on Chaco. You'll recall that Richard Wetherill *et al.* spent much of the terminal 1800s and earliest 1900s excavating the archaeology of Chaco Canyon, particularly Pueblo Bonito. The materials were hustled off to the American Museum of Natural History in New York, where they've resided ever since, and researchers will periodically yank a bone or something out of the collection to poke and prod. This time they yanked a whole bunch of bones out, and poked and prodded at the genetic level using the latest in state-of-the-art tools and methods. Their results suggest that the golden age of Chaco was ruled over by a dynastic succession of individuals who passed the mantle from mother to daughter.

The idea that Chaco was ruled over by a series of mighty queens has a lot of appeal. Even if that's just one interpretation of the data, pretty much every other interpretation is at least pretty cool.

Here's the catch: because the skeletal materials were excavated without any of the scientific controls employed by subsequent archaeologists, they are considered by the museum to be absent scientific provenience and, moreover, absent legal affiliation with any existing tribes. The fact that we know everything you just spent a generous chunk of your precious life reading, including how Chaco is *inarguably* an important chapter in the grand narrative of Pueblo history, somehow doesn't enter into it.

The team wasn't required to conduct tribal consultation. Fine. But they also took that as their cue to leave the tribes out altogether, without even sending them a nice postcard about what they were up to. The tribes found out about how pieces of their ancestors' most intimate bits were dissolved into points on a graph the same way that everyone else did.

Half of my social media feed blew up with voices of cheer,

celebrating this innovative new method of investigation and the marvelous information it reveals about everyone's favorite mysterious old place. The other half blew up with voices of consternation and outrage over how the researchers blatantly disrespected the Indigenous community by ducking the topic of cultural affiliation via legalistic trickery and refusing to pay the tribes even the basic courtesy of a friendly chat.

For my part, I tried as hard as I could to remain centrist, objective, and un-opinionated. I was not successful.

As embarrassing as this is to admit, I've only been to Chaco Canyon once. It was during a snowy spring between a winter gig at Zion Canyon Lodge and my second season at the North Rim, after I'd fallen in with the subculture of backcountry ruin aficionados in that region. Even though I had done exactly zero research on the place, at that point, I still understood that it was special. It's a UNESCO World Heritage Site, after all—like Bears Ears should probably be.

It's also in the center of nowhere. The middle of the giant bowl that is the San Juan River Drainage Basin is the driest and harshest part—and what doesn't work in the ancient world doesn't often work any better in the modern world. Not for long, anyway (looking at *you*, Las Vegas). So, there aren't many metropolitan areas around Chaco Culture National Historical Park. Mostly small towns and other assorted settlements ranging from quaint villages to pastoral family spreads to dilapidated mining husks.

And natural gas wells.

My visit was in 2005, bumping along in a borrowed car for about twenty miles through a thick layer of snow down what was—and remains—an unpaved road. I didn't see any active well pads from the road to Chaco after I'd turned off the main highway, and there really aren't any within about a ten-mile radius. Yet.

The BLM's 2003 resource management plan (RMP) for the San Juan Basin allowed for 9,942 natural gas wells in the ten-thousand-square-mile bowl. Since the gas and oil deposits located closest to Chaco Canyon are mostly locked up in dense shale formations, most of the wells are located to the north, where extraction is easier. Nature is handy when it comes to imposing limits like these.

But the RMP that was drafted in 2003 didn't account for hydraulic fracturing, or *fracking*, which is the practice of using hydraulic pressure to blast apart subsurface shale formations in order to release their stored-up oil and gas so it can be extracted— and/or seep into the local water table. It was gaining popularity at the time, but still wasn't quite popular enough for the agency to take it into account when drafting the plan. When it did arrive about a decade later, thanks to a fracking boom that made my own grandparents' tap water flammable, developers immediately started shifting their gaze toward the oil-rich shale formations closest to Chaco Canyon.

The BLM, ever diligent, was prompted to commence pro- ceedings to begin the process of thinking about beginning to commence proceedings to amend the existing RMP, with the hope of having an amended RMP in place sometime before the next ice age.

The agency would continue to issue permits in accordance with the existing plan, of course—regardless of the technol- ogy being employed. The idea, I suppose, was to allow their string-pullers in the extraction industry to install thousands of notoriously controversial and ecologically destructive contrap- tions before putting the finishing touches on an amended RMP that said, in effect, Too Late Now.

Conservationists and local Indigenous residents cried foul, of course, and swung into action with a series of lawsuits. Of these, the lawsuit with the biggest punch cleverly—and accurately— accused the agency of failing to account for the gluttonous waste of water that fracking represents because, again, the existing RMP doesn't account for fracking *at all.* They scored a hit, and the hits haven't stopped coming since then. Legislation to protect the greater Chaco cultural landscape is fighting its way through Con- gress as I write this.

Back in 2005, I was eager to witness any one of the astounding astronomical phenomena associated with the place. There's a solar calendar on Fajada Butte consisting of three sandstone slabs and a set of spiral petroglyphs that records the four seasonal turning points with remarkable accuracy, although tourists haven't been able to access it for a long time. But the great houses are purportedly also built to align with things like solstice sunrises and lunar standstills and so forth, and I was eager to see some of that for myself.

Astronomical markers are a fascinating study. While we tend to think of the formalized sundial—that thing shaped like a pizza with one of its slices turned upward—as the *primordial* form of clock, the simple fact is that the oldest clocks of all are in the sky. The sun rises and sets at precisely the same spots on the solstices, the days and nights are exactly the same length on the equinoxes, the patterns of stars interpreted as different constellations by different cultures wander around the sky in annual migrations, and so on. If you can wrap your head around how these things move about, you can jam a stick into the ground and read its shadow almost to the minute. Or, of even greater value, you can make predictions about things like the best time (down to the day) to plant maize seeds in the spring so the young plants will be just the right height when the late-summer rains kick in. Or anything else of a temporal or calendric nature.

This is how you get astronomical markers. I've visited at least a dozen sites in the Bears Ears area where shadows fall on a rock art panel *just so* on certain days that are of obvious importance. I've even discovered at least one all on my own: a set of petroglyphs inside a narrow sandstone gap that creates an arrow, complete with arrowhead and fletching, on the winter solstice. I found that one by accident, and I still get a little giddy when I think about it. My friend Connie Massingale found another one totally by accident—at a fairly popular site, no less—just because she happened to glance in the right direction at precisely the right time on precisely the right day.

The subfield of study dedicated to these phenomena is called *archaeoastronomy*, and the more exuberant of its devotees can sometimes (read: often) become so obsessed that confirmation bias takes over and they start seeing astronomical markers everywhere they look. Which makes for some annoying presentations at research conferences. But that doesn't diminish the reality of astronomical markers themselves, which occur more often than you might think, and the ones in Chaco Canyon are outstanding—when you can find them.

What I found instead that wintry spring day was a lot of impressive architecture covered in snow. The sky was too cloudy to see the sun rising or setting in any case, and even if the sky was crystal clear I certainly wasn't going to see a major solar alignment on a random day in early March. But the structures blew me away. I was the only fool who'd risked the gnarly road out to Chaco during a snowstorm that day, so I had the place all to myself as I wandered from great house to great house.

I would see architecture like that again about eight years later, albeit in smaller and more dilapidated form, about as far from Chaco as one can get in the greater Mesa Verde region.

As with nearby Dark Canyon, Beef Basin—where the veil between the Fremont and Pueblo worlds appears to have lifted during Chaco's breakup—is another place that I hope readers of this book don't feel hereby inspired to go and see for themselves. Not because I'm afraid the place might become crowded. There's basically no chance of that. But because you'll very likely regret it.

My first experience with the place was an interagency inventory conducted in 2013, which included personnel from two national parks and the BLM. We took a pair of brand-new Jeep Rubicons out there, blowing a total of three brand-new tires in the process. I blew a tire in my own vehicle following the same route a couple of years later. The very year before writing this chapter, a team of researchers had to be rescued from the place when their vehicle gave up entirely.

This can partly be blamed on the tendency of federal agencies to buy poorly manufactured American vehicles on account of "fleet agreements," which is why I've had to use my Tacoma to help rescue stranded backcountry personnel more than once. But in the case of Beef Basin, it's more the place than the means of conveyance. Imagine a rocky dirt road that's more rocks than dirt or road, some of them sharp enough to puncture ten-ply tires and *all* of them eager to roll and bounce merrily away the moment they detect the presence of a tire or boot. You can much more comfortably take a sure-footed horse, if you've got one, although then the vehicles attempting to negotiate the road will undoubtedly spook the horse and create a whole new set of problems for you.

The first serious archaeological inventory of Beef Basin and the surrounding landforms was conducted in the early 1950s by the University of Utah. They don't say much in the resulting reports about travel conditions, although they do comment that the area was "relatively undisturbed by amateurs" until not long before they began working there. Professional archaeology in the United States was beginning to tilt away from purely academic "look and see" investigations, and toward an ethos of salvage and preservation.

Passage of the Historic Sites Act in 1935 is a good example of this. It was enacted by Congress primarily as a means to organize the increasingly numerous national monuments, national parks, and historic buildings and battlefields under the direction of the National Park Service and the Secretary of the Interior—which it did. But it also included language that declared, for the very first time in American legislature, that "it is a national policy to preserve for public use historic sites, buildings, and objects of national significance." What this effectively meant was that historic preservation should be regarded as part of the government's responsibility, something at which the Antiquities Act had only hinted. Included in the Historic Sites Act was authorization to survey and note significant sites and buildings, which later became codified as the National Historic Landmarks Program—and, later still, was subsumed into the National Register of Historic Places following the 1966 passage of the National Historic Preservation Act.

At the same time, in the wake of the Pecos Conference and its eponymous culture-phase sequence, standardization became the primary focus in the realm of academic archaeology. To that end, Harvard University conducted a second survey of Alkali Ridge from 1931 to 1933, an area first described by Kidder during his extensive investigations of southeastern Utah in the early 1900s. In 1941, Deric Nusbaum—he of *Deric in Mesa Verde*, now all grown up and doing archaeology of his own in Gila Pueblo, Arizona—was sent to the White Canyon area of modern-day Natural Bridges National Monument, as well as Butler Wash to the east of Cedar Mesa, in a deployment similarly tasked with shoring up the accumulated data of standardized archaeological science.

Nusbaum, who would later change his name to Deric O'Bryan after his mother's maiden name, worked in the upper portions of White Canyon and collected forty-five tree-ring samples from several sites. A few years later, Carnegie Museum archaeologists also collected tree-ring samples from White Canyon during the Kay-Rial Expedition, although unfortunately the samples just say "Natural Bridges area" on their labels, so useful applications are nil. Altogether, this was some of the last formal work conducted in the Bears Ears area until the Glen Canyon Project, which would change the face of American archaeology forever.

During the following year, the National Park Service conducted surveys throughout what they called the greater Blanding area, focusing on the Beef Basin, Fable Valley, and Dark Canyon Plateau areas (but not the interior of Dark Canyon itself) north and west of Elk Ridge. The portion of the survey focusing on Beef Basin and Fable Valley was severely cramped by a lack of adequate maps, and was in any case geared primarily toward gathering information for a recreation study of the Upper Colorado River Basin—not toward inventorying its resources, and certainly not toward preserving them.

The result was increased recreational visitation of the area, which increased even more when this was immediately followed by construction of roads and jeep trails by local ranchers and the federal government.

Just to highlight how much things have changed since then: a 1959 issue of *The Desert Magazine* included an article called "Discovering Fable Valley." It's told in the typical voice of wilderness literature in the post-Teddy Roosevelt/pre-Ellen Meloy era. I bring it up here because it also includes descriptions and photos of a number of archaeological sites, narratives about how to reach them, and—just in case that wasn't enough—a map. All this in the sort of magazine you could pick up and browse while getting a haircut.

The very next article in that issue is a biographical write-up of an artist named Howard Bobbs, who specialized in capturing the glory "that was once the Indians" by painting it. According to Bobbs:

> Indians are given a white man's education but the white man doesn't follow up by accepting them. When they finish school they are neither fish nor fowl.* The whole process is one that disintegrates their tribal life. All we as painters can do is capture the glory that once was theirs and preserve it on canvas.

...which inspires clenched fists, until you realize that this was an admirably progressive viewpoint for a member of the elite Santa Fe art world at the time. It was basically a holdover—or maybe a borrow-over—from the ethnographers of John Wesley Powell's time, who often sought to record the details of Native American cultures before cultural assimilation and/or literal genocide drove them into extinction. It's an offensive position to take nowadays, but a well-meaning one to take at the time, especially during a decade known for focusing its attention on white picket fences and just about every other white thing you can imagine.

And yet, within a single decade, even Bobbs' well-meaning sentiment of "paint the Indians before they're gone" would become outdated and uncouth. A new generation of preservationists was on its way up, and they weren't looking to make

---

* A similar sentiment would appear much later in the book *Neither Wolf nor Dog*, which was recently made into a pretty enjoyable film.

paintings of anachronistic *glory* and whatnot. They had something more dynamic in mind.

Back in Bears Ears, the professional archaeological projects (so: not including jeep tours of Fable Valley) conducted between the 1930s and early 1950s also served to train a new generation of archaeologists. Academic archaeology's increasing obsession with standardization and scientific rigor coalesced with salvage archaeology's increasing obsession with trying to preserve as much irreplaceable material heritage as possible. They were eager to get started.

They wouldn't have long to wait.

Chapter Seven: The Cliff Dwellers

mentioned in the Introduction—and have thereafter tried to avoid saying outright—that the reason most people outside the immediate vicinity have any notion of Bears Ears archaeology at all is because of its ancient architecture. That's the stuff adorning magazines and coffee-table books, and reaps most of the *upvotes* and other internet currency on social media. When people talk about Bears Ears being "loved to death," a phrase whose precise origins I can't guess at, they're usually talking about people visiting the area's iconic cliff-ensconced structures to marvel at them, take photos of them, and occasionally do inexcusably horrid things like climb on top of them or perform preposterous New Age rituals inside them.

That last one is a bigger problem than you might imagine.

The term *Cliff Dwellers* was the preferred nomenclature for the ancient Pueblo peoples as a whole during the early days of Neil Judd's work in the area, before Earl Morris and A. V. Kidder started complicating things. The word *Anasazi* was later applied to them, and some people still use it, although it has been labeled as problematic and duly anathematized by the majority of researchers in favor of more respectful language like *Ancestral Pueblo*. The classic story is that it's what the Diné called the ancient denizens of the area when early archaeologists asked them about who built the great pueblos and cliff dwellings there, and it means approximately "old enemy." It speaks to the often-strained relationship between the two groups.

I've also heard a different story. Arnold Clifford, a Diné botanist and geologist, comes from a family whose origin centers upon the Chaco area, where Richard Wetherill set up shop and did his most extensive digging and trading. Wetherill employed a lot of Indigenous locals in his efforts to excavate the place, paying them to empty rooms and burials, and when more literate archaeologists and ethnographers showed up in the waning days of his operation they often heard these locals throw that word around. But they weren't using it for the people who'd built the structures they were pilfering, according to Clifford; they were using it for Wetherill himself. *He* was "Anasazi." That's why they used it whenever someone pointed at him.

What they were saying was, in so many words, "Here comes that asshole again."

Still, it was not until the 1930s that the term *Anasazi* started to appear in the archaeological literature, which frames a nasty pitfall for this story. Why the long pause? In any case, it was officially codified by Kidder in a 1936 paper and stuck around for the next fifty-five years in the technical literature. It died an official death in a 1991 meeting at Santa Fe's Museum of Indian Arts and Culture, where the *Ancestral Pueblo** was born, although *Anasazi* still limps doggedly toward its eventual death to this day.

In the archaeology of the early 1900s, the Cliff Dwellers and the Basketmakers were the two vanished "races" that preceded the modern Pueblo peoples. Which is all the more curious when you consider that the Pueblo III period, in which all the most iconic and repeatedly photographed cliff structures were assembled, extended only between AD 1150 and 1350 or so, making it second

---

* This term has its own problems, as pointed out to me by Steve Lekson—who was part of the 1991 meeting in Santa Fe. It assumes "by fiat" that all archaeology in the Southwest moved inexorably toward modern Pueblo, which is by no means the case. When members of the Diné community grumble about how components of their own ancestry can be traced to many so-called Ancestral Pueblo cliff dwellings, they aren't lying.

only to the Pueblo I period for shortness and, generally speaking, a very small slice of the total history of the Pueblo world.

Although the final period in the Pecos culture-phase sequence is Pueblo IV, the final one for full-time occupation of the Bears Ears area is Pueblo III. That's when everyone appears to have hightailed it out of there. It was initially described in the Pecos classification as being characterized by the emergence of large communities, highly elaborate artistry, and specialization of crafts and social functions. It is during the Pueblo III period that the iconic cliff palaces of the Southwest appeared, including the one literally called (by white people, anyway) Cliff Palace in Mesa Verde; as well as Betatakin and Keet Seel in Navajo National Monument, and Defiance House in Glen Canyon, among innumerable others.

It was the remarkable preservation of Pueblo III cliff structures—tucked, as they are, into sometimes enormous protective alcoves—and the equally remarkable puzzle of their "abandonment" that first attracted the attention of formal researchers. Many of the earliest reports by government surveyors describe spectacular buildings with a wide variety of intriguing items left behind, as if their occupants had only just departed. In the decades following the inaugural work of the late 1800s, archaeologists have come to appreciate the last century and a half of Pueblo occupation in the San Juan region as having witnessed more localized changes over a shorter span than in any previous era.

Of all the major changes that came with the Pueblo III period, the shift in settlement strategies are the ones I find most intriguing. For about six hundred years, farmers in the Bears Ears area lived adjacent to the areas they farmed, journeying to fresh water sources when needed. And then, during the early 1200s, many of them began doing just the opposite—living by their water sources and journeying to their fields. Settlements often aggregated around springs, in a possessive posture that contrasts markedly from what looks almost like a taboo against settlement in direct proximity to springs in earlier periods. Which makes sense on its own. Even without knowledge of bacteria and other microscopic creepy crawlies, it doesn't take a whole lot of experimenting to realize that eating, drinking, washing, and defecating all around the local water source is correlated with a lot of upset tummies.

This preference for settling near predictable domestic water sources, coupled with a concomitant increase in highly defensible storage structures, is highly suggestive of interpersonal or inter-group tensions. The breakdown and fragmentation of the Chaco world following the dizzyingly quick rise and fall of the capital Aztec was brutal, and there was no longer any sort of centralized political entity to organize a Pax in the post-Chaco era.

With this shift in location came shifts in settlement size. Mesa Verde's exemplary Cliff Palace, for example, contains 23 kivas and about 150 rooms. Lesser known to most non-specialists is Yellow Jacket Pueblo, in far southwestern Colorado just over the border from the Bears Ears area, which had at least 195 kivas, 600 to 1,200 rooms, and about 20 towers. Yellow Jacket, built and occupied between the AD 1000s and the late 1200s, remains the largest conglomerated "town" in the Mesa Verde region, second in size only to Aztec but without showing any signs of being a regional political center. Like the cliff dwellings of Mesa Verde, these towns of aggregated domestic roomblocks and ceremonial structures expanded greatly during the Pueblo III period, and again the most likely explanation is people huddling together to weather the breakdown of Chaco.

This is also when formal "kiva" kivas appear in the material record. They were first studied in an archaeological milieu by Jesse Walter Fewkes, one of the earliest people in the field to make the effort to inform his archaeological work by spending a lot of time talking to present-day Pueblo peoples. Although we can be certain he wasn't allowed to see many (if any) rituals taking place inside them, Fewkes was nonetheless shown around some formal kivas at the Hopi villages, and somewhat hyperbolically concluded that they were *the* signature architectural component of the Pueblo world. Thus did kivas enter the literature, cloaked in equal parts data and bombast.

Although not a major character in the archaeology of the Bears Ears area itself, Fewkes is another foundational figure in

Southwest archaeology as a whole. He was the first person to use a phonograph to record testimonies and stories from Indigenous people, focusing mainly on the Hopi and Zuñi peoples in the early 1890s. Nor did he stop with mere ethnographic data—he also focused a lot of awe and effort on music. Fewkes' recordings of Indigenous songs are still being studied and appreciated by ethnomusicologists and other like-minded types to this day. He was also one of two professional archaeologists (the other being Hewett) who befriended Lucy Peabody and encouraged her campaign to create a national park at Mesa Verde.

The idea of the kiva in Southwest archaeology is a powerful one, as Bill Lipe once explained to me, and it traces back to Fewkes and his interpretation of small household "kivas" at Mesa Verde as simply earlier versions of the large clan- and sodality-centered communal kivas he was shown at Hopi villages. This interpretation endured for about one hundred years, until Steve Lekson finally blew it apart in the 1980s. Lipe himself concocted a concluding summary on the issue toward the end of that same decade in a study on the social scale of kivas, arguing that "social propinquity counts for something in social interaction." In other words, and this is a gross oversimplification, the more communal form of what eventually became Hopi kivas appears to have developed as groups of people gathered and lived closer and closer together.

Trade wares, including the Kayenta-area polychromes that started to appear in the Bears Ears area in the late Pueblo II period, are not uncommon in early Pueblo III sites but become extremely rare in later ones. In the Four Corners region as a whole, long-distance trade appears to have become less and less common through the Pueblo III period, with communities seemingly becoming more isolated from each other over time.

Meanwhile, people appear to have exchanged pottery within their own *local* communities more and more frequently, including during large communal rituals. Possible explanations for intensification of local trade coincident with de-escalation of long-distance trade are numerous, but among the more plausible is that of buffering against subsistence shortfalls.

In the Pacific Northwest, *potlatch* ceremonies—large get-togethers featuring extravagant exchanges of goods—are believed by some to have evolved from earlier gatherings in which local communities that experienced a bounteous year could swap for goods with other local communities that hadn't. The overall leveling effect of this system of localized reciprocity meant that each settlement would always have enough to eat regardless of how micro-environmental niches performed.

In the Southwest, micro-environments were extremely variable during the Pueblo III period, when droughts of five or ten years could have markedly different and drastic effects on the "niches" in which Pueblo people grew their maize. It might rain like crazy in one canyon while the canyon next door remained bone-dry. Similar exchange patterns may well have been in place in the Bears Ears area, with maize and trade goods making their way between local settlements based on whose crops had come in that year and whose hadn't.

For that matter, the origins of the mighty Chaco world probably weren't much different. It appears to have started out as a food bank or reciprocity reservoir that erupted when climatic conditions suddenly went from sere to sodden. But there weren't any region-wide systems in place after Chaco and Aztec came crashing down—or, at any rate, there's no evidence of any—and whatever local systems were keeping things going in the northern San Juan, they didn't stop the entire area from becoming totally depopulated by the end of the 1200s.

This occurrence has engendered no small amount of focus and noise since its discovery by Euro-American researchers. Where everyone went isn't much of a mystery—go and visit the Pueblo of Hopi, or Acoma, or Taos, or any of over two dozen others and say hello. The bigger question is *why*.

In the heartlands of the Bears Ears area, most people moved off the mesa tops and into the canyons during the early to mid-1200s. In any case, everyone was gone well before AD 1300. Back in the central Mesa Verde portion of the greater San Juan region, all the large communities were also vacated by at least a decade prior to 1300.

At Salmon Pueblo, the residents who walked away in the 1280s left a tantalizing story behind. Salmon was first abandoned by its Chacoan builders just about the same time Aztec East was built, giving some researchers like Steve Lekson the impression that it was a "false start" before the new capital came into full stride. Salmon was subsequently reoccupied by locals, who hung around until its end. When the place was formally investigated by Cynthia Irwin-Williams in the early 1970s, she discovered the charred remains of several adults and about twenty children in the topmost portion of a ceremonial tower. She and her colleagues immediately concluded that these individuals were roasted alive inside the structure and then feasted upon.

However, more recent investigations have revealed that the people were deceased before being burned, and showed no signs of butchery. It was far more likely a funeral pyre, probably for individuals who'd died from malnutrition caused by whatever it was that spurred the region-wide depopulation in the first place. When investigation of the privately owned site resumed in the early 2000s thanks to a partnership with Archaeology Southwest, it was revealed that pretty much the *entire* pueblo was intentionally burned by the people living there when they left, making it a symbolic act rather than a violent one.

Something similar happened in Peru in about AD 1000, when weather patterns in South America tanked at the same time those in North America surged. The Wari, one of the earlier entrants to the list of imperial Andean civilizations that stretched from Olmec to Inca, were big on show. Atop a towering mesa called Cerro Baúl in the Moquegua Valley, the disputed borderlands between their territory and that of a rival state called the Tiwanaku, the Wari constructed an enormous colony—including the largest *chicha* or maize-beer brewery known from all of antiquity. Archaeological evidence suggests the brewery had a maximum output capacity of about 475 gallons *per batch*; that the brewing was all done by women; and that greater and lesser elites from both Wari and Tiwanaku societies gathered there to partake.

The empires of both Wari and Tiwanaku went into rapid and massive decline by the early 1000s, most likely as a result of the flipside of the climate weirdness that drenched the arid Southwest at the same time, with the Tiwanaku packing their stuff and departing first. This left the Wari contingent all alone atop a huge mesa with no enemies to entertain and/or taunt, crumbling social infrastructure back in the capital, and the largest brewery in the known world sitting nearby.

It was a party like no other.

When it was over, the Wari burned the brewery to the ground, ceremonially smashed their *karos* or drinking vessels, in the smoldering remains, and left. Minus the small difference of hundreds of gallons of ale, what happened in major population centers like Salmon Pueblo toward the end of the thirteenth century was probably about the same.

Again, archaeologists still aren't exactly sure why this mass depopulation happened—if that's even what it really was.

For a long time, the biggest explanatory contender was drought, since a *nasty* one set in about 1275. But people had already commenced their widespread skedaddle at least a few decades prior to this. By the time the megadrought of the late 1200s set in, the Bears Ears area was effectively empty. And, anyway, these folks were no strangers to drought. Far worse ones had taken place in previous eras. Fancy statistical modeling of the drought itself indicates that the land could still have supported a considerable population (in general, that is; the issue of wily microclimates would still be a factor). So, even during the megadrought of the late 1200s, local farmer-foragers in the Bears Ears and central Mesa Verde areas would've probably been just fine—most of them, anyway.

On the other hand, climate certainly played some role in the decision to leave the area. Based on my own team's research on the subject, many of the farmers in at least the Cedar Mesa area relied upon stored soil moisture from winter snowmelt to sprout and sustain maize crops until the summer monsoonal rainfall allowed them to complete their life cycle by filling out their cobs. However, reconstructions of local precipitation levels via tree-ring analyses show that this bimodal yearly pattern broke down between the years 1250 and 1450.

With that in mind, longtime Bears Ears and Chaco archaeologist Tom Windes once explained to me with some gravity about the explosion of a super volcano called Samalas in about AD 1257. When volcanoes explode, aerosols (suspensions of fine solid particles or droplets in the air) are released into the upper atmosphere, where they reduce the amount of solar radiation reaching the ground surface. When Krakatoa blew in 1883, the aerosols and other deep-Earth tidbits it spewed forth wreaked total havoc on the global climate for nearly a decade. Tambora's eruption in 1815 was even worse. Scholars believe the bicycle was invented because Tambora caused so many crop failures that horses became too expensive to feed. And both of these eruptions were high school science-fair volcanoes when compared with Samalas.

So, that could also be a factor.

The prime mover may also have been political collapse. The downfall of Chaco, a system of community organization that encompassed the entire Pueblo world, would have been like a mountain falling into the sea—not just a single splash but a series of reverberating sociocultural tsunamis.

Whatever the prime mover was, it was *big*. Big enough to have a similar effect in the Great Basin, where the Fremont largely walked away from their own farms at about the same time. Although they didn't leave their scattered agrarian homesteads in order to densely aggregate into larger ones, like their Ancestral Pueblo cousins. They abandoned agrarianism altogether.

After apparently reverting back to a foraging lifestyle, the Fremont just sort of disappear from the archaeological record. Some scholars think they migrated east into the Great Plains and/or north toward caribou country. Others think they were incorporated into the Numic Expansion, making them ancestral to extant speakers of the Numic language family—like Ute traditionalists of Bears Ears, who also believe that to be the case.

The Hopi Tribe also claims ancestral affiliation with the Fremont, and there's good reason for that as well. The horned serpent motif that was (and remains) essentially synonymous with the Pueblo communities in toto is found in Fremont rock art throughout their archaeological culture area. What's more, friend and fellow backcountry devotee Aaron O'Brien has shown me petroglyphs in lower Comb Wash—*way* down south in the Bears Ears area—that are inarguably Fremont. Thus, the ties between the Fremont and Pueblo cultures are strong, deep, and extend well into one of the most significant places the latter dwelled before they aggregated into communities like the Hopi villages.

My best guess is that there isn't any singular "this is what happened" scenario. The evidence suggests that some of the Fremont were indeed incorporated into the Numic Expansion, while others appear to have joined the Pueblos (or were at least present in Pueblo territory right before they all bounced), and others still headed out into the plains.

As for the Ancestral Pueblo who left Bears Ears itself, they never intended to stay away forever, and it's a certainty that they and their descendants never stopped visiting. I will come back to this. For now, however, let us shift focus to the west, where the archaeological and cultural legacies of Bears Ears bubbled together in a different cauldron: Glen Canyon.

By the middle of the last century, the American public had grown increasingly concerned about what was being done—or, rather, was *not* being done—for the preservation of archaeological resources.

Attempts to balance economic concerns, military requirements, and these increasing preservation values included passage of the Reservoir Salvage Act of 1960. It mandated preservation of

historical and archaeological data wherever feasible and authorized the Park Service to pay for it. The act did little in the way of
establishing penalties for those who violated it, and many considered its protections inadequate. Its only predecessor, the Historic
Sites Act of 1935, did even less. These, along with the Antiquities
Act, were the only applicable federal laws when the mighty Glen
Canyon Dam Salvage Project commenced in 1956.

The historic circumstances leading up to the Glen Canyon
Project (the "Dam Salvage" bit is usually dropped outside technical reports) are threadbare and aggravating. In sum, following
Major John Wesley Powell's impressive and rigorously scientific
survey of the Colorado River corridor in the 1870s, the Major
submitted numerous reports warning about the dangers of
drought in the "arid regions" of the Intermountain West. His recommendations came down to three pivotal points: don't sell any
more farmland that doesn't abut reliable water sources; set property boundaries in terms of natural watersheds rather than arbi-
trary lines on a map to avoid competition over streams; and don't
rely on private enterprises to devise and develop water projects.

Nobody paid him much attention at the time, which is a
shame in its own right, but his vision of communities constrained
by water rather than mindlessly expanding and *then* trying to find
enough water was ignored with special force. The planning and
centralized regulation involved in his recommendations was—
and still is, in some circles—anathema to the American notions
of free settlement and free enterprise.

With Glen Canyon Dam a sure thing, following years of
wrangling and the successful efforts of conservationists to block a
dam farther upstream in Echo Park, two separate but principally
related aftermaths sprouted forth: the fire and fury that marked
the subsequent environmental movement in the West, and a leviathan archaeological salvage effort.

The Glen Canyon Project consisted of an enormous survey
conducted jointly by the Museum of Northern Arizona and the
University of Utah along the Colorado River and some of its
major tributaries ahead of the flooding of what would come to be
called—more than a little ironically—Lake Powell. The National

Park Service, the MNA, and the U were all connected through the Interagency Archaeological Salvage Program, which initially sponsored the project; and it involved numerous government agencies, other museums and universities, and tribal members, in addition to a ton of professional archaeologists. The project started at Hite, at the confluence of the Dirty Devil and Colorado Rivers, and finished in Page, Arizona, the southern extent of the proposed reservoir, 186 miles below.

Much of the work was conducted by boat, with field crews floating from place to place and hopping out to conduct survey or excavation along the shore. My oft-mentioned friend, colleague, and mentor Bill Lipe worked on the Glen Canyon Project for four field seasons as a crew chief. He had "the big boat," as he tells it, so he and his crew did the excavations; while his colleague Don Fowler—prolific writer of the history of Southwest archaeology— had "the little boat and one guy," so he was responsible for the pedestrian survey.

Nowadays, that latter activity accounts for almost all professional archaeology in the States. This often strikes non-archaeologists almost as hard as the notion that we aren't allowed to keep what we find (no, seriously—we get asked that a lot), but it's true: mostly what we do is walk. As archaeology continued to tip away from destructive analysis and toward preservation and resource management during and after the Glen Canyon Project days, it became more about *inventory* than *investigation*. About finding out what's there—mostly so that developers, federal agencies, or the public can avoid destroying it.

Back in the late fifties and the dawning days of the Glen Canyon Project, excavation was still viewed as the principal and basically only means of discerning useful data about the past, with survey being conducted largely in order to show people where to sink their shovels.

Theoretically speaking, the taxonomic culture-history approach in American archaeology was still going strong, with attempts to define developmental material-culture phases and large-scale archaeological "cultures" firmly in the vanguard. However, although what came to be called New Archaeology was still several years in the future, some of its earliest glimmerings were beginning to show in the published literature—as well as in the minds of the new generation of archaeologists tasked with carrying out the Glen Canyon Project. So-called New Archaeology was a set of ideas that calcified in the 1960s around the central goal of making traditional archaeology more scientific. These included quantitative techniques, adoption of models for explaining behavior, and a general shift away from simply building chronological sequences toward explanations of cultural function and environmental adaptation.

To that end, and sensing where the field was headed, Jesse Jennings—archaeology professor at the University of Utah, as well as the man in charge of its portion of the project, which represented three-quarters of it—made an explicit goal of addressing substantive questions about local historic and prehistoric cultures during the project's orchestration. As Lipe expresses it, these included the search for solid, quantitative evidence of pre-ceramic adaptations; defining the spatial and temporal relationships between material cultures like the Mesa Verde and Kayenta branches of the Ancestral Pueblo (and, where possible, the mysterious Fremont); and using these same methods to expand our knowledge of more recent doings by the Paiute, Navajo, and historic white folks. It was thus that the Fremont-Pueblo boundary was determined to be a real and dynamic phenomenon.

All of this is frankly admirable, although Jennings himself could be something of a curmudgeon, particularly when it came to tricky issues like gender. As one of his former students— now a retired professor himself—explained it to me during my archaeological field school in Range Creek, Jennings used to say that it was impossible for women to ever be field archaeologists because "their high heels would poke holes in the sites."

Meanwhile, at the exact same time that boatloads of shirtless men were shuffling from one excavation to another, pioneering river guide Georgie White was taking boatloads of whooping guests on lengthy excursions down the Colorado right behind them. In 1952 she became the first woman to row the full lengths of Marble Gorge and the Grand Canyon, and made an even bigger name for herself not long after when she concocted the idea of lashing three rubber rafts together for better stability in big rapids. Most other river guides scoffed at her, loyal as they were to wooden dories since the days of Powell, but in the eyes of the general public her crafts seemed both safer and more fun. She began taking paying customers on the basis of this notoriety. Although little-known outside the roiling world of river rats, the rapids at Mile 24 in the Grand Canyon are named Georgie Rapid in her honor, and Bill Lipe never fails to mention her in his talks and presentations about the Glen Canyon Project.

While Jennings' stance against women in the field remained firm, the Museum of Northern Arizona bucked the trend in their portion of the project area when they brought on four graduates of a program run between 1946 and 1957 by Girl Scout leader Bertha Dutton, a former student of Edgar Lee Hewett. Dutton's program, dubbed the Dirty Diggers, was modeled on the field schools that Hewett conducted by and for people like Kidder and Morris. A cooperative agreement between the Girl Scouts of America and the Museum of New Mexico allowed her to create a mobile camping program designed to introduce young women to Southwest archaeology, which soon expanded into a full-scale field school at Pueblo Largo. Among other things, Dutton impressed on her students that archaeology was a systematic form of scientific inquiry rather than a hunt for pretty treasures— something that a lot of people still don't seem to understand.

The site they investigated was a large Kayenta-branch habitation dating to the Pueblo III period, with eighty-one rooms, fifteen courtyards, and five kivas. Stein, along with Hatch and Diehl, catalogued all the artifacts, most of them being potsherds. Ceramic analysis dated the site to the Tsegi phase of the Kayenta area's culture-phase sequence, inhabited between about AD 1260 and 1280. In other words: at or just after the point when everyone left the Bears Ears area.

The ceramic analysis they conducted on Paiute Mesa and the hundreds of other sites comprising the full Glen Canyon Project assemblage was also geared toward anchoring the site in the greater landscape of the Glen Canyon watershed, including Bears

Ears, another explicit goal of the culture-ecological approach that was accreting in archaeology at the time. Regional approaches to archaeology weren't the norm in those days, since everyone was far more concerned with using material taxonomies to create local historical sequences, although nowadays we would hardly dream of thinking about an archaeological site as if it existed in a vacuum.

Attempting to tease apart the impossibly complex interconnecting threads of modern globalization is a one-way ticket to the kind of headache you read about in obituaries, but even in ancient times people didn't live in self-sustaining little bubbles. Parrot feathers and chocolate residue in Chaco and Bears Ears testify strongly enough to this. And Southwest archaeologists were finally beginning to think this way during the Glen Canyon Project. To that end, the National Park Service was intentionally vague about the project's boundaries, and extended considerable flexibility to project personnel about where field investigations could be conducted. A letter to the University of Utah, cited often by Jennings and others when writing about the topic, stated:

> You should not concern yourself only with the land which will actually be flooded... I believe you should instruct your [crew chiefs] to look over all the lands adjacent to the canyon which give promise of being of importance in any field of investigation. We are very anxious to know just what archeological, historical, and biological resources exist in the Glen Canyon region.

Any archaeologists or other field scientists reading this book are probably crying right now. When discussing my concerns about funding for a research project with Lipe, one time, he jovially remarked that I wouldn't be the first if I held a bake sale.

Taking full advantage of the flexibility and seemingly limitless funding on offer from the NPS, project directors and crew chiefs investigated much of the lower San Juan River corridor, including the aptly named Red Rock Plateau that forms the triangle-shaped wedge where the San Juan and Colorado Rivers meet.

Thus began the Cedar Mesa Project, all but unrivaled to this day in the annals of Bears Ears archaeology.

As Bill Lipe explains it, his initial interest in Cedar Mesa had to do with learning more about the Early Basketmaker period, especially how and where they were able to live and thrive as early farmers atop that high and dry plateau. Following a reconnaissance survey in 1967, he secured a grant from the National Geographic Society to conduct additional surveys, excavate a few Early and Late Basketmaker sites, and attempt to re-locate sites originally found by Wetherill (as Nels Nelson had done in the 1920s).

That initial phase of work was done as a field school for the State University of New York (SUNY) in Binghamton, a tiny city just north of the Pennsylvania border and about equidistant from New York City, the Adirondacks, the Finger Lakes, and pretty much everything else in the state of New York that's worth visiting. Lipe was a professor there, at the time. In a bizarre coincidence, I know the place too.

The urban center of the part-suburban/part-feral area of my own upbringing to which I often refer through clenched teeth? That's Binghamton. I grew up in the countryside bordering that tiny little city. Upper-echelon classmates of mine would often joke about how "SUNY B" was their top choice if they ever decided to get a degree in misery.

Binghamton University, as it's now called, boasts one of the most impressive and respectable archaeology programs in the country these days, dedicated primarily to the very thing this book is attempting to accomplish: public scholarship. What are the odds?

The project expanded between 1971 and 1975, with a grant from the National Science Foundation and R. G. Matson jumping on board. Their research design, innovative for its time, included seventy-six randomly located sample *quadrats* (survey sections) and associated canyon surveys within five of twenty major drainage units, supplemented by systematic inventory and tree-ring sampling in Grand Gulch and McLoyd's (formerly Ruin) Canyon—and augmented by judgmental selection of sites to be more extensively inventoried and mapped. It was the greatest and most ambitious cultural resource inventory ever conducted in southeast Utah purely for the purpose of inquiry.

The Cedar Mesa Project is the stuff of legend. The legacy of Turkey Pen Ruin, which gave researchers their first glimpse of how deep into history maize farming extended in the Bears Ears area, continues to this day. They also dated the exquisite Moon House complex, one of only two individual sites singled out by the Trump administration when they enacted their reduction of Bears Ears National Monument. It turned out that most of the structures at Moon House were built in the AD 1260s, making it the last-known habitation in the immediate Cedar Mesa area until my friend and fellow Bears Ears enthusiast Ben Bellorado found a few more recent ones—all of them on the eastern fringes.

Lipe and his crew also had to clean a ton of trash out of the interior rooms of Moon House because Boy Scouts from Moab had been camping in them. I would also learn from other local archaeologists that Boy Scouts used to camp inside an enormous cave in the Butler Wash area with a lovely Pueblo III structure in it, absolutely trashing the place in the process. I simply cannot wrap my head around this. I was a Boy Scout myself, back in the boondocks that orbit the greater Binghamton area in upstate New York, and if we so much as dropped a candy wrapper where a leader could see we could look forward to twenty push-ups in the mud.

The Cedar Mesa Project also included development of a local chronology, and they estimated that the population of Cedar Mesa during any of its occupation periods was between about 750 and 1,500 people—or about the same as the average resident population in a single block in Manhattan. You could fit them all on a fancy cruise ship, *twice*. Cedar Mesa's total size is about four hundred square miles, which sounds like a lot until you realize that's just twenty miles long by twenty miles wide, so the environment there could sustainably support a population of between two and four people per square mile. Which sounds perfect to me.

When Lipe and Matson revivified the CMP in 2008, a big portion of it involved zeroing in on great house communities and the presence or influence of Chaco in the Bears Ears area. Winston Hurst and Edge of the Cedars State Park Museum curator Jonathan Till joined them in these efforts, and at one of these sites they found a fourteenth-century Hopi ceramic sherd. Cedar Mesa, you'll recall, was entirely depopulated by the 1280s at the absolute latest, and the Hopi didn't start producing their gorgeous coal-fired Jeddito Yellow Ware pottery—of which this find was an example—until the following century. And that was at Hopi itself, which is a good two hundred miles south of Cedar Mesa.

In other words: they never really left. Not for good, anyway. The presence of historic Hopi ceramics at archaeological sites in the Bears Ears area long after they'd supposedly "abandoned" the place testifies to its continued importance and usage in their cultural geography. Winston's find was far from the only one; the original CMP gang found an entire Jeddito vessel tucked underneath a boulder. (I would probably have fainted.)

The Hopi concept of Ancestral Pueblo archaeological sites as *footprints* is among the more elegant ideas about history that I know of. Better by leaps and bounds than regarding them as diagnostic garbage piles or, worse, as treasure chests. Instead, Hopi traditional concepts of archaeology center around regarding it like breadcrumbs that tell the story of ancestral peoples—their own, and ones they share with other groups—who moved and migrated all over their known world. Archaeological sites are not "abandoned," in other words, but a dynamic element of living memory.

Pueblo of San Juan anthropologist Alfonso Ortiz once famously averred that "the Anasazi [*sic*] didn't disappear; they're running bingo parlors in the Rio Grande Valley." Nowadays it's casinos rather than bingo parlors, as well as an incredible restaurant in Albuquerque, but the principle is the same. They never really left.

The Ancestral Pueblo weren't driven out of their masonry communities by invading Numic- or Athabaskan-speaking marauders, as some researchers used to surmise. They weren't wiped out by an asteroid, like the dinosaurs, although a volcano or some other climate-altering bugbear probably did play at least some role. And no, they were definitely not the lost tribes of Israel who arrived in a land of backwards heathens and taught them how to do masonry before getting killed and eaten—nor did they hop back into their UFOs and return to Betelgeuse.

They had, it appears, simply moved out of the northern San Juan and Chaco Canyon areas for a while until things in the post-Chaco world cooled off. Their becoming the largely egalitarian Pueblo societies we know today was probably what Lekson and others think was a deliberate rejection of the intense hierarchies of that once-mighty system, much like how the post-Classic Maya seemingly walked away from their megalithic city-states in a spirit of "well, that's enough of that." And they were almost certainly planning to return to places like Bears Ears at some point. Communal occupations included houses made of stone, where people might live for several generations on end, but the big picture was always one of movement.

This is why I don't make much of the so-called final depopulation of the Colorado Plateau. Knowing what I know, now, I balk at the purported finality of it. Whatever the impetus was for the widespread depopulation of settlements across the Colorado Plateau at the end of the 1200s—and, remember, it was big enough to affect the Fremont in the Great Basin as well—doing so still wasn't entirely out of character for people who routinely walked away from their settlements only to walk right back to them a few hundred years later. The Hopi even have stories of people burying caches of seeds and other goods in ceramic jars for whomever occupies an "abandoned" site next, and the fact that some of these caches are found at Pueblo III sites in places like Cedar Mesa casts further doubts on this being their final bow.

Like Bill Lipe before me, my first job as a professional archae-ologist was also in Glen Canyon. I was a seasonal field tech for the Park Service, there, during the 2010-2013 field seasons, and getting around by boat is still the most common way for archae-ologists to do their jobs there—although now the boats whip over the water some hundreds of feet above where those first ones were. And it says a lot about how things have changed that I was hired into that position by ethnographer Rosemary Sucec, who was then head of Cultural Resources for the Park Service there.

The term *cultural resources* refers to any environmental components of not-purely-utilitarian importance to people. This includes material things from history, to be sure; but it also includes songs, stories, traditional practices and rituals, and so on. Despite this, and somewhat annoyingly, the term is almost always used as a fancier way of saying *archaeological resources*, and this is no less true with the Cultural Resources division of the NPS in places like Glen Canyon. Having an ethnographer in charge of that was a treat, chiefly because she actually cared about the tribes and how they felt about management of said resources.

My first season was an absolute blast. My immediate supervi-sor and I, often with our charming full-time volunteer (a Vietnam vet and retired cop named D. W.), would spend up to a week at a time living off the Park Service boat and monitoring archaeo-logical sites from the shore. Sometimes we'd bring fishing poles along—this was before the mercury levels in the striped bass of Lake Powell had become better known—and, occasionally, kayaks. We roasted marshmallows. We had "mandatory swim breaks" when it got too hot during the day. And I learned a ton. When people talk about how easy government workers suppos-edly have it, I feel guilty about my memories of that first season, because it certainly isn't the norm.

I also got to help out on the curious case of Trent and the Descending Sheep site. I learned a lot from that, too.

At the beginning of the second season, I became gravely ill. This was about a week after my second-ever trip to the Bears Ears area, where I spent a blissful few days camping atop Cedar Mesa and exploring all the canyons that weren't rendered inaccessible due to snowpack. It was my first time seeing House on Fire, which has since become so popular—essentially serving as a *sacrifice site* for the rest of them, although you're not supposed to say that in polite company—that cars will occasionally stretch down the highway for up to half a mile away from the trailhead.

That memory became a beacon, a source of intense heartbreak, and ultimately an impetus to return to the Bears Ears area to pay off a debt that I incurred while trying to survive the next three years.

It came on very suddenly, when I woke up the fourth or fifth morning of the season in employee housing and couldn't get out of bed. The sheet and blanket felt heavy. I felt heavy. I turned my head. My tent was wadded all over the floor. I couldn't remember why. I must have been tired. I must have intended to shake it out and roll it and put it away in the morning. I couldn't remember getting home. I couldn't remember where I was, at first. Or *who* I was. I made my way into work at HQ, and slipped further and further out of touch.

By the end of March, I could hardly walk. I couldn't remember words, and had trouble speaking when I could remember them. I became easily lost. I experienced a constant headache and extended panic attacks, and my mind was encapsulated in what I can only describe as a nearly impenetrable haze. I became depressed and despondent, almost too scared to drive a car and too fatigued to get out of bed. I managed to keep my job, somehow, and I regularly drove myself to the hospital, which didn't help matters any because it gave lazy quacks the impression that I was either exaggerating my symptoms or faking them. I thought I was going crazy or dying, or both.

I visited thirteen doctors over the next five months, and was preemptively diagnosed with a cornucopia of ailments, including Ménière's disease, rheumatoid arthritis, chronic sinusitis, hepatitis, Epstein-Barr virus, syphilis, HIV, fibromyalgia, and lupus. In following with conventional, scientific medicine, the initial diagnosis is the hypothesis stage, after which comes the experiment stage: testing. I was tested for all these conditions and more, and the results all invalidated their respective hypotheses.

At that point all but one of those doctors diagnosed me as having anxiety/depression, and concluded that my symptoms were psychosomatic.

When it came time to test *that* hypothesis, they did so by drugging me to the gills and then spinning me back out the door. Best-case scenario, it cured me. Worst-case scenario, it made me not care about being sick anymore until the sickness itself killed me. Problem solved from their end, either way.

To spoil the surprise, I was eventually diagnosed with the neurological manifestations of Lyme disease, a clinical diagnosis that was confirmed with a battery of serological tests. But we only reached that point after I flatly told my series of dumbfounded doctors they were wrong and, along with the help of some diligent friends and a skeptical psychiatrist, continued to insist on ever more comprehensive testing. Had we not pursued that course, I would still be stuck with a diagnosis of anxiety/depression and a benzodiazepine addiction (the withdrawal syndrome from which is almost as unbearable as Lyme itself). That or I'd be dead.

Medical professional number fourteen turned out to be a physician assistant fresh out of medical school, and therefore hadn't yet begun to accumulate the mental beatdown that is working in the American medical field. His top priority was still alleviating the patients' suffering rather than staving off lawsuits by insurance providers for, say, ordering expensive tests for Lyme disease in a region where "everybody knows Lyme disease doesn't exist." That was the excuse the rest of them all gave while they were doping me up—and making me totally bankrupt.

What followed was roughly three whole years of hell—eighteen months of aggressive antibiotic treatment, including intravenous Rocephin injections for a few months, followed by another eighteen months of recovering from the damages. The feeling goes beyond one's ability to articulate. Most feelings do, of course, what with their being subjective in nature and all—but sometimes you can hope for a modicum of common ground. This one shoulders aside common ground like a turbo-powered glacier.

That last trip to Cedar Mesa in 2011 was seared into my sizzling brain like a cattle brand. As soon as I was approximately self-manageable again, the following year, I began my own series of pilgrimages to the place. Dissociation made it hazy at first, totally disconnected, not at all textured or *real*. But I connected with the place more and more with each trip.

It was the only place that worked like that, with me. No other "home" felt like home during the worst of it, and mostly they still don't.

Toward the end of that first summer, when I finally received a diagnosis that made sense, I went to see a behavioral health counselor for some advice on how to deal with this wretched new reality. She had a lot to give, a lot of it rather suspect in nature (there's a lot of misinformation about what Lyme disease is and how it works, even among professionals in other healthcare fields, and I for one did not find massage or aromatherapy helpful in the slightest). However, one piece of advice I found extremely useful, and I recommend it to anyone going through anything traumatic: keep a journal. Even if you never go back and reread the thing later in life, the act of expression is, in itself, cathartic.

My entries track an unmistakable pattern. In the early pages, ones with content like "I can't focus on reading so I'm becoming addicted to television shows [sad face]" or simply "THIS BLOWS" are occasionally punctuated with things like "camped in Comb Wash—had no energy to hike, but felt happier." Over the course of two journals and some four hundred pages the ratio gradually shifts, like a slow-motion seesaw, from mostly the former sorts of entry to mostly the latter sort.

Nor is this a declivity into idyll. The visits weren't always fun, and they weren't always pleasant, especially in the earlier half of what I could probably call the Lyme period of my life. I was thirty, in the best shape of my life before it happened, and now I often couldn't hike for more than a few dozen feet before collapsing face-first into something hard or spiny. I once suffered a full-blown panic attack because it started to rain. Dissociation, which accompanies most traumatic experiences whether there's a neurological component or not, was an almost constant state in those early days, which caused me to have doubts about the reality of anything pretty or calming or interesting that I saw, which made me panicky and depressed all over again.

But I kept at it, with an ironclad fixation on how blissful and perfect that last trip in early 2011 had been, as if the act of repetition—like a mantra; like prayer; like, if I'm being honest, addiction—might cause that experience to occur again. A ritual to summon the past back into reality so it can replace a really sucky present.

That didn't happen, of course. Such a thing is impossible.

What happened instead was the very slow, very gradual displacement of horror by something else. Something a bit more powerful.

Chapter Eight: The New Foragers

Traditional Native American cultural narratives are often said to include some version of the phrase "we have been here since time began." The more I look into this threadbare happenstance—and the more I hang out and chat with Native friends and colleagues—the more I'm starting to think this is less a universal Indigenous constant than an academic straw man. It's almost always followed by something like: "However, scientific evidence shows... (*chortle, nudge, eyeroll*)."

Casting a broader ethnographic net sheds an interesting light on the subject, given how much the American Southwest and Mesoamerica were in contact with each other during the distant past. How else would we be finding macaw feathers in northern Bears Ears and *Theobroma cacao* residue in ceramics at Chaco?

In the K'iche Mayan creation story, the *Popol Vuh*, the creator deities from the sea (Plumed Serpent) and from the air (Heart of Sky) got together to create the world out of the void. They sought to introduce some race of beings into this world that could appreciate its beauty, worship and respect its creators, and, of utmost importance, keep track of time.

Their first efforts were comprised of a mishmash of elements, but the resulting creatures couldn't form words and weren't quite smart enough to mark the passage of time or even remember their own names, so they were sent into the wild and became the non-primate animals. The creators tried again, this time using mud, but the results looked ugly and soon crumbled into the water—fossils. A third effort followed extended consultation between Heart of Sky and diviners called The

Grandparents, and they carefully carved figures out of wood. They could talk, in a sense, and they cared for and nurtured each other; but their minds weren't quite sharp enough to retain memory of the creators or appreciate their creations, so they were allowed to be killed off by flooding and other animals. The survivors, who are almost but *not quite* human, are the monkeys and other nonhuman primates.*

Finally, Plumed Serpent and Heart of Sky succeeded at making human beings out of *masa* or cornmeal, underscoring the sacredness of maize in Mayan culture and implying that human beings are really just sentient tamales (which sounds fine to me). Here, at last, was a creature that could appreciate the world and its creators, and perform the crucial task of keeping track of time. Hence the Mayan obsession with calendars, including the Long Count, which accounts for five graduating cycles of time—not unlike the way we count days, months, years, centuries, and millennia—adding up to 5,125-year cycles. And no, their calendar didn't end in December of 2012 any more than our own calendar "ends" on December 31 each year. It just started a new cycle.

Now think again about that phrase "we have been here since time began." What if it isn't intended to mean since the universe boiled into being so much as since time began *for them*? Which is to say: the place where their existence began.

The Hopi creation story asserts that they emerged into this world through a *sipapu*, or place of emergence located at the confluence of the Colorado and Little Colorado Rivers, after three previous worlds became decidedly unpalatable. The *Diné Bahane'* or "Story of the Navajo (Diné) People" also tells of emergence into this world from previous ones, totaling five instead of four—although most of them seem in agreement that they came from the north—where, in the first world at any rate, dwelled a figure named Winter Thunder. And one version of the Ute creation story involves the half-man, half-wolf creator deity Sinawav trekking to their homeland in the Colorado mountains with a bag full

---

* If you think that sounds weirdly similar to an 1859 bestseller by Charles Darwin, you're not alone.

of magical sticks slung over his shoulder, into which his brother Coyote cut a hole out of mischievous curiosity, so that as Sinawav traveled, most of the sticks—transforming into people—leapt out of the bag and became different groups across the landscape.* The ones that made it all the way to the sacred valley without falling out of Sinawav's bag became the Ute peoples.

None of these stories include the notion that the people telling them sprouted sui generis, at the place where they now live, at the dawning of the world. They talk instead about how they arrived at their points of origin. The places where their respective histories begin.

Told through the articulating lenses of both material and cultural history, the Bears Ears area was the convergence point of at least three nomadic peoples—Ute, Paiute, and Diné—sometime between about AD 1300 and 1600. The oldest tree-ring dated wiki-up poles (first two groups) and hogan beams (third one) all date to about 1600, but that just means those are the oldest identifiable examples of structures that never included durable adhesive elements like mortar or nails to begin with. My childhood tree house *did* include nails, and it fell apart within a year.

At least twenty-five—and probably closer to thirty—Indigenous nations claim ancestral connections with the Bears Ears area. An ethnographic study conducted in 2002 for the nearby Canyons of the Ancients National Monument included the Ute Mountain, Southern, and Uintah-Ouray Ute Tribes; the Pueblos of Hopi, Zuñi, Acoma, Cochiti, Isleta, San Felipe, Santa Ana, Santo Domingo, Jemez, Laguna, Sandia, Zia, Nambe, San Juan, Picuris, Pojoaque, San Ildefonso, Santa Clara, Taos, and Tesuque; the Jicarilla Apache; the San Juan band of the Southern Paiutes; and the Diné. And these are just the ones with official recognition by the US government.

---

* Another version has Sinawav giving Coyote the bag to carry to the sacred valley—with, given Coyote's nature, similar results.

To simplify all this, many researchers write instead about language families—e.g., Numic speakers, Athabaskan speakers, Uto-Aztecan and Kiowa speakers—in the manner of Romance languages, Germanic languages, Sanskrit languages, and so on. The study of linguistic evolution and transition as a function of geography can serve as a useful tool for reconstruction of population movement. Caution is warranted, however, in that this is still a Western concept for interpreting non-Western history. The best tool, as always, is asking Indigenous people themselves. They'll tell you if they want to.

Other researchers have had some success in studying modern and ancient DNA to reconstruct population movements, in which case Indigenous populations are more objectively referenced in terms of DNA haplogroups. The trouble—some of it, anyway—with using genetic data to reconstruct history is that DNA isn't cultural. It doesn't believe in anything. It just codes for a particular assembly of biological structures and, to a certain extent, behavioral expressions. My own genetic makeup, for example, is one-half Italian, which says nothing about my preference for hoppy beers or the fact that I speak Italian about as well as Brad Pitt in *Inglourious Basterds*. My DNA doesn't say anything about how I, or the world around me, actually identify *me*, and this is no less true for everyone else—including people that aren't walking around anymore.

This is why taking a DNA test to prove that you're one-sixteenth Cherokee or whatever, is offensive nonsense. And the opposite is also true. Ancestry that points to only a small handful of DNA haplogroups can include dozens or scores of cultures, all of them having contributed beliefs, social practices, and even personal quirks (e.g., my late maternal grandfather and I share a weird love for horseradish that appears nowhere else in our known family tree) that are impossible to detect at the molecular level. In an ethnographic work that would become one of the most important cornerstones of the Bears Ears movement, it is stated thus: "Although researchers tend to focus on the origins of the Navajo's Athapaskan [*sic*] ancestry, the ancestry of the Navajo likely incorporated many different peoples, cultures, and cultural traits."

While the precontact ancestors of today's Diné and Ute communities did not herd sheep or ride horses, for reasons I hope
I don't have to explain, these traits were nonetheless readily
adopted from other groups, going on to become important—even
sacred—elements of their respective cultures by the time written
Anglo-American history commenced. Other examples abound.

To simplify all this, and for other reasons that will become
clearer as the modern story of Bears Ears unfolds, I go the
language-family route in this book.

I introduced the topic of ethnography earlier, and I've made a
few references to the practice since then. Most of what follows is
gleaned from one ethnographic source or another, the principle
source being the work of my friend and former supervisor Rosemary Sucec. Oral histories and personal interviews with members of the tribes helped fill out the rest.

The traditional homeland of the various Southern Paiute bands
covers much of what is now south-central Utah, northern Arizona, southern Nevada, and southern California, where the
Pahrump Paiute and Timbisha Shoshone Tribes live still.

There were upwards of thirty different subgroups of the
Southern Paiute Tribe at the time of contact, including the Kaibab
(of the Grand Canyon region), Kaiparowits (of the Grand Staircase-Escalante region), and San Juan (of the Bears Ears region)
bands. Nowadays, owing to the vagaries of federal bureaucracy,
these are all subsumed within a mere five federally recognized
tribes.

Prior to the contact period, they traditionally practiced an
annual cycle, what anthropologists call a *seasonal round*, very
much like a lot of other Indigenous peoples did (and, in a few
cases, still do). Winter was all about finding a location where
the snow was deep, firewood was in plentiful supply, and there
were plenty of pine nuts. Spring meant the beginning of hunting and gathering, because cached stores were usually empty by
then. It also meant the planting of gardens after they'd adopted

horticulture. Summer was the time to hunt big game and gather seeds, fruits, and berries. Late summer and early fall meant harvesting, storing food, and beginning to rebuild stores of pine nuts. Fall was a high-mobility time, comprised of moving around to hunt or gather precious resources to prepare for the harsh days ahead.

Early Southern Paiute homes reflected the transient nature of this type of settlement strategy. During the winter, many tried to live in caves or built houses by leaning juniper posts against the horizontal limb of a tree. For the rest of the year, they sufficed with a dome-shaped or circular brush enclosure, whose earthly remains are ungodly difficult for archaeologists to correctly identify in the field.

Even then, you can't always be certain what you're looking at. Given the San Juan Basin's location at the periphery of the ancestral Paiute, Ute, and Diné cultural cores, communities of mixed cultural heritage comprised of traits from all three developed in or near the Bears Ears area with some regularity. Studying the various cultures of the area and reading historical accounts thereof is how I first became aware of the borderlands phenomenon manifested there.

In the Hayden Survey records, for example, William Henry Jackson noted a Ute band situated in the middle of Montezuma Canyon who had "considerable corn planted." Somewhat later, in his 1938 report to the US Geological Survey, Herbert Gregory observed that "present-day Piutes [sic] practice agriculture in Cottonwood Wash, and some of them return to their old homes in Montezuma and McElmo Canyons, especially in the winter." He also noted that certain areas in Allen Canyon, on the Manti-La Sal National Forest within the once-and-future boundary of Bears Ears National Monument, were referred to as "Piute Park" and "Piute Basin" by the locals—despite Allen Canyon being, then and now, Ute territory.

This was all brought home to me in a particularly fun way when I was working in the Bears Ears area for SWCA Environmental Consultants on behalf of the BLM back in 2016. One of the survey areas was located on the Butler Wash side of Comb

Ridge, and there my crew and I discovered a historic sheep corral. There were historic-period metal objects, as well as chipped stone tools, a combination often found in early-historic Native American sites because they saw no reason to stop using their traditional technology just because there's also shiny new stuff around. Everything about it said historic Diné.

I contacted local archaeologist Winston Hurst to ask if he wanted to revisit the site with me, just to make sure I got it all right, and during the revisit we found three additional features: a small stand of axe-hewn trees with historic can fragments and another chipped stone tool a little way upslope; a second corral on a steeper ledge several hundred feet to the south; and the highly eroded but unmistakable remains of a hogan—a traditional Diné structure that looks rather like a yurt made of wood and earth—near the bottom of the wash below the two corrals. Near the hogan we found an inscription on a sandstone rock face, also highly eroded and difficult to read. We were able to make out the name "Mikesboy." Winston confirmed that Mikesboy is an old Blanding-area name that refers to the progeny of a San Juan Paiute man named Jim Mike. We returned to the site a third time accompanied by another expert named Jay Willian, and his keen eye found some tiny horse petroglyphs and a few other components that were subsequently recorded.

Returning to the name Mikesboy: again, that's a Paiute name. On a boulder beside a hogan, which is traditionally Diné, and below some sheep corrals *and* what Jay identified as Ute or Paiute wiki-up rings. What Jay and Winston then explained to me was that Ute and Paiute families sometimes hired Diné folks to build hogans for them because they were such practical structures for the area, their having picked up the idea from living in the shadow of Navajo Mountain for a few generations following hostilities with the incoming Mormons. I never would have known otherwise—I would simply have assumed we'd found a historic Diné sheep camp and left it at that.

It was then I began to understand Jackson's confusion when he found the Utes in Montezuma Creek tending fields of maize. Bears Ears creates communities unique unto itself.

As for the name's progenitor, it turns out he's a pivotal figure not only in local history and culture, but with regard to several of the topics and individuals covered in this book. In 1908, William Boone Douglass was in Cortez, Colorado, conducting a survey for a planned reservoir and examining the possibility of building a road that might allow people to drive to newly minted Mesa Verde National Park. While working in the area, he was commissioned by the Park Service to conduct a formal survey of Natural Bridges National Monument to serve as a supplement to Byron Cummings' informal ones on behalf of the University of Utah. Douglass hired a local Native guy to help with the inventory of Bridges, a San Juan Paiute named Mike's Boy, who later took on the name Jim Mike. Jim "Mike's Boy" Mike was born in about 1873 and lived with his father Moenkopi or "Big Mouth" Mike in the Paiute Canyon area when he was a young man. In his elder years, he often claimed that he'd heard the blasting being done by frustrated but determined Mormons at the Hole-in-the-Rock while the family was moving from the Kanab area to the Blanding area in 1879-80.

While inventorying the natural bridges of Natural Bridges with Douglass, Jim Mike mentioned that he knew of a natural bridge even larger than those. According to historian Thomas J. Harvey in *Rainbow Bridge to Monument Valley*, Douglass remarked that "if this bridge exists, and I believe it does, it should beyond doubt be preserved… Mike's Boy says no white man has ever seen this bridge and only he and [unreadable] Indians knows its whereabouts." After a few false starts, including an attempt by John Wetherill to divert interest in the place, Douglass organized an expedition to find Rainbow Bridge.

John Wetherill, Byron Cummings, and Neil Judd joined them on the trail a bit later, after visiting Betatakin Ruin along the way. Cummings had already heard about the giant natural bridge and was planning to visit it anyway, retaining John to help guide them there (hence his trying to steer Douglass away from getting there first). Being the amiable character that he was, he'd decided they should join forces. Cummings and his party retained their own Native guide named Nasja Begay, and Douglass brought along

Jim Mike. Together, they negotiated on foot and horseback the serpentine sandstone area stretching between John's place and what would come to be called Rainbow Bridge.

Jim Mike returned to Rainbow Bridge in 1974. However, instead of riding on horseback and negotiating winding sandstone canyons for four days, this time he was transported to the Bridge via boat on the steadily-filling Lake Powell. The National Park Service had hitherto honored Nasja Begay as the sole official guide on the expedition, owing to consternation between Douglass and Cummings' crew members, and a plaque commemorating Jim Mike was finally added thanks to a 1960s campaign by a Blanding-area rancher named Clarence Rodgers. The NPS boated Jim and his family to the Bridge just ahead of installing the plaque.

Not altogether surprisingly, it turned out Jim Mike had never received the fifty dollars he was promised by Douglass for acting as guide, so the acting NPS superintendent also presented him with a crisp fifty-dollar bill during the ceremony. In response, he evidently muttered something about how there should probably be some interest by then.

As for whether or not the site that we found and recorded is associated with old Jim Mike himself, the chances are slim—chiefly because, according to Winston, he couldn't write. Chances are it was one of his sons, the name Mikesboy having passed from a translated title—meaning simply Son of Mike, like in Scandinavian names like Nels Nelson—into American legality as an official surname.

In 1872, about the year Jim Mike was born, a reservation was established by executive order in Nevada, to which only the Moapa band of Southern Paiutes moved. Other Paiute bands would be confined to small reservations throughout the state. However, in a curious twist compared with how these things usually go in American history, the San Juan band of Southern Paiutes living in the Bears Ears area were never confined to reservations at all.

This would turn out to be both a blessing and a curse.

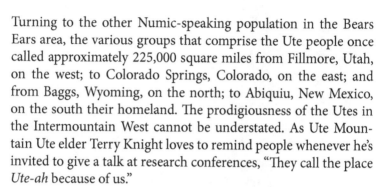

Turning to the other Numic-speaking population in the Bears Ears area, the various groups that comprise the Ute people once called approximately 225,000 square miles from Fillmore, Utah, on the west; to Colorado Springs, Colorado, on the east; and from Baggs, Wyoming, on the north; to Abiquiu, New Mexico, on the south their homeland. The prodigiousness of the Utes in the Intermountain West cannot be understated. As Ute Mountain Ute elder Terry Knight loves to remind people whenever he's invited to give a talk at research conferences, "They call the place *Ute-ah* because of us."

At least eleven different Ute bands existed at the time of European contact, including the Moache, Capote (*Kapota*), Weeminuche, Uncompahgre (*Tabeguache*), White River (*Parusanuch* and *Yamparika*, and incidentally where the name of the Yampa River comes from), Uintah, Pahvant, Timanogots, Sanpits (or *San Pitch*), Moanunts, and Sheberitch. Of those bands, the ones historically associated with the Bears Ears area are the Moachi, the Capote, and the Weeminuchie, now consolidated through a dog's breakfast of federal tinkering and meddling into the Uintah-Ouray—officially the Ute Indian—and Ute Mountain tribal organizations.

In deep historic times, they were prolific hunters of elk, desert bighorn and mountain sheep, wild turkey, rabbits, badger, porcupine, wildcat, beaver, and bears in and around the Bears Ears area prior to the post-contact era. Deer were of utmost importance, as they provided food, shelter (from skins), and tools (from bone and antler). Favorite deer-hunting places included Elk Ridge and the La Sal, Abajo, Navajo, and Sleeping Ute Mountains. Hunters would take deer and antelope in a variety of ways, including stalking, ambush attack, driving them into prey enclosures and/or over cliffs in the manner of Folsom bison hunters, and—after horses were introduced—running them down on horseback.

Animals that were traditionally considered sacred or otherwise culturally important, and were therefore never hunted or killed, included snakes and coyotes. The latter is kind of a big deal. Coyotes are, unfortunately, on the list of varmints for whom assisted extinction is officially sanctioned in the US in order to save one or two cows and, thus, ensure the continued ecological devastation of overgrazing in the Intermountain West. It's a wonderful system. Happily, it turns out they are also ridiculously adaptable, and they've reacted to eradication efforts in an almost laughable manner.

Simply put, coyotes have evolved to increase their birth rates whenever their population feels pressured. And the way they detect and measure such pressures is amazing: their iconic yips and whines act as a sort of local census. If those calls aren't answered strongly enough by nearby packs, it triggers an autonomic response that results in production of larger litters.

This isn't true of other major American predators like grizzly bears, wolves, or mountain lions, which is why efforts to eradicate them have worked so well (you've got this to thank next time you're playing vehicular pinball with a horde of scrambling deer). The successful eradication of these other predators has created ecological gaps, and—nature having proverbially harsh views on vacuums and all—the yipping-census strategy of coyotes has helped them to prodigiously fill those gaps.

In other words, thanks to a delightful quirk of evolution, efforts to wipe them out have resulted in *more coyotes than ever*. I can think of few other reasons to respect them as the ultimate tricksters, and thus they appear in numerous Ute and other Native American cultural narratives.

As hunters and gatherers in mountainous and upland zones, early Ute groups living in and around the Bears Ears area followed their own annual migratory cycle relative to the seasons and associated availability of foods—whether on the branch or the hoof. The highland areas, for example, were used in the summer; and in the winter the Utes would move to the lower and warmer plateaus and canyons south of the mountainous highlands. Following the introduction and incorporation of horses into Ute tradition, they would also make occasional hunting forays out into the plains during the fall, when the bison were nice and fat.

Much can be said about Ute culture and horses, and I've got limited space here to do it any sort of justice. Their adoption was momentous. No dressage* riders were these—Ute riders and their horses took to each other like a long-separated duo who'd been reunited at last. The latter allowed the former to expand their seasonal circuits, to carry more items as they traveled, to improve and increase trade relationships, and to embrace horse-back warfare, as well as the noted expansion of hunting strategies. Ute petroglyphs depicting horses are found all over the Bears Ears area, particularly in Cottonwood Wash; and—even cooler to me—historic Ute "racetracks" have been found in various locations as well, including between the Bears Ears themselves.

The archaeology of horses and horse-related things in the United States remains wide open for study, by the way. Almost nobody is doing it. My friend and colleague Kristina Stelter studied the archaeology of Viking horses for a master's degree in Britain and then tried to apply her findings here, only to discover that there was virtually no foundation on which to build. I really cannot fathom this. In the Bears Ears area alone, I've seen Ute and Diné petroglyphs of horses so detailed you could tell what sort of knots they'd used in the tack.

Also of interest to me, given how much I think about food, historic Ute practices in the Bears Ears area often included earthen ovens consisting of a four-foot-deep hole lined with stones. A fire was built on top of the stones, and food was placed in layers of damp grass and heated rocks on top of the coals. These items would then be covered with dirt to cook overnight. Early Paiute groups were known to do something similar with agave in places like the Grand Canyon.

It's a sensible practice, because there are few things that act as better insulators than the ground itself (hence the practical nature of pit houses), and you can leave your food to cook while you do other things because it's unlikely to be stolen by anyone who isn't crazy fast with a shovel. I've heard of other people

---

* I always thought they should rename dressage to "horse maneuvers." It would sound so much better on network television.

practicing similar cooking strategies to this day, especially in Mexico. And Edward Abbey's lightly fictionalized autobiography *The Fool's Progress* includes a tale about how he cooked a goat in this manner for a big party at a rented house in New Mexico—just before burning the place down.

In the precontact period, some of the Ute families in the Bears Ears area lived in dome-shaped willow houses throughout the year, but mostly they employed tripod- or conical-shaped homes with a three-or-four-pole construction referred to by most ethnographers as *wiki-ups*. Tepees were later adopted from Plains tribes, offering a more portable housing option well-suited to the Utes' mobile lifeway, and a few local archaeologists have developed a keen eye for finding historic Ute sites by spotting the rings of rocks used to help prevent the poles from splaying outward like a giraffe on a frozen lake. They're hard as hell to detect with an untrained eye.

Outside of horses, other domesticated animals associated with deep Ute history include the dog and the goat, but although turkey husbandry was practiced by the Ancestral Pueblo in other parts of the Bears Ears they do not appear to have been adopted into Ute lifeways. I can think of at least one good reason for this: turkeys were mainly foddered on maize kernels, and Ute traditions revolved around foraging rather than farming. Moreover, historic Ute peoples were traditionally very mobile before being relegated to reservations, and neither Pueblo turkeys nor Spanish (and, by adoption, Diné) sheep are well-suited to this. Goats are. And dogs, for their part, were very important to precontact Ute families as pets, camp scavengers, and limited-energy beasts of burden—about 0.12 horsepower, I would say—before the introduction of the horse.

The Diné and Apache Tribes living in the Southwest today speak languages that are part of the Athabaskan language group, which appears to be historically centered in western Canada. Some of the dialects spoken by Indigenous groups still living in the icy white north retain enough linguistic overlap with Diné that conversation between them is still possible.

Incidentally, the word *Navajo* as applied to the Diné is a Spanish pronunciation of the Tewa word *navahu'u*, which means "farm fields in the valley," or so most linguists believe. The Spanish referred to them as *Los Apaches de Nabajó*, meaning roughly "Apaches who farm in the valley," testifying to the facts that the Spanish recognized the close ethnolinguistic affiliation between those two tribes, and the Diné had learned and adopted agriculture by the time the Spanish arrived. Which is slightly better than being called *Indians*, since at least it derives from another Indigenous language, but only slightly.

The reason for their being characterized as valley-farmers is because agriculture has been a central component of Diné culture and heritage for at least the last three hundred years, after they acquired the practice from the Pueblos. Almost every family on the Navajo Nation raises some amount of their own food, with many families able to subsist on their farmed produce for weeks or months at a time. Maize and squash are the staple crops, with potatoes, beans, melons, pine nuts, and tree fruits (Navajo peaches are spectacular) supplementing them. Prior to that development, however, the Diné practiced a sustenance lifestyle similar to that of other nomadic or seminomadic peoples: foraging for wild plants and hunting game.

They still do a lot of that, too—especially in places like Bears Ears.

Although archaeologists agree that Athabaskan speakers were comparatively late arrivals in the northern Southwest, they disagree substantially on when they arrived and by what route they traveled. Three temporal windows have been suggested: AD 800–1000; AD 1200–1400; and concurrent with the 1540 arrival of the Spaniards. Various migration routes have been postulated, including an intermountain route downward through western Colorado and eastern Utah. Linguistic data suggest that the two southern Apachean language groups split from Diné about five hundred years ago, but archaeologists disagree as to whether the two groups split before or after their arrival in the Southwest region.

All of which is to say: scientists have a lot of ideas, and not many are in total agreement with any others outside of the Diné having come from "someplace up north."

Meanwhile, their own origin story posits that the current and historical homeland of the Diné people in the Four Corners region represents their fifth world of occupation, and included in that narrative are components of ancestry in that same icy white north where other Athabaskan speakers still live—e.g., the afore-mentioned figure known as Winter Thunder.

The Navajo Nation—you can always tell what sort of person you've met at a bar in Flagstaff by whether they refer to it as "the Nation" or "the Rez," the latter being what the Diné themselves most often call it because they're not trying to win points for being really hip—includes portions of present-day Utah, Arizona, and New Mexico, covering more than twenty-seven thousand square miles. As with the Ute and Southern Paiute cases, the Bears Ears area was and is peripheral to their primary historic homeland of the Diné. Despite this, Diné presence in that area has increased dramatically over time: according to the last official census, self-identifying Navajos presently make up more than half the population of San Juan County.

The Navajo Nation states on its website that its own archaeological evidence dates the earliest Diné sites in the Southwest to the early 1300s, based on tree-ring evidence. It goes on to speculate that at least two additional earlier centuries would have been necessary for such an archaeological pattern to emerge. Other Diné oral histories hold that their ancestors spent time "emerging through four levels of worlds, to currently reside in the fourth level, the 'glittering world,'" according to the Navajo Nation Tourism Department. They believe that holy beings created mountains, rivers, canyons, and other landforms so they could be inhabited—and their resources used—by people; and that these holy beings currently live, answering prayers and acting as guardians, within the most special of those landforms. Bears Ears is one of them.

The Diné never really functioned as a big, unified group prior to being forced onto a reservation, but were instead delineated by extended families or clans who enjoyed autonomous control and influence in their respective areas. This was a problem for Euro-Americans, who assumed a level of centralized rule that simply did not exist—and so, naturally enough, they imposed one. The acquisition of sheep from the Spanish further complicated territoriality issues, as increasing sheep herds meant expansion of land-usage by local groups for grazing. When coupled with the adoption of agriculture from the Pueblos, this precipitated increasing population density and an expanding territorial base that hasn't really stopped being a problem.

As with every other Indigenous group in the broader region, the earliest contact between European and Diné individuals was with the Spanish *entradas* of the 1500s. According to exploration maps drawn at the time, their territory extended much farther north into Utah than is presently designated by the legal reservation boundary, all the way up past Moab to Green River.

The relationship between *los Apaches de Nabajó* and the Spanish was typical of the time: the Spanish conquered and enslaved the Diné for mining labor, and the Diné conducted raids and armed warfare against Spanish colonies and military outposts. This continued right up until the Spanish turned power in the region over to the Mexican government in the early 1800s.

Although the title of this chapter is a tongue-in-cheek reference to the occupation of the Bears Ears area by foragers—some of whom would, nonetheless, become agriculturalists at one point or another in their respective histories—this is also a fitting place to discuss what was happening in the Pueblo world between the late 1200s depopulation of the Colorado Plateau and the arrival of the Spanish. Since the pueblos of Hopi and Zuñi are the ones represented in the Bears Ears Inter-Tribal Coalition, I'm choosing to focus on them, although it is of crucial importance to underscore that they are the chosen representatives of at least twenty-two other Indigenous groups in the Bears Ears conservation battle.

The Pueblo of Hopi is comprised of twelve villages on what

are called First, Second, and Third Mesas, representing most of the southern escarpment of Black Mesa in northeastern Arizona. Voluminous ethnographic work has been conducted with the Hopi, some of it in the form of hippie screeds that don't bear mention here or anywhere else. I'm not even sure what books to recommend over others, for the curious and insatiable, although you can't go wrong with Pueblo of San Juan (*Ohkay Owingeh*) author and scholar Alfonso Ortiz.

Precontact Hopi society is noted for its artistic murals and pottery, mining of metals and salt, and understanding and use of coal, as well as remarkably effective dry-farming strategies. They developed and farmed strains of plants with particularly deep taproots, including maize and beans, and planted in areas with large quantities of aeolian or wind-blown loess soils that had less runoff after rain and more permanent springs than other soils in the area. Studying this process, and asking Hopi farmers about it, is how my team and I were able to make some pretty good guesses about how the Hopis' ancestors practiced dry farming in the Bears Ears area. Although Hopi farmers utilized other methods of agriculture as well, and still do today.

The Hopi footprint concept indicates that the Hopi consider all archaeological sites to be traditional cultural properties. "Ceramics, architecture, and shrines are some of the tangible signs that reveal the path of early Puebloans," according to Rosemary Sucec, for whom I worked in Glen Canyon during my first stint as a professional archaeologist. Some pictographs and petroglyphs are recognized by modern Hopis as clan symbols, passed down through numerous generations. Areas referred to as "habitation" or "residential areas" by archaeologists are known as "resting places" to the Hopi, and some of these resting places were noted like map symbols in the petroglyphs and pictographs for other migrating Hopi to interpret. When a group left a resting place, they would leave seeds (typically maize, squash, and beans) in granaries or even sealed and buried pots for use by the next group who stopped there.

Oral histories provided by Hopi informants are remarkably (although not surprisingly) consistent with the archaeological record of the region that surrounds and includes the Bears Ears area. According to the Hopi, the first people to emerge into the present world were the *Motisinom*, from whom many Hopi clans are descended. The *Motisinom* are associated with what are called the Paleoindian and Archaic periods in the Pecos Sequence.

Their term for the Ancestral Pueblo is *Hisatsinom*, and debates have roiled over whether or not this should be the official term. It's a pretty-sounding word, and it is at least derived from a Pueblo language—as opposed to *Anasazi*, which is not only incorrect but patently insulting to Pueblo peoples. The problem with *Hisatsinom* is that it's a Hopi word, and that doesn't always sit well with people from other Pueblos.

Most of my friends have got stories about crazy happen-stances that occurred in direct or indirect articulation with the Hopi or their ancestors. It happens when you hang out with the sort of people that I do. I herein recount the following one because it took place during the darkest and most dismal days of my nightmarish health woes, and it shined the first light of hope into the suicidal depression that accompanied my ague.

My supervisor, known throughout the Park Service for her work with the tribes, took every opportunity she could to have tribal elders and educators visit the NPS-administered lands of Glen Canyon to see how the agency was getting along with the task of babysitting their sacred heritage. On this particular occasion, a group of about half a dozen elders from Hopi came to visit for a week so they could walk around inspecting sites and chatting with Park Service personnel. I couldn't go on the trip, being barely well enough to walk, so I stayed back to do some work in the office. Where the radio was.

At the end of the visit, the elders sat around in a circle near a kiva at one of their ancestral home sites to perform a closing prayer, but not before informing their hosts that it's not uncommon for this practice to, as it were, precipitate a rainstorm that was meant to provide water to the surrounding thirsty landscape. It was mon-soon season, and they were holding their prayer late in the after-noon, so in point of fact it was extremely unlikely for there *not* to be a rainstorm. And there was; right on cue; and to nobody's surprise.

However, it did catch everyone a little off guard when the radio crackled to life with frantic back-and-forth messages between some tourist and law enforcement—something about a houseboat that had flipped over. Those things are basically barrel-shaped, so although it's unlikely for one to act like a barrel and roll over, it certainly can happen. A microburst from a nasty rainstorm caused two houseboats to do just that in September of 2017, causing one unfortunate woman to lose an arm. This was probably what happened, with high winds and/or a motor left on during the anchoring process having pulled the boat far enough onto its side that it capsized. The incident was just up a side canyon from where the cultural resources party was moored, so they decided to go and see if they could be of assistance.

What they found is not easy to explain. To anchor a houseboat to shore, you run lines (ropes) from either side at a 30- to 45-degree angle onto the shore, where you either bury the special sand anchors or wedge them into a tree or boulder. In addition to keeping the craft tightly pulled against the shore, this also keeps it from swinging too far to either side. And they'd done that. The anchor lines extended outward from about halfway along the houseboat on both sides, and the anchors were firmly set. The houseboat itself, meanwhile, was upside down. It had flipped *lengthwise*.

If you've seen the film *The Dark Knight*, that scene where an eighteen-wheeler flips lengthwise on account of textbook Batman shenanigans wasn't CGI, like a lot of people think. It was real. And it took a huge steel piston and a sizable TNT boost to make that happen. Houseboats run about seventy feet in length and somewhere right around fifty thousand pounds. They're almost exactly the same weight and dimensions as a quality mobile home—which, in a sense, they are. This means that they are both bigger and heavier than an empty long-haul trailer, and have the added bonus of the suction effect of water. They are also notably devoid of huge steel pistons and TNT.

In other words, what had happened shouldn't be possible. Even the sort of microburst that can turn a campfire into a ten-thousand-acre wildfire in less time than it takes me to accidentally burn a marshmallow shouldn't be able to cause something that big and heavy to flip end over end. But it did. With dozens of witnesses, including the thoroughly befuddled family who were all safely on the beach when it happened. When I spoke with Susec about this incident while writing it up for the book, she recalled it as an alarming, yet powerfully demonstrative demonstration of their spiritual capacities, "not untypical when working with tribal spiritual leaders."

Back on the scene, the Hopi elders exchanged sheepish glances with each other. One of them even apologized.

As for the Pueblo of Zuñi, the area they currently occupy lies in western New Mexico, just west of the Continental Divide on the banks of—not surprisingly—the Zuñi River. The area traditionally used by the Zuñi extended some thirty-five miles east and northeast into the high-rising and also appropriately named Zuñi Mountains; and fifty miles west and south into lower, drier lands that make up the surrounding landscape.

Similar to Hopi creation stories, Zuñi oral tradition states that they were created in the fourth world or "womb." They describe how the Zuñi emerged onto this world's surface from a hole in the Grand Canyon along the Colorado River, just below the mouth of the Little Colorado River, which became a problem for the National Park Service when they tried to wrap their heads around the distance between the canyon and the Pueblo of Zuñi itself. The NPS decided it was too far away, and declined to allow the Zuñi to include the Canyon in their traditional cultural practices, to which the Zuñi responded by shrugging and then carrying on with those practices anyway.* This has subsequently changed, and it is now documented as a Traditional Cultural Property.

---

* Octavius Seowtewa and some of his fellow Zuñi community leaders recently made a wonderful documentary about this called *An Ancient Journey.*

From there they went south to the San Francisco Peaks near Flagstaff and then east to Canyon Diablo, following the Little Colorado River toward their current home. Somewhere along the Little Colorado River, the Zuñi split into four groups: one went north, which is why the Zuñi are affiliated with Capitol Reef and Grand Staircase-Escalante; one went south and never returned; one went straight to Zuñi; and the last went southeast to Escudilla Peak, then northeast to the El Morro Valley, and finally arrived at Zuñi from the northeast. Throughout their migrations—sometimes splitting into groups, sometimes accommodating others—the Zuñi ancestors were always searching and heading for their "middle place," or the center of their world.

Traditional Zuñi cultural narratives also include a remarkable relationship with the fossil record. Although they never mined for coal to fire that pottery, like Hopi potters, the Zuñi are nonetheless more closely associated with the mining of minerals than probably any other Native American tribe. Their creation story is reflective of that intimate relationship with their geomorphological surroundings.

They, like the Hopi and Diné, view this world as the last (or, at least, the latest) in a series. When this world was created, it was covered with water and wracked with earthquakes. The earliest people were amphibian in nature, as all the first creatures were basically slaves to the water, so their own version of the hero twins—the children of the Sun—used lightning and fire to dry out the land so that all creatures could step upon it and dry out. But soon the predatory ones grew to immense sizes, with great gnashing teeth and even wings in some cases. The twins stepped in once again, blasting the land with lightning and fire from the sky until the monsters were all gone, setting the stage for humans and the animals we know to spread across the surface of the world.

Anything about that story sound familiar? It's an almost literal reading of the geo- and paleontological records that are laid bare in the stratified canyons of the Colorado Plateau. It starts with the lifeless stone of the lowest Precambrian strata, moving upward to the marine fossils of the Cambrian explosion that occur in the mid-level limestones of the Grand Canyon (including the crinoids that people have long used as naturally occurring stone beads). Stuck into the next layers up are the great beasts of the Triassic and Cretaceous periods, followed by what we now understand to be an asteroid-induced vanishing act by same, and followed in turn by the bones of more recent and recognizable upper-Pleistocene creatures. The Zuñi have taught this scientifically accurate interpretation of this stratigraphic record for over a thousand years.

Meanwhile, it took until the mid-1800s for European scientists to officially agree that *things get older the farther down you go.*

Building an ethnographic record on which to base one's interpretations of material history is nothing new to archaeology, of course. When trying to understand the Ancestral Puebloans of the national monument that would eventually bear his name, for example, Adolph Bandelier simply looked at how Puebloan people of late-1800s were living and then projected that backwards.

However, there's an obvious fly in that ointment: Pueblo communities of the late-1800s had existed in a post-Colonial space for several hundred years, at that point. Indigenous peoples of the modern world were not living fossils in his time any more than they are today. Reading the archaeological record in the literal terms of the ethnographic record was therefore problematic, so the overcorrection for a long time was to focus on the materials themselves and just ignore what the descendants of their creators had to say about them. Human interpretations can be flawed and biased, after all—even by people who demonstrably know what they're talking about. Ignore the people, therefore, and focus on the quantifiable data!

That wasn't exactly a great solution, either. What it boils down to is, in effect, stripping the humanity right out of one of the most humanistic of sciences, to the smug satisfaction of a lot of quantitative archaeologists right up to the present. This is like bragging that your lemonade is pure and wholesome because it isn't tainted with any lemons. Some sort of middle ground was needed.

Heading into the 1980s, one method archaeologists increasingly used to help link the static archaeological record with the dynamic behavior that created it was *ethnoarchaeology*, literally the study of people who practice behaviors similar (if not identical) to the ones being studied.

Among its other benefits, ethnoarchaeology got a generation of archaeologists out of offices and holes in the ground, and forced them to interact with people of different cultures—which is frankly a good idea for anyone. It was also a way to introduce more thorough, intimate levels of understanding into a science that was formerly concerned only with identifying, classifying, and chronologically ordering old stuff without much consideration for the actual humans that created it.

The practice of ethnoarchaeology is largely credited to an influential professor named Lewis Binford, who—like me—did poorly as a student in high school but excelled when he began studying topics that piqued both his interest and cynicism. In the late-1960s, after helping to kickstart what came to be called *New Archaeology*, Binford turned his focus on the Middle Paleolithic (ca. 300,000 to 30,000 BP) in Europe. When he couldn't make heads or tails of some of the fossil bone assemblages, he decided to follow a group of Nunamiut hunter-gatherers around in Alaska to see if their behavior might shed some light on the subject. Sure enough, the curious patterns of bone disposal in Middle Paleolithic sites resolved themselves into a logical depiction when he saw how the Nunamiut were doing it, including the observation that big bones full of marrow were hauled back home for processing while smaller, more easily butchered ones were processed in the field. It made perfect sense the moment he saw real people doing it.

Binford's subsequent publication effectively overturned the earlier assumption, called (and I'm not making this up) the Schlepp Effect, which postulated that heavy animal bits were processed in the field while lighter ones were carried home for processing at one's leisure. That publication, titled "Willow Smoke and Dogs' Tails: Hunter-Gatherer Settlement Systems and Archaeological Site Formation," also set a yet-unbroken precedent for how a lot of archaeologists title their work.

This was in the heyday of what came to be called the New Archaeology, a term dating back to 1966, when Binford and his students were trying to interject some science into the science of archaeology—although Binford himself bowed out of those theoretical debates when he turned his focus toward ethnoarchaeology. The research design of the Glen Canyon Project included early components of the New Archaeology toolkit, like emphasizing quantitative data and shifting away from sweeping generalizations about local chronology, but it was mostly Binford and his gang that cast the theoretical framework in iron.

Funnily enough, Binford's dual-pronged insistence on scientific objectively and the use of ethnoarchaeology spawned what could be considered rival gangs of theorists. Focusing all of one's research energies on teasing apart the processes that shaped the archaeological record earned for its practitioners the moniker Processualists. Meanwhile, focusing all of one's research energies on living, breathing human beings in order to interpret that same record kicked open the door to postmodern critiques about how, in such a setting, total objectivity isn't actually possible—enter the Post-Processualists. They haven't stopped bickering since.

Meanwhile, the part of this saga that I think carries the greatest ongoing importance is that of talking to Indigenous people instead of treating them and their ancestors as nothing more than data points. Whether this idea was a result of the civil rights movement or simply a development that independently arose after it, it gained a lot of steam right about the time I was born.

Still, it's worthwhile to mention that there were outliers before this behavior started nudging toward the norm in Southwest archaeology. Long before, in fact. Here's good old Nels Nelson back in 1921 in his official report on the Cartier Grand Gulch Expedition:

> From earliest reports, the native life has been described as of "exceedingly low type"...and their country inaccessible. There is an unfairness in this judgment, for the native mind fostered in this environment is filled with complex ideas (Navaho, etc.). Again, one has only to note what happens to a

white man who goes in there to live for some time. His usual conventions and conveniences are of very little value; and little by little he disposes with one necessity after another. His mind may be cleverer than ever before, and yet to judge by his own exterior he may look like a degenerate. Who knows but that the same forces which draw men away from the usual and prosaic and which sometimes claim them for the rest of their lives, also drew the aborigine and held him. The mysterious, the unknown, is never attained without its price.

I can't stress this strongly enough: that paragraph appears in a *technical report* written and submitted to the American Museum of Natural History by a professional, academic archaeologist. It would take another fifty years before that attitude went from outlier to nearer the bulk of the bell curve.

Scrutinized through the lens of modern scholarship, it does have its troublesome elements, like the uncomfortable comparison between ancient Native Americans and modern Caucasian social dropouts. But, again, it was written in 1921, and in that regard it was remarkably ahead of its time. It brings Indigenous and mainstream American people onto the same level, however clunkily, and suggests—almost appallingly for the time—that the former are neither degenerate savages nor noble savages so much as...well, people.

As Standing Rock Sioux author and scholar Vine Deloria Jr. often pointed out in his books and essays, one of the best ways to understand people is to understand what makes them laugh. "Laughter," he wrote in *Custer Died for Your Sins*, "encompasses the limits of the soul. In humor, life is redefined and accepted. Irony and satire provide much keener insights into a group's collective psyche and value than do years of research." I couldn't agree more.

Although I didn't give it enough consideration at the time, this was first brought to my attention by one of my earliest professors of cultural anthropology, when he carped over and over about how ethnographies on Native Americans never included anything about their humor. He found this to be of particular grievousness in classic ethnographies of the Diné, but a broader survey of classic scholarly and mainstream literature on Native American cultures reveals a yawning void where the topic of humor is concerned. Odd, right?

This comes up in a great way in the classic film *Smoke Signals*, which I always recommend as a primer for white people that want to understand Native American cultures better but aren't yet ready for the heavy stuff. In one scene, main character Thomas Builds-the-Fire is relating to his friend Victor Joseph a humorous story about a fry-bread-eating contest, and Victor rebukes him for it. "Don't you even know how to be a real Indian?" Thomas admits that he supposes not, so Victor decides to instruct him. "First of all, quit grinning like an idiot," he admonishes. "Indians ain't supposed to smile like that. Get stoic."

The joke is on the audience, of course. That's how Native Americans are largely perceived in mainstream culture, thanks to philosopher Jean-Jacques Rousseau's "noble savage" myth and its modern iterations like *Dances with Wolves* (Victor doesn't fail to mention that, either).

Humor is, and has always been, extremely important to the Indigenous peoples of North America and elsewhere. Given things like their ability to respond to attempted genocide by increasing their numbers, for example, coyotes seem almost designed by nature to be regarded as tricksters—and among all the Bears Ears-affiliated tribes you'll find no end of ribald Coyote stories. But it isn't just Coyote who fills the trickster role. To the Desána of southern Columbia, it's a female turtle. Among the Yąnomamö of Venezuela and Brazil, it's a bird. In eastern Ecuador it's an anteater. Moving farther afield: to the Irish it was Lugh; to the Greeks it was Hermes; among the Norse (and, increasingly, Hollywood) it was Loki; Kitsune in Japan; and so on.

For the Akan and Bantu-speaking peoples of western, southern, and central Africa, the trickster is a spider named Anansi, who must resort to cleverness and trickery because of his small size. When a bunch of Africans were enslaved and imported to the Americas, their trickster came with them, evolving and adapting to the local environment by taking the form of another small-statured creature that must resort to cleverness and trickery: Br'er Rabbit.

Outside of cultural narratives, the social role of tricking or "clowning" also developed in many Native American cultures as a way of both focusing on a given problem and addressing it socially as a means to resolve tension. In the words of Lakota holy man John Fire Lame Deer, "Coyote, Iktome [a Lakota-specific trickster], and all clowns are sacred. They are a necessary part of us. A people who have so much to cry about as Indians do also need their laughter to survive."

The gravity of that pronouncement cannot be overstated. Humor is a powerful weapon. The more you can inject humor into otherwise serious topics, the easier they are to digest and, thus, understand. Moreover, if you can find a way to laugh at your enemies, it erodes some of their own power. I learned this lesson myself, over and over again, when I was battling and then recovering from the god-awful depredations of Lyme.

As Bill Bryson said of Lyme disease in *A Walk in the Woods*, "If undetected, it can lie dormant in the human body for years before erupting in a positive fiesta of maladies. Symptoms include, but are not limited to, headaches, fatigue, fever, chills, shortness of breath, dizziness, shooting pains in the extremities, cardiac irregularities, facial paralysis, muscle spasms, severe mental impairment, loss of control of body functions, and—hardly surprising, really—chronic depression." All true, I can assure you—especially that last one.

In all my subsequent research on the topic, I cannot find a single confirmed case where someone has died from a Lyme infection. What you find instead are suicides. Lots of them. According to one estimate,* 1,200 or more suicides per year can be attributed to Lyme and associated diseases. That's out of an annual total of about 40,000 suicides in our country, meaning that upwards of three percent of all suicides in the United States may very well be a result of Lyme or Lyme-like infections. That's

---

* A 2017 study for the journal *Neuropsychiatric Disease and Treatment* by physician and researcher Robert Bransfield.

what happens when a bacterium specializes in wholesale assault on your nervous system.

For me, humor was a big help in staving this off—at least as big as staring at my photos and fervently hoping that I would, someday, be able to hike on Cedar Mesa again.

Cedar Mesa never stopped serving as a sanctuary for me. The very last happy memory I had was from March of 2011, when I spent a blissful week camping and wandering around there and elsewhere in the Bears Ears area. Memories of that trip spun through my head like an audiovisual mantra, keeping me focused on the fact that full recovery meant that I could do that again. I periodically drove there to remind myself that it was real, and I always felt a little bit better during and after those pilgrimages.

The rest of the time I relied on humor.

I didn't get through that awful time by being a Tough Guy. I got through the way Br'er Rabbit would—weakened, vulnerable, and totally reliant upon cleverness and mirth. That's how you best an enemy that's much stronger than you are. Fellow conservationists and other activist types would do well to remember that.

Hence the importance and power of figures like Coyote, alternating cleverness with lechery, greed, cheating, gluttony—pretty much all the Big Seven—representing the purely spontaneous and reminding us that there is laughter to be found amid tears. Joseph Campbell, researcher and specialist in myth who famously described the hero's journey (the narrative arc that comprises something like ninety-nine percent of all stories in American pop culture), described the role and function of the trickster in particular as the character that "breaks in, just as the unconscious does, to trip up the rational." Tricksters break down walls. They either help or force you to deal with things you'd rather not deal with.

Hence also my old professor's taking umbrage with classic ethnographies on the Diné that include no mention of their sense of humor or its importance in their cultural narratives. Hopi people, unless I've been hallucinating all this time, seem to spend as many of their waking hours as possible being jovial, to the point where a popular T-shirt in northern Arizona bears the slogan

"Don't Worry, Be Hopi."* Among the Zuñi, the clown society or *Ne'wekwe* (literally "mud-eaters") is among the most important groups, their behavior often described as lewd, comical, and alarming all at once—rather like the tales of wacky Greek philosopher Diogenes or eccentric Zen monk Ryōkan, but with more social and ritual importance.

My favorite practical example comes, of course, from the Bears Ears area. During his archaeological investigations there in the 1920s, Neil Judd and his crew were approached by a Ute man on a horse who indicated that he was curious what they were up to. In those days, archaeologists targeted burials as often as possible because they were sure to contain whatever material goods the respective culture considered most important, which is how early archaeologists earned the justifiable stereotype of being socially sanctioned grave robbers. Through elaborate gestures and a halting command of the local Ute dialect, Judd explained that they were digging up dead people. The Ute fellow nodded his acknowledgment.

Judd, remembering that Indigenous locals often knew more about such things than white newcomers like himself, implied that he would happily pay the Ute gentleman in exchange for knowledge about where they might find some other burials to exhume. Agreement followed, money changed hands, and Judd was led on a tortuous and fantastic journey of his own through scrambly washes, dense piñon and juniper stands, denser sagebrush, and all the rest that southeast Utah has to offer until he was totally lost.

Finally, after what seemed like hours of this, they emerged at a clearing.

It was the Bluff cemetery.

---

* Flagstaff-based Hopi artist and musician Ed Kabotie likes to perform that as a song, and you can find him doing so online if you look around.

Chapter Nine: The Conquerors

In the year AD 711, the Moors of northern Africa invaded Spain. Don't ask me why. They conquered Spain's resident population of Visigoths and pushed northward, making it all the way to France before they were repelled in 732 by Charles Martel and his stalwart Frankish knights. What followed was a few hundred years of wrangling between different Islamic colonizers vying for control of southern Spain while Christians in the north kept trying to retake it for themselves.

Architecture, food, clothing, artistic styles, and the Spanish language itself were all heavily influenced and altered by Arabic elements during this time, which is why the letter *H* now appears in so many Spanish words despite being totally useless. The Moors finally fell to Spanish re-conquest of their Cordoba caliphate in 1236, and the other Moorish strongholds slowly but inevitably fell like widely spaced dominos (don't try too hard to picture that) until their last city, Granada, was captured by King Ferdinand V and Queen Isabella I in 1492.

If that year suddenly sounds familiar, there's your reason. That same year, they agreed to fund a risky journey proposed by a blowhard foreigner to find a round-the-world access route to the riches of the Indies. This would allow Spanish trading vessels to avoid having to sail around Africa—the Cape of Good Hope was to fifteenth-century ships what a wood chipper would be to a Boy Scout canoe—or deal with the pesky Arabs in the Middle East, at whom they were still a bit sore.

Christopher Columbus had first pitched his clever idea to access the Far East by sailing due west to the Italians (Columbus, whose given name was Christoforo Colombo, was himself an Italian), and no, they didn't turn him down because everybody thought the Earth was flat and he'd fall off the edge. Every educated person in Columbus's time and place knew the Earth was round, ever since it was proved by the Hellenistic Greeks in the third century. Ironically, there are more imbeciles in America *today* that believe in a flat Earth than there were in fifteenth-century Italy.

The reason the Italian nobles turned him down is because it was a half-baked plan that involved no small measure of risk and was, moreover, headed up by a guy well-known for being a raging scumbag. They wanted nothing to do with him or his deranged machinations.

The Spanish, on the other hand, were flush with power and pride from having finally retaken their own lands after seven hundred years under colonial rule. Their mood was decidedly more receptive to wily schemes. Moreover, there were now soldiers wandering all over the Spanish countryside with no official enemies to kill, and that was starting to become worrisome. Columbus's proposal to the Spanish Crown was a potential solution. Worst-case (and most likely) scenario, this pompous fool disappears into the briny deep, taking a whole bunch of tooled-up and really bored murderers with him. Where's the downside?

Two months and at least one near-mutiny later, Columbus and his three ships landed in some still-unknown location on an island in the Bahamas known to the Indigenous inhabitants as Guanahani, and then bounced around the area a bit. He established a colony in what is now Haiti, the first European settlement in the Americas since the Norse had tried to settle Newfoundland some five hundred years before, and then returned to Spain with a handful of captured Indigenous slaves in order to underscore both his success and lack of moral fiber. He made three later trips, gaining a reputation as one of the most repugnant people in history by forcing women into sexual slavery and cutting men's hands off when they didn't meet his sensational gold quotas. Eventually, even the Crown got tired of his antics and arrested him.

The result was basically a long, drawn-out war between Europe and the Americas that lasted for hundreds of years. The Spanish, who'd only recently shaken off the yoke of colonial rule by the Moors, proved the old adage that what the oppressed often want isn't equanimity and harmony so much as the power to do some vengeful oppressing of their own. The kids getting bullied on the playground very rarely fantasize about everyone holding hands and being friends, after all, so much as going all Karate Kid and kicking seven shades of hell out of the bullies—I know this because I was one of them. And while the Spanish conquest and colonization of the "New World" was soon joined by the French, English, Dutch, and Swedish, it's the Spanish whose crosses-and-cannons form of colonization had the biggest impact on the fifteenth-century American Southwest.

The Spanish reached the Southwest by way of Mexico, or New Spain, in 1540 in the form of conquistador (the literally Romanticized version of "conqueror," which sounds better than the slightly more accurate "pillaging marauder") Francisco Vázquez de Coronado and his army. They were looking for the fabled Seven Cities of Gold, collectively called *Cíbola*, which supposedly lay far to the north of the Aztec's territory in Mexico. The origins of the myth are murky, but the rumors were further fueled by reports from the unlikely survivors of a disastrously failed attempt to establish colonial settlements in Florida just over a decade earlier. One of those survivors deserves special attention.

Sometime in 1527-8, a Moorish slave from northern Africa known as Esteban—although also called Estevanico (which was not a reference to his size so much as a condescending way the Spanish referred to enslaved people)—arrived in Florida with Spanish explorers and became embroiled in a series of outlandish adventures. After failing to locate villages full of gold near modern-day Tampa, and enduring all manner of maladies and attacks by crocodilians and Native locals, the beleaguered Spaniards slaughtered their horses, melted the metals in their tack, and made crude boats on which to escape across the Gulf to Texas—where they were immediately set upon by more of the same. Following all this, the enormous party of invaders was reduced to just four men, including Esteban and one Álvar Núñez Cabeza de Vaca.

What happened next is one of the greatest and weirdest adventure stories in American history. Cabeza de Vaca (literally "Cow Head"), along with his three companions, explored much of Texas and parts of northern Mexico, New Mexico, and Arizona, developing sympathy and curiosity for the Indigenous peoples of the region as they traveled. He would make peaceful overtures, including offering medicine for the sick, and thereby settle into a given neighborhood. While there, he would ask shrewd questions and take careful mental notes about the tribes in neighboring areas, learning as much as he could about their languages and customs. Armed with this knowledge, he and his companions would be peacefully received when they moved on to the next area. Sometimes they would be accompanied by befriended Native people wishing to help guide them there.

In this way, Cabeza de Vaca used ethnography as a functional tool for leap-frogging from one place to another without getting killed, until he and his small crew finally arrived safely in Mexico City ten years after the Tampa incident. When he sailed back to Spain shortly thereafter, he published an account of his exploits, which included such colorful chapter titles as "How We Departed After Eating the Dogs." It is now a classic of historic adventurism, as well as a bittersweet register of a number of tribes that were wiped out between then and now, including one that he found using the hot-rock method to cook stew inside hollowed-out pumpkins. Genius.

Meanwhile, Esteban stayed on in Mexico, and his knowledge of Indigenous peoples to the north made him invaluable for whoever led the next incursion thereto. He was thus deployed back into the American Southwest in 1539, accompanying one Friar Marcos de Niza in a search for—*sigh*—fabled cities full of gold. You can't beat Spanish conquistadors for consistency in the face of relentless disappointment. Traveling ahead of the friar, and decked out in beads and macaw feathers, Esteban cut an impressive figure when he arrived at the Zuñi village of Hawikuh.

The synopsis of what happened next is that the Zuñi were

impressed with Esteban at first; and then somewhat less impressed with him; and then killed him.

According to Zuñi oral histories and lore, he took on haughty airs and began demanding food and women. According to Spanish written histories, Esteban and his party were attacked on sight. Some scholars believe that it was because Esteban announced that he was an advance party for a group of powerful white men, which gave the Zuñi the impression that he was scouting for slave-raiders (ironically enough, given his own status in that regard). And still another account by Professor Juan Francisco Maura of the University of Vermont speculates that he wasn't killed at all, but that he and some Zuñi pals faked his death so that he could go free from his own slavery.

I like that last version the best. It may be the minority view on the subject, but it's the one with the greatest appeal. Besides, Esteban had accompanied Cabeza de Vaca throughout the greater Southwest for six years, during which time the two developed and refined methods of approaching Native American groups without offending or enraging them. And then he got to Zuñi and started demanding that they drag women to his quarters? Really? That's just the sort of story you'd make up if you were him and you wanted racist Spaniards to believe you'd gotten yourself killed doing something stupid.

Coronado and his party followed the very next year, *still* hoping to find cities made of gold, after Marcos de Niza apparently told him that they did indeed exist because Esteban was killed when he tried to enter one of them. Maybe. Niza said something to save face, at any rate, and it emboldened Coronado to co-invest with Spanish viceroy Antonio de Mendoza in a northward expedition involving three hundred Spaniards, more than one thousand "pacified" Indigenous Mexicans, and accompanying armies of horses, pigs, and cows.

They hit the Zuñi town of Hawikuh first, where Esteban had supposedly been killed, and subdued the place with their superior firepower. They found precisely no gold.

The frustrated Coronado dispatched additional expeditions throughout the region, including a trip to the Grand Canyon by

García López de Cárdenas. If you watch the IMAX film in the National Geographic Visitor Center in Tusayan, you can see him being led to the rim by a friendly Native guide and falling to his knees to praise God for creating such an exquisite wonder.

In reality, de Cárdenas thought the Grand Canyon was a grand pain in the ass. After finding himself unable to make it down the South Rim to the Colorado River with his severely dehydrated men, something thousands of tourists do on-foot every year, he was forced to return to Coronado's outpost at Zuñi.

Shortly thereafter, the Spanish fought their first officially named battle, the Tiguex War, named for the Tiwa region of the Rio Grande. Cárdenas would end up being the only member of the Coronado Expedition to be convicted of war crimes on account of the brutality he perpetrated on its behalf.

Coronado, meanwhile—having pacified the region to his satisfaction and still eager to return with enough booty to justify the expensive expedition—set off on yet another harebrained search for cities of gold. The seven golden cities of Cíbola had turned out to be so much hot air, but surely the newly swirling rumor of a city of gold called Quivira on the far side of the Great Plains was believable! I haven't the faintest idea why it never occurred to the Spanish conquistadors that rumors of cities made out of gold "over there, like *way* over there, just keep going and you can't miss it" by local informants might be of suspect intention, but apparently it didn't.

So, Coronado set off across the plains toward modern-day Kansas or Nebraska, and you can probably guess how many cities of gold he encountered before giving up. He returned to Mexico in 1542, now significantly less wealthy and popular, and the Spanish weren't seen in the American Southwest again for four decades.

About this time, ideas about the existence of fabled cities of gold began, finally, to lose their appeal. According to a few sources,* topmost among reasons the Spanish were convinced

---

* My favorite being the imminently readable *Four Corners: History, Land, and People of the Desert Southwest,* by Kenneth A. Brown.

of the existence of Cíbola were rumors that a gold-laden ship of refugees had escaped the Moors and sailed west to a mysterious land. Once there, they "built a utopian community of unimaginable wealth and sophistication." And then, what, never sent so much as a postcard back to Spain? Doubt was creeping in at last.

Enter Juan de Oñate y Salazar, a half-Basque born in 1550 in the colony of New Spain. In 1595, he was chosen for the principle tasks of organizing the resources of the acquired territories to the north to see if they could yield anything of value other than imaginary cities of gold; and capturing a traitorous criminal named Francisco Leyva de Bonilla, who'd made an unauthorized excursion into the Great Plains (in search of *guess what*) that got all but one of his men killed. Oñate was also supposed to spread Catholicism, if he happened to get around to it.

Thusly charged, Oñate marched north to recolonize what is now the American Southwest and expand the colonies already there. His retinue was four linear miles long, being comprised of over one hundred families and their personal effects and something like seven thousand animals. The cloud of dust they raised could be seen from a considerable distance, like a smoking volcano that was somehow drawing closer by the day. Not surprisingly, when Oñate and his enormous gang started arriving at Pueblo communities along the Rio Grande, they were all freshly abandoned. Frustrated, he decided to halt for a spell and send a much smaller detachment to find some Native people and, somehow, convince them that the Spaniards came in peace.

To demonstrate those peaceful intentions, they converted the Tewa residents at the Pueblo of Yunque to Christianity—and then kicked them all out. Winter was coming, after all, and it was getting cold outside. God would look after the newly baptized and homeless Tewa, surely.

In 1598, Oñate led another expedition to colonize the area. Between the first incursion and this one, European diseases took a massive toll on local populations, and populations at the Pueblos were greatly reduced in size. They were further reduced when missionaries herded people together in order to make them easier to missionize, consolidating most Towa, Tiwa, Keres, and Tewa peoples from the area south of Albuquerque to an area north of Santa Fe, where Coronado had first established a settlement that Oñate now occupied.

This chapter of Southwest history is sometimes characterized as a war, but it wasn't that exactly. It was terrorism on a near-continental scale. Thousands of people were put to death under Oñate's command, and many of the survivors were given gruesome souvenirs—severed hands, severed feet, and so on—to show everyone else what happened when you defied the mighty Spanish by committing unspeakable acts of betrayal like, for example, being stubbornly Native. In 1599, he and his forces almost completely destroyed the ancient Pueblo city of Acoma in retribution for their having killed a nephew that he rather liked after a skirmish over the taxes Acoma hadn't paid. All but two hundred of the two thousand or so residents of Acoma were slaughtered, followed by much cutting-off of hands and feet for the surviving adults and a future of slavery for their kids. That'll show those people with no experience of even the concept of taxation what happens when they don't pony up!

This is probably the thing for which Oñate is best known among modern historians, chiefly because it was the reason he was banished from New Mexico, being found guilty of extreme cruelty toward the Indigenous residents (along with murder, rape, disloyalty to the Crown, and—I'm not making this up—theft of property). That trial took place in 1614, by the way, over a decade after he'd stepped down as governor. Spain was trying to pin the blame for the civil unrest that led to the Pueblo Revolt of 1680, to which I'll return momentarily, entirely on Oñate in much the same way that the Mormon Church would later pin the Mountain Meadows Massacre entirely on John D. Lee. Oñate was fined six thousand ducats, or about a million bucks in modern US currency, and sternly told not to do it again.

Amazingly, considering he'd been found guilty of biblical levels of heinousness and got off criminally lightly, Oñate tried to appeal the conviction in 1622. The King was not amused.

Even more amazingly, the state of New Mexico had a statue of this barbaric swine erected outside the Rio Grande Visitor Center in 1994. In 1997, not long before the four-hundredth anniversary of his arrival, someone cut the right foot off the statue, leaving behind a note that said, "Fair is fair." The rest of Oñate's statue was finally removed during the nationwide protests against people like him in June of 2020.

A lot of what we know about the history of the Southwest, that doesn't come from archaeological science or Indigenous oral histories, comes from the diaries of the Franciscan monks who accompanied these Spanish conquistadors. The term that would later become the territorial and state name, Utah, was first mentioned in the 1620s by the Franciscan missionary Father Gerónimo de Zárate Salmerón in the form of *Yuta*. The word *Yuta* referred to the Ute people as a whole; the various Ute bands were not differentiated by the Spanish until the eighteenth century.

Given its downstream impact on the specific history of the Bears Ears area of Yuta, the Pueblo Revolt that took place forty years later deserves attention. Following the ugliness and tension kicked up by the Tiguex War, the various Pueblo peoples weren't too happy to see the Spanish once again taking up residence in the Rio Grande Valley and extending their noisome biblical tentacles throughout the region. Oñate had to put down a revolt at the Pueblo of Acoma almost immediately, where he killed or enslaved hundreds of its residents and sentenced all men over twenty-five to have a foot cut off.

This did nothing to make the Pueblo people happier about having the Spanish around.

They were subsequently forced into an *encomienda* system whereby they were compelled to provide food and labor to the Spanish, while access to water and arable lands to farm were restricted. The Bible-thumping Spanish also waged an ideological war on all forms of Indigenous religion, outlawing kachinas and traditional dances, and burning traditional religious items as they had with the incredible Mayan codices in Mesoamerica (look it up). Theocracy increased throughout the region, to the growing consternation of both the Pueblo communities and the Spanish Crown, with Franciscan missionaries vying with Spanish officials for power while the Indigenous locals got slapped around by both.

Things finally came to a head following a drought in the 1670s that caused famine throughout the Pueblo communities and increased raiding by other hostile tribes who were also starving. The Franciscans turned to the Crown, in what I cheekily think of as the equivalent of modern agribusiness types screaming anti-federal sentiments and then begging for subsidies when the weather turns crappy. In 1675, the re-emboldened local Spanish government arrested almost fifty medicine men from several Pueblo communities for practicing "sorcery" to try and bring back the rains, ordering four of them to be hanged (one committed suicide before the sentence was carried out) and the rest imprisoned. People from a number of Pueblo communities stormed Santa Fe and demanded the release of the prisoners, including one from the Pueblo of San Juan (*Ohkay Owingeh*) named Popé. Because most of the Spanish soldiers were off fighting other Native people at the time, the governor had to accede to their demands.

It was Popé who largely engineered what happened next. He spent half a decade carefully getting people from forty-six different Pueblo villages on his side and readied them for a mass, collective revolt. Among those who joined up were the Zuñi and Hopi, the two Pueblos with the closest cultural ties to Bears Ears, although not all the Hopi villages were on board. The village of Awatovi elected to side with the Spanish, for the understandable reason that they thought the revolt would either fail or simply result in a much larger wave of enraged Spanish coming up from Mexico in retribution (which did eventually happen). Following the revolt, they paid a heavy price for this hesitance.

A consortium of messengers met in secret at the Pueblo of Taos in the spring of 1680, and were deployed by Popé to all the allied Pueblo villages with news that the uprising would occur on the first night of the new moon the following August. They ran from village to village, carrying deerskin depictions of the orders with them, giving future historians and running enthusiasts a delightful image for paintings and book covers. They met again in August, when Popé gave them each a knotted maguey cord and told them to once again run to all the participating Pueblo villages. The knots acted as a countdown: one for each day until commencement of hostilities. Timing was crucial. Although outnumbering the Spanish by at least two to one, Popé and the other organizers knew that the Pueblo peoples would undoubtedly lose in a typical series of pitched battles in which the Spanish had time to fortify and make repairs in-between. They were relying on the element of surprise.

Nothing doing, as it turned out. After a pair of runners from Tesuque named Catua and Umtua delivered their knotted cords to the Pueblos of Tanos, San Marcos, and La Cienega, leaders from the same hastened to Santa Fe to warn the Spanish. Like the nervous folks of Awatovi, they probably thought that if the present installment of Spanish horses and cannons didn't put down the uprising, more would be along shortly. There was simply no telling how many Spaniards were waiting down south. It's one thing to throw rocks at a hornet's nest hanging on your gutter where you can clearly see its size, and quite another to piss off a wandering group of them when you have no idea if their reinforcements number in the dozens or the thousands. The two runners were arrested and tortured by the Spanish for details about the revolt, and the Pueblos of Tanos, San Marcos, and La Cienega—likely motivated by guilt over this—ended up joining the revolt after all.

Luckily for Popé and the loyal Pueblos, this betrayal took place just two days before the revolt was scheduled to happen, so they hastened to kick things off immediately before the Spanish could organize their defenses. It started on August 9 at Tesuque, home of the captured and tortured Catua and Umtua, and the following day it swept across the Pueblo world. Missionaries who'd resided near or within the participating Pueblo communities were killed en masse, and the revolutionaries used captured Spanish horses and weapons to blockade Santa Fe so the replenishing supply caravans that annually arrived from Mexico via the Camino Real ("Royal Road") couldn't get to it. Then they turned to the city itself.

The battle of Santa Fe involved about five hundred Indigenous attackers versus two hundred Spanish settlers, and the resulting siege was an ugly one. Settlers who managed to escape the fray fled south to the Pueblo of Isleta where they hoped to meet up with other Spaniards, only to find that they'd fled south to try and meet up with the annual resupply caravan and warn it.

Before long, Santa Fe had fallen. The Spanish were kicked out of the Southwest, making the Pueblo Revolt the only successful major uprising against European colonists by Indigenous peoples. The people residing in the Pueblo communities that survive today, twenty-two of them in all, still mark the occasion—sometimes with marathons dedicated to Catua and Umtua.

Following the revolt, the Spanish attempted to immediately reconquer their lost colonial tract in 1681. It didn't work. Then they decided those grapes were sour anyway, and that was that until twelve years later, when fears about what may be happening to the saved and baptized Native souls they'd left behind inspired them to try and retake New Mexico again. The fact that the French were advancing westward from the Mississippi River Valley and making them look really bad had, of course, nothing to do with it.

In their absence, Popé ordered everyone to scrub themselves of the filth of all things Spanish and/or Christian—figuratively and literally, as it turns out, in the form of symbolic bathing rituals. They razed churches and missions to the ground; rid themselves of horses, sheep, and cattle (non-Pueblo tribes in the region were only too happy to generously take them off the Puebloans' hands); rid themselves of Spanish tools and weapons (again, the ones that weren't outright destroyed were given good homes); and, apparently, dealt with nonparticipants in places like Awatovi in the manner of traitors everywhere.

And then, finally, the followers of Popé relaxed. And had a good look around. And realized that they were now completely surrounded by other tribes that were heavily tooled-up with the Spanish horses and steel that they no longer possessed.

This is an important lesson for all my reactionary readers, out there. You cannot go backwards. Not unless *everyone* goes with you.

When the Spanish made their foray back into New Mexico in September of 1692, under the direction of Diego de Vargas, the Pueblo occupants of Santa Fe sued for peace—provided the Spanish help them deal with the Apaches, the Utes, etc. They were only too happy to do so. The rest of the Pueblo villages surrendered to the Spanish within a couple of months.

While the Spanish went to make war on the Apaches, promising to return all peaceful-like when they were through, some of the Pueblo elders began to ask uncomfortable questions like, "So, outside of a friendly handshake, what *exactly* is stopping them from making war on us as well?" By the time de Vargas headed north once more in October of the following year, the collective Pueblo attitude toward their presence had once again soured. The Spanish—some eight hundred settlers, soldiers, and priests, plus the usual retinue of animals—sat outside Santa Fe in the plummeting autumn temperatures for eleven days, before de Vargas finally lost it. After the short and decisive Battle of Santa Fe 2.0, the rest of the Pueblo community in the Rio Grande region hastened to make peace once again.

Of note, the Spanish did not militarily reassert themselves with the Hopi as they did with the Pueblo villages of northern New Mexico—principally because of the Hopi mesas' remote location in northeastern Arizona. Moreover, attempts by Spanish missionaries to convert the Hopi to Christianity never really succeeded either, and the Hopi people successfully resisted every subsequent political or religious overture until finally the Spanish just gave up. As a result, the Hopi villages became refuges for a lot of other Pueblo people unwilling to reconcile with the Spaniards after they'd kicked them out of the Southwest once already.

Those Pueblo peoples within the Rio Grande region, Pueblos that remained firm in their suspicion that the Spanish were just trying to lure them into another Oñate-style bloodbath, packed up and fled. Some went north to the lands of their ancestors, according to some oral histories, hiding out in places like Mesa Verde and Bears Ears. Most of them went to Spanish-free Hopi, according to both traditional and archaeological knowledge. Others, perhaps as few as a couple hundred, headed for the northern borderlands of the Dinétah or *Navajo Homeland*. This took place in what historians (white ones, anyway) call the Gobernador period in Diné history, with the event and its rippling effects being known afterward as the Dinétah Phenomenon.

It went about like this: the Pueblo refugees made haste to defensible locations along mesa-top rims and atop isolated boulders in far-northwestern New Mexico, constructing masonry structures of between one and half a dozen rooms called *pueblitos* or "little pueblos," often in the form of towers or cliff dwellings. Chances are that they constructed these tight little settlements in defensible locations to ward off attacks from the Diné—and a feared Ute-Comanche alliance that liked to charge down from the north on occasion—just as much as from the Spanish. However, it didn't take long for the two groups to patch things up and begin blending their traditions, practices, beliefs, and even families.

I've heard a few researchers argue that this was the genesis of "Navajo culture" as the world now knows it, although that strikes me as a little sophomoric. Adaptability has always been a hallmark of Diné tradition and heritage (e.g., sheep and silverwork), probably more so than any other group with which I'm familiar.

In any case, modern Diné scholars and community leaders claim ancestral affiliation with the archaeological sites that I, for official reasons, keep calling Ancestral Pueblo. This historic episode is part of the reason why.

Another part, as explained to me by Steve Lekson, is the immense gargantuan that was Chaco. The Diné have some pretty specific stories about the heyday of the Chaco/Aztec world, suggesting that either Diné forebears were there or that some of the Chaco diaspora wound up in the Diné cultural lineage—or both. Oral history, specifically a tale about a figure called the Gambler, ties into this idea, and Diné archaeologists insist that Chaco wasn't "Ancestral Pueblo" so much as a melting pot where various Native American groups blended or were forged—not unlike Bears Ears, for that matter, but with more top-down *oomph* behind it. Physical evidence doesn't conclusively bear this out, to their annoyance, but the pueblitos are certainly real.

There were only about fifty of these tiny pueblos constructed during this time, at least that we know of, and they were only inhabited for about fifty years before their occupants decided it was safe to return to their respective homes in the Rio Grande region. If you know where to look, you can still find a bunch of them dotting the landscape in the northern tracts of the Navajo Nation, just so long as you also don't mind potentially running afoul of far-flung Diné sheepherders (who all carry rifles) or their ubiquitous sheepdogs (who don't need to).

After that, things became remarkably tranquil in the colonial Southwest. The Spanish had learned that Native people can only be pushed so far, that God wasn't necessarily on their side, and that those same Native people knew some handy stuff about how to live in places where rain will sometimes fall halfway to the ground and then evaporate right before your baffled eyes (meteorologists call this a "virga weather pattern," presumably because "bastard weather pattern" was already taken by hurricanes). The Spanish took care. They even started to model their own villages after the layouts and dynamics of the Pueblos, since it all seemed to work so well for them right up until, you know, the Spanish showed up.

The Pueblos, for their part, had learned that if you can't beat 'em, join 'em. They adopted the Spanish language as their lingua franca or, for you fantasy buffs out there, "common tongue" to facilitate relationships between each other and the colonists. They took bits and pieces of Spanish religion and infused it into their own, which is why it is now possible to watch Catholic-flavored public rituals being performed at places like Acoma. The Spanish brought chilies and tomatoes from their colonies farther to the south, as well as peach and apricot trees from Spain. They also brought honeybees, which is probably the one that sounds weirdest of all to non-historians. Technically speaking, honeybees are an invasive species—the four-thousand-or-so species of bees indigenous to North America never included them until they escaped from Spanish colonial beekeepers.

All this and more the Pueblos adopted from the Spanish, and everything started to look harmonious after all. For the Spanish and the Pueblos, at least—but the rest of the tribes in the surrounding region saw their increasing chumminess as offensive and infuriating. And, remember, they had a lot of Spanish horses and steel of their own. Raids on Pueblo and Spanish villages increased momentously during the late seventeenth and early eighteenth centuries.

By the 1760s, the costs of reinforcements and repairs in New Spain began to outweigh the benefits, turning the place into a net-loss asset for its colonizers. Newly crowned Charles III had ascended the throne in a time of turmoil and upheaval in Spain, and the travails of New Spain were an added cost that he was loath to endure. Rumors of corruption in their distant province only made matters worse. After all, few things are as frustrating as sending buckets of water to put out a fire just to see wealthy chumps running away with the buckets. Iron-fisted reforms were required so that the colonies could help pay for the motherland's problems rather than adding to them.

The king dispatched a pair of heavies named Don José de Galvez and Marqués de Rubí to straighten the place up—the former to enact governmental reforms and the latter to focus on civil and military infrastructure. In addition to extensive construction and development, they also sought to buffer the economic shortfall by exploring the surrounding areas for silver and, if it turned out that wasn't enough, build upon those explorations by connecting the struggling Santa Fe with the stronger and more prosperous missions in California. A trade route was needed, which would operate in a manner not entirely unlike jumper cables connecting a dead or dying battery with a strong one. What's more, it had to thread its way around the hostile Apache and Diné territories (the Utes and Comanches were mostly to the north and east). Which brings us back to southeast Utah.

The first official Spanish expedition into the San Juan River corridor at the foot of the Bears Ears area was led by Juan María Antonio de Rivera in 1765, in order to learn about the peoples they hadn't yet encountered, map the area, and look for silver (the

Crown having finally learned its lesson about phantasmal cities made of gold). Unique among European explorers of this and preceding eras, Rivera didn't travel with a military attachment, and supposedly never fired a shot in combat. Like Cabeza de Vaca and Esteban, he relied on the bold tactic of treating the Indigenous people whom he encountered with respect. They weren't looking to establish a new colony, after all. They were just looking for a trade route, and maybe a few places to mine some precious minerals in order to help stop the bleeding overseas.

The first of his two expeditions followed the San Juan to the present-day locations of Aneth and Bluff, and the second penetrated the canyon country all the way to present-day Moab, which is how Spanish Valley got its name. In fact, it was from Rivera or his immediate successors that just about everything in the region with a Spanish-sounding name first acquired it. The Dolores River is a shortening of Rivera's *el Río de Nuestra Señora de Dolores*, or the River of Our Lady of Sorrows. Subsequent explorers Dominguez and Escalante made mention of the *Sierra La Sal* or Salt Mountains in their journals, as well as the *Sierra Abajo* or Low Mountains on the horizon to the south. The San Rafael Swell is named after the patron saint of travel. One other landform also started to appear on hand-drawn maps just south of Sierra Abajo: *las Orejas del Oso*.

The next and historically most important Spanish expedition was that of Franciscan friars Silvestre Vélez de Escalante and Atanasio Domínguez, when they were tasked with establishing an overland trail between northern New Mexico and California. Their journey commenced in 1776, the same year the British colonies did what the Spanish colonies would do themselves in about forty more years, and it lasted roughly one year. The upshot is that they never did find a route all the way to California, but the specifics of their journey are pretty incredible. Like Rivera, they didn't bother with a military escort, and the whole of their company was just eight men—including a mapmaker named Bernardo Miera y Pacheco. The subsequent (and now called "Old") Spanish Trail, which is really a spaghetti plate of numerous pathways between Santa Fe and Monterey, was only possible because of his maps.

Interestingly enough, given their obtuse obsession with spurious cities made of gold, the Spanish were the first to make the connection between the crumbling architecture of Southwest archaeology and the Indigenous locals living nearby. During the Domínguez-Escalante expedition, the pair and their crew stopped and recorded what are now called Escalante and Domínguez Pueblos, currently managed by the Canyons of the Ancients Visitor Center and Museum in southwestern Colorado. They note in their journals that "there was in ancient times a small settlement the same type as those Indians of New Mexico, as the ruins which we purposely inspected show." All that "lost civilization" stuff arrived with American settlers somewhat later, part and parcel of the assemblage of grim fairy tales that was Manifest Destiny.

Royal decrees from the Spanish government forbade trading with local Native Americans in and around the settled territories, during this time—although that certainly didn't stop all of them. But it did mean that the law-abiding among them had to obtain their goods from traders in Chihuahua, far to the south, and often at greatly inflated prices. That changed when Mexico won its independence from Spain in 1821 with the Treaty of Córdoba.

Between 1829 and 1830, now-Mexican explorer Antonio Armijo led yet another expedition to find a trade route between Santa Fe and Los Angeles, passing through northern New Mexico and Arizona just to the south of Monument Valley. Unlike his predecessors, Armijo was more than willing to barter, trade, and otherwise engage with the region's Indigenous inhabitants in friendly ways. Armijo thus succeeded where others had failed, and the pathway that he forged was in continual use for the next two decades.

But trade between Mexicans and the Indigenous peoples of the Southwest was never an altogether friendly affair, given the latter's feelings toward the former since the 1500s (they saw little difference between Spanish-speaking Mexicans and Spanish-speaking Spaniards). Trade with various Ute communities was good, but their Comanche and Apache neighbors had grown

particularly adept at raiding and laying waste to Mexican settlements. Moreover, after gaining independence, Mexico had
internal strife aplenty to contend with, and teetered often on the
verge of civil war. They could spare little attention for the sparsely
settled northern borderlands of their new country.

Because of this, Armijo's trade route was the only lifeline the
residents of what is now New Mexico had. They were essentially
cut off from Mexico by distance and hostile locals, and became
entirely dependent on trade with the United States instead. That
was one source of the trouble to come.

Meanwhile, in order to stave off or at least buffer attacks by
the Comanches and Apaches, the Mexican government decided
to sponsor migration of United States citizens to what was then
called the province of Tejas. This was the other source.

The idea was to expand settlement into the Comanche's territory in the western portion of the province. For their part, the
American settlers took a long look at *eastern* Tejas, realized that's
where all the good farmland was located, and settled there instead.
English-speaking people from the eastern seaboard began surging
into what is now eastern Texas, prompting the Mexican government to backpedal pretty hard on encouraging American settlement in that province as a whole. They discouraged it even harder
in 1829 when they abolished slavery, which should be celebrated
as an early victory for human rights in North America—if only
slightly tainted by the fact that it was done to make slave-zealous
American settlers consider settling someplace else.

What it made them do instead was revolt.

Antonio López de Santa Anna took over as dictator of Mexico and went to put down the revolt in what would be the proud
but very short-lived Republic of Texas, killing Davy Crockett and
some others at the Alamo before being defeated by General Sam
Houston. Texas allowed themselves to be annexed to the United
States, President James Polk (in between sessions of browbeating
the Brits into handing over Washington and Oregon) offered to
buy Alta California and its dependent child Santa Fe from Mexico, and then things broke apart into a calamity called the Mexican-American War. It lasted all of two years, and by the end of

it the United States border looked pretty much like it does now. Among the veterans of that war was Ulysses S. Grant, who would have to shoulder a weapon once more when the United States tried to tear itself in half just two decades later.

Of greatest relevance to the Bears Ears area is what happened afterward. As they had once done in eastern Tejas, settlers from the United States now swarmed into the Southwest region, and they weren't too pleased to find the place still chock-full of Mexicans and Indians. The Treaty of Guadalupe Hidalgo, which had officially ended the war, promised US citizenship to all Mexican citizens living within the newly conquered territory—and, believe it or not, under Mexican law the Native Americans living in that territory were also considered Mexican citizens. Remember when I mentioned how a lot of early Southwest anthropology was aimed at delineating "our Indians" from "their Indians"? This is where that all started.

To the issue of Mexican farmers being displaced by incoming American settlers, the federal government responded with a whole lot of not much; but to the issue of Native people and their rights as full-fledged citizens, their response was a bit more animated. Indigenous people weren't citizens, whatever the treaty said—they were hostiles. This is where young Theodore Roosevelt picked up the lesson that he would shake off in later adulthood. Native Americans weren't granted United States citizenship until the 1930s, and a lot of stuff happened between the mid-1800s and then.

Physical evidence of the Spanish presence in the Southwest is sparse these days, outside of obvious things like place names. But it's around. The most notable examples are the missions that weren't totally destroyed, like the one at Pecos Pueblo where Kidder did so much of his investigating, and people will occasionally find isolated Spanish artifacts like crosses, crushed helmets, and coins. There are also inscriptions that Spanish explorers, soldiers, and friars carved into rock faces, the densest collection of them being the one at El Morro National Monument in New Mexico. And, just occasionally, people find them elsewhere. This very thing happened in Glen Canyon not long before I was stationed there and began my prolonged battle against stupid Lyme disease.

Following the momentous and history-making Glen Canyon Project that preceded the flooding of Lake Powell, the major focus of American archaeology shifted from research to management—i.e., the treatment of historically or culturally significant stuff as resources to be protected, exploited, or destroyed according to whatever makes the most sense at the time. This would have huge implications for the field of archaeology as a whole, particularly in terms of how we make a living.

But that emphasis on management means the bulk of American archaeology has shifted away from research of ancient things as means to reconstruct the past for purposes of scientific whimsy, and toward treating them as resources to be cataloged, monitored, and used as sparingly as possible.

This still allows many of them to be "used" in some decidedly uncouth ways, of course. I recently saw a loathsome social media screed about how cultural resources "are only RESOURCES if they're USED," which serves as its author's justification for selling maps of places of extreme cultural and scientific sensitivity to local ATV enthusiasts. This is linguistic trickery of the "depends what your definition of *is* is" variety, most often employed by hipsters and armchair philosophers (and the occasional commander in chief) to prove things about reality that would give reality itself a migraine.

Still, the engorged emphasis on preservation over exploitation in archaeology also means that the majority of archaeological knowledge is, these days, of a distinctly preservationist bent. Bears Ears archaeology—and Bill Lipe in particular—had a lot to do with this, at least in the Southwest.

Based on the lessons he learned running the Cedar Mesa Project, Lipe published a paper in 1974 titled "A Conservation Model for Archaeology" in an issue of the technical journal *Kiva* that stated in clear, unequivocal language that "archaeological research on any particular segment of the past is based on a non-renewable resource, and one that is being rapidly eroded." He called for "slowing down the attrition of the resource base" and all but demanded public outreach and education. In later publications, he extolled the growing acceptance of ecological approaches in archaeology, and paid a lot of rope to the notion that this might, maybe, possibly mean that conservation of regional ecosystems is just as important to preserving the human story as it is to *keeping it going a bit longer*. To that end, he called for stewardship and management of archaeological resources.

That really does mean everyone, by the way. Effective stewardship and management of archaeological resources means trying to keep them around for the benefit of everyone past, present, and future who loves them, can learn something from them, and/or considers them sacred. Hence my old boss Rosemary Sucec inviting a group of Hopi elders to offer their firsthand appraisal of how the Park Service was looking after the material heritage of their ancestors. There needs to be more of this, and for cultural resources beyond just the archaeological ones.

In the wake of the Glen Canyon Project, the NPS assumed management of 1.7 million acres surrounding Lake Powell as Glen Canyon National Recreation Area. As weird as it sounds, the impounded waters of Lake Powell only encompass between thirteen and fifteen percent of the Glen Canyon NRA, depending upon current water levels. So, no, not all of the cultural resources in Glen Canyon were drowned when it filled—not even close. Those that remain above the bathtub ring are practically innumerable, especially considering the San Juan Arm of the reservoir where it reaches into Bears Ears, and the NPS is tasked with looking after all of them while also looking after the sorts of people that same reservoir tends to attract. This is where Glen Canyon's role in preservationist archaeology starts looking like a dog chasing its own tail.

Vandalism is, to put it criminally mildly, a problem at Lake Powell. During my tenure there, I got to witness ancient granaries used as fire pits, the roof beams from thousand-year-old cliff structures used as firewood, and more than a few petroglyph panels repurposed as canvases for puerile jackasses—as in the case of Trent and the Descending Sheep site. Being an archaeologist there is gut-wrenching. Most of your job consists of taking careful notes while watching things you love get steadily destroyed.

Nor is the situation any better for places that don't have obvious archaeological resources. Nearly every wall of friable sandstone that's approachable from a beach where watercraft can land is so thoroughly littered with imagery and lettering—most of it carved into the surface—that many of them look the way newspapers would if you read them through a kaleidoscope.

To combat this, the Park Service created a program in 2005 called the Graffiti Removal and Intervention Team (GRIT) overseen by the agency and staffed by volunteers. Their task, briefly, was to live aboard a donated houseboat for a week using chisels and wire brushes to score the inscriptions off. They typically focused on one small area at a time, working carefully and methodically, giving every impression that their task would be completed in about fifty thousand years or so. It was funded for a mere three.

In 2006, a GRIT volunteer leader and boat pilot named Jim Page made the discovery of a lifetime. What he spotted, almost totally obscured by erosion and some idiots named Rob and Kathi, was the phrase *Paso por Aqui año 1776* inscribed in scrolling, semicursive letters. This discovery was made some 230 years after it was scratched into the wall, and it isn't easy to spot without someone pointing it out for you. I know this personally.

By the end of my first year as a seasonal archaeologist at Glen Canyon National Recreation Area, or GLCA as it's known in the biz, I at least had the diagnosis on what was turning my brain into porridge and my life into hell. Aggressive treatment wouldn't begin until I fetched up in Colorado to convalesce with some dear friends after the season ended, and the first early inklings of recovery wouldn't make their appearance until early 2012 when I was able to start making successful camping trips to Bears Ears again. Back in the summer of 2011, I was simply loaded-up with enough meds to maintain a more or less normal life and prevent things from getting any worse.

This did not, of course, mean that they were getting any better.

In addition to going after its victims' joints—hence being so often lumped into the same etiological category as arthritis, which is degeneration of the cartilage that keeps bones from scraping against one another—the Lyme or *Borrelia* bacterial genus has a sweet tooth for the trigeminal nerve system. This is the frontal-cranial nerve associated with things like biting and chewing, and although it doesn't directly control or affect the nearby control centers of balance and sight it can certainly *in*directly affect them when it becomes severely inflamed.

If you want to know what that feels like, go for a ten-hour boat ride on very turbulent water and then try sitting in a chair reading a book. The chair will give every impression of bucking around like a rodeo bronc, and the words—when you discern words at all—will chase each other around the pages like turbo-charged ants. And that's the baseline feeling, mind you. Compounding this was the fact that riding in boats in very turbulent water for upwards of ten hours at a time was, itself, literally my job much of the time. To say it was unpleasant would be an act of understatement tantamount to treason. It was like a never-ending bad acid trip.

In just such circumstances was I taken on a trip to visit Paso Por Aquí, or "the 1776 Panel" as we were calling it, to see what all the fuss was about. I know I was there, because I took photos. What I remember, however, is my immediate supervisor having a good laugh while pointing straight at it and watching my eyes dance all around it like a cat transfixed by a tumble dryer. I have absolutely zero memory of managing to descry the words in person.

Again, for the record, depression often appears near the top of the list of Lyme symptoms. I can't imagine why.

When I returned for a fourth and final season at Glen Canyon, most of the nightmares of the previous year had dissipated into nebulous silhouettes rather than hard, discrete memories. More and more of them were being crowded out by an expanding gallery of better (if not always *pleasanter*) memories from places like Cedar Mesa.

I dipped my toe into Beef Basin during that season, on an interagency resource inventory cobbled-together by Susec and some colleagues in surrounding land management agencies, thereby adding the remotest corner of the Bears Ears footprint into my personal realm of experience. Beef Basin was no exception.

I recalled once already how the road into that fabled realm of harshness devoured a total of three brand-new tires on two Jeep Rubicons the NPS had acquired just months before. It was also late springtime, so the cedar gnats that are often little more than a nuisance on Cedar Mesa took the form of dense, whining black clouds of evil in the slightly lower and wetter Basin. Then there was the day we all got to learn from a pair of backcountry rangers from Canyonlands—who get to ride dirt bikes, by the way—how one goes about retrieving keys that are locked inside a Rubicon using only what the desert provides...

I also got to sleep in the yard of a historic guard station, not far from the outhouse, although that wasn't quite as bad as it might sound. Evenings were spent inside the main structure, mostly listening to the higher-ups spin yarns about the shenanigans they've encountered as agency personnel.

Three years later, arsonists attempted to burn that guard station to the ground in what authorities suspect was an act of protest against the BLM. Two other backcountry BLM structures were targeted between then and May of 2017, when Interior Secretary Ryan Zinke arrived to cursorily tour Bears Ears National Monument as part of a mandated review process.

Shenanigans indeed.

Just before and during the time that I was working at Glen Canyon, researchers from a number of institutions conducted a series of analyses on Paso por Aqui to establish its authenticity, including lidar, photogrammetry, and the slightly more prosaic task of comparing the writing style with examples like El Morro.

The results were unanimous: the phrase, which translates as "we passed this way in the year 1776," was indeed written by some Spaniard or other in that very year. Which could only mean it was someone from Dominguez and Escalante's party. It is the earliest concrete (that is: sandstone) evidence of European presence in Utah.

To protect it, the Park Service first tried employing the always popular obscurity strategy: they kept their mouths shut about where it's located and hoped that nobody would find it. But, again, it's located in an area where people were already inscribing scores of names, doodles, sports logos, and other portrayals of humanity at its finest. A nearby sign that warns about the legal consequences of vandalizing natural features on National Park Service land is, itself, pretty thoroughly vandalized.

So, right about the time the Bears Ears conservation battle was reaching a fever pitch just to the east, NPS personnel finally caved and installed a heavy metal gate around the inscription. My friend and former coworker Erik oversaw its installation. He fondly remembers having panicked seizures every time it seemed like the wind was going to swing the very heavy gate into the rock face as it dangled beneath a hovering helicopter.

About a year later, my friend and colleague Kate Hovanes assisted the Old Spanish Trail Association in submitting a proposal to have Paso Por Aquí added to the National Register of Historic Places, mere eligibility to which is enough to earn considerable protections for a lot of archaeological sites. It was accepted in 2018.

Chapter Ten: The Wranglers

The history of land battles in the western United States is a fun one.

Settlers of the Intermountain West decided upon arrival that there were two great evils they'd be well rid of: Indians and government. The savvier among them took a sideline position and let their two enemies duke it out between themselves, offering a jab here and there whenever they thought one of them might come out of the fight a bit too strong. But mostly they just grumbled.

The wild, wild West in the post-Civil War era wasn't the dusty forum of daily shootouts so often caricatured in films (except in weird little pockets like Frisco, Utah—a mining town that boomed between 1875 and 1885 and, in its short golden era, boasted about one murder per day). I'm hardly the first person to point this out. Instead, people worked the land, ranched and drove cattle, did their level best to ignore John Wesley Powell's stern warnings about water management, and grumbled about Indians and government. With minor adjustments in terms of culture and technology, that's basically still true.

What brought the earliest Anglo- or Euro-American people into the Bears Ears area was, for the most part, trade. During the 1820s, trappers and traders started venturing into the greater Utah Territory and interacting with the Native Americans who lived there. Such figures as Etienne Provost, Jedediah Smith, William H. Ashley, and Antoine Leroux regularly traded, traveled, and intermarried with the tribes, often changing alliances with local tribes and bands to keep pace with ever-changing political and economic conditions in those uncertain days.

And then came the Church of Jesus Christ of Latter-day Saints. They're mostly known to non-LDS individuals as Mormons, so-called because the word itself appears in the title of their holy tract, the Book of Mormon—deriving in turn from the name of a land where the prophet Alma purportedly preached and baptized. The LDS church emerged out of what I've come to think of as America's first major identity crisis in the early 1800s, while the United States was busily pursuing Manifest Destiny and, suddenly, many Americans began to wonder who they really were.

Mormons have always been an industrious lot. Famously so. Their symbol is the beehive, for a number of what turns out to be incongruent reasons, having much to do with biblical history and honey production (and the Masons), but it works as a near-perfect metaphor for their collective mindset in any case. All their settlements were built—initially, anyway—on a grid system where the streets were numbered in terms of direction and distance from the temple. Living for a handful of years in Salt Lake City, I've frankly grown to love this. When a friend says, "I live on 243 South, 600 East," or some such thing, I can navigate there from pretty much anywhere without having to pester Google. What's more, the primary city streets are quite broad, thanks to orders from prophet Brigham Young that they be made wide enough that a wagon team could turn around "without resorting to profanity." If you make a wrong turn in a Utah city, U-turns are often a piece of cake.

When the Mormons came west after being driven from Missouri, having gotten there after being driven from their point of origin very near to where I was born in upstate New York, they didn't arrive in the shambling, ragtag fashion of a lot of homesteaders. Or in the fierce and independently stalwart attitude of others, as characterized in Ole Edvart Rølvaag's novel *Giants in the Earth*. Or in the manner of Oregon Trailers dying one by one of dysentery in the school computer lab. They came like bees—communal, hardworking, and brimming with solidarity. In a few publications, famed western wilderness and history author

Wallace Stegner describes Mormon caravans as "villages on the march, villages of sobriety, solidarity and discipline unheard of anywhere else on the western trails."

That "sobriety" bit has an interesting edge to it, vis-à-vis Mormon industriousness. Thanks to the booming 1820s trade in beaver pelts, some English-speaking trappers and traders were already in the Utah Territory when the Mormons arrived in 1847. And the Mormons had already decided that strong drink was a mocker, thanks to founder Joseph Smith's "Word of Wisdom" tract that became official doctrine in 1835. But finding clean drinking water was always a problem for westward explorers in places like the aptly named Salt Lake Valley.

So, when the Mormons arrived and decided to settle there, leader Brigham Young—who replaced Joseph Smith after he was assassinated in Illinois—immediately directed the creation of a brewery, setting the precedent for production and sale of beer so weak in alcohol content you find yourself racing against your own bladder to catch a buzz off the stuff. It wasn't *meant* to get people drunk. It was meant to be an alternative to lousy water.*

Speaking of water, it was also Stegner who praised the early Mormons for realizing and fully appreciating the immense importance of water in the American West—something that others pointedly failed to do, sometimes to this day. In a lovely little book titled *The Sound of Mountain Water*, he put it thusly: "On their very first day in Salt Lake Valley [the Mormons] made their peace with one of the West's inflexible conditions—they diverted the water of City Creek and softened the ground for a potato field, and thus began Anglo-American irrigation on this continent, admitting what Indian and Spaniard had already had to learn."

---

* Bishop Arnold of Soissons pulled the same trick in France during the early AD 1000s, encouraging local peasants to drink beer instead of well water because of its "gift of health" (and, although they didn't know it at the time, lack of deadly pathogens). After this tactic saved a bunch of lives during a particularly virulent outbreak, Arnold was canonized by the Catholic Church as a Patron Saint of Beer—one of over thirty, believe it or not.

The "Indians" of the Bears Ears area did not, so far as we know, practice irrigation so much as an ingenious method of dry-farming—at least on top of Cedar Mesa and Elk Ridge. But Stegner's words also echo another odd element of Mormon history in the arid lands: with the exception of Spanish colonists in the post-Pueblo Revolt era, Mormons were far more willing than most Euro-Americans to sit down and listen to what Indigenous inhabitants had to say about how to successfully live there.

This fact is often surprising to many non-LDS individuals, given the Mormon canonical belief that Native Americans are really the fabled Lamanites (one of four ancient peoples, along with the Jaredites, the Mulekites, and the Nephites) from the Book of Mormon, who colonized the Americas in the distant past. They were the wicked and savage assailants of wealthy Hebrew prophets, the forefathers of the Nephites, who traveled to the Americas by boat in 600 BC. For their transgressions against better (read: *whiter*) colonists, they were "cut off from the presence of the Lord" and cursed with "skin of blackness" so that they would not be enticing to the randy Nephites. A firmer foundation for systemic prejudice I can hardly imagine.

But the fact remains: as they made their way toward the Great Basin, Brigham Young admonished his followers to be kind and respectful toward whatever Lamanites they happened to encounter. Jacob Hamblin, who came to be known as the "Buckskin Apostle," was almost superhuman at this. By the mid-1850s, he'd established himself as an employer and dear friend of the Paiute and Diné communities in the region of southern Utah and northern Arizona, and was often deployed to soothe Mormon-Native hostilities with his impressive geniality.

Much of this goodwill would be shaken apart, however, with the Mountain Meadows Massacre of 1857, when Mormon settlers attacked and butchered several families aboard a wagon train bound for California. Many of the Mormon settlers were dressed up as Paiutes during the attack in a *very* grim predecessor of the modern "red face" practiced by imbeciles at some sporting events. It was a horrific event. Several days into the attack, a group of Mormons under John D. Lee jettisoned their Paiute costumes and lured some of the survivors out under a white flag, and then killed almost all of them.

The federal government of the United States (all thirty-three of them, at that point), already leery of the Mormons and their developing autonomous theocracy in the Utah Territory—and moving troops in their direction to set up US Army camps for this reason—reacted about how you might expect. Brevet Major James Henry Carleton was assigned to investigate the crime and bury the bodies, and he reported the following (credited as "A Correspondent") to *Harper's Weekly* for the edition on August 13, 1859:

> I am writing no tale of fiction; I wish not to gratify the fancy, but to tell a tale of truth to the reason and to the heart. I speak truths which hereafter legal evidence will fully corroborate. I met this train [of California-bound settlers] on the Platte River on my way to Fort Laramie in the spring of 1857, the best and richest one I had ever seen upon the plains. Fortune then beamed upon them with her sweetest smile. With a fine outfit and every comfort around them, they spoke to me exultingly of their prospects in the land of their golden dreams. To-day, as then, I ride with them, but no word of friendly greeting falls upon my ear, no face meets me with a smile of recognition; the empty sockets in their ghastly skulls tell me a tale of horror and of blood.

This is the sort of thing you get when you conduct a bloodthirsty massacre in secret during a time when mass media coverage is a real possibility. The article concludes with a summary of Carleton's interview with the local Paiutes, who reported to him that the orders came down from Brigham Young himself, although it's hard to know whether or not that part is true.

Legal proceedings related to the Mountain Meadows Massacre were halted when a "war" with a grand total of zero casualties ensued on account of the federal army's presence in Utah, Brigham Young was forcibly replaced as governor by a presidential appointee named Alfred Cummings, and Utah came under nominal military occupation. The investigation resumed after things had settled down a bit, and John D. Lee was summarily executed for it in 1877. He was the only one. He died screaming churlish imprecations about betrayal.

Lee had eluded prior capture by building a ranch and ferry service at the bottleneck between Glen and Grand Canyons, naming the ferry service after himself—which sounds like a poor way to elude capture, all things considered. The place is now managed by the Park Service, including the historic orchards.

Outside of this specific incident, what primarily characterized the second half the 1800s in Utah was a shoving match between the locals and the federal government over the topics of polygamy (a foundational practice that they were loath to relinquish) and land rights. The former was finally resolved with a series of congressional hearings in 1904-1907, although there are still fundamentalist holdouts here and there that continue the practice. The latter is not likely to be resolved before the sun winks out.

In 1859, in the midst of all this, the US Army dispatched Captain John N. Macomb of the Topographical Corps out of Santa Fe to explore the San Juan River country, including the Bears Ears and Moab areas. Officially charged with finding a practicable route to bring supplies between Santa Fe and the southern Utah settlements in case hostilities with the Mormons erupted once more, Macomb's mission also included finding the confluence of the Green and Colorado Rivers, surveying the region transected by the Old Spanish Trail, and generally filling in one of the largest remaining gaps of geographical knowledge in the American West—the very last being the Grand Staircase area just to the west.

Although Macomb apparently did a swell job of inventorying the Bears Ears area and surrounding region, the outbreak of the Civil War distracted him from publishing a formal report of his efforts. Ever. Instead, in 1876, he put forth a rather less-than-formal report that was culled from the journals of expedition members and from letters to his wife. This is why members of the Hayden Survey were so taken aback when they got to Mesa Verde and saw a bunch of enormous masonry structures that nobody had bothered telling them were there.

Although Macomb did not keep formal records of the expedition, his 1876 report stands as a benchmark in scientific knowledge of the San Juan region.* Early geologist John S. Newberry was a member of Macomb's retinue, and conducted a number of investigations that included the discovery of at least one new species of dinosaur and a whole bunch of geologic and archaeological wonders. He also sported the sort of beard that would make modern hipsters weep into their IPAs. It was on this expedition that Newberry also became the first geologist to examine the Grand Canyon.

Macomb also conducted the first serious investigations around the Abajo Mountains, and it was probably he who first started putting *las Orejas del Oso* on official government maps. Newberry, meanwhile, made some of the earliest speculations about the former inhabitants of the innumerable archaeological remnants in the area and describing them as, in Macomb's retelling, "evidently built by the Pueblo Indians." Subsequent investigations conducted by members of the Hayden Survey documented a myriad of Ancestral Pueblo sites, accomplishing the dual task of kick-starting both professional archaeology and rampant looting in the region.

The earliest full-time, non-Indigenous settlement in the Bears Ears area was established by Peter Shirts (alternately spelled "Shurtz" by some historians), an excommunicated Mormon. In 1887, Shirts built a home where Montezuma Creek meets the San Juan River not far to the east of modern-day Bluff. Shirts moved the rest of his family there from Michigan soon after, but they left him there and hoofed it back to Michigan when rumors of an impending Ute attack made its way to their ears. So far as we know, it never happened—or, at any rate, nothing happened that Shirts couldn't survive.

In 1878, LDS church leaders decided to establish a colony on the Colorado River near modern-day Bluff, ostensibly to improve relations with the Native Americans in the region after an earlier

---

* You can read all about it in the excellent 2010 book *Exploring Desert Stone* by Steven K. Madsen.

effort had spectacularly failed in the Moab area but also because the pesky federal government was busy deploying its own regiments there in the form of people like Macomb. An exploring party was sent first, traversing a route through the Arizona Strip to John D. Lee's ferry (presumably operated by someone else at the time) and then across the Navajo Nation. They met with Shirts in early 1879, and Fort Montezuma was established just below McElmo Wash.

The goal of the advanced party was to sow crops for the much larger party that would be taking the shorter—and, as it turned out, harsher—route directly across the Glen Canyon country the following year. They took note of the cantankerous attitude of the "Sandy Juan," as a lot of river rats still call it, and planted exactly one small garden that fairly quickly died.

The San Juan Expedition—known more commonly as the Hole-in-the-Rock Expedition, for what will soon be obvious reasons—commenced in the fall of 1879 and, after many a rugged league through the Grand Staircase-Escalante region, pitched up against a menacing sandstone wall in Glen Canyon. The subsequently named Hole-in-the-Rock route involved widening a narrow opening in the sandstone bedrock of the cliff face above the Colorado River, building a road down the cliff face itself, crossing the mighty river, and then gouging and grading another road up and out the other side. A combination of manual rock removal and blasting was used to widen the cleft, and later accounts by elderly Indigenous residents like Jim Mike include testimony about having heard the blasts. It took until the end of January 1880 before the work was completed, and thereafter the party could progress by carefully lowering the wagons through the new gap and ferrying them across the Colorado River.

On the east side of the Colorado, the settlers had to create yet another new road, a steep and narrow cut angling up the face of the cliff and then running along a sandstone shelf. The work was tedious and exhausting, and not a little dangerous (especially in the winter), but not one person died during the whole operation.

As much as that reads like a throwaway line tacked onto the

story like a modern journalistic factoid, it's pretty incredible when you think about it. Compare it with the Donner Party.

Still, given their ingenious and tireless fortitude in Glen Canyon, they were nonetheless stymied by Cedar Mesa's Grand Gulch. Stumbling along old Native trails, hopping "from spring to spring" as an ethnobotanist friend of mine puts it, they hit the gulch in much the same spirit of de Cárdenas when he reached the Grand Canyon: with a jolt, a long look, and much grumbling. But still they would not turn back, and instead kept trying to follow the faint trails of prehistoric and more recently historic Indigenous locals, camping at what are now called Cow Tank and Dripping Springs.

Emerging from Grand Gulch after this harrowing leg of their journey, the explorers mistook the nearby Abajo Mountains, which they called the Blues, for the La Sal Mountains nearer to Moab, which they called the Elks. Hence the name Elk Ridge for the lofty mesa on which the Bears Ears formations sit.* Just a few years ago, and based entirely on its name, the Forest Service decided to "reintroduce" elk to the area—to the considerable mirth of local archaeologists and historians, all of whom agree that there never were any elk on Elk Ridge before the Forest Service put them there.

Anyway, having gained the top of Cedar Mesa, the expedition then turned east, soon topping out on the mesa's highest point—now called Salvation Knoll for this very reason—where they could see the mighty Comb Ridge, natural border between cultural worlds for millennia and their last challenge before reaching the sweet sanctity of…well, of the place where the advance party had failed to make even a single tiny garden survive. I'm sure they were thrilled to discover this.

Albert R. Lyman, who arrived in Bluff in about 1881—his mother was pregnant with him in Fillmore during the San Juan

---

* At least, that's the story according to an article in *Blue Mountain Shadows* by local historian LaVerne Tate. Heidi Redd of the Dugout Ranch and Don Irwin of the Forest Service both insist that Elk Ridge is named for the long-defunct E.L.K. Ranch.

Expedition, and thus couldn't join in; they moved to the area afterward—was one of the earliest local Anglo figures to explore the area and take careful notes of his explorations. In his oral history, recorded in 1970 by the San Juan County Historical Society, Lyman discusses excavations made at the Bluff Great House in the 1890s, as well as two prehistoric roads that he recognized around the turn of the century, making his efforts some of the earliest kinda-sorta formal archaeological work in the Bears Ears area.

Lyman was also a prolific writer, and his *History of San Juan County 1879-1917* is nothing short of lyrical. Check out this sample, where he attempts to characterize the deep history of the area:

> The shattered fortress keeping mute sentinel over the pass or crossing, and the white skull still holding the axe that split it in twain, hold alike to their coveted secrets. We know that a nation left their castles to crumble, and their farms to grow wild with cedars and brush; and though we gaze longingly at the worn lintles [*sic*] and marks of human fingers in the mud-daubed wall, we are forced to give it up as a sealed volumn [*sic*].

Not exactly flawless, but fun to read.

The Mormon expeditionary contingent would have to build additional roads as they traveled, including one from the top of Gray Mesa to the valley below it; one from the top of Clay Hill Pass down to Whirlwind Bench; and one up and over Comb Ridge at San Juan Hill. Big and rocky landforms, those. I can't even begin to imagine the toil.

By April 6, 1880, most of the settlers had reached Cottonwood Wash and chosen to stop their journey there instead of traveling another eighteen miles to the fort and failed garden at Montezuma Creek. They named this location Bluff City, the latter half being dropped over time because a city it is certainly not. It would take another 137 years for the community of Bluff to be officially incorporated as a town. The first settlers surveyed the future town site of Bluff and, in what I can only describe as a spirit of delirious hopefulness, laid out farming grids and town lots.

With the tentative establishment of Bluff City, running the newly settled region was the next order of business. San Juan County was officially incorporated in 1880 from Iron, Kane, and Piute Counties by the Utah territorial legislature. San Juan County court jurisdictions, judges, clerks, county commissioners, and an assessor and collector were all named by late April of that year, a prosecuting attorney assigned in September, and a postmaster appointed by December. All this within a year of the Hole-in-the-Rockers arriving safely at a place where the local river wildly fluctuated between a lowly trickle and a raging torrent, laughing mightily at attempts to grow crops anywhere it could reach. No crops at all were raised in Bluff City in 1881 because of this, compelling LDS president John Taylor to send an emissary named Edward Dalton to try and lift their spirits like a proselytizing Patch Adams.

Meanwhile, although the original plan was to farm—and *only* to farm—the Mormons knew a lucrative idea when they saw one, and they soon enough did. A mining boom took place along the San Juan in 1883, starting with actual mines in Colorado and then making its way downstream in the form of speculation and rumor. The community of Bluff City, being a natural outfitting point, lurched back to life. In the spring of that same year, the English-owned Kansas and New Mexico Land and Cattle Company moved some seven thousand bovines onto the range north and east of Bluff City, raising hackles among the locals.

By 1885, owing to difficulties with the irrigation ditches, general lack of water, and poor crops, some of the residents began moving out into the surrounding county to find better farming and grazing lands. People were starting to give up on the place. This was not helped by the tempestuous river flooding yet again in 1884 and washing away dams, channels, and—in case there was any doubt about the nature of the San Juan before it was tamed by the damming craze of the mid-1900s—the entire community of Montezuma Creek. The settlers near Bluff City considered moving to several nearby locations, but complications such as land prices and/or land-ownership issues forced them to look farther afield. Exploring parties investigated Recapture Canyon, Mustang Mesa, White Mesa, and the south and north forks of Montezuma Canyon, all of them pretty far from Bluff City, because of the aforementioned British cattle barons. I don't really know when Bluff City became just Bluff, but my heart tells me it was probably when people started wholesale abandoning it.

In 1887, work commenced to establish a new town at the request of stake president Francis Hammond. The new town was originally going to be named Hammond for this reason, but it was later renamed Monticello in honor of Thomas Jefferson's estate. What followed was an eight-year battle between town builders and the Brits that owned the Kansas and New Mexico Land and Cattle Company. What emerged was 320 acres of fenced-off property filled with crudely constructed homes, although better-constructed private homes, a meeting house, and an irrigation ditch were built not long after. The Blue Mountain Irrigation and Manufacturing Company, later known as the Blue Mountain Irrigation Company, was organized in 1888 in Bluff and built the ditch for the residents of Monticello in what was probably a spirit of equal parts relief and jealousy.

The Mormons were not the first Euro-Americans to settle in Monticello, however. The so-called Northern Route of the Old Spanish Trail, established in 1831 to avoid the Diné and their lands, passed through modern-day Dove Creek before turning north in what would become the outskirts of Monticello. Thus, when the Mormon pioneers got to the future town site of Monticello they found roundup grounds where loose cattle and deer amiably grazed beside each other. Chances are they were originally constructed by Mexican sheepherders, who'd decided the lush green fields on the flanks of the Abajos were more amenable to their lifestyle than the harsher conditions around Santa Fe. Mormons elsewhere in Utah were also in the habit of hiring Mexican and Basque sheepherders after they'd taken up the practice, considering both groups to be the undisputed champions at the task, and many of them passed through the area as well.* The cattle came afterward.

Nowadays, you won't find much in the way of Spanish or Hispanic relics testifying to their former presence in the Bears Ears area, apart from the occasional *dendroglyph* or *arborglyph*, which are historic carvings on aspen trees that can still be seen today. Early sheepherders in the Southwest seemed to love carving their names and other images into the papery white bark of aspen trees. To my knowledge, the best examples in the area are found in the La Sal Mountains, closer to Moab, where keen eyes can sometimes spot a few that are downright pornographic ('twas a lonely business, sheepherding).

Back in 1886, a Mormon exploring party also zeroed in on the potential for agriculture and livestock on White Mesa, located just south of the Abajos. This location, known only as "Sagebrush" by the local Diné, would not be settled as a new town until 1897 due to Monticello's needs shoving it onto a backburner. Walter C. Lyman and his brother Joseph would end up being its founders, although they didn't name it after themselves, instead naming it after the wife of its first male resident—hence its originally being called Grayson instead of Lyman.

The town's name ended up being changed after a wealthy guy from the East offered to donate a library of one thousand books to any town in the West that agreed to change its name to his own. Which sounds weird enough on its own, but it gets even weirder. Another town, the town of Thurber, jumped at the chance shortly before the patriarchs of Grayson could, so they cut in for half the books by changing their town's name to that of the wealthy weirdo's wife's maiden name—Blanding.

---

* For reasons lost to history—or, at any rate, reasons I can't seem to find—Basques were hired in great numbers to the north and south of the Bears Ears area, but not within it. This makes for a curious hole in the map of Basque-American history at their monument and history center in Reno.

The Abajo Mountains turned out to be a better and more manageable water source for the economic development of the area, which encouraged additional settlement around its major drainages. Mormon colonists obtained legal rights to water in those drainages through various channels, and established a viable agricultural economy centered on the burgeoning communities of Blanding and Monticello. The Homestead Act of 1862, the Desert Land Act of 1877, and the Enlarged Homestead Act of 1909 further encouraged the development of these communities by providing access to inexpensive public land for private exploitation. This is where the practice of settling canyon heads to prevent access to the public lands within them got its start in southern Utah.

This all led to yet another in the endless series of backwoods culture-fusion elements characteristic of the Bears Ears area, in the form of a tense but dynamic patchwork involving Mormon and gentile "cowboy" cultures that endures to this day. And from this comes one of the most colorful legacies in the West.

As Albert Lyman tells it in his transcribed history of the earliest early days of the area, tensions roiled to the point where Wild West-style gunfights began to occur as the two cultural components jostled for control. "The gunmen in and around Monticello," he recounts, "made living so difficult and so dangerous, adding so many special unpleasantries on the side, that it is claimed most of the big boys and young men carried concealed weapons for an extreme emergency."

There were lawmen, of course, although most of them were unpaid and only worked behind the badge some of the time—rather like volunteer fire brigades. The first-ever paid sheriff in San Juan County assumed the post in the mid-1880s, a fellow named Willard George William Butt—or, more informally, Dick Butt.

Besides having a name that would earn him superstardom on modern social media, the man was preternaturally successful at just about everything he attempted, including law enforcement and a number of different business ventures. He was also near-universally praised as a fair and decent guy. But he didn't stick around the immediate area for long, and by early the follow-ing decade Dick and the rest of the Butt family had relocated to Verdure, where he could more closely monitor his sawmill, dair-ies, beef cattle, and so forth.

Amid this quarrelsome medley already "sufficiently fruitful in raising hell," in Lyman's words, appeared a booze joint called the Blue Goose Saloon, where "fire-water was sold" and "question-able practices and genuine coarse times prevailed." That phrasing brings a nostalgic tear to my eyes. I was a bartender for about ten years, and that's the best summation of the practice I've ever seen.

The Blue Goose was founded and initially run by William "Latigo" Gordon in 1896 as a way to divert mischief-causing cowboys into a centralized location, not entirely unlike round-ing up unruly steers, but of course it didn't really work out that way. What happened instead is more like what spaceships do with planets in sci-fi movies: they whipped around inside its orbit, picking up a gravity assist in the process (in this case the *specific gravity* of ethanol), before propelling back outside to cause even more mayhem.

The first effort to close the saloon came within a year of its opening, and it's become a Utah standby ever since—they raised the price of obtaining a liquor license higher than Gordon could afford. A little under a decade later, in 1904, a local moonshiner named Bartolo Jaramillo and his wife Lupe began selling their spirits out of a log cabin that they creatively christened the Blue Goose. They were busted during the fun little experiment the United States had with attempting to ban alcoholic beverages—the one that more or less resulted in the creation of organized crime in America as we now know it—and the Blue Goose Saloon once again disappeared into memory.

And then, in 2015, the old Bar TN property in Monticello was purchased by Jim Brandt and turned into the Old West RV Park. With the property came a rather crumby-looking house at the northern corner, and when demolition commenced they found a hand-hewn log cabin hiding behind its walls: the last iteration of the Blue Goose. Efforts are apparently underway to have the thing moved to Main Street and stabilized as a historic attraction.

Meanwhile, back in the 1930s, a young attorney named Fred Keller decided to memorialize in song the elbow-rubbing Mormon and cowboy cultures in Monticello with a ballad called simply "The Blue Mountain Song." It's a hoot. You can see Keller's typed-up version on the Library of Congress website, and it includes the following:

My home it was in Texas.
My past you must not know.
I seek a refuge from the law, where the sage and pinion
    grow.
....

I chum with Latigo Gordon.
I drink at the Blue Goose Saloon.
I dance all night with the Mormon girls and ride home
    beneath the moon.

While all that was going on, settlers of every variety in the Bears Ears area experienced their own shares of conflicts with the Indigenous residents that already called the place home—namely Ute, San Juan Paiute, and Diné groups and families. Tensions increased as the Anglo and Indigenous communities disagreed on topics such as grazing areas, water usage, and the ever-moving target of settlement locations.

Some of this tension was preemptively addressed just after the entire surrounding region fell into the hands of the United States following cessation of hostilities with Mexico, when Fort Massachusetts was established near the base of Mount Blanca just over the border in Colorado. But the Ute locals, having become a dominant force in the region through shifting allegiances and other clever strategic means, were not happy about either the military fort or the increasing numbers of settlers in their territory. Hostilities flared in the Ute War of 1854–1855, starting with a violent flare-up at Fort Pueblo on the Arkansas River and culminating with major Ute losses in a number of skirmishes throughout Colorado and northern New Mexico. Subsequent treaties were established between the US government and the Capote and Moachi bands in 1855, with all the inherent longevity such treaties tended to have.

Major conflicts involving Ute war parties continued across the region, ramping up considerably once the end of the Civil War saw many veterans and refugees from the East flooding into the West. The situation boiled over in southeast Utah for the first time with the Pinhook Draw fight of 1881, in the foothills of the La Sal Mountains. Mainly the result of escalating insults and little personal conflicts between traders nearer to Monticello, a small group of Ute men killed a pair of white guys and emptied out the trading post run by one of them before torching the place and heading south. An exhaustive running battle commenced, with the Ute side drawing a mounted posse from western Colorado into Pinhook Draw, assuming advantageous firing positions before the posse got there. It worked—ten white posse members lost their lives to Ute gunfire, while only three of the latter group were killed. It is, of course, now remembered as a "massacre" for this reason.

Not long before all this, the Uintah Ute Reservation was created in the northeast corner of Utah by an executive order from Abraham Lincoln. Nobody was forcibly corralled onto it at the time, mostly because of federal troops being distracted by a little dustup back East, but when the Civil War ended there was an invigorated push to get as much of the public domain as possible into the hands of veterans as a combination "thank you for your service" and "take *that*, Indians." The Ouray Reservation was created in 1880 for the forcibly relocated Uncompahgre band, bringing the total Ute reservation lands to more than four million acres. The two reservations later merged into the Uintah and Ouray Reservation.

Which didn't mean a whole lot to local Ute residents, at the time, who were spread all over the Intermountain West and preferred to stay that way. As the post-war land rush caused more and more of the type of conflicts presented above, however, increasing numbers of them were killed in clashes with well-armed state and federal forces. By the middle of the 1880s, many of the Ute people still living outside the reservation were resignedly willing to discuss that option after all.

Leaders of the Southern Ute bands in Colorado were told by a consortium of Indian agents and Colorado senators that they could move back to their ancestral homelands in southeastern Utah as a condition of the General Allotment or Dawes Severalty Act of 1887, which aimed to make agriculturalists of all Native Americans by providing allotments of farmable land. Despite their not being agriculturalists to begin with, they flooded back into southeastern Utah to quit fighting and take up farming. These efforts to find lands for Ute families with suitable agricultural potential eventually converged on San Juan County, where a number of them moved (or returned, in many cases) to stake their claims.

The deal sounded almost too good to be true. And it was. Local Mormons and gentiles alike became incensed, and fought back by lobbying state and federal government officials to prevent the seizure of "their" land by Native Americans—a situation that would repeat itself with only a few significant changes just over a century later. Pressure from the Mormons and their duly hired state officials culminated in Congress failing to ratify an agreement, and most of the Utes were forced to move back to Colorado once again. But not all of them. The ones who'd settled in the remote hinterlands of Montezuma Creek and Allen Canyon stood by their stakes and were never forced to leave them. This would have some interesting repercussions down the line.

Conflicts between white settlers and Diné people in the Bears Ears area were also inevitable. Starting as early as 1861, while most of the US Army was busy trying to kill other white Americans who didn't want to give up their slaves, some of them found enough free time to begin scheming toward removing the Diné from all of their homelands in the greater Four Corners area. To that end, they launched a full military campaign against the Diné and their linguistic cousins, the Mescalero Apaches, destroying their homes and gardens and killing their livestock. The survivors were forcibly relocated to Fort Sumner and Bosque Redondo in New Mexico.

Nearly ten thousand men, women, and children were forced into the long walk to Bosque Redondo, a considerable distance from wherever they started and about three hundred miles from the farthest points. Approximately two hundred of them died before they even made it there. Another two thousand or so would perish over the next four years due to disease, poor planning on the part of their federal overseers, crop failures and infestations, and suicide.

They were also forced to subsist on such nutritionally vacuous fare as canned lard, condensed milk, granulated white sugar, and bleached white flour—all because those food items are white, and white = good. I wish I was kidding about that. So-called Indian fry bread is a result of this, which is why traditional Indigenous chefs like Sean Sherman are openly opposed to the stuff.

A few of the Diné managed to escape or evade the heinous roundup, hiding out in places like the Grand Canyon and around Navajo Mountain, the most famous one being Hoskannini ("Angry One"), the exact whereabouts of whose hideout remains unknown to this day. A few historians have even proposed some of the deeper, darker canyons of the Bears Ears area as potential locations for Hoskannini's hideouts, although there isn't a whole lot of evidence to support this.

While not as broadly famous as Hoskannini, a Diné leader named K'aayélii ("One with Quiver") was born right around 1801, near a spring at the head of a canyon atop Elk Ridge—both of which are now named after a corrupted spelling of his name, "Kigalia." As one of the principal Diné leaders of the region, he and his band traveled all over it, ranging as far as the La Sal and Henry Mountains and the Uncompaghre Plateau. He also managed to hide out from the inhumane roundup and ethnic cleansing of the Long Walk, taking refuge with his people in the deep, dark canyons that lurk behind the Bears Ears.

Another of the most influential Diné leaders from this time, Chief Manuelito, was also born in the vicinity of the Bears Ears formations themselves, although he spent most of his storied life in the Chuska Mountains within the present-day Navajo Nation boundary in New Mexico. He was a prodigious raider of Mexican settlements during the early 1800s, owing largely to an impressive talent for rallying different bands together. He was also disliked and feared by many Ute, Comanche, Apache, and Pueblo leaders for this very reason. After he and his troops were herded into Bosque Redondo, this talent served him and his people well when Manuelito cobbled together a unified voice against the oppression visited upon them by the federal government there. He also helped frame the 1868 treaty that ended their ghastly internment.

That treaty is a story unto itself, and I've barely got time or space to do it justice here. At the internment camp, the Diné were pressured to assimilate to American culture—that is, to adopt American-style agriculture, as well as individualism and Christianity—in the manner of people in internment camps throughout history (right up to the present day, in the case of Chinese Uighurs). But that first one presented a problem almost immediately: Bosque Redondo is too harsh to farm. That's why it wasn't densely settled already. Assimilation or no, they were destined to starve, as were the sheep on which they'd come to depend.

Word of the horrid conditions at Bosque Redondo spread, and the federal government couldn't ignore the mounting criticism. Kit Carson, harsh and heartless architect of the roundup, caved to sympathy in 1866 and ordered that no more prisoners be sent there. Negotiations between Diné leaders and federal government officials began shortly thereafter, with Generals William Tecumseh Sherman and Samuel F. Tappan stepping in for the United States.

The negotiations staggered, at first. It was fierce pleas and encouragement from Diné women that kept the process alive, just as their knowledge of weaving and genius methods for keeping their hearty Navajo-Churro (or four-horned) sheep alive had helped keep the people themselves from perishing during their internment. Little mention is made of this in most history books, chiefly because patriarchal hierarchy was another piece of the "assimilation" package and federal officials would therefore only deal with men—twenty-nine of whom signed the resulting treaty in 1868. In 2019, the US government agreed to give one of only two extant copies of the treaty to the Diné for their own curation, and then-current Navajo Nation President Jonathan Nez made mention of this during a speech he gave at a fundraising dinner a few months later. It was from this speech that I learned the treaty process wouldn't even have been possible without the women's involvement.

The treaty of 1868 also established the original borders of the Navajo Indian Reservation, defined at the time as the thirty-seventh parallel in the north, a straight line running through Fort Defiance in the south, another straight line running through Fort Lyon in the east, and longitude 109°30' in the west. It was a rectangle, in other words, roughly one-third the size of the current Navajo Nation's footprint.

Their sovereignty finally acknowledged through that treaty, the Diné were allowed to return (that is: walk) back to their homeland. Manuelito returned to the Tohatchi area in the Chuskas, where he succeeded Barboncito—a famous Diné spiritual and political leader who also helped frame the 1868 treaty—as principal chief of the region. He was appointed as head of the newly minted Navajo Tribal Police in 1872, and went on to accomplish much in the name of his people. In 1980, the Navajo Nation established its most prestigious scholarship in his honor.

Although the Diné were finally released from captivity and allowed to return home in 1868, the history that followed was largely characterized by the same problems that plagued them before they were shuffled into a concentration camp in the first place. In fact, the last big "relocation" effort foisted on the Diné in the Bears Ears area took place in the early 1950s, when tensions erupted between them and local white cattlemen following a winter drought that necessitated expansion of grazing areas to feed their respective animals. In the first—and, so far as I can tell, only—instance of southeast Utah locals working together with the BLM, they targeted Diné sheep and shepherds on public land for violating one spurious thing or another, rounding them up into trucks and burning many of their hogans in the process. All were deposited on the south side of the river.

The very small number of distraught and angry Diné residents who could afford a lawyer promptly hired one, camping out in his backyard in Salt Lake City while the courts deliberated, and they were ultimately awarded one hundred thousand dollars for their lost livestock (total, that is—not apiece). The judge said some really harsh things about the BLM and their complicity in this nefariousness, the Diné caravanned back to their waiting families on the south side of the San Juan, and that was that.

The upshot of this tale is that the state of Utah succeeded in bulldozing scores of Native American families out of San Juan County a mere seventy years ago and at a cost of one hundred thousand dollars in 1950 money, or just a tad over one million dollars today. Meanwhile, the county spent just under half that much to hire San Diego-based attorneys to help maintain ATV access for three miles of Recapture Canyon just a couple of years ago, according to an investigation by friend and *Salt Lake Tribune* reporter Zak Podmore, so they haven't stopped spending big piles of taxpayer money on efforts that are demonstrably idiotic and pointless (Recapture remains closed to ATVs, and the county is now at least two-thirds Indigenous). I can't help but think of the conquistadors and their obstinate efforts to find cities made of gold...

So, the Diné had to endure the same sort of group- and boundary-juggling that plagued Ute peoples in the same region, albeit with slightly differing outcomes.

Tensions inevitably rose when the latter were being jostled back and forth between southeastern Utah and southwestern Colorado, and they erupted into full-blown conflict in 1914, when Tse-Ne-Gat—also known by the Anglicized name Everett Hatch—reportedly killed Juan Chacon, a Mexican sheepherder, within the boundaries of the Ute Mountain Reservation. Tse-Ne-Gat was the son of Ute chief Old Polk, and he refused to turn himself in to authorities because he believed his life was already in enough danger. Old Polk took Tse-Ne-Gat and the rest of his band to hide out in the shadow of Navajo Mountain, while newspapers around the country circulated the tale of terrifying rogue Indians still at-large in the region. After ten months, a posse of twenty-six cowboys and three sheriffs was formed to go after Old Polk. The arrest attempt included them coming upon the camp and startling them into a gunfight in which two Ute men and one white man were killed.

Another chief named Posey was camped out nearer the San Juan River at the time. Posey was half-Paiute and half-Mexican, and had married into the Ute Mountain band, although he refused to live on the newly minted Ute Mountain Reservation and chose instead to occupy the vicinity of Allen Canyon with other Ute holdouts. When the gunfire erupted, he hastened his own men to Polk's rescue.

Heavily biased journalism tainted stories about the incident in local and regional newspapers, painting the Ute and Paiute bands alike as murderous savages and prompting Brigadier General Hugh L. Scott, Chief of Staff of the United States Army, to travel to Bluff. Scott eventually captured twenty-three "hostiles," including Tse-Ne-Gat, Old Polk, Posey, and Posey's son, all of whom were brought to Salt Lake City for questioning. All but Tse-Ne-Gat, who was taken to Denver for trial, were released by authorities by April of 1915. Tse-Ne-Gat was acquitted of all charges, which enraged settlers throughout the Four Corners area, although it's worth noting that several who testified on his behalf were Blanding (or Grayson, at the time) Mormons.

Journalists once again leapt into the fray and looked for fires that needed extra gasoline dumped on them. They continued to portray both Indigenous groups—and now Posey, in particular, since every good piece of editorializing needs a villain—in very negative terms, and generally stoke the anger of the locals. Posey's band of about one hundred Ute and Paiute members was gaining a fearsome reputation. Tempers flared again when two young members of his band robbed a sheep ranch on Cahone Mesa, and the aggression stirred up by the newspapers pushed it all even closer to the edge.

The accused turned themselves in and stood trial, but were allowed to return home after they contracted food poisoning while in custody. The two boys then returned to stand trial without incident. However, after hearing guilty sentences passed their way, they managed a daring daylight escape when the sheriff took them out to lunch partway through the proceedings.

When the public found out about the escape, a gang of locals went in pursuit of both the convicts themselves and Posey, having decided that Posey was synonymous with all things Native and problematic in the region. This was the start of what would come to be called Posey's War, although it was really a defensive action taken by a mixed Ute and Paiute group fleeing their homes and attempting to escape to the rough canyon country around Navajo Mountain, which had served as a safe haven for so many different groups before.

Thanks to ongoing efforts by journalists to depict Posey and all other Ute and Paiute people of the Bears Ears area as bloodthirsty monsters, including a *Times-Independent* piece with the title "Piute Band Declares War on Whites in Blanding," then-governor of Utah Charles Mabey felt publicly justified in using a military scout plane to bomb them from the air. The US military told him no, thankfully, which is why the Bears Ears area remains blessedly free of bomb craters.

Other newspaper articles included ludicrous yarns about Ute terrorists attacking the town of Blanding in full war regalia, Posey and his band robbing banks, and so on. All of this culminated in yet another posse forming up to chase after Posey.

The pursuit came to a head on Comb Ridge, and when Edward Abbey later penned a fictional "Battle of Comb Ridge" in *The Monkey Wrench Gang*—where his titular characters try to stop the building of Highway 95 between Blanding and Natural Bridges—it takes place in almost the exact same spot. Most of Posey's band surrendered, although Posey himself was among those who refused and disappeared into Comb Wash instead.

Posey's band were trundled off into a barbed-wire compound erected in the middle of Blanding, a sort of makeshift POW camp, where they learned that Posey was dead. And here is where Jim "Mike's Boy" Mike comes back into the tale.

The official story is that Posey died of blood poisoning caused by the gunshot wound in his hip, his body being found at the bottom of Comb Wash by his pursuers, and most historians report it that way. Jim Mike was there, having been among the San Juan Paiute component of Posey's band. As he told it to Gary Shumway in a 1958 oral history: "They didn't shoot him. He wasn't shot. He was poisoned with flour and he had flour on his hands... They shot him after he was dead, that was false. He was in the cave, he was in the cave, dead, afterwards [they] shot him. That's what they killed him with—bread." It goes on like that. According to Jim Mike, the Ute community as a whole has never bought the story that Posey was wounded by a gunshot to the hip and, thus, easily captured by his pursuers before dying of infection from the wound. So far as I can tell, they continue to believe that he was poisoned. The cave to which Mike refers is unknown to me, but there's a few of them strewn throughout the upper Comb Wash area so it could have been any one of them.

In any case, Posey and the son of one of the original two perpetrators were the only casualties in what journalists bombastically labeled a war.

Posey's band was released from their stockade after his body was brought into town. Marshal Jesse Ray Ward took control of the body, ordering it buried in an unmarked grave so as not to be molested by the posse—to no avail, as it turned out. His body was exhumed at least twice by posse goons and others who wanted their photographs taken with the corpse (and people think Instagram invented the concept of idiots posing with things they shouldn't be posing with).

Just over one hundred years later, a trio of psychotic so-called revolutionaries also made their way from southwestern Colorado into the Bears Ears area in a hail of gunfire. In May of 1998, three Cortez locals—Jason McVean, Robert Mason, and Alan "Monte" Pilon—stole a water truck in Colorado, loaded it with firearms and explosives, and started toward Utah with the alleged (according to some sources, anyway) intention of blowing up Glen Canyon Dam. Their plans to attempt this all but impossible daydream were thwarted, however, when they were pulled over by Officer Dale Claxton. Whether or not it was because the vehicle was stolen, or had a broken taillight, or whatever became a moot point when one of the men stepped out of the vehicle and opened fire on Claxton before he could even unbuckle his seatbelt. A barrage of high-powered rounds nearly blew him apart. The trio then abandoned the truck and fled, wounding two Montezuma County sheriff's deputies en route just for good measure.

The biggest engagement, nicknamed The Battle of the Bridge by journalists, took place on June 4 when shots were fired at a Utah social worker who'd stopped by Bluff's now-defunct swinging bridge for lunch. San Juan County deputy Kelly Bradford immediately went to the area to investigate, and took two bullets upon arrival (he survived, thankfully). Helicopters, SWAT teams, and even trackers from the Navajo Nation Police—no reason not to go with the best—swarmed the area. It was mayhem. There's an archaeological site in that general vicinity with a set of kiva depressions in it that were utilized as ad hoc foxholes.

When the assault on the assailants' position finally occurred, however, they found Mason already dead, either by his own hand or someone else's. He was in a makeshift bunker surrounded by explosives. Pilon's remains were found a year later by a group of hunters. McVean would remain missing until 2007, when a cowboy from Blanding discovered his skeleton, a bulletproof vest, a backpack full of bombs and ammunition, and a rusty AK-47 in the vicinity of Cross Canyon.

In the heart of Bears Ears, BLM rangers found a cache of ammunition and survival supplies in a remote alcove not long after the shootout occurred. And just this past year, I had the personal displeasure of finding a collapsible rifle mount—the kind sharpshooters use to fire from a prone position—discarded on a butte with an excellent view of the lower portion of a popular driving route for tourists. History comes alive.

Back in the 1920s, the fracas with Posey served as an excuse to corral the remaining Ute holdouts into an allotment system. An order from the Interior Secretary demanded that the surviving members of Posey's band and Old Polk's band cease their nomadic hunting and gathering (which is to say: traditional) lifestyle and settle on allotted parcels in, respectively, Allen Canyon and Montezuma Creek. These spots were supposedly chosen for the dual reasons that they contained numerous Ute settlements already, and the white people didn't seem to want them, although the biggest reason is the same one employed by teachers who always try to split up the troublesome kids. As reported in the *Moab Times-Independent*, "the two bands which are not friendly [toward white homesteaders], will be located some distance apart."

What remained of the San Juan band of the Southern Paiutes just sort of disappear from known history, at this point—although the people themselves certainly didn't. What is now called the Arizona Strip—the stretch of land straddling the Utah/Arizona border between Lee's Ferry and St. George—was originally called the Paiute Strip. It was set aside as a reservation for the Southern Paiute people as a whole in 1907, but then taken back away from them in 1933. To this day, no fewer than three Southern Paiute bands are legally considered consulting parties in matters of resource management in the Grand Canyon and Grand Staircase-Escalante areas. But not Bears Ears.

In 1954, the federal government officially removed the San Juan Band of Southern Paiutes from the list of federally recognized Native American tribes, supposedly owing to their no longer having enough members to qualify. This decision was reversed forty-five years later, although they are now federally recognized as the San Juan Southern Paiute Tribe *of Arizona*. Their official headquarters is in Tuba City on the Navajo Nation, and in 2000 the Diné and San Juan Paiute Tribes signed an impressive treaty— the first one drafted and signed entirely by Native American tribes in nearly two hundred years—setting aside approximately 5,400 acres of reservation land for the latter party. That treaty, amended in 2004, needed only to be ratified by Congress in order to finally establish a permanent homeland for the San Juan Paiutes.

They're still waiting for Congress to get around to that.

Meanwhile, the majority of San Juan Paiute people today live in what they call the Southern Area, clustering mostly around Tuba City and the Hopi mesas. A few San Juan Paiute families still have homes near Navajo Mountain—also known as Paiute Mountain, or *Ina'ih bi dzil*, in their own language—an area whose importance to Indigenous groups of the Four Corners region is rivaled only by the Bears Ears themselves. Others live in the Blanding and White Mesa areas.

Unfortunately, the San Juan Paiutes are largely a "forgotten" people outside of their own homes and families, blessed by never being corralled into a reservation but cursed to obscurity by that same happenstance.

As far as I can tell, nobody from the San Juan Paiute Tribe was ever given allotments when they were doled out to Ute refugees in the Bears Ears area, although some—like the Whiskers family—ended up owning parcels there nonetheless. But life on allotments didn't really fit the traditional Ute lifestyle, either, which included the aforementioned seasonal round that extended across entire landscapes depending upon the season.

Some of them tried farming, which worked well enough, but their tendency to farm at a subsistence level rather than a market-economy level meant that better-equipped and more experienced white neighbors competitively excluded them into insolvency. In response, some took to herding cattle and sheep. But free use of the range had come to an end, at least for them, and all the lands surrounding their allotments were controlled or owned by the Forest Service, BLM, and private interests.

In 1938, the Ute community filed a lawsuit against the US government for a sum of forty million dollars (I'm not sure how they arrived at that number) for the mounting troubles associated with losing nearly all their lands in southeastern Utah. The lawsuits languished until a Salt Lake City lawyer named Ernest Wilkinson and his firm stepped in to help them in the 1950s, and they wound up settling on a final reparation sum of thirty-two million dollars, which was split roughly in half between the northern tribe at Uintah-Ouray and the southern tribe at Ute

Mountain. Through various machinations and legal wrangling with the new locals, the southern contingent succeeded in using some of these funds to establish and grow the Ute community located atop White Mesa just to the south of Blanding. The town itself is now called White Mesa, fittingly enough, and is a de facto outpost of the Ute Mountain Ute Reservation.

Eventually, White Mesa attracted many of the struggling Ute families from Allen Canyon and Montezuma Creek, who saw in the growing community a better future than allotment life would allow.

White Mesa also attracted a uranium mill.

Thus, in the wake of the most egregious ugliness visited upon the Ute Tribe in the Bears Ears area, what developed were allotments. It didn't really work out, at least not the way it was supposed to, but it also wasn't all bad—some were bartered into crucial improvements for the community of White Mesa, while others are still held in optimal locations for protecting resources from private development or federal overreach. So: a mixed bag.

For the Diné, it was trading posts.

Trading posts have a deep history in the Bears Ears area and surrounding region, with the earliest one having arguably materialized in the narrow bottleneck of Marble Gorge between Glen and Grand Canyons when Mormon leader John D. Lee was sent there to avoid prosecution. This had repercussions all its own. But the inception of what would become trading posts as, in effect, an institution can be squarely pegged to 1868, when the Diné were allowed to return home from Bosque Redondo. Like the Ute individuals and families living just to the north of their new reservation, the Diné were relegated to an environmentally meager tract of land, and then abandoned to their own fate—along with the heinous whimsies of often-corrupt Indian agents.

Meanwhile, following a wave that would be weirdly repeated almost exactly one hundred years later, a rapidly increasing number of Americans suddenly became quite interested in Native

American arts and wares. And the Navajo Nation was—and, in the continental United States, remains—the largest Indigenous reservation, which makes it pretty easy to find. The topmost item was Diné textiles, usually intricately woven blankets that steadily morphed into rugs, which were selling for up to $50 apiece (or about $1,500 in today's money) all through the 1800s.

What emerged was, not surprisingly, also a mixed bag. On the one hand: traders helped broker cultural shifts that helped make the tumultuous part-traditional/part-alien nature of reservation life a bit more tolerable, mostly by facilitating input and flow of money and technology from outside. On the other hand: this process itself, broadly categorized as *technology transfer* by anthropologists, also precipitated the erosion of Diné tradition by fostering dependence on things like non-Diné foods that continue to have dour impacts to this day.

The latter is the socioeconomic equivalent of the producer-consumer relationship that makes it more worthwhile to hunt a caloric condenser, like a deer, than attempt to eat a thousand apples—the deer has already done that for you. It's a wise economic decision. But apples don't give you tapeworms, and it's uncommon for them to run away and/or try to kick you to death if you don't make a clean shot. Similarly, devoting a thousand hours of labor in a given season to growing a garden for your family yields a bunch of vegetables, assuming the weather cooperates; but devoting that same thousand hours of labor to a gorgeous and very sought-after Two Gray Hills or Storm King rug yields enough calorie-dense sugar, flour, and lard to make a year's worth of fry bread. Again, it's a wise economic decision. But the vegetables don't increase one's risk of obesity and type 2 diabetes. Hence, again, a lot of Indigenous-kitchen traditionalists are increasingly hostile toward fry bread.

Still, the history of trading posts vis-à-vis the Diné is largely a positive one. There were unscrupulous, unethical, and even tyrannical traders, to be sure, but (oddly enough, given how such things usually go) the market itself often weeded them out. When a trader or trading-post operator turned out to be a four-flusher, the Indigenous artisans and craftspeople simply shrugged and found a different one. The majority of them developed healthy and fruitful relationships as a result, and most traders strongly encouraged the Diné to retain as much of their traditional culture as they could—both for their own sake, and because it meant the trader could keep hocking "traditional Indian goods" to other white people with a straight face. Either way, it was beneficial more often than it was detrimental, and the trading post grew into a combination of community-gathering place and liaison space between worlds.

I got to experience the modern equivalent of this in 2010, not long before I left Flagstaff to try my hand at both graduate school and long-term debilitating illness. One of my best friends is a woman I met in archaeology classes at NAU with the cool moniker "K. C." (and no, she didn't call me "R. E." and still doesn't), who'd grown up with a father who was—and, as far as I know, remains—a Native art trader. Hanging out at her dad's old shop in Flagstaff all through that year before I left was mesmerizing, partly for the goods themselves and partly for the stories I heard. Stories of tribal gatherings, foods whose names I can't pronounce, and literal adventures on literal dusty trails to trade with people who don't speak a lick of English.

The biggest and most enduring lesson was that it's all about relationships rather than commerce. Mainstream capitalism teaches that if you aren't willing to minnow into bondage with scumbags, you'll lose the game to those who are. Indigenous artists and craftspeople of the Southwest, on the other hand, are apparently far more willing to take a financial hit to work with a lower-income trader who also happens to be a kind and respectful individual. Which *should* kick the door open for sociopaths who excel at pretending to be kind and respectful just to take people for a jolly ride, but it doesn't. I guess they're more strongly drawn to places like Wall Street and Washington, DC.

For her part, K. C. elected to stop being actively involved in the trading business with her father when she dove into the field of archaeology. Not because there was a conflict of interest, of course—her father is very much the kind and respectful individual of mention, who doesn't do things like trade in illicit antiquities. But she's very perspicacious, and didn't want to give any false impressions nonetheless. She is now a full professor living several states away, and I only get to catch up with her and her lovely kids when we both make it to the same conferences. Her father's trading post in Flagstaff is also gone, and largely nudged aside in my mind by memories of her selflessly looking after me during the horrific earliest stages of my ailment. When I close my eyes, however, I can still usually see it. Lots and lots of turquoise.

The first trading post in the Bears Ears area went up almost the moment Mormon settlers arrived, when Amasa Barton and some partners established one at Montezuma Creek in 1880. The tempestuous San Juan River had its own opinions about this, as it often did, and the trading post was moved to an area about nine miles downstream from Bluff within a couple of years. Barton himself was murdered in an act of vengeance in 1887, after he beat a Diné boy nearly to death for stealing a mere pocketful of wool, and run of the trading post was taken up by other Bluff locals. It went defunct by the end of the 1800s, for reasons unknown to historians but probably having to do with the river, and its ruins molder still.

The second one was established on a secure sandstone ledge a good hundred-or-so feet above the riverbank at Mexican Hat. Most sources suggest it was first built in about 1907 by Zeke Johnson, Charles Bernheimer's local guide and the man most closely associated with Natural Bridges National Monument, and an iteration of it is still in operation to this day. Other trading posts sprang up in and around the Bears Ears area during the early 1900s at Aneth, Bluff, and Navajo Mountain. Richard Wetherill established one in Chaco Canyon, for better or for worse (mostly worse).

Richard's genial and conservation-minded brother John established a trading post at Oljato, not far over the river from Bears Ears within the Navajo Nation, from which the storied 1909 expedition to Rainbow Bridge was launched. John, his impressive polyglot wife Louisa, and their business partner Clyde Coville moved their trading operations southward twenty miles to

Kayenta in 1910, where they built a new trading post that became almost legendary in its own right.

Louisa Wetherill would spend much of the next twenty-two years in Kayenta carefully and lovingly amassing notes for a biography of Wolfkiller, a kindly Diné friend who'd helped them build that first house and trading post at Oljato. Nobody would publish her book at the time, however, owing to a combination of the subject being an Indigenous person and the author being a woman. Her efforts were finally acknowledged in 2007 with the publication of *Wolfkiller: Wisdom from a Nineteenth-Century Navajo Shepherd*, compiled by prolific historian (and she and John's great-grandson) Harvey Leake.

In sum, and not without exceptions, the historic trading-post era that extended between the shuttering of Bosque Redondo and the Great Depression was a more-or-less happy one. Then things took a turn.

Most historians identify this time period as the "Closing of the West," although, as postmodern critics often point out, this concept only meant closure of limitless range acquisition by wealthy white men. Women, Hispanics, freed African slaves, and Native Americans who struggled daily to maintain agency and identity in the Intermountain West didn't really count. The date where most historians stick the pin is approximately 1890, although it really began with a series of catastrophes a few years prior.

Following cessation of efforts between US citizens to murder each other (it's weird to think about how recently the Civil War was fought), and the successful—and very stupid—eradication of most of the apex predators and *all* the bison from the vast western frontier, a cattle boom took place. The grasses of the Great Plains were open for business, and apparently eternally regenerative. Most of the money required to finance the enormous herds that started spilling out all over the left-hand half of the United States came from wealthy outside investors, which is how the lands around Bluff became occupied with cattle owned by British people. Theodore* Roosevelt got in on the action by purchasing a ranch and a respectable host of beeves for eighty thousand dollars in what was then the Dakota Territory.

This was the era of the cattle barons. Ranchers on the Great Plains wrangled and herded about six million head of cattle into market by the 1870s, which undoubtedly means there were even more of them free-ranging around that never made it there. It didn't matter. When your cow-punching operation amounts to the equivalent of a cartoon money vault, you hardly notice when a few thousand coins roll out through cracks in the wall.

The problem of overgrazing became almost immediately apparent, however—at least to those paying attention. While American bison could certainly make short work of a broad swath of grassland, they and the North American landscape had co-evolved over innumerable seasons to handle one another's behaviors. Not so cattle, which did most of their evolving in the Indian subcontinent.

Making matters worse, the new breed of homesteaders were bringing with them Joseph Glidden's new invention called "barbed wire," which turned much of the expansive-but-not-in-finite public domain into a dizzying maze of private and open sections. And sheep were an annoying factor, one for which Roosevelt had a special lifelong hatred. And then a financial crisis erupted in the East, which began dragging beef prices downward. And so on.

But all that was nothing compared with what good old Mother Nature had in store for the cattle barons and their hubris. Historians often refer to it as the Great Die Up.

The winter of 1886-87 began in the Great Plains in mid-November with unseasonably early and fierce snowfall, which didn't let up until almost Christmas. Christmas Day saw temperatures of negative thirty-six degrees Fahrenheit. By New Year's Day it was negative forty, at which point it doesn't matter if it's Fahrenheit or Celsius because that's the abysmal place where the two

---

* He hated the nickname "Teddy" because his beloved and deceased first wife used it as a term of endearment.

temperature systems intersect. This was immediately followed by a blizzard, just for good measure, and temperatures didn't rise above zero degrees Fahrenheit again until well into March. About one hundred people froze to death in Kansas alone. Cattle died in the tens of thousands.

This series of events coincided with the earliest rumblings of the American conservationist movement, which made its biggest early public appearance with the first publications by Theodore Roosevelt's Boone and Crockett Club in (of course) 1893. Although Roosevelt's involvement in the movement is often pinned squarely on his love of hunting, and for good reason, it's safe to assume the dire fate of his own cattle outfit during the winter of 1886-87 was a factor as well. He called it a "perfect smashup" in a letter to Congressman Henry Cabot Lodge, and reported being "utterly unable to enjoy a visit to [his] ranch." That would sound pretty tame coming from anyone else, but remember that this is a guy who once paused during a speech to beat someone up for shooting him and then *continued with the speech.*

Cattle no longer fully occupied the open range after that devastating winter. An 1897 act of Congress gave the federal government administration over grazing on public lands, and a follow-up bill in 1905 organized the Forest Service within the Department of Agriculture. Things limped along thus until the next great depression, often capitalized as the Great Depression, which came about thanks to a stock market crash in 1929. Its effects were felt in the Bears Ears area shortly after.

In the years before the 1930s, there weren't a whole lot of restrictions on grazing in public lands, outside of the tacit ones that followed the calamitous winter of 1886-87, and large-scale ranchers effectively took control of much of the prime pasturages in the area. The Taylor Grazing Act of 1934 changed all that, regulating the use of public grazing land and establishing the Grazing Service. The intended purpose of the act was to stabilize the often economically volatile livestock industry, as well as to stop the misuse and abuse of public lands through regulatory control of those lands by the Grazing Service. In anticipation of this, major livestock owners in the Bears Ears area applied for grazing permits that totaled nearly seventy-five percent of San Juan County.

With the Depression in full swing, and the prices of beef and wool at all-time lows, most area ranchers couldn't afford to pay for those permits to continue grazing their animals on public lands. As if that wasn't enough, the state of Utah also experienced a drought in 1934 that was so bad it dried up water holes and springs that had never gone dry in living memory. In many places, the grass simply didn't grow that year. The Grazing Service stepped in at that point, offering to buy all the "surplus" stock above the number they decided was a good fit for the depleted ranges.

A sheep-reduction program followed soon after, one with racist overtones in how it was applied on the supposedly sovereign Navajo Nation just across the river. It was first proposed in 1933, before the above tale of cow-related woe, as a voluntary program in which Diné sheepherders could enroll themselves if they wished. In 1935, it became mandatory, and US government officials purchased—at prices they determined—more than half of the sheep on Dinétah to haul away and slaughter. Protestors were arrested.

Women on the Nation were hit hardest of all, because more of them were dependent upon sheep for their sole source of livelihood (weaving legendarily gorgeous blankets and so forth) than were men. That market all but evaporated, and the majority of trading posts throughout the region—already in trouble, like every other venue of commerce, thanks to the Depression—died as a result.

Worse still, with shipping costs being what they were, many of the purchased animals were slaughtered right there in front of the people who'd come to consider them sacred.

Imagine someone from a faraway land deciding that dogs are a drain on *your* household economy, forcing you to take a few dollars in exchange for your beloved canine companions, and then shooting them on your front lawn.

That was the end of the beginning of what would develop into the American conservation movement, and its thread braids together with the history of Southwest archaeology in a poignant way.

The Taylor Grazing Act allowed for the establishment of the Department of the Interior and the Grazing Office to manage grazing on non-Forest Service lands. In 1946, one year after the end of World War II, the Grazing Office was combined with the General Land Office, which had overseen the sale of lands since 1849, to become the Bureau of Land Management or BLM (the same acronym as the social justice movement Black Lives Matter, which occasionally makes for some lively misunderstandings on social media). These acts gave the Secretary of the Interior authority to limit grazing on public lands, with administration of grazing allotments being overseen by the newly formed agency. This helps explain how and why the Ute allotment debacle occurred the way that it did in the Bears Ears area.

The end of World War II brought a lot of other changes to the United States, including an ardent devotion to economic growth. "America at this moment," said Winston Churchill between drinks in 1945, "stands at the summit of the world." The economy was booming. Babies were booming. And whatever expedited economic development was unilaterally endorsed and encouraged, regardless of what the consequences might be. Consequences are things that happen to other people! Dam all the rivers! Mine all the minerals! Drill all the oil! We won't stop until there's a car in every driveway and a TV in every home!

This was a time period known to historians as the Great Compression, owing to the phenomenon of wage compression—that is, reduction of income disparity—that occurred between about 1945 and the early 1970s. Economic inequality between the richest and poorest citizens shrank to a gap that was practically razor-thin compared to the abyssal chasm it comprises now. Although a lot of factors went into this inequality-compressing, economists give the lion's share of credit to progressive taxation, with slightly lesser shares going to unionization, price and wage controls, and a widespread sense of post-victory solidarity. I can hardly imagine what any of that was like.

By such means, the economy grew by about thirty-seven percent during the 1950s, and with it came a cultural backlash against the rationing of the war years in the form of consumerism. That's not an easy term to define, but the essence of a consumption economy—as opposed to a production economy—is prioritization of meeting the whimsical wants of *customers* over the practical needs of *citizens*. Mainstream culture in the United States swung madly toward the customer or consumer end of that spectrum during the post-war boom. By the end of the decade, despite representing just six percent of the world's population, Americans were consuming roughly one-third of its total goods and services.

Promotion of consumer goods exploded during this time as well, more than doubling between 1950 and the early 1960s, and the formerly nascent and localized practice of "advertising" mushroomed with startling haste toward the assaulting ubiquity that characterizes it today. Forests were converted into newspaper ads and billboards advertising the latest trendy gewgaws that would themselves wind up as garbage in ever-increasing piles where the forests used to be.

People who sensed that this might not last forever were branded as unpatriotic or, worse, as communists. The former would get you ridiculed by certain types, the same as it does now. The latter could destroy your life.

Trouble doesn't take long to brew in a stewpot of reiterative wastefulness, however, and soon enough the consequences shrugged-off during the Boom Years started making themselves a little harder to ignore. Rivers, for example—being principally defined as moving water and, thus, fundamentally resilient to things like catching fire—started catching fire. Wilderness, formerly considered rather noisy places on account of various choirs of songbirds, became quieter and quieter. The very air itself started looking awfully brown.

Out of this sprang a resurgence in the slumbering conservationist movement, along with the emergence of environmentalism in US culture—the latter being commonly defined as a more obtrusive and (understandably) emotional version of the former. My colleagues and I tend to identify as conservationists rather than environmentalists, given a tendency to conduct research and work with nonprofits rather than chain ourselves to trees, although the distinction is largely moot. I've certainly taken part in a protest or two. I don't know many conservationists who haven't.

Political and social responses to these developments are legion. According to the Environmental Protection Agency, most major environmental statutes were passed between the late 1960s and early 1980s. Environmental protection laws were popping up with almost the same fecundity as billboards.

To give just one example: inspired by conservation pioneers like Theodore Roosevelt and spurred by the eruption of environmentalism, Interior Secretary Stewart Udall launched what he called the Third Conservation Wave. At its core was the philosophy—although I'd call it more of an observation—that natural resources are finite components of larger systems on which all life ultimately depends. Accordingly, in his opinion, the role and function of land management agencies is to manage these resources carefully and intelligently. Udall personally oversaw the creation of four national parks, six national monuments, eight national seashores and lakeshores, nine national recreation areas, twenty national historic sites, and fifty-six national wildlife refuges during his eight-year tenure.

On an interesting side note, it was also Udall who forced the owner of the Washington Redskins to desegregate his team, the very last in the NFL to do so, by threatening to kick them out of their NPS-affiliated stadium if they didn't. It's only too bad he couldn't do anything about their name while he was at it—that would take a bit longer.

The influence of America's growing conservation movement was also felt in American archaeology, during this time period. As archaeology became increasingly institutionalized and data-collection methods improved, concerns about how little was being done for the preservation of archaeological resources grew apace. Material culture in general, and Indigenous material culture in particular, was still largely regarded as treasure to be collected, data to be mined, or very old garbage to be cleared away so something new and shiny could be built.

Granted, the Antiquities Act dates all the way back to 1906, at least partly in response to observations by Kidder and Cummings of the rapacious looting taking place in southeastern Utah. It was created to respond to practices like those by making them illegal. But the Act itself doesn't pack a lot of wallop, outside of giving presidents the ability to create or enlarge national monuments in order to protect things worth protecting. It does mandate a fine of up to five hundred dollars and/or up to ninety days in jail for excavating archaeological sites on federal land without a permit, but in many of the cases where it was cited the litigants appealed on the grounds that its wording was unconstitutionally vague. Besides which, as both economic inflation and the market for illicit antiquities grew, five hundred dollars became less like a catastrophic forfeiture and more like a business expense.

There was also the nonprofit National Trust for Historic Preservation, which was founded during the stretch of time between the Antiquities Act and the midcentury conservation movement (specifically in 1949) by congressional charter. Their mission is to "engage America's diverse communities in preserving and sharing the stories and places that matter to them." That's an impressively bold mission statement for its time, especially the part about "America's diverse communities," and they continue to strive toward that goal to this day. In 2019, they included the Bears Ears area on their list of America's 11 Most Endangered Historic Places, which is nice—but, again, that doesn't do a whole lot with regard to protective legislation.

This is where the Reservoir Salvage Act of 1960 comes back into the picture. Although it didn't accomplish much in terms of protecting archaeological resources beyond telling the NPS to cover the tab, it did begin to establish several archaeology-themed job positions within the federal government. Of all the steps taken to compel land management agencies to take the management and protection of archaeological resources more seriously, that was one of the biggest.

Then came the biggest step of all: the National Historic Preservation Act (NHPA) of 1966. Section 106 of the NHPA required that federal agencies consider the effects of any development project on historic properties that are included on the National Register of Historic Places. It is compliance with Section 106 of the NHPA that drives the overwhelming majority of contracted archaeological work in the present day, which is why it's sometimes nicknamed the Care and Feeding of Archaeologists.

In 1969, NHPA was followed up by the National Environmental Policy Act (NEPA), which included an umbrella requirement that federal agencies consider all potential environmental effects of projects undertaken with some component of federal involvement. This involvement can mean funding, or that the project is taking place on public lands, or requires federal oversight, or whatever. Given that the environment includes both natural and cultural resources, this has obvious implications for archaeology, although satisfaction of the demands of NHPA Section 106 is often assumed to be more than adequate in any case. This became an even truer assumption starting in 1972, thanks to an executive order that greatly expanded its preservation powers.

With Executive Order 11593,* the purview of Section 106 of the NHPA was greatly expanded as agencies were directed to consider effects not just to places listed on the National Register of Historic Places, but to places that were simply *eligible* for it, and to develop standards for determining that eligibility. That's a big task. As cultural resource law guru Thomas F. King writes in *Thinking about Cultural Resource Management: Essays from the Edge*, "no agency is really fully staffed to carry out Section 106 review in accordance with the regulations on every one of its projects." For that reason, many private-sector cultural resource management

---

* Both NEPA and EO 11593 were creations of Republican president Richard Nixon, by the way, which points up how frustratingly partisan environmental protection has become in recent years.

(CRM) firms have materialized to help government agencies and, by extension, development project proponents comply with the requirements of NHPA. That's the easiest way to earn a paycheck if you've got a degree in archaeology.

Of course, the one blanket qualifier for everything that's potentially eligible for the National Register of Historical Places is that it has to be *historic*. The National Register stipulates that "properties that have achieved significance within the past fifty years shall not be considered eligible" unless they are of "exceptional importance." This has been handily inverted to mean that anything fifty years old or older needs to be considered potentially eligible for historic preservation, which is unfortunate because fifty years is *nothing*. It means that an embarrassing amount of inventory and curation funding gets punted off onto stuff that your own parents probably threw into the trash when you were a kid.

On the bright side, the fifty-year rule also makes for some fun gift-giving traditions on the fiftieth birthdays of archaeologists themselves. Embalming fluid is a favorite.

Because of all this, local BLM officials began taking a greater interest in management and preservation of archaeological resources in the Bears Ears area by the mid-1960s. In the early 1970s, they contracted with the Museum of Northern Arizona to conduct a series of cleanup and salvage operations in and around Grand Gulch, then and now the crown jewel of Cedar Mesa. They awarded another contract to the MNA in 1976 to assess the archaeological resources in areas being considered for addition to a newly created Grand Gulch Primitive Area, with the Glen Canyon and Cedar Mesa Projects' own Bill Lipe at the helm.

These and similar projects represented efforts to prevent looting and vandalism beyond what had already occurred, and were conducted in anticipation of recreational usage being most intensive inside the canyons. It was a prescient move, which is not something people often say about the BLM, and they deserve accolades for it. Recreation has indeed escalated dramatically in the Bears Ears area, and it is indeed focused mostly within the canyons.

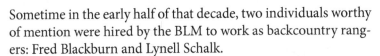

Sometime in the early half of that decade, two individuals worthy of mention were hired by the BLM to work as backcountry rangers: Fred Blackburn and Lynell Schalk.

Fred Blackburn appears throughout this book, and with good reason. He wound up getting so interested in the recent and ancient history of the area that he has become one of its most celebrated historians. Recognizing the disparity between the written records that (sometimes) accompanied the artifacts associated with the earliest archaeological work in the Bears Ears area, Blackburn and his team—including Vaughn Hadenfeldt, who would go on to become a legendary local hiking guide and one of the area's most vociferous conservationists—effectively invented the process of "reverse archaeology" to try and fix it.

Before all that, however, Fred was a BLM ranger who mostly chased pothunters, many of whom were obnoxiously bold in the 1970s and '80s. According to him, they would occasionally leave human skulls in prominent places just to taunt local archaeologists and law enforcement personnel alike. While cleaning out the Recreation Shed for the Manti-La Sal National Forest, back in the summer of 2016, my coworkers and I found some disturbing old photographs taken by Fred which depicted exactly that. What steered him toward historic preservation in the first place was an episode involving Bill Lipe, who was in the same place running the Cedar Mesa Project—and, with some consequence, trying to help Tom Windes get a local looter arrested—at that time.

Another of the photos that we randomly found on that shelf in the Manti-La Sal Rec Shed depicted four gorgeous little ceramic vessels that Fred had discovered in 1973 while helping the foreman of the TY Cattle Company move some cows out of heavy forest so that it could be chained. As he recounted the story to me back in 2016:

> This was the first pottery I had ever found, and I wanted to keep it, badly, but being a ranger and supposed to be protecting this resource created a dilemma of ethics. Bill Lipe was

working in the area at the time and I contacted him… Had I not done this, my life and career would have taken an entirely different direction! What Bill did for me was to teach me that the information was way more interesting than the object, creating a life-long interest in the Kayenta Puebloan people. Bill told me that at that time it was the northernmost example of pure Kayenta presence. Would not be surprised if that has changed by now…

And it has, of course. There are now *hundreds* of recorded instances of Kayenta presence in both the Bears Ears and Grand Staircase areas. I've recorded some of these artifacts in the course of my own work, and they are simply gorgeous. Fred's find was definitely among the first in the modern era, however—and it started him down a path that has yielded an incredible wealth of historical knowledge and preservation advocacy ever since.

Then there's Lynell Schalk. She worked as a lead ranger for the BLM in the 1970s, and was one of the first women to serve in law enforcement for the agency. In a 2005 interview for *Archaeology* magazine, Schalk told of how her standing order was a pointedly vague "go out there and stop the looting." She and her coworkers pursued looters on horseback and on foot, in trucks and in helicopters, and were out on patrols almost constantly.

Dealing with looters was only a small portion of their daily challenges, of course. The landscape itself, only marginally developed to this day, was still wild and fierce.

Still, probably the biggest challenge BLM rangers faced in those days was what to *do* with the looters once they'd spotted them. The only law in existence to prevent looting, back then, was the Antiquities Act, with its increasingly meager fine and supposedly unconstitutional vagueness. Looting wouldn't be made into a felony until 1979. Nor were the rangers allowed to carry guns, at least not at first.

In the end, it took a story about Schalk and her colleagues in the *New York Times*, followed by an angry letter to Interior Secretary Cecil Andrus by none other than Edward Abbey, before they were allowed to carry weapons when confronting what were often heavily armed looters. Abbey, a frequent visitor of the Bears Ears area, cloyingly referred to Schalk as a "girl-ranger" in another, more scathing letter he wrote expressing support for the BLM ranger program in general and for the greater need to preserve the cultural legacy of the entire Southwest.

One of the recipients of that letter was Senator Orrin Hatch, the longest-standing Republican senator in US history. Hatch drew considerable attention with a public comment in 2017 to the general effect of "Indians aren't smart enough to know how to properly manage land," which sent many non-bigoted people into an understandable rage. He finally retired at the end of 2018, prompting the *Salt Lake Tribune* to name him 2017 Utahn of the Year in satirical recognition of all the awful stuff he had accomplished in his forty-two-year stretch as a result of "his utter lack of integrity that rises from his unquenchable thirst for power."

Senator Hatch, who apparently didn't read past the headline, promptly shared the news story on his Twitter feed along with a heartfelt thanks to the *Tribune*. Always read past the headline, kiddos.

Thanks largely to all the historic preservation and environmental laws of the 1960s and early 1970s, CRM archaeology exploded in the 1980s. From that point right up to the present day, efforts conducted by universities, museums, and independent researchers represent only a small fraction of the total work that falls under the general heading of "archaeology."

Research by those sorts of institutions still goes on, of course—much of it following the classic formula of one group of people poking and prodding at the material history of *other* people in order to answer what often turn out to be asinine questions. "After spending five whole years and literal buckets of grant money analyzing thousands of animal bones excavated from hunting grounds that were sacred to the people now huddled together on a crappy reservation nearby, we have determined to a confidence interval of 0.99 that ancient Californians preferred fresh deer meat over rotting fish. Most of the time. Except when they didn't. More research is required to further refine these conclusions." (Fine work, lads. You're a credit to your kind.) But most of what comprises archaeology in the United States, these days, is conducted as a protective measure within the domain of CRM.

That shepherding of the field and its focus hasn't come without its own downsides. As Thomas F. King notes in a few of his publications, CRM is "a fancy term for trying to take care of what's important to people for cultural reasons." Again, this includes far more than just archaeological materials. It includes songs, stories, styles, rituals, and traditions. It includes languages. And it includes places that are considered culturally important or sacred to people whether they include archaeological materials or not. But few people working in the field interpret "cultural resources" as anything other than a complicated way of saying "archaeological stuff." This, in turn, means that the specific practice of CRM archaeology can potentially enable undertakings that don't impact material history but do impact culturally important places.

On the bright side, the inverse of that argument is just as valid. Archaeologists in the United States are gradually coming to recognize that cultural importance extends well beyond material history, and to endorse the positions of people who think of entire landscapes as important or sacred. That lesson would be expressed in a bold way on December 28, 2016.

Tracking the growth and development of the world of CRM, in the past several decades, is a utile way to track the growth and development of the world of American archaeology as a whole. The Glen Canyon Project and its impact has been discussed ad nauseam already, but it was just the first of three major projects identified and explained to me—and in publication—by Bill Lipe as exemplifying the biggest changes in the field thus far.

The Dolores Archaeological Project, or DAP to those who were on it, was one of the largest federally funded archaeological projects in US history. It took place between 1978 and 1985, and was carried out ahead of damming the Dolores River downstream from the town of Dolores in southwestern Colorado, just over the state border from Bears Ears, resulting in the creation of McPhee

Reservoir—where my friends from the area like to bring their fishing gear when they feel like drinking beer outdoors. After it was over, many of the DAP crew members wound up settling in the local area.

Numerous sociopolitical occurrences took place in the time between the Glen Canyon and Dolores Projects. Occurrences like the civil rights movement.

For a start, the emergence and spread of second-wave feminism* caused massive surges in the hiring of women throughout the private economic sector, including the field of archaeology. By the time I got into my own undergraduate program at Northern Arizona University, women had begun to outnumber men in a number of such programs. My undergraduate and graduate advisors were all women. In fact, as of this writing, there are three supervisors between me and the topmost brass in the CRM firm for whom I work, and all three of *them* are women.

When I asked a friend in Mancos why she thought archaeology had become so appealing to women, she responded (jokingly, I assume) that it was probably all to do with Indiana Jones. "Half of us have a crush on him. The other half want to discredit and outshine the thieving bastard."

This was also the era of the American Indian Movement and the Native American Rights Fund, when authors like Vine Deloria Jr. of the Standing Rock Sioux started publishing the sorts of acerbic things that I will never be able to resist quoting.** The American Indian Religious Freedom Act of 1978 secured Indigenous access to sacred sites—although the National Park Service still held firm to some of its own views on this, particularly with regard to which tribes had access to which sites—as well as

---

* First-wave feminism dates to the late 1800s, and at least one of its impacts on the field of archaeology was the creation of Mesa Verde National Park (see Chapter Four). The effects of third-wave feminism on the field have yet to be tallied up.

**Among my favorites: "Custer is said to have boasted that he could ride through the entire Sioux Nation with his Seventh Cavalry, and he was half right. He got half-way through."

the freedom to practice their religious ceremonies without legal interference.

This meant that archaeologists needed to include Native American consultation in their research designs, especially when those research designs were components of large projects conducted on public lands. As a result, archaeologists were compelled to go back to the way things were in the earlier part of the 1900s—before insistence on scientific objectivism mostly kicked them out—and actually talk to Indigenous people (with the unfortunate flipside effect that it also revivified what Steve Lekson calls the "pots = people" conceit of the early culture-historians). It was forced, and consisted largely of checking the box that says CONSULTED WITH TRIBES on federal regulatory documents, but it was a start.

This is where CRM-flavored archaeology confers a definite advantage over classic archaeology. It doesn't seek to give voice to historic or ancient people through the interpretation of their material heritage so much as *lend* them a voice in legal proceedings related to use and management of public lands. This is what all environmental regulations do, to one extent or another. Redwood trees and spotted owls can't vote, and neither can dead people (not legally, anyway), but natural and cultural resource legislation prevents them from being totally ignored.

The best mainstream depiction of this is probably the classic *Simpsons* episode titled "Lisa the Skeptic," in which the titular bookish saxophonist campaigns to make the developers of a new mall allow for an archaeological inventory ahead of construction. Hijinks ensue. At one point, Homer utters what I believe is the finest example of what often characterizes opposition to resource-protection laws: "You can't stop progress 'cause of some moldy old bones!"

This, in turn, precipitates all sorts of fun follow-up questions about exactly what constitutes *progress* and exactly whose *moldy old bones* we're talking about.

In most cases, compliance with cultural and natural resources legislation is just an added expense for the developer. This isn't a big deal with small-fry projects like putting a new door on a restroom in a national park, or putting up a sign nearby that says "Stop pooping in the bushes, you cretins—we fixed the door!" But there is an economy of scale involved, here. The bigger the project, the bigger its impact footprint, the more the contractor has to pay to deploy teams of specialists to make sure they aren't going to blast through a pyramid or whatever.

Those costs aren't usually enough to shut down a project, because developers aren't stupid and they know enough to build such expenses into their budgets in the first place, but simply paying for a cultural resource inventory (that is: investigation and assessment) can still be pretty expensive. And that's assuming the archaeologists don't find anything unexpected or special. Things can get *really* interesting when they do.

Case in point: back in the mid-2000s, a team of archaeologists discovered that the proposed location of a transit station for the Utah Transit Authority was also the location of an impressive Fremont village. The state of Utah took the side of numerous outspoken preservationists, pressuring the UTA to utilize any of a handful of other equally good locations for their railroad games. At first, anyway. But business is business, and Utah is Utah, so it didn't take much wheel-greasing for the state to reverse that position and support a land-swap deal that would switch the location of the site from public to private (this is a contingency that's allowable under NEPA in certain circumstances). It would destroy the site, of course, but it would also net the contractor building the station—and the agency overseeing their actions—a sweet stack of cheddar in the process. They promised they'd try to be nice about it.

Into this fray stepped Kevin Jones, my good friend and fellow conservationist who happened to be Utah's state archaeologist at the time. He and his two assistants, Ron Rood and Derinna Kopp, vehemently opposed the action on the grounds that it was blatantly unethical and more than a tad criminal to go *abracadabra* and make public land into private land, spiriting its public-ness away so its resource content wouldn't be a public issue anymore. Both NEPA and NHPA would still apply, after all, because UTA is funded in part by the federal government, so the fix still wouldn't (or shouldn't) sidestep those laws. Most local and regional Native American tribes also concurred with the state archaeologists' opposition, including the Ute Tribe, who identify the Fremont as their ancestors.

In response to all this, the UTA pulled some more strings, and in 2011 the three state archaeologist positions were removed.

Note that I didn't say the *people* were removed. The positions themselves were removed. Imagine if simply doing an important state-level job the way you're supposed to do it was enough to piss off the sort of people who are powerful and corrupt enough to make the job disappear.

To this day, Utah doesn't have a full-time state archaeologist. But it's not like there's anything in Utah that warrants having one, right?

As for that transit station: given all the hubbub and protests and whatnot, the UTA agreed to relocate it farther to the north— only to get into serious trouble with the feds for subsequent noncompliance and, believe it or not, damaging yet another three-thousand-year-old archaeological site. Oops. As restitution for their naughtiness, the state agency was ordered to set aside $250,000 (roughly twice the combined yearly salaries of the three dissolved positions) for archaeological conservation efforts.

Conspiracy theorists often believe that government agencies are capable of successfully executing enormous, complicated, and clandestine projects with seamless efficiency. Those of us who've had any experience with those agencies find this amusing.

In the Bears Ears area, these laws were brought to bear against the BLM in a history-making case. Cows have grazed allotments there since grazing allotments were invented, and about a century's worth of trampling, manure, invasive plant species, and once-standing prehistoric architecture knocked over by itchy bovine rumps testifies to this in almost every corner of the place. In 1990, a consortium of conservationists and wilderness advocates decided they'd had enough.

The BLM was legally challenged over failure to adequately account for the impacts of grazing in their blanket resource management plan for the Comb Wash allotment, where cows were busily wreaking havoc in lower Arch, Mule, Fish Creek, Owl Creek, and Road Canyons. According to NEPA, an environmental impact statement (EIS) is required for potentially environment-impacting practices like the doling out of grazing leases on federal lands, and the BLM insisted that the overarching impact study comprising the RMP was just fine—the same as they would say about the issue of fracking near Chaco a little over a decade later. The challengers disagreed, with some arguing that most of the RMP was copy-paste boilerplate that didn't consider specific impacts to specific localities at all. You'd be surprised how often that does happen.

One BLM employee even made the mistake of owning up to this, explaining that he only took amount and condition of forage into account when he set livestock numbers in the canyons. Things like water quality, wildlife habitat, soil erosion, scenery, and recreation weren't considered at all. He later tried to retract his testimony.

The plaintiffs, comprised largely of a number of conservation organizations, insisted that a separate EIS be done for specific impacts from grazing. They offered up the Grand Gulch Primitive Area as an example of the ecological benefits incurred when grazing is disallowed, and I would add to their testimony that I selfishly prefer not having to drink manure-flavored water while backpacking there.

The defendants, comprised largely of agribusiness lobbyists and affiliated fluffers, countered primarily on the basis of precedent. It's a slippery slope, they contended—if a bunch of damn environmentalists succeed in removing cows from five canyons that have little forage and lots of archaeology, they might go from there to kicking cows out of other beautiful and fragile public lands!

Wouldn't that be a shame?

That "slippery slope" argument is a funny one. You'll see it in legal cases all the time, particularly those that are even moderately publicized. As if behavior invariably snowballs. This is the same thinking behind the concept of gateway drugs, engendering impressively coruscating arguments about how allowing people to smoke marijuana is how you end up with an entire generation of heroin addicts.

Factual evidence often skews the other way, of course, but that's not a roadblock so much as a speed bump. Facts rarely shift the zealous.

Anyway, the case dragged on for about three years, and in the end it was a big win for the plaintiffs. This was the first time a federal judge in the United States ever considered the environmental impacts of grazing, and the extent to which having cows on public lands is in the best interests of the public. Imaginative strain was not required on the part of the judge; the case was simply a matter of compelling the agency to interpret the law in a less shady manner.

Of course, political legislation being what it is, a lot of these laws are open to rather shady interpretation indeed. Take the word *undertaking*. The NHPA process requires consideration of impacts to the environment from *undertakings* conducted by federal agencies, including consultation with stakeholders like Native American tribes affiliated with the associated lands and/or resources.

Most agency personnel interpret that in the most logical and straightforward way possible, in the same way that any sane individual defaults to a commonplace definition of *eating* or *breathing*.

Then there's the Army Corps of Engineers. When considering the construction and operation of the Dakota Access or Bakken Pipeline for pumping oil through land considered culturally important to the Standing Rock Sioux—for, among other reasons, its being a source of their drinking water—the Army Corps decided that doing so didn't quite fit their own definition of *undertaking*. They also hacked the proposed area of potential effect into itty bitty pieces instead of dealing with it as one big one, applied their own special definitions of "historic properties" and "cultural resources," and performed a few other handy prestidigitations in order to consider themselves legally compliant without having to consult with stakeholders.

The local Sioux community and other stakeholders respectfully disagreed with the Army Corps, as you might imagine they would, and weren't the least bit overjoyed about being left entirely out of the process. You've probably heard a few things about what happened next.

Standing Rock is one tip of a multifaceted iceberg, whose expansive subsurface extends back to the 1968 founding of the American Indian Movement, one major component of which is that Native Americans became a lot more animated in examining and criticizing archaeology's role in helping destroy their heritage through the process of "research." This growing struggle for sovereignty and voice also resulted in increasing numbers of Indigenous people wanting to take an active role in that research rather than criticizing it from the sidelines. The field was dominated by white people, of course—and, numerically speaking, still very much is—but Indigenous people were interested in getting more directly involved in what was, when you get right down to it, research and preservation of *their* history.

Thus, by the time of Lipe's third example—the 2002-2010 Animas-La Plata Project, which also occurred just over the Utah-Colorado border from Bears Ears but nearer to Durango—Native Americans were starting to fill positions as professional archaeologists.

Indigenous fieldworkers have been a component of Southwest archaeology since the days of Richard Wetherill, of course, who often hired (with varying levels of success) his Diné neighbors to help him pillage archaeological sites. But Indigenous archaeologists are in a different class. Theirs is the multivariate and tricky practice of using science to study and/or help protect the material record while simultaneously including paradigms and perspectives rooted in traditional cultural knowledge. It's an impressive task to tackle, and it attracts some impressive characters for that very reason.

This was brought home to me in a personal way when I was working as a bartender in Flagstaff in 2006, just about a month before my first trip to Grand Gulch. Early in the evening, a Hopi fellow a little older than me came in to have a short draft before going home. He noticed a fairly prominent tattoo on my arm, identified it as symbolizing "water sign" to himself and his ancestors, and proceeded to grill me over what it was doing on my body.

I nervously explained that it was modeled on the design that adorned the first piece of ancient pottery I'd ever found. I couldn't take the potsherd itself, because that was both immoral and illegal, so I'd borrowed the design instead. It symbolized my commitment to studying and helping preserve things like that piece of ancient pottery for the rest of my life, or at least for as long as people might hire me to do so (again: I was tending bar, at the time).

He found this answer an acceptable one—far better, at any rate, than the answers often provided by people with faux-Maori sleeves or dreamcatchers in decidedly unhandy places—and introduced himself as an archaeologist with the National Park Service. I was floored. The concept of a "Native American archaeologist" seemed to me about as likely as a "Hatfield-McCoy" or a "canine mailman." It would take many years of training and research before the preceding paragraphs fully sank in, and at the time I was simply dumbfounded. He got a kick out of that.

This is how I first met Lyle Balenquah. We would unexpectedly reconnect with each other eleven years later, thanks to the magnetic power of Bears Ears.

Some of what I'd been doing in that interim involved learning harsh lessons about American culture and our horrendous medical system. Quite apart from my research goals, the Bears Ears area had become a sanctuary for me. I never stopped daydreaming about those final pleasant memories of the place that I'd made back in 2011, just before falling ill, and much of my academic efforts were an excuse to keep going back there to make sure they stayed real.

The earliest portion of my horrific four-year experience with Lyme disease began while I was working in Glen Canyon as a seasonal archaeologist, and from there it followed me to Salt Lake City where I was scheduled to attend grad school. I deferred the first semester, for the hopefully obvious reason that my brain was a puddle of mud and *it was graduate school*, but thereupon learned that I would have to attend anyway. You'll never guess why.

I was working in what's called the Federal Pathways program, which awards full-time benefits to seasonal employees who are actively working toward a graduate degree. This proved a timely boon when I was diagnosed with Lyme and wound up needing about eighteen months of aggressive treatment, including about three months of intravenous antibiotics that necessitated sporting a catheter in my left forearm (scaring away all romantic interests, save one—and we're still friends because of that). That's the sort of thing that can catch you a lot of grief from bullies and dimwits when you're in high school, but one would think such mentalities wouldn't make it all the way to graduate school. One would be wrong.

I was in no condition to be pursuing a master's degree. I was, in fact, unable to negotiate shoelaces fully three days out of ten. And, with a small handful of exceptions, the students and faculty with whom I had to share that environment never missed an opportunity to remind me. Yet I had to, because withdrawal from the graduate program would also disqualify me from the Pathways program and its associated health insurance.

The thing is, this being the United States and all, even federal health insurance only knocked the price of my treatment and therapy from outrageously exorbitant down to merely exorbitant. My savings were completely depleted by about the one-year anniversary of falling ill. Rich relatives weren't an option, because I don't have any; and personal loans weren't an option, or at least personal loans with interest rates lower than cruel-and-unusual, for basically the same reason. However, student loans most assuredly were an option, just so long as I remained a student.

In other words: although I was mentally and physically and (increasingly, given the circumstances) emotionally crippled, I had to stay in school or I would lose the ability to pay for the medical treatments that were keeping me in the general vicinity of functional. I would end up in the same boat as many others of my generation, owing more money to my own government in the form of student loans than I would ever agree to pay for a house that doesn't include turrets and a drawbridge. But at least I'd be alive to whine about it.

On the other hand, the plan to conduct research that would keep me in and around the gorgeous and therapeutic Cedar Mesa worked like a charm. My sweet-natured classmate Michael Lewis helped me draft a couple of grant applications, and our equally sweet-natured advisor Joan Coltrain offered to endorse and direct the project. That's how I wound up studying the archaeology of agriculture, and why I know so much about Ancestral Pueblo dry-farming strategies in the Bears Ears area. Moreover, thanks to a couple of grants from the U's Global Change and Sustainability Center, I now had funding for gas and food to live out of a tent the way I had in northern Arizona half a decade before. Which was more than good enough for me, given where I was able to live.

I often say that the three surest steps to happiness in life are 1) find what you really want to do, 2) find where you really want to do it, and 3) find someone else to pay for it.

So, I spent as much time as I could in the Bears Ears area camping and wandering around, only this time I did so with a notebook and little glass vials for collecting water samples. I still had a lot of trouble with things like balance and depth perception, which can be slightly troublesome in a place that's celebrated for its canyons and cliff walls—but the more time I spent out there, the better I felt.

I also discovered that my sense of direction, or "internal GPS" as a dear friend likes to call it, was all but totally busted. Balance and depth perception both came back to me as the healing process winnowed on over the next few years, and even my malfunctioning short-term memory—one of the worst and most common grievances associated with all neurological afflictions—

eventually returned to almost normal. But not that first one. To this day I've got the uncanny ability to get hopelessly lost in any space bigger and more complicated than a gas station.

This made the whole "throw away the map" principle of turning the known into the unknown less like an exciting practice and more like a constant challenge, and I started amassing maps like a cartographic hoarder. Not that it helped a whole lot.

One lovely autumn week during the latter portion of this time, I decided to hike into Grand Gulch via the same route that I'd used during my first trip there back in 2006, in order to bliss out on some therapeutic nostalgia—and, if there was time, collect water samples for my research. During the time between that first trip and falling ill, I'd gone to visit the Bears Ears area on at least a dozen occasions, although I never went back into Grand Gulch. I don't know why. I suspect it's because of the burdensome innate compulsion we all have for novelty. I'd been there, after all; I'd done that. But I'm more often addicted to routine than I am to novelty, to the annoyance of more partners than I care to tally, so of course I was bound to return eventually.

I'm more inclined to think that long pause was the result of not wanting to spoil a perfect memory. My first trip to Grand Gulch stands out as one of the highest points of my life.

Having read about the place in various writings by David Roberts, Ann Zwinger, and a few others while living at the North Rim prior to commencement of undergraduate studies at NAU, my eagerness to see the place boiled over during my first semester back at school. I didn't realize this at the time, but it was also one hundred years (and five months) after passage of the Antiquities Act.

It took weeks and weeks of planning, which I'd never really done before. Trips into the backcountry prior to that one had consisted mostly of Grand Canyon coworkers shoving a beer into my hand with a hearty, "What are *you* doing this weekend? I've got an idea…" It was my first attempt at the sort of logistical thinking that can get a person killed if it isn't done properly—as I would learn ten years later in the summer of 2016 when, despite being older and wiser and more careful by far, a flash flood in the lower Gulch nearly brought my tale to a quick and crunchy end.

One thing I figured out during the planning stage for that first trip was that, owing partly to my upbringing and partly to my own idiosyncratic quirks (although in what proportions I cannot guess), I was still very much a cheapskate. Dinner was the same thing every night: boil-in-bag rice with a pouch of Tasty Bites heated beside it in the same water, then I'd pour sugar and cinnamon into the rice-infused water and have that as a sort of backcountry horchata. Cheap and easy, compared with those commercial freeze-dried affairs, except with about a third the calories. It was also in the weeks leading up to the trip that I realized every gas station, fast-food joint, and convenience store in the country has piles of little single-serving condiments just sitting there for backpackers to grab. The best and rarest of them are good honey and good hot sauce; stuff your pockets with those whenever you get the chance.

Of course, as Sancho Panza famously quipped, "the best sauce in the world is hunger." Forget to pack enough calorie-rich food on a backpacking trip and you'll learn this, too.

The plan was to stash my backpack safely in the woods some-where near the Kane Gulch Ranger Station, drive down to the Bullet Canyon trailhead and leave my rusty 4Runner there, and then ride my newly acquired and also rusty mountain bike along the highway back to where the backpack was waiting. I would camp someplace nearby for the rest of the night (which you can't actually do, by the way), and start into Grand Gulch via Kane bright and early the next morning. And I stuck to that plan—right up to the part where I was supposed to start the backpack-ing part bright and early the next morning.

Instead, pumped up from the mix CD my girlfriend had burned for me and even more pumped up for the trip itself, I set off that very night. In the pitch dark. Into a deep and winding canyon* that I'd never visited before.

Because of Grand Gulch's increasing popularity at the time

---

* I've never been able to wrap my head around the difference between a *canyon* and a *gulch*, and no amount of browbeating can convince me that Grand Gulch and Kane Gulch aren't a commingling pair of canyons.

of that first trip, my going there over Thanksgiving was at least partly motivated by a desire to avoid other people, the bulk of whom would presumably be doing things like eating turkey and screaming at each other about politics. I needn't have bothered, in any case. Popularity is a relative metric, and by 2006 the upper third of Grand Gulch was getting popular *for Grand Gulch*. The only other person that I encountered on the mesa top, a certifiable Old Timer who'd hiked every nook and cranny of the Bears Ears area since I was in diapers, cracked jokes about this when I met him. "It's getting popular in the Davy Crockett sense," he assured me. "But it only feels crowded to grumpy folks like me. It'll probably never be *crowded* crowded."

As of this writing, that was almost exactly fourteen years ago, and I would definitely say that it's starting to get "*crowded* crowded" now. Or maybe I'm just becoming grumpy, too?

The main thing that I got for my planning back in 2006 was ice that froze over during the night, although on the plus side it didn't snow while I was down in the canyon bottoms. And the mice, which can be pestilential to the point of maddening in upper Grand Gulch, never showed. And there weren't any of the loathsome little monsters known locally as cedar gnats, my top candidate for the national bird of Hell. It was almost unimaginably serene.

When I dropped back into the gulch for a few days in 2013, much had changed. I had trouble remembering what it was like in any case, thanks to my still being a good way behind the finish line of the healing process. I should also explain right now that, in many—if not most—cases of neurological affliction, that finish line is what mathematicians call an unapproachable limit. An event horizon. Zeno's paradox. As with heartbreak, you never completely get over it; the roar just gets quieter and quieter, until it's drowned out by other things. But it's still there.

Again, I can get lost in a supermarket. That's how I know I'll never be completely over it.

Still, I'm a bit of a shutterbug, so I had photographs of that first trip. I even brought some of them with me on the second one.

What I didn't bring was a GPS, having not realized how badly my senses were buggered, and I ended up getting lost. I didn't even know such a thing was possible inside a canyon, given that they are great geological furrows with steep walls on either side. That's like a bowling ball getting lost in a gutter.

Nevertheless, I somehow managed it, and I ended up a day late climbing out. I'd had to filter water from a big puddle with my bandana, which made me feel oddly proud. And I'd outstripped my store of food, of course—which lent the whole thing a pseudo-religious air, as if I'd spent several days stumbling and fasting in a gigantic cathedral. And, in a way, I had.

I emerged in a state of dizzying bliss. There was no girlfriend and no mix CD awaiting my return, that time, but I still felt better than I had in almost three years. In retrospect, it was the first time that I felt truly *happy* since the summer of 2010.

I wasn't exactly okay, yet. Far from it. But I finally started to believe it was possible.

Chapter Eleven: The Pillagers

The first pillaging of the Bears Ears area was by what are variously called looters, pothunters, or grave robbers (this last is, of course, not to be confused with professional archaeologists—or at least not anymore). There were two major surges in antiquities looting in southeast Utah, one in the late 1800s and the other in the mid to late 1900s, the first one occurring because of a perfect storm of coincidence: an economic depression occurred in the 1890s following a series of developments that undermined the public's confidence to the point of panic. Confidence that was already more than a little strained following the devastation that precipitated the so-called Closing of the West by about 1890.

Kicking the party off was the collapse of Reading Railroad in 1893,* which precipitated a stock market plunge in the East. At the same time, the explosion of settlement and farming in the West had what should have been predictable results, with outputs of crops like wheat and maize doubling between 1870 and 1890 while the nation's population only increased by a third—causing prices to plummet in the glut. In some cases, wheat prices fell well below the cost of production, and a common response was to produce still more wheat—i.e., add to the surplus—in order for farmers to hopefully sell enough to make ends meet.

President Grover Cleveland initially responded to these calamities by ignoring them, believing that business cycles

---

* Someone really needs to investigate what the planets were up to that year.

operate naturally and are best not meddled with. But he cared a great deal about the nation's depleted gold reserve, deeply drained by the Sherman Silver Purchase Act and lavish spending by the previous Congress. Realizing these two contingencies might touch each other in the fullness of time, President Cleveland scrambled to rescue the gold standard, but in so doing he created a jagged rift in the Democratic Party and let the already tense populace know just how bad things had gotten. Their already-strained confidence shattered. The resulting Panic of '93, as it's sometimes called, kicked off one of the worst depressions in American history.

Meanwhile, in the years leading up to this economic plunge, some of the earlier players in this book had busied themselves alerting the nation—and, as evidenced by Nordenskiöld, the world—to the rich and wondrous world of Four Corners archaeology. There were the photographs and drawings by Jackson in the Hayden reports, the artifact collections of McLoyd and Graham being shown off by Reverend Green, the sensational adventure-and-excavation exploits of Moorehead in *The Illustrated American*, and the collections and publications of the Wetherills and their friends and sponsors. Treasure, it seemed, was all over the place in the Four Corners area, and there weren't any laws forbidding its extraction and sale. In those circumstances, turning to the practice of looting to hopefully put food on the table made a lot of sense, and many people did so—including Earl Morris's father.

The depression of the 1890s lasted until about 1897, although recovery from an economic slump isn't felt in all areas or all sectors of the economy at the same time, and its effects can reverberate almost indefinitely. The mortgage-linked recession of 2008 was "resolved" by about 2012 thanks to gutsy bipartisan action by GW, Obama, and a small army of advisors and economic specialists; but the downstream effects of that panic were still being felt when the pandemic-linked recession hit. One of those lingering effects was the creation of the Tea Party, in revolt against using taxpayer money to bail out Wall Street. Another one was the Trump administration.

While the post-1893 Panic economy was looking more like the post-2008 Recession economy on the national scale, conditions in southeastern Utah limped along in tandem. Passage of the Antiquities Act in 1906 had a quashing effect on the illicit antiquities market that made looting a much less profitable enterprise, so it trickled down to only those few individuals and families who'd gotten totally hooked on it. But it didn't go away altogether, and some of the blame rests with the field of archaeology itself.

Following the kindly Dean Cummings' departure from the University of Utah in 1915, care and feeding of the U's museum collections fell largely to another professor, Andrew Kerr, who added substantially to those collections by hiring San Juan County locals to dig sites on his behalf. One of them was the grandfather of Earl Shumway, who would later go down as the most notorious looter in the region.

By such means did pothunting linger on, although I can find little evidence to support the contention that it was ever more than a pastime activity for a small number of locals after the market dried up following the late 1800s depression. In any case, it seems to have declined somewhat in popularity by the early to middle 1900s. And then, starting in the 1970s and going well into the '80s, it surged again—and for reasons that are altogether different and more culturally embarrassing.

What would now be decried as cultural appropriation of Native American traditions began to occur first among the hippies, cultural descendants of the beatniks in the 1960s. They decided that rejection of modern values and toxic technophilia was our only salvation and, therefore, we should act like the wise and noble Indians acted: living lightly on the land, respecting nature in all its guises, and wearing lots of beads and feathers. (The real Native Americans, meanwhile, were busily trying to get jobs and political sovereignty.) They routinely made pilgrimages to seek spiritual guidance on reservations, bringing nothing to contribute except hungry mouths and generally making a nuisance of themselves. Frank Waters' history-ethnography effort *The Book of the Hopi*, published in 1963, generated a full-fledged cult following that had gangs of motley fools converging on the ancient stone towns of the Hopis and other Pueblo peoples like a visiting plague. The 1969 film *Easy Rider*, not so much a celebration of the hippie movement as a eulogy for it, featured scenes at Taos Pueblo for this very reason.

It was about this time that nigh-ubiquitous Southwest Indigenous character Kokopelli began appearing in more and more places in mainstream culture than just Santa Fe, although "Kokopellimania"—as some have called it—didn't reach its full zenith until the 1990s. Meanwhile, the so-called New Age movement came to full flower in the 1980s, and some of them flocked to Indigenous spiritual practices as well, chummed in by what Native scholars call "plastic medicine" peddlers writing books and selling Native American-looking gewgaws alongside Chinese incense and Tibetan prayer beads. One salty archaeologist I know calls them "crystal bangers," and has ever since they and their faux-Indigenous practices started popping up at archaeological sites in the Bears Ears and Sedona areas during this time period.

Nor has Native American art and regalia ceased being hip in mainstream American culture to this day, despite widespread misunderstandings about its actual symbolism. Take dream-catchers, for example—those little wooden hoops with crisscrossing strings and feathers dangling beneath. As their name implies, their traditional function (one of them, anyway; their full traditional significance is *really* complicated) is to catch bad dreams the way that a spider catches flies, in order to keep them from going forth into the world and manifesting as reality. Thus, hanging one from your rearview mirror only makes sense if you sleep in your car, and wearing one on your body during daylight hours makes even less sense. I once knew a bleach-blonde girl with an enormous dreamcatcher tattoo that can only be seen in full when she's naked, knowledge of which compelled me to crack so many jokes about her love life that we're no longer friends.

This surging interest in Native American crafts and practices was also accompanied in the 1960s and '70s by the aforementioned American Indian Movement, which included the 1969 seizure of Alcatraz and 1972 occupation of the Bureau of Indian

Affairs headquarters in DC. Mainstream culture wasn't unaware of all this. The cover of the July-August 1972 issue of *Art in America* featured a close-up image of a stereotype Plains warrior festooned with neon on a trading post in New Mexico. Inside, the issue focused on Native American artists. The magazine didn't have much impact, socially speaking, although I personally love it for its inclusion of an article by Vine Deloria Jr. But it reflects the growing consensus among its intended audience. An elaborate headdress or ancient polychrome bowl were trendy accompaniments to the Maxfield Parrish print hanging in the parlor.

So, the second major surge in pothunting in the Four Corners was a lot like that of wildlife poaching: providing illicit paraphernalia to a market comprised partly of wealthy collectors looking to expand their array of trendy baubles and partly of half-educated rubes who thought it might help their cockamamie rituals work better. Impacts to the local archaeology weren't overly dissimilar from those caused by poachers, either with carcasses ripped apart and then laid to rot after the precious sought-after portion was wrenched free.

Local archaeologists, conservationists, Native Americans, and other people possessed of sanity and feelings decried this eruption of widespread looting. A young Tom Windes was the archaeologist for the Manti-La Sal National Forest in the early 1970s—one of the very first Forest Service archaeologists in the county—and remembers when he tried to bust somebody for looting before the passage of the Archaeological Resources Protection Act. He'd found a Blanding resident digging on Forest Service lands in '72 and, with help from Bill Lipe, managed to get the guy fined seventy-five dollars for violating the Antiquities Act.

The perpetrator turned out to be a friend of the district ranger, who was a bit of a pothunter himself, and Tom was consequently hounded out of the area. I've borne witness to more recent versions of this. Tom ended spending the bulk of his career doing dendrochronology in Chaco Canyon, where he's practically a legend, before finally returning to the Bears Ears area to conduct tree-ring sampling with a group of volunteers called the Wood Rats.

Darrel Lyman—also of Blanding—became the first person prosecuted and convicted under ARPA after it was enacted in 1979, being given a fine of $1,500 (half of it was subsequently suspended) and two years of probation in exchange for testifying about an accomplice in the looting of the midden at Turkey Pen Ruin. His accomplice, Casey Shumway, pleaded not guilty, and thus became the first person to be tried in a courtroom under the new law. He ended up with a verdict of not guilty because, if you can believe it, the judge and jury decided on their own that since a midden was technically a trash pile it wasn't really an archaeological resource.

Ironically enough, Casey Shumway was instead found guilty of Malicious Mischief (USC 1361, Title 18) for destroying federal property, a crime that carried a stiffer penalty than ARPA at the time.

The biggest fish of all was Earl K. Shumway. He grew up in Moab, a distant cousin of the Casey Shumway mentioned above and son of DeLoy Shumway, who'd learned the fine art of looting from his own father, who'd learned it from Professor Kerr. Earl was first indicted on four felony counts of violating ARPA in 1985 at the age of twenty-five. During and after the trial, he established a reputation for himself by openly bragging about how much money he made looting, how he always carried a gun in case he needed to shoot any cops, and how he littered all of his looted sites with empty Mountain Dew cans.

In 1986 he was busted again, and, in order to avoid a prison sentence, named a long list of fellow looters that led to a series of raids on homes and trading posts around Blanding—in which two of the county's three commissioners were netted. Young Earl was released, and went right back at it. He met and convinced a helicopter pilot named Michael Miller to help him in 1991, and another helicopter pilot named John Ruhl agreed to fly the two around in search of sites to plunder (Earl's father had taught him how to spot likely sites from the air). This gave the added advantage of an airborne lookout while they were digging. His exploits became the stuff of legend—especially his treatment of skeletons.

During this time, mostly in response to the two county commissioners getting busted, a few locals in Blanding convened a series of meetings to discuss ARPA and their resentment of it. In a 2009 study on looting and arrests in the Four Corners for the journal *Crime, Law, and Social Change*, researcher Jennifer Goddard cites a pair of local newspaper editorials published in 1985 that serve as apt descriptors. The first one stated plainly that so-called professional archaeologists were wrong in their contention that continued pothunting would mean the loss of many archaeological sites over the next few years, resulting in their being "without a job," and that they would "have to learn as much as the pothunters know in order to understand this." The second one attacked federal legislators for being duped by what it called "inexperienced plunderers (aka archaeologists)," and attested that we wouldn't know anything about "Anasazi culture" if it wasn't for the careful work of local pothunters. You can't make this stuff up.

Meanwhile, Earl was busted yet again in 1994, and at his 1995 trial he was convicted thanks to DNA evidence taken from a cigarette butt. What awaited him this time had *teeth*.

While ARPA added a bit of judiciary potency to the "antiquities" component of the Antiquities Act, another bill had passed between Earl's 1985 and 1994 brushes with the law: the Native American Graves Protection and Repatriation Act, or NAGPRA. To this day, it remains the fiercest piece of federal legislation regarding archaeological sites and materials in the United States.

That law came about largely because of a Native American woman named Maria Darlene Pearson, also known as Hai-Mecha Eunka ("Running Moccasins"), a Yankton Sioux activist who'd simply had it with how Indigenous remains were treated by looters and professionals alike. Her husband worked for the Iowa Department of Transportation, and when both Anglo and Native remains were found during road construction in the 1970s the Anglo remains were quickly reburied—while the Native ones, specifically a mother and child, were sent to a lab to be studied by some eager graduate student. Pearson furiously protested,

eventually obtaining the audience of the governor who consequently enacted the Iowa Burials Protection Act of 1976.

She didn't stop there. Taking the fight to national leaders,
Pearson's efforts resulted in the language written into NAGPRA
when it passed in 1990.

However, NAGPRA isn't without its own problems. For
one thing, as Thomas F. King loves to point out, its language is
"grounded in property law," directing federal agencies and museums to repatriate funerary items to the tribes that "own" them.
Outside of foisting Western concepts of ownership on cultures
that very rarely share them, this also engenders the obvious and
often infuriating task of legally establishing who, exactly, is a lin-
eal descendent. In some cases, this can lead to mutually beneficial
cross-cultural efforts. In others, it can be poisonous.

Imperfect law that still needs a lot of work though it may
be, NAGPRA is still a big step in the right direction. And it certainly packs a wallop. Punishments for a *first offense* can include
$100,000 in fines and a year in the clink.

With that potent decree now in force, Earl Shumway became
the first to feel its fangs. The judge made special note of Shumway's
treatment of infant remains, going as far as trying to enhance the
punishment by invoking the "vulnerable victim" clause, and sentenced him to six and a half years in prison with a $3,500 fine.
He was beaten nearly to death by a group of Native Americans
while being transported to prison, which should appear in the
dictionary under *schadenfreude*, and died of cancer shortly after
serving his sentence.

So ended the reign of Earl K. Shumway, called by true crime
blogger Jim Fisher the "John Dillinger of Archaeological Looting." But the looting itself continued.

By the early 2000s, the BLM decided enough was enough, and
teamed up with the FBI in what came to be known as Operation
Cerberus Action, named for the three-headed dog that guarded
the gates of the Underworld in ancient Greek mythology—his
most recent mainstream appearance being a walk-on cameo as
Fluffy in *Harry Potter and the Sorcerer's Stone*. They targeted a
down-on-his-luck man with a history of mental problems named

Ted Gardiner to go undercover as a looted-antiquities buyer, in full cop-show fashion: wires, hidden cameras, traceable bills for purchases, and so on.

What followed was several years of information-gathering that ultimately led to a massive series of raids in 2009. The feds particularly targeted beloved Blanding physician Dr. Jim Redd, whose wife Jeannie was—and, for all I know, still is—a passionate and addic-ted looter. During the undercover investigation, Jeannie openly talked about a site she had looted known as Baby Mummy Cave, where Dean Cummings had apparently found a handful of infant burials (which he chose to leave undisturbed) during his own work in the area. Local archaeologist Winston Hurst visited Baby Mummy Cave soon after it was looted, where he found that coyotes had gotten to—yes—an unearthed infant and torn a few bits off, which he sadly bundled together and reburied within the site.*

Remember, horrid mistreatment of infant burials is what filled the judge with fire and fury in Earl Shumway's trial in 1995. Candidly talking about rummaging around in a place where, according to her own voice on the official record, "five babies were buried" should have shifted the crosshairs squarely toward Jeannie Redd. But it was her husband the authorities wanted most. Understanding why that is requires a bit of a run-up.

As near as I can tell, the most likely answer is something psychologists call *narrative bias*, or the tendency of people raised on repetitive story structures to carry an expectation of those structures into real life. The most common story structure in our culture is the narrative arc that begins with equilibrium, then conflict is introduced, a bunch of action takes place, the conflict is resolved with some major change having taken place (the main character learns a lesson, or gets the big prize, or whatever), and it ends with a return to equilibrium in a world made slightly better—or, in the case of a tragedy, worse—by whatever happened

---

* That particular story appears in *Finders Keepers: A Tale of Archaeological Plunder and Obsession* by Craig Childs. Whether he was cleaning up after Jeannie or some other looter is not known to me.

during the arc. When real-life events don't adhere to a recognizable storyline structure like that one, people often just tune them out.

Wars are a handy way to wrap your head around this. World War II, for example, had all the elements: beginning, middle, and end; a big conflict with what is still touted by its victors as a satisfactory resolution; genuine heroes; and, of greatest importance, genuine villains. This is why you can find enough movies, TV shows, and books about World War II to fill the warehouse at the end of *Raiders of the Lost Ark*.

Compare that with the war in Afghanistan, which doesn't fit a classical narrative structure in *any* of those senses. A study conducted by Rasmussen Reports in July of 2018 revealed that as many as forty-two percent of Americans didn't even realize that war was still going on. No clear beginning/middle/end, no conflict resolution (obviously), no clear heroes, and no clear villains have effectively made it into a non-story to them. I can only imagine how our men and women in uniform feel about this.

The villain is of greatest importance in narratives of a martial nature. You can have a military or law-enforcement action with no big heroes, and Cerberus certainly doesn't have any of those. But you'd better have a big villain, or people might get funny ideas about your story—or, worse, ignore it altogether. A poor local boy hunting for a quick buck wouldn't do, in this particular story, and a woman doesn't fit the culturally prescribed bill either. You need an evil and socially powerful man, a Snidely Whiplash or a Lex Luthor, even if that means you've got to create one. And they certainly tried to, with dire consequences.

I know a few of the folks who participated in the Cerberus raids. What they saw in many of them turned their stomachs. It was like scenes from the reality television show *Hoarders*.

In addition to dressers and cabinets filled with exquisite Ancestral Pueblo artifacts, other common finds included mountains of fly-ridden fast food containers, ashtrays of every conceivable construction that were almost always overflowing, plates of rotting food, punch- and kick-holes in walls and doors, dead plants, dead *pets*, and—this part helps explains the rest—meth paraphernalia.

It turns out the Snidely Whiplash-like villain hiring teams of professional goons to help steal golden idols before the dashing hero can steal them himself is largely a myth on both conceptual sides. I've mentioned before how the idea of archaeologists as people who primarily snatch ancient treasures and bundle them off to museums is antiquated. We want to solve the mysteries of the past, reconstruct patterns of behavior, and/or help Indigenous peoples in resource preservation and cultural sovereignty battles—none of which is especially conducive to being thing-obsessed.

Many of the serious archaeologists I know think of artifacts not as treasures so much as annoyances, believe it or not, leastwise because they often require expensive curation efforts. So many artifacts end up in curation facilities—museums, universities, state and federal storage facilities, and so on—that professionals in that corner of the realm have begun referring to it as a "crisis."

The chasm between reality and the other side of the myth gapes just as wide. Serious collectors of antiquities aren't interested in most of what looters in the Southwest dig up. A fully intact turkey-feather blanket or an exquisitely decorated kiva jar, sure—but the chances of unearthing either of those during routine pothunting are vanishingly small. Instead, the bell curve of looting is principally composed of two camps: those who do it for fun and/or to spite the government and the tribes, like Earl Shumway; and squalid addict types, who know they can only get about fifty dollars for a corrugated Pueblo II jar on the local black market and that's just fine with them. Fifty bucks pays for enough junk food, PBR, and meth to survive at least another week or two.

And here's where the local community has good reason to despise the legacy of Cerberus. Meth addiction—drug and alcohol abuse in general, for that matter—is a big problem in any impoverished community in the United States, regardless of the dominating ethnicity or presence of churches or whatever all else, because the root problem is socioeconomic. It's the same in rural communities as it is in inner cities. Substance abuse and base violence are more strongly linked to economic distress and disparity than to any extraneous variable, like skin tone or local culture, because in our country we teach people that poverty is deplorable. In addition to brown air and burning rivers, that's another fun spinoff from the legacy of consumerism.

I grew up in a rural mobile-home community and went to a high school peopled mostly by well-off suburbanites, so I felt the sting of this nearly every day of my adolescence until I grabbed my diploma and fled to New Orleans. Hence the quote—variously attributed to either John Steinbeck or Ronald Wright—that the poor in America see themselves "not as an exploited proletariat but as temporarily embarrassed millionaires." According to the American Dream, anyone can start out from anywhere and rise to glittery opulence, the flipside of the myth being that anyone who *doesn't* do that has failed because of some fatal flaw on their part.

This is how you get enormous numbers of people insecure enough to hate themselves for bullshit reasons that are totally outside their control. And *that* is how you get a lot of abusive and self-destructive behavior.

So, it turns out San Juan County has some drug problems, just like every other community in America where economically challenged people of every conceivable stripe watch the Kardashians on TV and then hate themselves for not being that lucky. And addicts have trouble holding steady jobs, even when the local community has steady jobs for them to try to hold. And in small towns there isn't much of a market for things like stolen car stereos because everybody knows everybody and "say, didn't Phil over on First Street just have his car broken into yesterday…?" But ancient artifacts don't belong to your friends and neighbors, and people with money are typically inclined to collect things even when they don't need them.*

---

* Trust me on this. Working as a country club bartender in Flagstaff, I once got to visit a wine cellar with an estimated worth of over a million dollars

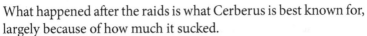

What happened after the raids is what Cerberus is best known for, largely because of how much it sucked.

Gardiner had been given the codename SU 6129, and was promised up to $7,500 a month, plus expenses, for helping gather information that helped lead to the busting of looters that he befriended during the operation—keep that last part in mind. When the raids occurred, Dr. Redd was treated to a lengthy interrogation straight out of HBO's *The Wire*, with federal agents reportedly asking him which of the shovels in his garage he used to dig up bodies (remember, his wife was the looting fanatic; he just went along with it good-humoredly, although that doesn't make him completely innocent, either). They told him he was going to lose his medical license, and probably go to jail forever, and much else besides.

Given my hardscrabble background, I've had more than a few encounters with the law. And yes, believe it or not, much of what you see on cop shows really does happen. Pairs of officers play Good Cop/Bad Cop in order to manipulate people into admitting things they would never dream of admitting otherwise. They'll purposefully leave you sitting handcuffed in a squad car or a holding cell for a very long time while they busy themselves making phone calls, scrutinizing the incident report, slowly stirring their coffee, or however else they can legally stall so that you'll gradually become so uncomfortable that you break down and confess to every crime ever committed. And they'll bully you with "possibilities" that range from unlikely to literally impossible. A younger me was once apprehended on suspicion of attempted shoplifting, and the arresting officer explained how not admitting right then and there that I was a red-handed bandit was technically obstruction of justice—a felony charge with a minimum sentence of ten years in prison. He honestly thought I was stupid enough to believe that.

—just the wine cellar, mind you; not including the house sitting atop it— owned by a guy who's allergic to sulfites and, thus, doesn't drink wine.

And that was the straw that broke Dr. Redd's back. They filled his head with possibilities so horrible (and, with sober retrospective thinking, also patently ludicrous) that they pushed him beyond the place where you believe full confession is your only escape route and into that dark abyss where another one presents itself. He took it.

Dr. Redd committed suicide by sitting inside his Jeep with a garden hose running from the exhaust into the interior.

The punishment for his wife, the pothunting enthusiast who is on record for having looted a site literally named for the presence of buried infants, was the guilt of dealing with his death. Her actual charges were piffles. Subsequent reports on the investigation materials show how the feds had amassed considerable evidence to convict a total of twenty-six individuals, including Jeannie Redd—but not her husband. They went after him the hardest, driving the man to take his own life, and it was all a bluff.

The blowback from the death of Dr. Redd alone was both awful and totally avoidable, but it didn't stop there. A salesman and artifact collector from Albuquerque named Steven Shrader, who was also a defendant in the case, flew home to visit his mother in Illinois and then shot himself in the chest (at an elementary school, for some reason). Not long after that, Ted Gardiner—who had, remember, befriended many of the people he was trying to help bust in order to earn their trust—spiraled into a depressive psychosis and shot himself in the head.

Jeannie Redd ended up with three years of probation and a two-thousand-dollar fine, mostly because the judge felt sorry for her after the suicide of her husband. Eleven of the other twenty-five living defendants pleaded guilty to felony charges, eight to misdemeanor charges, and six of them had all charges dropped. Not one of them went to prison. The looming horror for which Dr. Redd and Steven Shrader had killed themselves turned out to be a slap on the wrist.

In a 2007 brief about site stewardship for the NPS, Arizona State University archaeologist Sophia Kelly concluded that so-called big stick methods of archaeological protection "are often met with hostility and prove ineffective in the long run." This was certainly the case with both the 1986 and 2009 raids in Blanding, which bellowed the fires of local resentment toward land management agencies while doing a whole lot of nothing to stymy pothunting.

More to the point, according to a few local buddies of mine, the raids inspired a surge of purely vandalistic looting as a form of enraged protest. I can't see how that counts as a victory.

Call me a bleeding-heart liberal if you must. Many of the proud rural folks with whom I grew up never miss a chance. But I've simply had way too much education—and I don't just mean education in the classroom—to believe that the solution for criminal behavior is always heavy-handed penal bullying.

My childhood home was in the backwoods of the drizzly Northeast. Before his untimely death in 2016, my adolescent bestie and I would while away long weekend hours chopping wood in his barn while grilled to the gills on some chemical or other; or tearing around wilderness trails on ATVs and blasting guns at stuff; or finding some other illegal but entertaining distraction to pass the time. Blanding-based archaeologist Winston Hurst expressed some of these same sentiments in a fantastic autobiographical article he published in local history magazine *Blue Mountain Shadows* in 2011, where he tells of starting out with a "feral childhood" before ending up as—in my opinion, at least—an exemplary and much-celebrated local researcher.

I escaped my own feral childhood chiefly because of luck. I was lucky enough to have parents who genuinely wanted to see me succeed and a best friend who enjoyed reading books as much as he enjoyed things like rebellious vandalism and mayhem. Thanks to that early encouragement in intellectualism, I was lucky enough to fall in with the sort of kids who'd learned that dressing well and turning in straight As are effective ways to hoodwink society into looking the other way when you disappear into the woods with a half-keg and a sack of weed. And thanks to the lessons I learned from *those* kids, I was able to pass myself off as a decent member of society until, in true "fake it 'til you make it" fashion, I emerged out the other end as a scientist and author with a handful of college degrees.

If a single one of those major dominoes, or any of about a million tiny ones, hadn't fallen exactly the way it did I would probably be living the sort of life my dear old friend Dann was living when he died tragically at thirty-eight: working graveyard shifts in a warehouse, paying child support to an ex-girlfriend, and constantly battling with a variety of addictions.

I'm no better than anyone else who grew up in American poverty, in other words; and they're no worse than me. Most of them just aren't as lucky as I was.

As for the local community in San Juan County, professedly ground zero for graverobbing and every other kind of awfulness visited by human beings upon each other, my own experience varies somewhat from that conception as well. I have yet to live in Bluff, which is odd considering that it's by far the most openly liberal and weird of the towns bordering Bears Ears—but I have lived in both Blanding and Monticello. I remember both towns having what I consider some of the same small-town/rural problems that also plagued the one where I grew up, for sure, but I also remember the people in both towns being mostly friendly and welcoming.

Case in point: I shared a house in Blanding with a partner who'd arrived there a year before me, after interning for a summer in Canyonlands and deciding she was in love with the area. A day or so after moving in, there was a knock at her door—and there before her stood, by her estimation, the entire town. "Welcome to Blanding! Here, try some of my famous Jell-O* casserole. I see you could use a couch; I've got one at home I can bring over. How are you fixed for microwaves?"

I should note at this point that she is openly queer, with an

---

* LDS and Gentile friends alike will sometimes refer to the Mormon-populated stretch from Calgary to the Sierra Madres as the Jell-O Belt.

abundance of visible tattoos and piercings, and hair that is often dyed a decidedly unnatural hue—sometimes more than one. Based on the stereotypes we'd both heard about Blanding, a crowd of locals appearing at her door wasn't likely to bear offers of food and furniture so much as torches and a length of rope.

So much for stereotypes.

Regarding illicit antiquities, there's also an interesting generational phenomenon that appears to be cropping up all over the country, where younger inheritors of looted artifact collections grasp the ugliness in their possession and rebel against it. Grandpa's milk crate full of pottery seems less like an heirloom than like participation in something wretched. They want to put it back, or give it to a museum or to the tribes, or otherwise rid themselves of it.

The problem, of course, is that headlining stories like that of Cerberus give a lot of these people the impression that they will be booked, cuffed, and hung from a high pole the moment they tell any figures of authority what they've come to possess. Which isn't even close to true, but that's the impression a lot of them have.

This is why museum employees in communities like those surrounding Bears Ears will occasionally show up to work in the morning and find a cache of artifacts sitting at the front door like a box of unwanted kittens. The treatment they receive is also approximately the same: a sigh, an eyeroll, and every effort to find them a good home. Some are retrieved by tribal authorities. Some end up in teaching collections.

The rest—often the majority—get added to the curation crises.

Anyway. So much for all that.

The pillaging of Bears Ears in the form of pothunting has a ton of tendrils, and I've covered only a tiny portion here, but it does seem to have begun as a direct result of economic desperation related to the depression of the mid-1890s. And then there was *the* Depression, the one that everyone calls Great, which killed most of the trading posts around the Bears Ears area—and a lot of other things, besides.

As the entire nation continued to suffer through the years of the Great Depression, the federal government set about the daunting task of establishing programs of institutional relief. As part of the resulting New Deal launched by President Franklin Roosevelt, various forms of federal aid arrived in struggling communities in the forms of food, money, or subsidized jobs. Western states generally received more financial support than eastern states, with Utah ranking ninth overall in federal aid per capita, and numbers of workers in Utah employed on federal relief projects was well above the national average.

Still, while the Great Depression had taken quite a toll on the state of Utah—as it had just about everywhere else—the problem of population density (specifically its lack) was a major stumbling block. Utah was simply too big, with too few people per square mile, to stage many of the sort of recovery efforts that were more effective in tighter-packed places like Massachusetts. Coincidentally enough, this preloaded social distancing came in very handy during the COVID-19 crisis.

Back in the Great Depression, the "solution" was intensified focus on land and resource usage.

This included road construction and maintenance, bridge construction, snow shoveling, wood chopping, and development of natural resources throughout the entire state. More specific to the Bears Ears area, Civilian Conservation Corps (CCC) crews constructed roads, fences, corrals, and flood control projects, culverts, telephone lines, and campgrounds, and were stationed in Dry Valley, Indian Creek, Blanding, and Monticello. The one in Dry Valley would end up being the very last CCC Division of Grazing camp to close in Utah after the United States entered World War II. Its life had been extended so that roads to vanadium deposits in eastern Utah could be constructed.

And here, at last, we come to the second pillaging of Bears Ears.

In 1937, the Vanadium Corporation of America began

constructing reduction mills to recover vanadium from carnotite deposits throughout the Bears Ears area and surrounding region. Only vanadium was being separated out of deposits at the time, although it co-occurred with uranium; that would come later. The Vanadium Corporation also built a mill around the same time just over the border in Uravan, Colorado. The first vanadium mills were built southwest of Blanding in Cottonwood Canyon, also in 1937, and their owner purchased land adjacent to Monticello in 1941 to build another vanadium mill—although this one was never built due to lack of funds. The Vanadium Corporation then purchased land adjacent to this incomplete mill in order to establish an ore-buying station, and eventually purchased the incomplete mill itself in 1942. They fixed it up, and operations commenced at the Monticello Vanadium Mill that very year.

The reason for all this sudden and surging interest in vanadium was the outbreak of World War II, although mining for it—and radium—had been occurring in southeastern Utah since at least the year 1900, especially around Moab. Vanadium is a steel additive, and it became popular for the war effort because small amounts of it can greatly increase steel's tensile strength and resistance to fatigue failure.

In 1943, the Vanadium Corporation sold the mill in Monticello to the Defense Plant Corporation, which was technically a federal agency despite having "Corporation" in its name. They expanded the mill, built a lot of additional housing for its workers, and then promptly decided they had all the vanadium they needed.

The federal government stopped purchasing vanadium by 1944, to the woe of mill employees in Monticello and elsewhere. Not long after, however, they began expressing some interest in its dangerously radioactive byproduct. They expressed even more after publicly admitting that uranium isotope U-235 was used as the fission catalyst in nuclear bombs. Happily, there were all these recently out-of-work vanadium miners who already knew the ropes.

Edward Abbey has some colorful anecdotes about the uranium boom that followed and its impact on the Bears Ears and

Moab areas. In his book *The Monkey Wrench Gang*, the character he calls Bishop Love wears a necklace with a chip of depleted uranium in it to show the sissy hippies and other tree-hugger types how harmless it is.

That really happened.

Calvin "Cal" Black, the person on whom Abbey's character is based, served as a San Juan County commissioner for twenty-two years before retiring in 1990. In all those years, he probably did more than any public official not named Orrin Hatch to fan the flame of environmental destruction in Utah. He was also one of the two county commissioners caught up in the looting raid of 1986, after being ratted out by Earl Shumway. Because of that chip of uranium he carried around his neck, Cal Black—a lifelong nonsmoker—ended up being killed by a tumor on his lung.

So, that's two entries for the *schadenfreude* slot in the dictionary.

The Four Corners region was one of the few areas in the state of Utah to enjoy an economic boom during the post-World War II period, thanks mostly to the federal government's compulsion to establish a domestic stockpile of refined yellowcake uranium. An ore-processing station was opened in Monticello, and uranium prospecting began in earnest in any potentially uranium-bearing exposures in the local geology. Major uranium mines started popping up in places like Lisbon Valley, Cottonwood Wash, and atop White Mesa—where the Happy Jack Mine was located. By the 1950s, the uranium boom had completely engulfed San Juan County.

Stories of extensive uranium deposits in southeastern Utah attracted hundreds of prospectors hoping to strike it rich. Claims registration fees jumped from $3,500 to $117,000 in 1954 at the San Juan County Recorder's Office. Increases in population and improvements in services and infrastructure were necessary, and Monticello ended up doubling its population to 2,500 in just three years. A million dollars' worth of buildings was constructed within city limits, including four new hotels and six trailer parks. To meet these needs, the water and sewer system was expanded at a cost of $500,000 and about a dozen new businesses ranging from dry cleaners to investment brokers were established, along with an expansion of the mill facilities themselves.

Similar growth occurred in every other sector of the local economy—including, and most notably, the human health sector. Everyone kept getting sick, for some reason.

It was also because of the uranium boom that development and expansion of the local transportation system occurred. A paved road was built between Monticello and Blanding by 1953, and in 1956 the road from Blanding down through Bluff and over to Mexican Hat was completed. In 1958, a mining company called Texas Zinc built the rollercoaster that is the Moki Dugway—a hair-raising series of switchbacks that climb up the southern edge of Cedar Mesa—in order to transport uranium from Fry Canyon to a processing mill in Mexican Hat via the road that runs down the spine of Cedar Mesa (now State Route 261). Pothunters, of course, took full advantage of the new roads, although so did recreationists—including ones who would later complain when these new roads were joined by newer ones.

Between 1952 and 1957, domestic production of uranium increased from 700 tons to 17,800 tons per year, and roughly forty percent of southeastern Utah was staked with uranium mining claims. Federal buying programs of the 1960s accelerated this already momentous growth, and the oil embargo of 1973 and its associated energy crisis kicked things up even more, as people suddenly grew concerned about our dependence on "foreign" energy sources. Federal subsidies flowed out once again, this time under President Jimmy Carter, keeping the uranium boom going for just a little while longer even though demand was starting to wane. The country had, by then, more than enough stockpiled for all the bombs we wanted to make (or so we thought at the time), and development of nuclear power plants had become unpopular.

They would become even more unpopular after Three Mile Island (1979) and Chernobyl (1986). But even by the mid-1970s, public awareness of the health risks associated with uranium mining and processing was spreading far and wide. A series of bills was passed to bring about regulation, angering people like Cal

Black no end, and a Nuclear Regulatory Commission emerged. Companies still in operation were responsible for their own cleanup under the direction of the newly formed commission, and were required to generate environmental impact statements per NEPA to address the effects of continued operation. Some of them did.

Others did what big corporations occasionally do when they're told to clean up their messes: file for bankruptcy and then just walk away. This happened in Moab, leaving locals with permanently contaminated water *and* the bill for trying to decontaminate it.

In total, American taxpayers became responsible for about $1.6 billion of remediation at abandoned mill sites, in addition to mounting hospital bills in places where uranium mining and processing were still chugging along—like the Bears Ears area. The mounting costs associated with the long-term effects of uranium milling, a more-than-sufficient stockpile of uranium oxide, and newly elected president Ronald Reagan's steps to eliminate federal subsidies resulted in a near-total collapse of the domestic uranium industry in 1984.

That's when things took a turn from the ominous to the horrific for the areas and communities that had become dependent upon the uranium industry, particularly Native American ones. As soon as the Atomic Regulatory Agency had what they considered a large enough stockpile of uranium to buffer whatever demands the Cold War might generate, they simply packed up and walked away from the mines. The breakdown of the domestic uranium industry and Reagan's elimination of subsidies meant a concomitant breakdown in cleanup efforts. By 1986, over five hundred mines on the Navajo Nation alone were abandoned, and nearly all of them continue to leak some measure of contamination into homes and water sources there as you read this sentence.

Although the mill in Monticello was shuttered in 1964, cleanup efforts there are technically ongoing. Long-term remediation initially included construction of an onsite waste repository; excavation and placement of contaminated soil, sediments, and other materials in the repository; and institutional controls on all of the above. The long-term groundwater and surface water remediation included construction of a permeable reactive-treatment wall for groundwater at the boundary of the site; construction of two off-location treatment cells; bio-monitoring; even more institutional controls; groundwater monitoring; and extraction and treatment of contaminated groundwater upon detection. Implementation of these efforts took place between 1991 and 2004, almost thirty years after the place closed down, but at least they commenced at all. Groundwater treatment and monitoring continue to this day.

The story with the White Mesa Mill, located about half an hour down the highway, couldn't be more different. Built in the late 1970s, it is now the only fully licensed and operating conventional uranium mill in the country—as its owners proudly boast on their website. In the 1990s, following abandonment of most primary uranium extraction, the White Mesa Mill shifted its operation toward a new source of revenue in the form of processing "alternative feeds" and discarding the resulting waste onsite. Alternative feed is industry slang for materials that have already been processed once, by the way, and in this case they include uranium-bearing wastes from other contaminated places around the country.

To put that another way: although processing virgin uranium from rocks ceased being economically feasible by the 1980s, the owners of the White Mesa Mill decided they'd keep the place running by processing the already-contaminated garbage and slag from other places in order to squeeze the very last drops of uranium out of them. Think of it like a coffee shop finding out that fair-trade laws and environmental regulations make the bulk purchase of coffee beans too expensive to turn a worthwhile profit, so instead they start buying garbage bags full of used grounds from Starbucks.

That practice would raise some eyebrows on its own, and I've tasted coffee in a few places that make me wonder if it's been tried before, but at least if those bags tear open during transport you'll get nothing worse than some brown stuff on the highway. Radioactive waste behaves a bit differently.

About three hundred Ute residents live a mere three-mile drive away—there's something about the combination of *three-mile* and *uranium* that makes me think dire thoughts, but I can't imagine why—in the White Mesa Ute community, where many of them settled after life on resource-marginal allotments proved untenable. Blanding, Bluff, and Monticello are all within twenty miles. Because of that whole "alternative feeds" thing, supposedly uranium-bearing but definitely radio-contaminated wastes were trucked into the place on highways that pass through these and scores of other communities along the way.

The White Mesa Mill officially closed in 2007, at which point it went into a *timely renewal* state—or, as normal people would put it, *standby*. Its owner, Energy Fuels, has lobbied heavily for work to resume there since the day it was closed. Their chief arguments seem always to swirl around economic benefits for the local community, making the place seem less like a radioactive garbage processer than an open-access treasure chest.

The math implied by that impression is a little tricky. Successful operation and timely shutdown of the mill in Monticello, for example, nonetheless resulted in an environmental mess that has cost taxpayers $250 million so far and isn't finished yet. Moreover, both it and the White Mesa Mill were identified as lead culprits in escalating cases of birth defects and cancer in a 2007 study by the Utah Department of Health, which was half the reason they put the latter one in standby that year (the other half being that the mill turned out to be operating under an expired permit). I've been around cancer some, having lost a few family members and one close friend to it thus far, and in addition to its being a devastating battle it is also invariably an expensive one.

I'm no economist, but I fail to see how putting a few dozen people to work gets an entire community over financial humps like those. Yet despite all this, the White Mesa Mill's operating license was renewed for ten years starting in 2018.

It gets even worse from there. In 2012 and 2013, reports generated and published by owners of the mill showed that it was emitting more of the cancer-causing pollutant radon than the Clean Air Act allows for businesses that are up and running, let alone ones just sitting there on standby. Radioactive spills also occurred in 2015, 2016, and 2017 as truckloads of the aforementioned alternative feeds were being transported there for eventual reprocessing when it resumed operations.

As of this writing, potential alternative feeds include five thousand barrels of processed uranium waste from Estonia. This is appalling in its own right, but it gets even crazier: the reason Energy Fuels would be acquiring all that radioactive waste from so far away in the first place is because the Estonian government decided it was too dangerous to store on Estonian soil. Make of that what you will.

Meanwhile, the first item of business mentioned on the mill's webpage at the time I drafted this chapter is a self-congratulatory screed on anticipated processing of ten thousand tons of radioactive waste from the now-defunct Sequoyah Fuels plant on the Cherokee Nation. A spokesperson for the company told the *Cortez Journal* that they were "proud to play a role in helping clean up the land of Native American communities." By, remember, hauling ten thousand tons of radioactive waste from one of them right to the doorstep of another so it can be reprocessed for trace amounts of leftover uranium, like a wino chugging from the spit bucket, before the now twice-processed radioactive waste gets buried underground right beside the only major aquifer in the area. Yeah—I'd be proud, too.

Remember also: radioactive spills occurred during the transport process in all three of the three years leading up to that transfer. How many strikes is that?

Until we can beam things from location to location like Scotty on *Star Trek*, that's going to keep happening at least once in a while. It's inevitable. And when problems are inevitable, you find ways to keep them as quiet as possible. This helps explain why the drivers' routes—and the mines, and the plants, and the processing mills—are located in or near socioeconomically depressed areas.

If that last fact sounds eerily familiar in shape, there's a reason. Situating things that are dangerous or horrible in or near places where they're only going to endanger people that don't have the economic, social, or political clout to do anything about it is a time-honored tradition. The repercussions of that tradition are occasionally so big, and so awful, they can land in a place like Bears Ears even when they occur hundreds of miles away.

Black Mesa is a mountainous upland plateau in northern Arizona. The Hopis have called it home for at least a thousand years, and its remoteness helped them to retain their culture and heritage while the Spanish were re-colonizing the Pueblo villages of the Rio Grande region. Called *Dziłíjiin* (Black Mountain) by the Diné, who have also made use of the mesa since their arrival in the region, its name comes from the innumerable seams of coal running through it. Beginning at least seven hundred years ago, people in the Hopi villages located there figured out how to use that coal to fire gorgeous yellow pottery. By the late 1800s, it had started to attract attention from others.

In 1882, President Chester A. Arthur created a rather sizable rectangular reservation in northeastern Arizona via executive order, neatly surrounding Black Mesa, "for the use and occupancy of the Moqui [Hopi] and other such Indians as the secretary of the interior may see fit to settle therein." This was how the Hopi Reservation came about, with only a tiny bit of prodding by an Indian agent named Galen Eastman, who feared that Mormon settlers would overwhelm the Hopi community if homesteading continued unchecked. Yet even Eastman was surprised at how big the 1882 reservation was, given that his own recommendation excluded the village of Moenkopi. Its creation was a bold and noble move, in other words, until one realizes that Arthur did so following a report from a government surveyor about dense coal deposits located between the villages of Moenkopi and Oraibi.

The only non-Native people living anywhere near there, at the time, were a few families of Mormon settlers and John and Louisa Wetherill. However, according to the Desert Lands Act of 1877 those settlers could, if they continued to inhabit and improve their stakes, purchase up to 160 acres apiece at $1.25 an acre. That was Galen Eastman's fear. This would also give them title to whatever mineral resources lay beneath those acres—unless, for some reason, those lands were removed from the public sector. President Arthur, a shrewd and wealthy businessman himself, thus created the original Hopi Reservation as a clever way of putting all that coal in the bank for later.

Meanwhile, the Navajo Reservation had expanded twice between 1868 and 1882, both times via executive order by President Rutherford B. Hayes and both in response to urging by Galen Eastman. That meant the Hopi and the Diné each had a rectangle-shaped reservation in northern Arizona in 1882, sitting directly beside each other. An executive order by President Arthur in 1884 set aside "for Indian purposes" 2.4 million acres between the Arizona-Utah border and the San Juan River, with some historians interpreting the vagueness of "for Indian purposes" to mean "for halting the southward expansion of Mormonism." Over the next several decades, the Navajo Reservation grew and expanded as a result of further presidential and congressional actions, until it completely encircled the 2.5-million-acre Hopi Reservation.

Sometime around 1895, President Theodore Roosevelt began making noise about federally protecting the wilderness and cliff dwellings of that region. According to historian Douglas Brinkley, Roosevelt believed the "fantastic barrenness, incredible wildness, and desolate majesty of the Navajo lands" needed to be protected—that, furthermore, Arizona business types were "unable to comprehend the concept of antiquities," and that Arizona should be "managed rather than mined." Roosevelt's vision would come true with President Taft's creation of tiny little Navajo National Monument by President Taft in 1909, just to the northwest of Black Mesa. His sentiment about resource management, meanwhile, went as unheeded as John Wesley Powell's sentiment about water management.

In the 1950s, the state of Arizona took a hard look at the coal reserves lying under the Navajo and Hopi Reservations, and decided the time had come to un-reserve them. A coalition of twenty-one energy development companies and their lobbyists pulled together to facilitate the task, results of which included the creation of the Navajo and Hopi Tribal Councils by the US federal government (so that the energy developers had smaller groups to squeeze and cajole rather than entire communities, as was the case before) and the 1974 Navajo-Hopi Land Settlement Act. That last piece of legislation divided 1.8 million acres of jointly owned Diné and Hopi land in half, drawing a hard political line where only a cultural one existed before. It was officially done to settle a "land dispute" between the two tribes, but was really done to facilitate mineral extraction. And here's where this already troubled tale nukes the fridge.

The establishment of the Tribal Councils was foisted on the tribes as a result of the Mineral Development Act of 1938, which stated that "lands within Indian reservations may, with the approval of the Secretary of the Interior, be leased for mining purposes, by authority of the Tribal Council or other authorized spokesmen for the Indians." In other words, Tribal Councils were created by the federal government because there had to be federally recognized Tribal Councils in order to authorize the leasing of reservation lands for mining purposes.

They were remarkably fluid in this regard. When, for example, the newly created Hopi Tribal Council opposed a 1944 attempt by Standard Oil to acquire an oil lease within the 1882 reservation boundary, a series of slick legislative acts rebranded almost three quarters of it as a Joint Use Area where Hopi farmers and Diné sheepherders both lived—and, therefore, not under either tribe's unilateral control—while also disbanding the Council.

Into this miasma stepped John S. Boyden, a Mormon bishop and former US attorney with a scheme to open Black Mesa up for major energy development. Just to give you an idea what sort of person he was: the international mining conglomerate Kennecott (you've maybe heard of them as operators of the mine that's busily poisoning the air and people in Salt Lake City) acquired Peabody Coal in 1966, and four years later Boyden moved his law offices to the tenth floor of the Kennecott Building in Salt Lake City where he could—symbolically—look down upon the Mormon Temple.

When the Navajo Nation Tribal Council sent Boyden

packing, he capitalized on bitter factionalizing between traditionalist and progressive Hopis to weasel his way in with them instead, effectively creating a new Tribal Council for the Hopi to replace the one that got dissolved back in '44. Then, when the aforementioned Navajo-Hopi Land Settlement Act came about, the "official" lawyer of the Hopi people strung them along while actually working for Kennecott-Peabody.

Starting in 1966, the year Boyden acquired his fancy new office, a series of leases for coal extraction by Kennecott-Peabody were signed by him on behalf of the Hopi—to their considerable surprise. By the time of the 1974 legislation, Boyden had secured for his *real* employer a rich swath of coal-bearing Hopi land and a slurry line—using the precious and irreplaceable water of the Coconino aquifer—across the Dinétah to a power plant near Page, there to be converted into air pollution in order to do what the turbines of Glen Canyon Dam are already doing just a few miles away.* When COVID-19 swept through the Navajo Nation with devastating consequences, reasons included wells and springs sucked dry for this abominable slurry line.

The coda to this story is a doozy. Although Boyden always presented himself as a humble country lawyer and humanitarian working on behalf of the Hopi pro bono, a lawsuit filed under the Freedom of Information Act by the Native American Rights Fund later revealed that he was handsomely paid by the US government out of taxpayer monies held in trust for the Hopis. How handsomely, you ask? The total amount over his thirty-year tenure as legal counsel for the Hopi Tribe was $2.7 million in mid-1900s money, or about $21 million inflation-adjusted dollars. And that's what he got from the government on behalf of the people he fleeced—it's probably safe to assume he wasn't working pro bono for Kennecott-Peabody, either.

The relevance of this tale to Bears Ears is that it kindled some fierce animosity between two tribes who trace key elements of their ancestry there. The sort of animosity that would make it

---

* That monstrosity, called the Navajo Generating Station, was finally shuttered in November of 2019 while I was editing this very chapter.

extremely unlikely for major factions from both to work together as members of, say, a historic and monumental alliance—which underscores how special it is that this did indeed occur.

Back in the Bears Ears area itself, I would be remiss if I didn't also mention one other form of pillaging that continues to occur. A seemingly innocuous but ultimately very destructive force in the welfare of both the natural and cultural resources of the area. Recreational tourism.

This topic deserves to be introduced in a chapter about pillaging because that's essentially what it is: people visiting unique, fragile, scientifically important and culturally significant or sacred places in order to get stuff—photos, or souvenirs, or simply experiences—without really giving anything back in return.

There are the backcountry archaeology aficionados, among whom I still count myself on my off days. They're mostly harmless, as I've said before, although that word *mostly* is a tricky one. Given the density and ubiquity of archaeological sites in the Bears Ears area, they also go absolutely everywhere.

Then there's the plant people, who've caught wind of the fact that some of the more out-of-the-way—and, for this and other reasons, less cow-ravaged—canyon systems still contain what are called *relic* or *fossil* ecosystems because of their near-total lack of invasive species.

The animal people look for animals. There are bears in Bears Ears, fittingly enough, and modern so-called hunters love to harass them into starving delirium by releasing gangs of dogs with GPS radio collars while they loaf around pretending that this somehow counts as outdoorsmanship.

The rock and dinosaur people both look for things that moved around a long time ago before settling down a bit. Hikers, backpackers, and trail runners look for places to get away from more crowded wilderness areas. Professional photographers look high and low, this way and that, for a chance to take the perfect shot of any of the above. Social media "photographers" follow closely in their footsteps for a chance to take the exact same shot. And so on.

The result is overexploitation, escalating volumes of trash and vandalism, and in some cases injury or death among the under-prepared. Josh Ewing, the current executive director of Friends of Cedar Mesa (FCM), is quoted in a handful of stories—in which the writers were pretty obviously hoping to write about the evils of development or looting—that the largest threat facing Bears Ears National Monument is tourism. All the way back in 1999, Jerry Spangler said in an article for the *Deseret News* that some fifteen thousand people per year were "scurrying through" its canyon systems. That number has since increased by an order of magnitude.

Spangler's article also included the following prescient sentiment: "Two decades ago, visitors to the area were experienced, well-prepared hikers and backpackers. Today's weekend warriors are just not as knowledgeable." The story goes on to recount an episode involving a woman who got lost in a very easily navigable canyon, one that even I couldn't get lost in, and kept calling the BLM offices in Monticello for directions out of the place.

Conversations I've had with Scott Edwards and Laura Lantz, who heroically served as the only two full-time rangers atop Cedar Mesa for over twenty-five years prior to retiring in 2019, often lament the increase of what they call "softer users" to the canyons. These include people who show up with a half-charged cell phone full of GPS points, a gas station Gatorade bottle, and about as much backcountry savvy as you'd find in a plush dinosaur.

Just a couple years ago, I went on a weekend hike through one of Cedar Mesa's most popular canyons (you needn't always have a place entirely to yourself in order to enjoy it, after all). Joining me was Jonathan Bailey, his partner Aaron, and a jovial middle-aged guy named Jerry who'd first begun exploring the area several decades earlier. As we hiked along, Jerry recounted a colorful encounter with Fred Blackburn, still a BLM ranger at the time, who accused him on-sight of being a pothunter. In Fred's defense, Jerry said, "it was totally understandable at the time, because back then people didn't really do the sort of thing we're out here doing today."

Which is true. Prior to about twenty years ago, it was almost unthinkable to imagine someone grabbing a backpack, a camera, and a sandwich, and heading deep into the backcountry in search of cool archaeological sites for no reason other than to visit them. Front-country sites were a different matter. One of the most popular Sunday picnic spots in the Bears Ears area during the early to mid-1900s was a site near Blanding called Five Kivas, which is how it got completely decimated. But getting into the backcountry takes considerable effort, and people that weren't Everett Ruess didn't often expend that effort to reach hidden-away archaeological sites unless they were expecting to haul away buckets of tangible booty.

Nowadays, however, it's an accepted and increasingly common recreational practice in the Southwest, and one that is ballooning in popularity. A few authors have referred to the internet era as the age of the end of forgetting, and it's eerily true. Ask any celebrity with a photo or a tweet they wish would just disappear. Information used to be lost all the time, and the annals of archaeology are brimming with examples—from "lost" Mayan temples to the piles of maps and photographs that went up in smoke when the *Illustrated American* office caught fire.

No longer. Even if it's an accumulation of tiny pieces of data over long stretches of time, it still does nothing but accumulate, and eventually you get thousands of people per year showing up at the Kane Gulch Ranger Station and asking the way to Panther Cave or Ghost House Ruin because they saw it in their social media feed.

Local artist JR Lancaster often grumbles about what he calls "the hatching of Baby Moab" in reference to the nigh incomprehensible overexploitation of that once sleepy little town just to the north. And it's a scary comparison.

It gets scarier when one realizes that the overexploitation of Moab is, at least partly, by design. The town of Moab, along with most of its associated residential areas, reside within Grand

County. According to state law, at least forty-seven percent of the take from taxation on tourism—specifically the transient room tax, or TRT, a county-wide tax on temporary lodging—must be directed toward "tourism promotion" in its respective county. In other words, almost half of what the county garners from tourists staying in motels, hotels, inns, hostels, and private campgrounds is required by law to be spent on attracting more tourists.

The engineering equivalent would be if half the surplus velocity generated by a runaway train was rerouted back into the engine to make the train go even faster. The long-term result isn't difficult to imagine.

According to the latest figures, as of this writing, Grand County collects more than five million dollars annually from TRT revenue. A little under half of that is required by law to be spent on promotion of even more tourism and recreation instead of, say, infrastructure. This is how you get a town built to sustain six thousand property owners sharing its roads, electricity, sanitation services, and drinking water with millions of tourists while *still* only being able to sustainably support about six thousand people.

Since the Spanish Valley portion of greater Moab extends into San Juan County, one way to release that pressure is to direct it southward, toward Bears Ears. And they are.

Local residents aren't powerless against this, although the fact isn't often enunciated to them. If you live in a place where tourism is increasing, and will undoubtedly continue to increase, you can prevent—or at least stymie—efforts to turn your beloved little burgh into Moab or Sedona by passing aggressive zoning ordinances. No businesses over a certain square footage, no use of water in excess of X cubic feet per day, etc. Head the bastards off before they even arrive.

But you have to act fast. The opportunity to do this in Blanding, Monticello, and Bluff is dwindling pretty quickly, as Bluff recently discovered in the form of one of the ugliest and most culturally appropriative eyesores I have ever seen. You have to kill Baby Moab *before* it hatches.

The extent to which the highly publicized Bears Ears conservation battle is, has been, or will be exacerbating these problems is difficult to calculate. It is exacerbating visitation, of course; that's not up for debate. But the biggest reason so many conservation groups jumped on the Bears Ears National Monument bandwagon, after a consortium of tribes created and proposed it, is because the proposal itself was at least partly a *response* to the already staggering increase of visitation over the past several decades.

According to figures I've pulled together from FCM and UC Boulder, the total number of visitors to the Cedar Mesa area increased from 2,800 in 1974 to over 50,000 in 2005; approximately tripled between 2005 and 2015; and then tripled *again* between 2015 and 2017. That's an almost literal depiction of exponential increase.

So, yes, coverage of the controversy has undoubtedly contributed to the number of visitors per annum, but the notion that it's doing so to an extent significantly greater than the established trend is a hard sell. For steepness of gain curves, it's tough to beat exponential.

This is a tricky gauntlet for me to navigate, not only because I'm an avid recreational hiker but because outdoor recreation is, by most measures, a good thing. Studies have shown that people exposed to the wilderness as children grow up to be well-adjusted adults more often than ones that aren't. So-called wilderness therapy as a practice—or, as it were, an industry—has its pros and cons, but outdoor recreation as a prescribed behavior for emotional malady goes back further than my own research can even reach.

I scored a lucky pair with my parents, in this regard. My mother was never exactly the outdoorsy type while I was growing up, but she always preferred camping to motels whenever we traveled. What's more, she trusted me when I embarked on my own forays into the wilderness—even after she figured out what my "intellectual" buddies and I were really getting up to, out there. She was at Woodstock, after all.

On the other side of that coin, my father was very outdoorsy while I was growing up, particularly in the realm of killing and eating wild things. I got way into hunting and fishing because of this. But he also seemed to have a bedrock loathing of sleeping outside, so instead of waking up at the manly hour of six or seven to set forth into the woods from camp, we'd wake up at the frankly offensive hour of five in order to reach the woods in time. Thus began a lifelong addiction to both outdoor pursuits and very strong coffee.

The problem arises when that wilderness is a target-rich environment, which simply means that it's full of the sort of stuff certain types of people are looking for. If birds are your thing, there's about a million places you can go to see wide varieties of the ones we haven't killed off yet. If (against TLC's advisement) you prefer chasing waterfalls, there may be as many as a dozen within driving distance of where you're sitting right now. But the archaeological splendors of Bears Ears exist in only one place. All of them. And they weren't built with tourists in mind.

Tourism is the one patch of common ground between people who are for and against elevated federal protection, in that both parties tend to despise it—and for good reason. It can be extremely destructive to fragile archaeological sites that can't possibly be reseeded the way you can with burned or clear-cut forests. This is what Lipe meant when he described ancient or historic material heritage as the epitome of a non-renewable resource. Barring some unforeseen weirdness in the space-time continuum, we're stuck with just the one.

Moreover, its impacts are invariably cumulative. An archaeological site can be stripped clean of artifacts—or have its standing architecture reduced to rubble—by a myriad of tiny impacts over a long enough period, even if only a tiny percentage of visitors are thoughtless or pestiferous. Think of it like this: if ten thousand people swing by Rising Sun Kiva in a given season, and only one percent take home a potsherd or stand on its roof for a selfie, that's one hundred missing sherds and one hundred times that an aging structure had to endure the weight of some sizable grinning swine standing atop it. Or two hundred in two years. Or five hundred in five. In ten years: total destruction.

To try to combat this, the agencies in the Bears Ears area are involved in popularizing and expanding a Site Stewardship Program through which volunteers "adopt" sites in order to babysit them once or twice a season. Of note, FCM has taken to supporting their efforts by gathering and training armies of volunteer site stewards on their own time and dime.

Most aggressively—and most controversially—they also endorse the practice of directing tourist traffic toward "visitor-ready resources" that are more easily managed and monitored than those in the deep backcountry. Handy examples of this practice include a site in Zion National Park called, appropriately enough, Sacrifice Rock. It's a car-sized boulder with some petroglyphs on it that was left in a conspicuous location to preserve its provenance (it's an astronomical marker) while simultaneously serving as a discussion point about visitation to archaeological sites. That discussion often focuses on inadvertent destruction: the rock art on Sacrifice Rock is getting harder to see every year, thanks to the obliterating effects of millions of loving hands, and it won't be long before they're totally erased.

For my own part, direct involvement in the Bears Ears conservation movement began, inauspiciously enough, when I realized that I was guilty of pillaging the place for its healing properties without really giving anything back, either. I credit this lesson to Scotty's dog.

I'd been in graduate school for just shy of three miserable years, enduring in about equal measure the awfulness of Lyme disease and the awfulness of intolerable tools who think "academics" is a catch phrase for "ego-battle arena." I would be rid of both forms of infection within a few months, when springtime arrived, but now it was only winter. And I was in Moab, cat-sitting for a lovely couple that I knew from school. My then-girlfriend Rex*

---

* Not her real name, obviously—her real name is Donna. But she's half-Iranian, and she went to high school in post-9/11 Florida, so it

came to visit over Christmas, called it the best Christmas she'd ever had up to that point, and absolutely loved the place. I hadn't the heart to tell her what it's like in the summer.

After she'd gone, I poked around Cedar Mesa, as I always do, but my heart was set on a canyon in the southern reaches of Needles just to the north of Monticello. I'd heard rumors of amazing rock art, and I couldn't shake them.

As it happened, I drove out there on a Sunday. This decision had dire repercussions. The approach takes one off the main highway onto a county road for about fifteen miles, and from there onto a dirt road for another five or so, and from there again onto a rugged two-track for several more miles before one reaches the head of the canyon. There was snow, but blessedly little of it—only enough to cover the ground in a thin blanket of white.

This, too, had dire repercussions.

After exploring all through the shortened winter day, I returned to my vehicle just as the sun was beginning to touch the horizon and made ready to return. I wasn't worried about getting lost because I was the only person foolish enough to drive out to that particular trailhead on a freezing Sunday afternoon just after Christmas, which meant I could easily follow my own tracks back to the highway. This I did, for about six minutes, until a sudden and horrifying *crunch* enlightened me to the fact that the sinuous path I'd followed wasn't a road after all. It was a creek bed. My morning drive over the ice had weakened it enough that my afternoon drive resulted in my truck breaking through, becoming instantly and hopelessly high-centered on the compacted ice in the middle.

I leapt out of the truck and had a look at the tires to see if I could wedge some sticks or something underneath them. And then laughed at myself for doing so. The tires were spinning lazily about six inches above muddy water whose depth I didn't even know.

---

didn't take her long to become tough as coffin nails in response to all the predictable harassment and bullying. Hence her Linnaean taxonomic name, *Donnasaurus rex* (sensu lato).

Then I looked at the rapidly sinking sun. And then I regarded the rapidly sinking temperature. And then I stopped laughing.

It's about fifteen miles along the horrible dirt road that I have since learned is, yes, a creek bed for most of the way, and I'd only managed to drive about two or three before turning my vehicle into a two-ton teeter-totter. On the other hand, it was only about a mile or two if I used my GPS to help me cut straight across the cow fields that separate the canyons from the main road. Moreover, if I stayed there to await help—which is what they say you should always do in such situations—it would get, I don't know, really *boring*. That was what compelled me to layer up and start marching through the gathering gloom toward a road that was, if nothing else, at least paved. It wasn't that I was already partly delirious from cold and hunger or anything.

All was well until about halfway across the snowy expanse, when I stumbled into a barbed-wire fence. They don't bother putting those on the background maps in consumer-grade GPS units, or at least not the one that I was using. It was so cold my hand stuck to the topmost metal wire as I was negotiating the fence, but I managed to get a leg over it, whereupon the bottommost wire reacted to the combination of weight and cold by giving a demonstration of what engineers call "fatigue failure." It snapped. I came almost straight down upon the top wire, and a barb, sharp and cold, stabbed deeply into my inner thigh.

Panic erupted. For all I knew, I'd just pierced my femoral artery, but I couldn't convince myself to take my pants off and check because I was more certain that I would instantly freeze to death. I marched on, severely limping, presumably leaving a dense trail of blood for the horde of hungry predators queuing up behind me.

It was pitch dark and some absurd number of degrees below freezing when I gained the main road, and only then did it finally occur to me that I hadn't seen or heard a vehicle on the thing the entire time I was hobbling toward it. My body was starting to switch gears from shivering to convulsing, the second-to-last stage before it just gives up, and I was also certain that I'd lost about...six, maybe seven gallons of blood. The highway was approximately thirty miles down the road from where I stood. About ten miles in the other direction was the Needles District Visitor Center, which was closed for the winter. I started walking toward the highway. I didn't know what else to do. Cold and hunger and loss of blood wouldn't allow me to think straight and do anything rational, like hike back to the truck and curl up under my emergency blanket.

I was thus engaged in the act of stumbling to an icy death when, an hour or two later, a pickup truck came around the turn in front of me and went zipping past. I heard a dog bark as it passed, its sound stretching out in audible Doppler fashion.

"AARRRrrrroooooooff..."

I didn't turn and look back. I assumed that I'd imagined it all. But the truck came to a stop, someplace behind me, and reversed back to where I was. I didn't wave my arms or even say much of anything as the driver unlocked the passenger door and ushered me in. I didn't utter more than a few marginally coherent words until we were back at his campsite and I was sitting beside his campfire. Then we started to chat.

It turned out the guy's name was Scotty, and although I forget his dog's name it is to her that I probably owe my life. Scotty didn't even see me when he went zooming past me along the road because it was dark as good espresso outside, and he was looking for the car of a friend of his. The two of them were planning to do some climbing in Indian Creek the following morning. But Scotty's friend hadn't shown up yet, so he was driving around looking for him in case he went to the wrong campsite. It was the dog that spotted me, and her bark that I'd heard.

Thusly warmed and slightly cheered, I limped off to have a pee and take a look at the mortal wound from which liters, buckets, *bathtubs'* worth of my life's essence were steadily pumping all night long—and saw a little red dot where the barb had punctured the skin, but only just, situated nowhere near any major hematic thoroughfares. I limped back to the fire and opted not to mention having finally contemplated the abyssal vastness that often extends between my imagination and reality.

Since Scotty's friend still hadn't showed, and it was getting late, he proceeded to cook up a handful of gourmet hamburgers that he'd brought along and gave two of them to me. He also opened the bottle of Maker's Mark that he'd brought for himself and his climbing buddy, and I had about half of that as well. And he had extra sleeping bags that he used to build a cozy nest for his dog, which he now offered to me while the true hero of our story kept herself warm by the fire, and when it was time to go to sleep I made them into a nest for myself while Scotty and his dog slept together in his tent. Not that it was easy for me to fall asleep.

Scotty's friend showed up sometime in the middle of the night, but he was still asleep the following morning when we rode out to rescue my stricken truck. Depressingly, it took Scotty all of forty seconds to yank my vehicle out of the riverbed with his winch. Bear that in mind, dear reader, and learn from my mistakes. Invest in a winch.

"By the way," he inquired whilst winching, "why archaeology?" My answer to this question changes just about every time I'm asked. What I said at the time is that I love hiking and backpacking to archaeological sites, investigating and taking photos of them, because it's fun to do and I've had a sweet tooth for abandoned places ever since I grew up in what was basically Sleepy Hollow. Becoming an archaeologist meant turning my favorite hobby into a job, as Confucius supposedly advised.

He sloshed this around like a savvy wine-taster. "Okay, so that's what you get out of it. But what do you do to give back?"

"Huh?"

"Well," he explained, unhooking the winch cable from my formerly stricken vehicle, "I'm a rock climber. And Indian Creek is some of the best crack-climbing in the world. I know a lot of people don't give a shit, they don't think much deeper than buying fancy gear and putting up routes, but I know these places wouldn't look very much like this if we didn't do something to look after them. So, I get involved in conservation stuff. Sign petitions and give money to Friends of Indian Creek. Do what I can to give back, you know?"

It turns out Scotty is more the norm than the exception.

Despite largely unfounded rumors about the destruction to archaeological sites wrought by climbers in places like Indian Creek, including social-media blathering from one or two notorious trolls within the archaeological community itself, climbers probably comprise the most ecologically conscious contingent of the various outdoor-recreation subcultures. My friend and occasional hiking partner Greg Child, known to the wider world as an Aussie-born mountaineer and author (and outspoken conservation advocate), put it to me this way: "There is a tendency to toss all climbers into the category of looter/pothunter/OHV vandal. Climbers are likely to be the most respectful group out there, if they are given info and education."

Scotty certainly bore this out, or at least he seemed to. I strained to hear his words, and respond somewhat intelligibly, over the sound of the winch.

I should mention at this point how hung-over I was. Half a bottle of Maker's Mark at the tail end of the previous evening's horrifying shenanigans will have that effect. All I could do was nod feebly and, in deference to having worked several seasons at Glen Canyon and seeing how Lake Powell visitors treat archaeological sites, mutter the following: "Well... basically, I get paid to take careful notes and photographs of things that I love while assholes are steadily destroying them. It's like house-sitting, which I'm supposed to be doing right now, except your job is to carefully monitor just how thoroughly the house is being wrecked by a sloppy and racist demolition crew."

"That sounds depressing."

"It is."

Back in town, the cats were happy to see me. Rex, on the other hand, was infuriated—having found my story not adventurous and cool so much as scary and idiotic. She hammered the point home by charging that I "don't give a shit about anyone else's feelings. People would miss you if you died out there, asshole. People who are dumb enough to care about you." Then she hung up.

I used to be proud of that sort of idiocy. I would tell stories like the one about Scotty's dog as if I were the greatest solo wanderer since Muir. A few of my friends, especially some of the ones

I knew from the North Rim, heartily agreed with that sentiment and then went forth in search of similar tales to tell.

There's a rich literature to support this trope, the one where the protagonist tramps into some great stretch of landscape to find something-or-other, and we consumed it all—from *Desert Solitaire* to *Kon-Tiki* to *Wild*—as if they weren't stories so much as instruction manuals. The trivial fact that friends and partners and family members might, you know, *cry* or something if we ended up as big red splotches on that same landscape just didn't figure into it.

The mystique we've created around the solitary white male badass character is a proof of concept for euphemizing ugliness. The ugliness of privilege, egotism, and selfishness. The ugliness of delusion.

Where this all reconvenes is the point that Scotty was attempting to make to a guy who was nearing total victory in a harrowing and nightmarish several-year battle with neurological damages from Lyme disease, was about to escape from graduate school for at least a little while and possibly forever, thought of himself as a solo adventurer and of solo adventurism itself as transcendent, and was so thoroughly beaten up and sickened from the escapades of the night before that he was practically hallucinating. His point, stated as gently as he could, was that people like me are pillagers too.

When I got home from Moab a week later, Rex still wanted to murder me for once again risking so much for so little, and she explained this in a way best described as *thorough*. She dumped me soon after, although we remain close friends to this day.

This was, you might say, a turning point. I knew I wouldn't be able to stop myself from charging off on zany walkabouts like a hopped-up hamster in a series of perilous mazes, and I've never really bothered to try. However, if I could steer that impulse toward efforts that yielded tangible benefits for the places I loved and the people for they it mattered most, I might just be able to pay down some of the enormous debt that I undoubtedly owed to places like Bears Ears—constant visits to which helped keep me from going off the deep end during approximately three years of multifaceted nightmares. The time had come to find some way to give back.

And I found one. Or, rather, it found me.

Chapter Twelve: The Builders

Efforts to create elevated* protection status for the Bears Ears area date back at least to 1934, when the 2016 monument footprint was part of an enormous proposed Escalante National Monument. Although efforts to protect the archaeology of the area date back to nearer the start of the 1900s, when Edgar Lee Hewett called it the Bluff District in a report to the General Land Office in which he called for preservation of the historic and prehistoric ruins of the Southwest. But the Escalante proposal of the 1930s is where the idea of legislative protection first set down roots.

Going back to the Great Depression of the 1930s: owing to a sparse population density that precluded the type of socioeconomic programs that worked in more densely populated areas, the principle solution proposed for the state of Utah was intensified focus on land and resource uses. And that meant *all* uses. Zion and Bryce National Parks were already established prior to the great crash, and their revenue streams suggested that use of the land through recreational tourism was as safe an economic bet as grazing or mineral extraction.

---

* Cultural and natural resources are both technically "protected" on public lands because laws like NHPA and NEPA ensure that they can't be wantonly destroyed in the name of development without at least some effort to understand the loss and mitigate that destruction. Elevated protection—as in a designated wilderness, or a national monument or park—effectively removes private development from the table altogether.

For this reason, a newly formed Utah Planning Board started eyeing tourist attractions along the Green and Colorado River corridors, and the Utah delegation heartily endorsed the idea. A report issued by the Board in 1935, following consultation with the Utah delegation, includes the following: "An extension of authority, especially of the National Park Service, would be beneficial to the people of Utah."

Nor was archaeology left out of the scheme, although sometimes it probably should've been. An article that appeared in the *Price News-Advocate* in the 1930s, for example, reported the "transplantation of the hieroglyphics of a dead race" from a rock wall near Hanksville to the Smithsonian. Some would argue that this *detracts* from the scenic and cultural value of a given area, of course, since rare is the tourist who goes someplace to marvel and take photos of big gaps where rock art used to be. And, as usual, there's the "dead (or lost, or vanished) race" thing, which must always come as a bit of a surprise to their descendants.

The original proposal of consequence was for a new national park in Wayne County, as well as a network of roads connecting the park, Bryce and Zion National Parks, Natural Bridges, and Mesa Verde. The Wayne County national park proposal dated back to the 1920s, when Ephraim Portman Pectol and Joseph H. Hickman of Torrey established a community organization called the Wayne County-wide Wonderland Club. Both men were subsequently elected to public office, taking their notions that Wayne County deserved recreational development as a "Wonderland" with them. This prompted an investigation of the intervening area in southeastern Utah, some seven thousand square miles in total, which was de facto proposed as a national monument—named Escalante after the Spanish explorer—in April 1936 to facilitate these recreational tourism developments.

The Wilderness Society praised the move, correctly identifying the proposed monument area as the largest roadless wilderness tract in the continental United States. Interior Secretary Harold Ickes championed the proposal, and digital copies of his map are still available from the Utah Division of State History, complete with what I assume are coffee stains. But opposition appeared almost immediately from parties arguing that the lands should remain under the auspice of the Taylor Grazing Act alone, without additional legislative bondage. Sheep and cattle herders, usually bitter rivals, agreed on this point and made it clear during a series of public hearings. Representatives for the Interior Department tried to assure them that sheep and cattle wouldn't be kicked off the land, while also pointing out that *maybe* the land had already reached peak productivity for grazing and, um, was *maybe* starting to suffer because of it...?

The response was breathtaking. During one of the public meetings, a representative of San Juan cattlemen took the position that eastern tourists would find livestock just as attractive as native scenery. Tourists, he admonished, "do not want to see a bunch of bobcats and wildcats." I can't even...

In any event, the opposition gained the upper hand and the proposal died. Subsequent discussions and wrangling, which involved Mesa Verde's own Jesse Nusbaum, added up to a battle over whether grazing or recreation was a better investment for the state of Utah. A 1938 compromise proposal, meanwhile, restricted the monument area to 2,450 square miles along the Green and Colorado River corridors, encompassing smaller chunks of the landscape around it. The Park Service felt confident that this would appease the grazing contingent—incorrectly, as it turned out.

The Utah delegation, bowing to pressure from the cattle-grazing and dam-building contingents, voiced fierce opposition to the new bill. They wanted, at the very least, a rider that required local approval for all such executive proclamations. When another public hearing was called in Utah, this time to discuss the proposed Antiquities Act amendment, its result only deepened the divide between the players. Reticence turned to threats. The Utah delegation increasingly saw the proposal to put the Colorado River corridor into the hands of the Park Service as nothing less than federal overreach, while the latter increasingly viewed the former's opposition as borderline treasonous.

The year before, President Franklin Roosevelt heartily endorsed the Wayne Wonderland National Monument idea.

Roosevelt created the monument in August of that year, giving it the more auspicious name of Capitol Reef. Nobody objected, as the Utah delegation and the state's grazing interests were still on board with the idea (it was Escalante National Monument they opposed), although there wasn't any funding available for its management. A historian named Charles Kelly offered to volunteer his services as the monument's custodian, as Zeke Johnson did for Natural Bridges between 1923 and 1941. Kelly in turn found himself increasingly alarmed at the US Atomic Energy Commission's seemingly limitless lust for uranium prospecting during the 1950s, and kicked off the campaign that would lead to its becoming a national park in 1971 largely to prevent it from being mined.

What happened next in the story of Escalante National Monument is one of those curious quirks of history. World War II, which had commenced with Hitler's invasion of Poland in September of 1939, failed to attract more than interested observation from the United States for the first little while, even after Winston Churchill famously begged "the New World, with all its power and might" to step forth and lend a hand in 1940. That situation changed dramatically in December of 1941, after Hitler's ally in the Pacific decided it might be fun to awaken a sleeping giant (in the words of Japanese Admiral Isoroku Yamamoto) with a surprise attack on Pearl Harbor. The giant wasn't thrilled. We officially entered World War II within hours of the attack, and soon enough the demands of national defense took precedence over everything else—especially where allocation of natural resources was concerned.

The Escalante National Monument proposal died in committee as a result, never making it off the congressional floor with a determined Yay or Nay attached to it, and wasn't reopened until a small portion of its total footprint was considered for recreational development in the 1960s. That portion became Canyonlands National Park.

Concerted efforts on the conservation front simmered down after that, at least in the Bears Ears area, while construction of roads to facilitate logging and uranium hauling—and, consequently, looting—ticked along at a steady but not altogether alarming pace. Then came the 1980s and an effort by the National Parks Conservation Association to expand the boundary of Canyon-lands out to the rims formed by the Green and Colorado River corridors. This effort gained traction in the 1990s under Super-intendent Walt Dabney, who considered it not an expansion of the park so much as its "completion." The park had already been expanded once, in 1971, but its boundary was still determined by politics far more than by environmental or topographic factors.

Most of the Utah delegation pushed back, not surprisingly, and the Canyonlands completion effort stalled out.

Along a parallel trajectory, Utah representative Wayne Owens took it upon himself in the 1970s to re-propose the can-yons of the Escalante River as a national park during his first term in Congress. He received little support, and so allowed the proposal to die on the vine, but he continued to campaign on its behalf in a personal way for the next twenty years. By the 1990s, when Dabney was busily trying to expand Canyonlands, Owens and the BLM had become allies in their efforts to turn the entire Escalante River drainage basin into a national conservation area, or scenic area, or recreation area—*something* that offered elevated protection. They got their wish in 1996, when President Bill Clin-ton incorporated this area into the 1.8-million-acre Grand Stair-case-Escalante National Monument, although getting that wish also helped light the fuse on a powder keg of local rage that would have dire implications later on.

Frustrated by the setbacks and roadblocks that stymied efforts to expand the boundary of Canyonlands National Park, advocates of elevated environmental protection were embold-ened by the creation of Grand Staircase-Escalante National Monument, and decided that campaigning on behalf of another national monument might prove a more effective strategy. Nobody bothered with this approach during the two presidential terms of George W. Bush, not being overly eager to attract atten-tion during his administration, but after Barack Obama took office in 2008 the conservation effort tentatively peeked its head out of the shadows. A draft legal memo was circulated within the administration that identified seventeen different areas that warranted consideration as possible national monument sites under the Antiquities Act, including sites in Utah's San Rafael Swell, Cedar Mesa, Desolation Canyon, and, of course, Canyonlands regions.

Among Utah politicians, Congressman Rob Bishop probably took the advisory memo on potential national monuments most seriously. To him, and to his constituents, it was a threat.

Conservationists were still hanging back, for the most part— but when President Obama was reelected in 2012, they sprang from cover. Having scored a second term in office, and with potential reelection now firmly off the table, the possibility that he would cement his legacy with something like a large national monument seemed likely. Concerted conservation initiatives, like the Greater Canyonlands proposal that sought to codify what Dabney characterized as the park's completion, began to catalyze. Bishop's defensive strategy started to catalyze as well.

While all of this was going on, Native Americans throughout the northern Southwest reached a point of frustration where they, too, were beginning to campaign more aggressively for protection of their ancestral and sacred lands and resources. Burns like that of the Black Mesa controversy still stung. Badly. As did the multitude of other destructive injustices perpetrated against them, including all the other places they consider sacred that were lost to "development," "progress," and/or "just because." This became a major rallying point in the American Indian Movement, the Native American Rights Fund, and other similar causes.

In the Bears Ears area, the graverobbing that had commenced and accelerated there following its popularization with the Wetherill and Hayden efforts did not go unnoticed by the tribes any more than by archaeologists. Going back to at least the end of World War II, a growing chorus of Indigenous voices publicly decried the rampant desecration of their ancestral burial places. Nor had they failed to notice when the effort to protect the place as a portion of the proposed Escalante National Monument failed.

When Robert Kennedy was running for president in 1968, the tribes invited him to a meeting in Bluff and begged him to do something to protect the innumerable natural and cultural resources of the area they all considered sacred. Whether he agreed to or not became immaterial when he was assassinated before the election even happened. The election went to Nixon—who, ironically enough, went on to draft EO 11593, thereby making it easier to protect those very places and resources under NHPA.

In 2010, Senator Robert Bennett asked the Indigenous people in San Juan County if they had any interest in how public lands were managed. I don't know what answer he expected other than "uh, *yes*?" Which is about how the Utah Tribal Leaders Association responded in March of that year. They requested "full engagement and consultation with local and regional tribes in county-by-county land use planning and legislative processes..." so long as the process provided early, honest, and transparent considering of rights and interests of the individual tribes. This represented the response by tribal leaders of the Navajo Nation, Skull Valley Band of Goshutes, Paiute Tribe of Utah, Uinta/Ouray Ute Tribe, NW Band of the Shoshone Nation, Ute Mountain Ute Tribe (including White Mesa), and the Confederated Goshute Tribe.

But the response from many tribal elders at ground level was a bit more gun-shy, for frankly understandable reasons: they were afraid to speak of the deeper connections they had to the landscape for fear of what might still get taken away. Members of what would subsequently crystallize into the nonprofit advocacy group Utah Diné Bikéyah (which means approximately "the Diné people's sacred homelands in Utah"), or UDB, hastened to address this. Along with a group called Round River Conservation Studies, they helped initiate the response to Bennett's request by doing things like interviewing off-reservation Diné elders—many of whom didn't even speak English—in a manner they'd find comfortable and respectful. After Senator Bennett was ousted later in 2010 by a Tea Party insurgency, these efforts simply continued without him.

It was also in 2010 that another advocacy group was founded in the Bears Ears area: the oft-mentioned Friends of Cedar Mesa. It was created by former BLM ranger Mark Meloy, widower of incomparable wilderness author Ellen Meloy, with the original intent of supporting and assisting the agency in its efforts on the eponymous plateau.

In the decade between their founding and publication of this book, FCM has operated and grown somewhat dramatically. They've become an effective watchdog group for state- and federal-level management, taking actively oppositional roles on topics like oil and gas leasing in sensitive areas. They've trained and utilized scores of volunteers for projects like trail maintenance, fence- and sign-construction, and archaeological site stewardship. They've even used their own accrued capital for contracting private firms to conduct cultural resource inventories and stabilization projects in the area, many of them with fund-matching grants from the agencies.

All this from an "office" that, until just a couple years ago, consisted of a pair of desks in the front half of a tiny brick building in Bluff.

Starting in 2012, FCM began cobbling together a skeletal development plan for what they call their Cultural Resources Defense Campaign. It's a three-pronged plan that consists of assisting local land management agencies in the areas of law enforcement, education, and site monitoring and recording. The last of these prongs includes the archaeology-focused projects already mentioned. The second includes an impressive fundraising campaign to purchase a building known affectionately around Bluff as the NadaBar* and turn it into the Bears Ears Education Center, their hub of operation since September of 2018.

As for assisting with law enforcement: starting in 2016, FCM partnered with land managers to begin offering a $2,500 reward for anyone with information leading to the conviction of looters,

---

* Location of the old Silver Dollar Saloon, which went defunct in the 1980s, after which it served as an art gallery and social gathering place— and, if the authorities asked, most definitely "not a bar."

vandals, and other ne'er-do-wells bent on perpetrating vileness toward Bears Ears' irreplaceable material history. In the words of current FCM president and long-time local adventure guide Vaughn Hadenfeldt, "hopefully twenty-five-hundred bucks is enough to entice one meth head to rat out another."

Getting back to the other fledgling nonprofit: by the end of their second year, the proto-UDB contingent had ramped up their ethnographic efforts and begun to engage politically as a voice for all seven Diné chapter houses (the administrative meeting places where Navajo Nation locals can gather and voice their opinions to their respective council delegates) within the state of Utah. They published a book of their results, with the punctual title *Diné Bikéyah*, and gauged its response as a metric for whether non-Indigenous people were interested in hearing what Native American elders had to say about land and resource management. A surprising number of them were. By the middle of 2011, they had seeded the idea for a Diné Bikéyah National Conservation Area in official correspondence with Utah State Director Juan Palma and Interior Secretary Ken Salazar.

In 2012, UDB was officially certified as a 501(c)(3) nonprofit organization, thanks in part to financial backing from Round River, and thereafter marched forth on their own. The first step was helping to facilitate a Memorandum of Agreement between the Navajo Nation and San Juan County to engage in an eighteen-month joint land-planning process, which then died on the vine for the usual political reasons. But UDB didn't cease their march, openly acknowledging the entire time that their backup plan was a national monument proposal should the joint planning process fail.

Officially, UDB's goal was to determine the most effective footprint for conservation imperatives in southeastern Utah that were consonant with Indigenous tradition and history. The result (one of them, anyway) was something that's variously called ethnographic or holistic mapping, which involved producing an ethnography that was massive in scale—pulling together traditional cultural knowledge from a range of sources—and generating a detailed map as a result.

To give just a small but important taste of what that included, ethnographic data collected by UDB from tribal elders identified the confluence of the San Juan and Colorado Rivers to be of almost incomparable cultural importance. This is borne out in the published literature as well, although I don't think it was ever synthesized before they did so in 2013. No fewer than a dozen publications by ethnographers and archaeologists from the late 1800s and early 1900s identify that confluence as Tokonabi* in the Hopi cultural geography, point of origin for two of their oldest and most revered societies.

The mighty Rainbow Bridge, that means so much to so many, is also located near Navajo Mountain and the San Juan-Colorado confluence. Navajo Mountain itself—called *Naatsis'áán* in Diné—is associated with the head of their sacred matriarch and "pollen figure," of which Black Mesa is the body and Balakai Mesa the lower extremities, according to oral histories collected into a 1941 Department of the Interior volume called, fittingly enough, *Diné Bikéyah*. The broken-up and canyon-cut riverine borderlands just to the north of the mountain are variously considered powerful, sacred, and forbidden.

The San Juan Paiutes, meanwhile, have considered the San Juan-Colorado confluence integral to their cultural geography from as early as AD 1300. One of the south-trending tributaries just east of the confluence is called Piute Canyon for this reason.

Thus, if you wanted to pinpoint a single place in southeastern Utah that is of paramount importance to nearly all the tribes associated with the region, the confluence of the San Juan and Colorado Rivers would be the one (the confluence of the Colorado and Little Colorado Rivers being its only tentative rival). The fact that it's currently part of Lake Powell is therefore a bit of a sore spot.

The enormous ethnographic project conducted by UDB resulted, in part, in a big map that clearly displayed immense

---

* Or *Toko'nabi*, or *Tokónabi*, or *Toko'navi*. This will happen when people from a different culture try to transcribe a word that's never been written down before.

cultural knowledge and importance. In 2013, the sum of their efforts was formalized as a report that formed the basis of a subsequent proposal for a 1.9-million-acre Diné Bikéyah National Conservation Area. The proposal was unveiled in an open house convened in Monticello in August of that year.

Nor were they alone in pushing for better protections in the Bears Ears area. Starting in 2012, and reaching critical mass in 2014, FCM started pushing for a national conservation area or monument that encompassed Cedar Mesa and the major drainages on either side of it. Their proposal totaled 707,000 acres, and included approximately 56,000 known archaeological sites, four wilderness study areas, and the Grand Gulch Primitive Area. Their goal was to get enough citizens on their side to warrant presidential action and, as in the case of Grand Staircase-Escalante, trigger an Antiquities Act proclamation that would neatly circumvent opposition by the Utah delegation. "Anywhere else in the world," as FCM executive director Josh Ewing explained it to the *Salt Lake Tribune*, "this region would be nationally protected, even without the archaeology."

The Crow Canyon Archaeological Center backed this effort by sending an open letter with 120 signatories to the Utah delegation on its behalf. In late 2014, a special double issue of *Archaeology Southwest Magazine*, edited by Bill Lipe, was created and published as a result—something that would repeat itself three years later, this time with me and a colleague at the helm.

And, of course, there was the Greater Canyonlands proposal, whose boundary included the Bears Ears area and quite a lot of the surrounding landscape as well.

All these mounting challenges to anti-federal sentiments were being closely monitored by Congressman Bishop, going back to the internal memo about potential conservation areas. With help from fellow Utah congressman Jason Chaffetz, Bishop's response was to draft and propose a congressional alternative that they hoped would prevent presidential action.

Starting in 2013, Bishop and Chaffetz spearheaded an effort called the Public Lands Initiative (PLI) around the stated goal of reaching a consensus for management of public lands in eastern and southern Utah. It was touted as a "grand bargain" designed to end public land disputes through cooperative agreements on land management from a bottom-up rather than top-down approach. This consisted principally of canvassing county commissioners and a few other stakeholders throughout rural Utah counties for about three years, including open house forums like the one where the Diné Bikéyah National Conservation Area proposal was formally presented.

In theory, the PLI was a wonderful idea. In addition to being more locally focused than any of the federal alternatives, it called for the identification of areas of critical environmental or cultural concern, suggested land exchanges and management plans for those and all surrounding areas, and even went a step further than most of the alternative proposals by calling for the creation of designated wilderness areas.

That's a pretty big deal. Officially designated wilderness sits at the very top of the hierarchy of public land and resource protection status. Since the Wilderness Act was passed in 1964, Congress has designated just over 110 million acres of public land as official wilderness, including the Dark Canyon Wilderness in southeastern Utah. Grand Gulch has been managed as a "primitive area" since 1970, which means there aren't any visitor services and you're not allowed to have campfires, but even the mighty Gulch isn't afforded the protected status of an official wilderness.

For these and other reasons, a lot of people were excited by the PLI, including conservation groups like Grand Canyon Trust, who poured a lot of hard work into gathering data for it from the very beginning. However, in their own words, "by mid-2015 it [had] become clear that 'consensus' was no longer Representative Bishop's goal." Something else was afoot.

Analysis of the steadily evolving bill by groups like Southern Utah Wilderness Alliance (SUWA) showed that the designated wilderness areas were being plopped down on top of areas that were already wilderness study areas, or WSAs, which didn't expand protective footprints at all—and, in a few cases, reduced them. It was also becoming painfully obvious that dissenting voices were being marginalized or left out of the process altogether.

Tribal representatives in Utah were eager to develop an agreement within the umbrella of the PLI process, considering it the most likely method of getting the elevated protections they were seeking through their own proposal. To that end, they made at least twenty-five presentations at PLI hearings and a series of trips to Washington, DC, over the same three-year period that other concerned groups were trying to help the process. But it wasn't long before many of these tribal representatives began complaining that they were mostly treated with derision and scorn, particularly Ute Mountain Ute councilwoman Regina Lopez-Whiteskunk, who was treated with derision and scorn *and* blatant misogyny.

Nobody from the Utah delegation made any substantive public comments about the tribes' input or the proposal they were suggesting, and although it was supposed to be included as one of the management alternatives in the San Juan County Commission's 2014 public hearing on their portion of the PLI, it never appeared. Its supporters responded by waging a write-in war, representing almost sixty-five percent of received public comments in San Juan County and forcing the commission's hand.

What the write-in campaign forced that hand to do was, in effect, extend its middle finger. They formally acknowledged the write-in data, and then simply ignored the results and went on in their usual fashion.

When the PLI was finally released in 2016, a lot of this shadiness started to make sense. For one thing, it called for the transfer of one hundred thousand acres of Ute Reservation land to the state for fossil fuel development, in exchange for other parcels in other parts of the state, all without the Ute Tribe's consent. A billboard was immediately erected near the Uintah-Ouray Reservation calling the PLI nothing more than a "21st Century Indian Land-grab" and, as of this writing, it's still there.

The PLI also called for increased development of uranium on public lands across the state, a number of other public-to-state land transfers that preferentially benefited developers over the public, increased grazing leases, and other ills besides. Moreover, when carefully scrutinized by legal scholars like the University of Utah's John Ruple, it turned out the actual wording in the PLI's so-called wilderness and conservation area designations made development *easier* rather than limiting or curtailing it.

It was becoming painfully clear that three years of public input had consisted of Bishop and Chaffetz inputting the amassed data straight into the toilet, at least where San Juan County was concerned. The only input that really mattered to them was from the usual cast of big-money political puppeteers.

Worse still, the PLI included a ticking bomb. One of its stipulations was that the Antiquities Act would henceforth not have any power whatsoever in seven counties in Utah, including all the counties with the densest and most outstanding archaeology. Similar legislation is on the books in Wyoming and Alaska, but their laws require congressional ratification of Antiquities Act usage (which, effectively, gives back to the legislative branch what Lacey's bill carved out for the executive) rather than preventing its usage altogether. Even the most ardent critics of the Antiquities Act hadn't gone *that* far, at least not successfully.

It was a bold move by Bishop, in other words—one that greatly pleased many of his constituents. It also helped the PLI's chances in Washington the way a sledgehammer helps a soufflé.

About a year before all that came to light, the tribes decided they'd had enough.

In the spring of 2015, tribal representatives convened a series of meetings in Towaoc, Colorado, within the Ute Mountain Ute Reservation. The results of the meetings were unprecedented. What ultimately emerged was the Bears Ears Inter-Tribal Coalition, a consortium comprised of Hopi, Diné, Zuñi, Ute Mountain Ute, and Uintah-Ouray Ute representatives—groups that share a long and occasionally very colorful history in the Bears Ears area. They had found a common cause: the 1.9-million-acre protection area identified by UDB. And they were ready to go to war for it.

The commonality of the Coalition's cause may seem fairly straightforward, on its surface, but two underlying elements nonetheless warrant additional consideration. The first is the tribes' respective histories briefly summarized in this book, particularly land-use/access tensions that have boiled out of foul vagaries like the Black Mesa coal conspiracy. These are entirely different groups, after all—or, legally speaking, sovereign nations. Shouldering all of that aside in order to work together on a shared goal speaks volumes about how special that goal is.

The second is a remarkable ethnolinguistic curiosity, one whose existence I hadn't even realized until UDB cultural resources coordinator Angelo Baca pointed it out. In the different languages of all the tribes involved in the Coalition—and, presumably, numerous others—Bears Ears is known as Bears Ears.

These aren't just different languages, although that alone would be enough. They represent entirely different language *families*, some of them as distinct from one another as Latin and Mandarin. Hence presenting my snapshots of regional tribal history in terms of linguistic affiliations. The Athabaskan-speaking Diné and Apache people, the Numic-speaking Ute and Paiute people, the Uto-Aztecan-speaking Hopi people, and the Zuñi-speaking Zuñi people (their language is entirely unlike any other in the known world) have different names for every other area, landform, waterway, animal, vegetable, and mineral in the region. But they all refer to those twin sandstone formations by their respective term for the ears of a bear. I know of no other such case, anywhere.

In early October of 2015, UDB began mustering allies in the archaeological community to help them in their fight. Former state archaeologist Kevin Jones was tasked with heading up the creation of a sort-of legal white paper comprised of statements from a selection of local experts about the archaeological importance—and need for protection—of the major landforms that make up the Bears Ears area. As Kevin put it, the effort centered on a need to "portray the resources of each of the geographic segments of the proposal in a clear and understandable way, for public presentations and testimony in hearings and meetings."

Somehow or other, I qualified. My testimony on what they were calling the Headwaters area, or the *high uplands* to geological nitpickers, was incorporated into Kevin's report and bundled in with UDB's ethnographic efforts for use by the Coalition. This was the first time UDB and I clasped hands, so to speak, although neither of us realized it at the time.

The collection and collation of those data by Kevin and his team all took place in about ten days, which is probably some sort of record. The Coalition submitted their "Proposal to President Barack Obama for the Creation of Bears Ears National Monument" on October 15, 2015. The response from the PLI contingent was to ramp up efforts to rally its own supporters against it.

The PLI was touted, as often and as loudly as possible, as "local" and "Utah-based;" while invectives like "outsiders" and "elites" were hurled at its pro-monument detractors. So far as I can tell, the goal was to get so many Utahns on the PLI side and opposed to the monument that Obama wouldn't dare designate the latter. And then, when that lopsided land grab disguised as a management bill went down like a lead balloon, there would be no elevated protections at all. The result wouldn't be the sweetheart deal for developers that the PLI was supposed to be, but at least business could proceed as usual.

Meanwhile, with UDB's vision for a conservation area now subsumed into the Coalition's much more aggressive Bears Ears National Monument proposal, FCM and the Greater Canyonlands proponents (namely SUWA and Grand Canyon Trust) wisely dropped their alternatives and jumped aboard. At about the same time, the All Pueblo Council, which had previously lobbied the Utah delegation and the Obama administration in support of the protections being proposed by both UDB and FCM, also submitted a revision steering their support toward the Coalition's proposal. The Bears Ears army was growing.

By early summer of 2016, journalists across the country started zeroing-in on the topic. Utah state representative Mike Noel responded by publicly calling the entire Bears Ears effort a sham, claiming that the only digging taking place at archaeological sites in southeast Utah was that of badgers. Jonathan Bailey and I had a field day with that one. He began sketching T-shirt and mug designs featuring badgers in full Indiana Jones regalia, and I started bringing a stuffed toy badger on my backcountry hikes so that I could pose it at sites in what I generously hoped were hilarious photos. Popular Utah-based political cartoonist Pat Bagley also noticed the gaffe, and a comic soon appeared lampooning it.

More aggressive ploys to undermine the monument effort soon began to pop up here and there in the surrounding area, one of them being the suspiciously sudden and conspicuously located sale of a 391-acre section of SITLA* land straddling the highway that passes through Comb Ridge on the south end. The sale of State Trust parcels is not directly connected with federal designations, at least not inherently, but this particular parcel straddles the highway that crosses Comb Ridge into the proposed monument boundary—its privatization would be a big thorn in the monument effort's side. Tellingly, the parcel was nominated for sale by the Bluff-based Hole-in-the-Rock Foundation (HIRF), an LDS organization openly opposed to the monument. Conservationists smelled a rat, and a public hearing was convened in Bluff to discuss the sale.

I had moved to the area following the potently self-reflective "Scotty's dog" incident, so I drove down from my then-home in Monticello to attend the hearing. It would turn out to be the foundational event in escalating my involvement in the Bears Ears effort.

After enduring questions and statements from a handful of concerned citizens, one of the HIRF individuals trying to broker the auction took the stand. He smiled an easy, relaxed smile, and told everyone that he understood how they felt. He even

---

* The Utah State Institutional Trust Lands Administration, overseers of State Trust lands in Utah. As part of a bargain upon entering the Union, each state has a generous handful of these whose sale they can use to support public institutions, schools, and so forth.

368 BEHIND THE BEARS EARS

cast flimsy deference toward the Diné woman who'd just said, in admirably terse language, that she doesn't trust people like him. He assured us all, with a lubricious smile, that he and his kind were nobody to fear. He then made a pawing reference to their journey to the area, ending with the observation that, upon arrival, "we got red dirt on our shoes and red dirt in our hearts."

That's the point where I snapped.

I've studied linguistics, as most anthropologists are required to do, and I know all about framing—the act of carefully arranging words in order to create an impression rather than convey a straightforward message. What's more, my first degree program at the University of New Orleans was in English literature and composition, and although I didn't finish that program I still learned a lot about poetry—the act of carefully arranging words in order to create a feeling. Political rhetoric is often nothing more than a clever combination of the two.

Take President Franklin D. Roosevelt, who famously said "we have nothing to fear, but fear itself," to a chorus of cheers that was so loud—and that echoed and resounded for so long—that almost nobody has quite realized how paradoxical it is. Fear is an emotion, after all. There is nothing to which we should feel an emotion except as a response to that particular emotion itself? That's a recipe for madness.

Nor is FDR's non-convergent catechism anything new. Ahead of the American Revolution, for example, people took to the streets chanting "No taxation without representation!" Since we now live under a representative form of government—a republic, in other words, and supposedly a democratic one—it's easy to post-hoc rationalize this slogan in those terms. But those things didn't exist in Europe or its colonies during pre-Revolutionary times except among a handful of French philosophers and, ironically enough, several tribes of what were then considered Native American "savages" (in particular the Iroquois nations). So, what did it really mean?

Nothing. It meant nothing. It just *sounded* good, so people took to the streets and marched to it.

Beware of this stuff. Minstrels and troubadours learned

long ago that they could lure dimwitted people into bed with clever-sounding nonsense, and this did not go unnoticed by politicians.

I expressed much of this in a *Salt Lake Tribune* op-ed the following morning, and my involvement snowballed from there. I wrote and published additional op-eds for a number of local and regional periodicals, after that—sometimes on my own, and sometimes with coauthor and fellow Flagstaff firebrand Bess Bennett. Our best coauthored piece appeared in an issue of the *Navajo-Hopi Observer*, a respected regional periodical that serves the Indigenous community of northern Arizona, which was exceedingly flattering to me.

Before long, I attracted the attentions of Jonathan Bailey and his own rather extensive social circle in the conservation realm, which is how we became friends and eventual colleagues. Friends of Cedar Mesa took notice of me during this time as well, and began tossing little research and advocacy projects my way—and then, as time went on, bigger and bigger ones. So did Archaeology Southwest, specifically in the form of their *Preservation Archaeology* blog, and my relationship with them also grew momentously from there. It wasn't long before I was considered one of the most outspoken Bears Ears allies in the local archaeological community, right alongside longtime BLM archaeologist Don Simonis and, of course, Bill Lipe.

In the interest of fair reporting, however, I should note that not all archaeologists are in favor of the monument. Some of the better-reasoned among them oppose it because they think the increased attention from pro-monument voices will do more harm than any elevated protections can reasonably mitigate. Others are opposed because they confidently believe in the power of watchdog groups and federal agencies to conduct effective and respectful resource management without elevated mandates to begin with. Still others think that creation and defense of the monument might ultimately weaken the playing position of the Antiquities Act, effectively tolling its death knell a mere 110 years after its creation.

Less well-reasoned examples include privilege-blind aversion to having to share favorite field destinations, the daunting terror that someone else might stumble upon better research topics or data, and so on. One particular specimen openly opposes the monument for no discernible reason beyond the fact that I openly support it and I once dated a girl that he liked.

The strongest and most judicious anti-monument sentiments in the archaeological community in those early days probably came from Winston Hurst, who grew up in Blanding and believes—along with me, in most cases—that heavy-handed authoritarian tactics rarely fix things. Look at the War on Drugs. It's done a great job of destabilizing a few South American countries and ruining the lives of thousands of mostly ethnic-minority Americans caught with enough marijuana to get a lab rat stoned for half an hour, but I don't know what else to say about it.

For that matter, look at Cerberus.

In a poignant essay written for Stanford's Bill Lane Center for the American West, Winston explains how top-down protectionist efforts equate to "an end run around the local populations who are most powerfully positioned to protect the land or abuse it." He's got a point. People tend to react to that sort of thing with hostility. Putting up a sign (and *nothing else*) that says "This Place Is Now Federally Protected" while fervently stoking anti-federalism in the local community is like threatening your dogs for growling at the cat and then locking them all outside together.

I happen to still be pro-monument, if you couldn't tell from the *book* I've written about it, but these are valid concerns. And they have worsened in alarmingly short order. Among conservationists, the worst-case scenario was creation of the monument just ahead of the swearing-in of an executive administration that would defund, reduce, and/or otherwise undermine its protected status after their highly publicized efforts had advertised the place to the entire world—which is exactly what happened.

Still, most of the archaeological community—in the surrounding region, at any rate—rallied to the side of the tribes, and with good reason. Yes, the place houses an abundance of interesting old stuff, but so does every other region that's played host to numerous human groups through the ages. The truly unique component is how the Bears Ears area has played a critical role in the growth and development of the field itself. There was Jackson and Holmes in the 1870s; followed by Graham, McLoyd, and the Wetherills (and, to a certain extent, Moorehead) in the 1890s; and then Nelson, and Bernheimer, and Judd, and Kidder, Cummings, Brew, Matson and Lipe, and so on—right up to the equally colorful characters of the present day. Never has the place waned in importance for the archaeological community, and never has it ceased to teach lessons. The history of the archaeology of Bears Ears is a coming-of-age narrative that traces an intriguing path from colonialistic treasure-hunting to cross-cultural collaboration.

In the end, a little over seven hundred archaeologists signed an open letter in June of 2016 urging President Obama to proclaim the national monument being proposed by UDB and the Coalition. Considering that the annual meeting of the Society for American Archaeology routinely boasts upward of five thousand attendees—enough, evidently, to drink downtown Austin nearly dry—that doesn't seem like much, but remember that archaeology is a regional science. Before the controversy started making national headlines, I spoke with a few Great Basin archaeologists who didn't even know what "a Bears Ears" is, and the Great Basin is practically right next door. So, yeah, that's an impressive turnout.

Later that same month, Interior Secretary Sally Jewell and some other DC dignitaries decided to hold a public meeting in Bluff to gauge the locals' feelings on the issue. It was a circus. The town of Bluff, with a population of around three hundred if you count the deer in people's lawns, played host to approximately two thousand people—all of them crowded inside and/or around the community center.

My job was to help corral the attendees and try to prevent hostilities from breaking out. They never did, thankfully, although they came close a few times—like when at least one local resident showed up just to scream hateful things in the faces of "outsiders" from such distant lands as a few hours up the road. People from the *Salt Lake Tribune* were on hand to enshrine that development, and a few others like it, but no actual blood was shed.

Jewell herself had arrived a few days before to go hiking. She wanted to see the landforms and archaeological splendors of the Bears Ears area for herself. So, FCM's Josh Ewing and Vaughn Hadenfeldt, along with BLM archaeologist Cameron Cox, took her on several ambles to see a few of them, and the effect it had on her was palpable. Josh has a photo of her on one of those hikes that he provided to the *Tribune* for their blanket coverage of the meeting, and the image alone warrants ear protection.

Back in Bluff, a lottery system was used to address the out-pouring of public sentiment, and selected speakers were given two minutes to address the assembly—which consisted of Secretary Jewell, Under Secretary of Agriculture for Natural Resources and Environment Robert Bonnie, BLM Director Neil Kornze, acting Assistant Secretary for Indian Affairs Larry Roberts, National Park Service Director John Jarvis, and Regional Forester Don Jirón. Some of my friends gathered up a handful of raffle tickets and shoved them into my hands. Others did the same for Kevin Jones, who ended up with about fifteen of them. Neither of us got to speak. After the event, Kevin commented that this is why he "doesn't play the lottery."

You can see all of the comments on YouTube. Some of them are impressive. Most of them are at least coherent. A few of them sound the way hip-hop diss tracks would if they were ghostwritten by kindergarteners.

Jonathan Till and Laurie Webster both managed to give arrestingly comprehensive full-length lectures on the archae-ology of the area in their two-minute slots. I have no idea how they pulled that off. I agree with Bill Lipe that it's *far* easier to be verbose than to be concise. The best I could do would be ninety seconds of sputtering followed by "…it's complicated."

Probably good they didn't pick any of my tickets during the raffle.

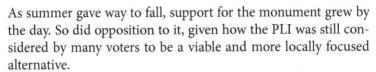

As summer gave way to fall, support for the monument grew by the day. So did opposition to it, given how the PLI was still considered by many voters to be a viable and more locally focused alternative.

Conservationists, legal experts, and just about anyone else who'd actually *read* the PLI suspected that it didn't stand a chance. They were right. The 114th House of Representatives retired for the year on December 8 without having bothered to vote on Bishop and Chaffetz's bill at all. Cheers were stifled, however, because by then something else had happened. Something of much greater consequence.

Reality-television star Donald J. Trump was elected the forty-fifth president of the United States on November 10, 2016—by a respectable margin of negative three million votes.

For Bears Ears, it was a worst-case scenario. If President Obama created the monument during his last two months in office, one of Trump's first acts—as avowed destroyer of everything his predecessor had accomplished—would be to attack it. The Utah delegation would make damn sure of that. The ensuing battle would attract yet more public attention, even while the elevated protections offered by national monument status were weakened or, worse, yanked away altogether. A lot of people I know threw the brakes on their Bears Ears advocacy efforts for this reason, hoping the outgoing president would take the hint.

The president, to his immeasurable credit, ignored them.

Following months of careful planning and consultation, President Obama proclaimed Bears Ears National Monument on December 28 as his final major act before leaving office. His proclamation protected 1.35 million acres, following as closely as possible the map drawn up during the PLI process. It also included unprecedented administrative management roles for the tribes in two distinct forms: a dedicated Bears Ears Commission, which would include one elected representative from each of the five Coalition tribes, and an advisory committee comprised of various local and tribal stakeholders. Responses from Native

Americans—the ones to whom I spoke, anyway—and traditionally left-leaning communities like downtown Flagstaff were mostly tearful rejoices.

Responses from traditionally right-leaning communities, like those of rural southeastern Utah, were precisely the opposite. Protestors flooded downtown Monticello almost immediately, bearing signs hastily emblazoned with slogans like "Rural Lives Matter" (take *that*, victims of racially motivated gunplay) and the slightly more popular "Trump This Monument." The response from the man himself would come soon enough.

Honestly, I can sympathize with the locals, especially after living there for a spell. Their track record of interactions with Big Brother makes for an uncomfortable read, as in the Cerberus debacle. And, as their abundant testimony at the public lands hearing demonstrated, they are largely in favor of elevated protections for their beloved region and its resources. They just want a more locally derived and locally focused version, like the PLI, an admittedly great idea whose own authors preemptively scuttled it with an enfilade of politics-as-usual.

Where we disagree is on the contention that state local government is, by default and unilaterally, a better option. This circles back to the issue of Moab and its current status as a compressed-spring canister that spews overcrowding and Jeep fumes instead of paper snakes. The local government is causing that, under orders from the state, by doing things like devoting at least forty-seven percent of tourism taxation toward advertising for even more tourism *by law*.

Moreover, it was state officials—not Patagonia, or Osprey, or the North Face, or Edward Abbey—who created the Mighty 5 campaign that helped turn portions of Arches, Bryce, Zion, Canyonlands, and Capitol Reef into the outdoor equivalent of sardine cans. Advocates of entirely stateside land management would do well to remember what Jim Stiles wrote in his *Canyon Country Zephyr* back in 2008: "Look at the locations of *all* SITLA lands adjacent to paved roads in scenic areas. That is your [state lands-development] blueprint for the future." I have yet to see him proven wrong on this.

Anyway, as a person born and raised "rural" myself, I still understand the wariness toward top-down government control. Having lived in southeast Utah and studied the local history, I understand it even more. Locals and out-of-staters alike agree that the Bears Ears area warrants elevated protections. Given the local culture and their open hostility toward the federal government, the PLI would have been the best method of accomplishing this *if* its final form wasn't so twisted and ineffectual. But it was. That left only two options: no elevated protections at all, or the national monument proposal. Blame Bishop and Chaffetz.

At 1.35 million acres, the monument was considerably smaller than the 1.9 million acres proposed by the Inter-Tribal Coalition, principally because Red Canyon and a few other places with small amounts of extractable uranium were excluded in the hopes that throwing such bones would satisfy the detractors from that particular realm.* The boundary also stopped way short of the San Juan-Colorado confluence, arguably the most sacred locality within the landscape to the local tribes (although the phrase "most sacred" is just about as essentialist and grammatically unsound as a phrase can get), for what I presume are political reasons beyond my realm of comprehension.

But there was something else at work with how the boundary was drawn: it almost perfectly matched the proposed boundary included in the now-defunct PLI. It was almost like a challenge. "If the Utah delegation was sincere about wanting elevated protections for everything within this boundary," it seemed to say, "then surely they'll have no beef with it."

Then there's a little tidbit that I've never seen covered in any news article, at least as of this writing, but which could have enormous downstream political consequences. In his 2016 proclamation, President Obama specifically says that the myriad of resources in the Bears Ears area "constitute one of the densest and most significant *cultural landscapes* in the United States" [emphasis added]. To my knowledge, this is the first official document of its caliber to recognize cultural landscapes as a thing.

---

* Spoiler alert: nope.

A little under a month after the proclamation, I was invited to the celebratory event in Monument Valley recapped in the introduction, where I was encouraged by Regina Lopez-Whiteskunk to tell my Bears Ears story.

I was then contacted by lawyers who would go on to sue the Trump administration for reducing the newly created national monument. If you already have an idea of the Bears Ears National Monument timeline, that means I was contacted by people involved in a lawsuit against Trump for attacking it almost exactly a year before he actually did so.

As the kids like to say: *si vis pacem, para bellum.*

The litigants in the case to come were UDB, FCM, Patagonia, Archaeology Southwest, Conservation Lands Foundation, the Access Fund, the Society for Vertebrate Paleontology, and the National Trust for Historic Preservation. They wanted me as an author—along with Bill Lipe, Ben Bellorado, private-sector GIS whiz Zack Scribner, Southwest rock art expert Sally Cole, and FCM's Josh Ewing—and database manager on a technical report that would accompany the lawsuit.

The format of that project was a thing of genius, and I wish I knew whom to credit for it. The plan was to separate the monument area into intuitive chunks based on major landforms, and then create a georeferenced bibliography that showed where existing research and literature was focused. That way, when the Trump administration attempted to remove some or all of any portion of those landforms from the monument, a volume of research and georeferenced data related to that landform would go into the lawsuit. We were basically stringing the place with conceptual tripwires.

The major stipulations were that we had to sign a nondisclosure agreement that held until the lawsuit finally launched, and weren't to include any technical data (location info, etc.) that might get us or anyone else into trouble under ARPA. So: publicly available literature only, and don't tell a soul what you're up to.

Madeline McGill from the Rural Utah Project offered a pithy take on this legal strategy when she learned about it a few years later: "I doubt [the Trump administration] was ready for that sort of unity. My impression of those people is that they think everybody thinks like them, in terms of the things that divide everyone. The idea of a unified group of Native Americans with white scientists and corporate businesspeople probably scared the shit out of them." We certainly hoped it would, when or if it was ever deployed.

During this period, organizers of the Outdoor Retailer (or simply OR) show decided to publicly vent their outrage over the state of Utah's constant attacks on public land by pulling out of Salt Lake City. The OR is a tradeshow for the outdoor recreation industry—the biggest of its kind—that used to pump millions of dollars into SLC's economy each year. Its new home is Denver.

Utah governor Gary Herbert characterized the move as a tantrum. I won't criticize him for that. It's an apt opinion, and he's allowed to have it. What I will say is that it doesn't seem any *less* of a tantrum than screaming about how it's "overreach" for the federal government to decide what to do with federal lands. Given its incredible canyons, arguably the greatest snow on the planet, about eighty different mountain ranges, and much else besides, the state of Utah could very well be the capital of outdoor recreation in the country. Instead, it's more like the capital of mining and extraction.

Imagine someone pointing at the most fertile portion of their land and saying, "Now *there's* a good spot for a septic tank—plant the garden someplace else."

Their impetus became clear in short order. Almost the moment he was sworn in, Trump ordered newly appointed Interior Secretary Ryan Zinke to conduct a review of all national monuments larger than one hundred thousand acres created since 1996 (i.e., big ones created by Presidents Clinton, George W., and Obama). The presidential order specifically directed Zinke to determine whether or not those monuments complied with the Antiquities Act, which stipulates the "smallest area compatible with proper care and management," and determine whether or not the monuments interfered with available uses of the land under the multi-use policy of federal land management agencies.

Zinke, for his part, promised a fair and objective review of all input from stakeholders and interested parties. The process kicked off with meetings between Zinke and the Utah delegation, the San Juan County Commission, and members of the Inter-Tribal Coalition, all of whom definitely count as stakeholders and interested parties—the major difference being the meeting with Coalition members only happened after they flew to Washington, DC, and demanded one. Zinke then went on a "listening tour" that included the Bears Ears and Grand Staircase-Escalante areas, during which he harshly scolded (on camera) Diné writer and community organizer Cassandra Begay when she asked him why he seemed to be ignoring Indigenous voices.

One aspect of the review process that nobody doubted—including, seemingly, some of its staunchest supporters—was the extent to which extraction industry lobbyists were pulling the strings. Investigations by the *New York Times*, *Washington Post*, and *Roll Call* uncovered emails, memos, letters, and other evidence of machinations by the oil and uranium lobbies. Uranium company Energy Fuels lobbied biggest and loudest for the shrinking of Bears Ears National Monument, starting well before the review process ever commenced, and the fact that they own the controversial mill just outside the White Mesa Ute community probably plays no small role in this. What's more, agency emails acquired by the *Post* showed that the Interior Department dismissed, downplayed, and/or outright redacted information about the benefits of national monuments, choosing instead to emphasize the economic values of mining, timber, and—of course—grazing.

As for public involvement, the review process included a comment period for each national monument under review, during which the public would be given a chance to weigh in. Tellingly, the comment period for most of them was sixty days long, which is thirty days shorter than the public comment period for draft resource management plans and environmental impact statements under NEPA (which is a different process, of course—but it's a useful basis of comparison). If that's not suspicious enough in its own right, the comment period for Bears Ears was only fifteen days. It takes me more than fifteen days to *read* most government reports that I've seen, let alone comment on them.

Not that the Interior Department expected to learn anything new from the public. Agency officials literally said as much during training seminars leading up to the comment period, with staffers being told that the public were most likely to be largely in favor of not altering any existing monuments. And they were right. Approximately ninety-six percent of the ninety thousand comments received during the comment period for Bears Ears were in favor of national monuments in general, with about half of them mentioning Bears Ears by name.

In fact, the total number of public comments received during the fifteen-day comment period was over half a million, but bundles of comments collected by concerned groups of citizens were displayed as single comments—hence the official figure of about one-fifth that amount. When the grand total was analyzed by the Center for Western Priorities, they found that closer to ninety-nine percent of all comments gathered during the fifteen-day comment window were in support of monument designations in general and Bears Ears National Monument in particular.

In other words, the Interior Department fully expected the public to be in favor of national monuments before receiving over half a million comments to that effect. It didn't matter. Agency officials had instead directed staff to figure out how much coal, oil, and natural gas—as well as grass for grazing and timber for selling—was made harder or impossible to access by the monument designations, according to an analysis by the *New York Times*. With those data in hand, outpourings of support for elevated protection from hundreds of thousands of American citizens could be ignored. And it was.

The resulting report is a humdinger. It contains a lot of "spin," according to an analysis by the Grand Canyon Trust, including umbrella statements about how national monuments curtail hunting, fishing, and plant- and firewood-gathering by Native Americans. All of that is true enough in the case of many national monuments, which underscores the need for a lot more multivocality in American conservationism, but *none* of it applies to the two monuments that ended up on the chopping block.

Zinke also propounded a novel perspective on how the Antiquities Act should be interpreted, saying that "while early monument designations focused more on geological formations, archaeological ruins, and areas of historic interest, a more recent and broad interpretation of what constitutes an 'object of historic or scientific interest' has been expanded to include landscape areas, biodiversity, and viewsheds."

Setting aside for a moment how both of the monuments that were subsequently reduced have geological formations, archaeological ruins, and areas of historic interest in such dizzying measure that I've seen maybe one percent of them after a decade and a half of near-constant exploration, I also question the assumption that "landscape areas, biodiversity, and viewsheds" can't possibly be of historic or scientific interest. Biodiversity wouldn't even be a *word* if it wasn't for scientific interest.

Several associated documents were released and then quickly redacted, and they are more starkly revealing than the official report itself. They include language about how the creation of Bears Ears National Monument "is unlikely [to have] impacted timber production" and that "more vandalism would have occurred" and "less archaeological research would have occurred" at Grand Staircase-Escalante without the monument designation. Excising them from the final report was, I suppose, a fun exercise in seeing how long it would take journalists to find them.

Welcome to the age of the end of forgetting.

In all, Zinke recommended minor or major alterations to Bears Ears, Grand Staircase-Escalante, Gold Butte, Katahdin, Northeast Canyons and Seamounts, Organ Mountains-Desert Peaks, Pacific Remote Islands, Rio Grande del Norte, and Rose Atoll National Monuments. Only the first two were advanced into the woodchipper.

This done, Zinke hopped astride his haggard horse, doffed his fresh-out-of-the-box black cowboy hat (backwards), and rode into ignominy as yet another member of Trump's cabinet hounded out of office by a litany of corruption charges.

As the year rolled onward, the noise generated by those of us working on the super-secret lawyers' report started to create its own sort of gravity. Among the results of this development is that Archaeology Southwest—one of the litigants in the case—bestowed upon me and Ben Bellorado the great privilege of co-editing a special triple-sized issue of *Archaeology Southwest Magazine* focused on Bears Ears.

In June of 2017, to help generate ideas about how the area was occupied and used at the landscape level during the full stretch of its history, Archaeology Southwest teamed up with FCM to sponsor and host an experts' gathering in Bluff. The cast was legendary. Outside of myself and Ben, it included Bill Lipe, R. G. Matson, Winston Hurst, Jonathan Till, Jay Willian, Fred Blackburn, Vaughn Hadenfeldt, Sally Cole, Bill Doelle, Don Simonis, Don Irwin—in short, every major character in this book who's still alive—and many others besides. Blackburn kept insisting that I take plenty of photos. "You'll never see anything like this again in your life," he assured me.

Absent from the meeting were then-current BLM archaeologists, who thought it might be wise not to be in a big room with a bunch of conservationists (arguably a good move considering how many of the locals already feel about them); the Indigenous archaeologists we'd invited, who simply couldn't squeeze it into their already bursting schedules; and a few cocky private-sector archaeologists who, presumably after gazing into a crystal ball, decided on their own that sensitive and legally protected information was going be thrown around like confetti. Which is awfully insulting to the local experts who did attend with the understanding that they, being *experts* and all, know what they should and should not talk about in public.

We convened for drinks and barbecue at Vaughn's house afterward, as often happens after big gatherings of interesting people in Bluff, and there I got to hear stories from some of the greatest figures in local science and adventure. I was especially enthralled with some of Fred Blackburn's tales involving early battles with looters in places like Mustang Mesa. This was when I discovered that looters in the 1970s and '80s liked to pose skulls near looted sites as a middle finger to archaeologists and law enforcement.

The meeting stretched through the entire weekend, and the resulting occupation maps became a prized highlight of the magazine. About halfway through the second day I had the honor of leading the segment on Research Priorities and Future Directions to generate ideas for research projects that FCM and other sponsors could fund, and I took the opportunity to tell the story of Trent and the Descending Sheep site from Glen Canyon. Laughter ensued.

Finally, near the end of the second day, Josh Ewing announced that we were going to talk about "monument and conservation topics." About a third of the attendees took their cue and walked out. As with the Indigenous community at the gathering in Monument Valley the year before, people who were opposed to the national monument itself but still wanted to take part in our massive research effort were not barred from attending.

Based on Zinke's conclusions—and, more extensively, pressure from the Utah delegation and the Sutherland Institute, a combination think tank and lobbyist farm whose operative goal seems to be keeping public lands out of public hands—Trump signed an executive order in January of 2017 reducing Grand Staircase-Escalante National Monument and *drastically* reducing Bears Ears National Monument. He flew to Salt Lake City to announce the monument reductions, standing before one of his typical gangs of rallying supporters, with an alternating set of Utah and US flags arranged regally on the steps behind him. You can see this in the press photos. What you can't see is the enormous crowd of protestors.

That very afternoon, outdoor industry leader Patagonia's website was slate black and emblazoned with the words: *The President Stole Your Land.* Underneath, in smaller letters: *In an illegal move, the president just reduced the size of Bears Ears and Grand*

Staircase-Escalante National Monuments. This is the largest elimination of protected land in American history. It was a bold and potent move for them to make, albeit a knee-jerk one that rubbed some people the wrong way.* Recreation titan REI followed suit, in a slightly more restrained manner, devoting a portion of its homepage to a statement about how they will "continue to advocate for the places we all love" despite the "loss of millions of acres of protected lands."

As for the reductions themselves: the revised boundary of Bears Ears is about fifteen percent of the 2016 one, and is comprised principally of a pair of management zones—one surrounding Indian Creek (the Indian Creek unit) and one surrounding Comb Wash and just enough of Cedar Mesa and Elk Ridge to include the actual Bears Ears themselves (the Shash Ja'a unit, after the Diné term for Bears Ears).

The new designation also excised tribal expertise from being a direct component of the monument's management, rubbing salt in the wound for the very people whose tireless work over several years represented the vanguard effort to get the place protected as a national monument in the first place.

First, the revised Bears Ears National Monument Advisory Committee, with twelve total seats, includes just two for "tribal interests" despite this being three fewer than the number of tribes in the Bears Ears Inter-Tribal Coalition. This, like the decision to give one of the tiny units a name derived from the language of just one tribe, is seen by a lot of critics as an effort to foment intertribal tension.

Second, the Bears Ears Commission, comprised of representatives from the five Coalition tribes, was written out of existence. Instead, the monument commission was remanufactured as the Shash Ja'a Commission, narrowing its influence exclusively

---

* Tribal members were particularly irate, since a whole bunch of presidents have stolen their land—usually in the name of development, but occasionally in the name of environmental preservation. Patagonia took the criticism face-on, to their immense credit, and they are now a sponsoring partner for both UDB and Natives Outdoors.

on that unit and cramming a seat for a San Juan County Commission appointee. There's no mention of an Indian Creek Commission at all.

From there, it gets a bit silly. President Obama's original proclamation includes the following: "Resources such as the Doll House Ruin in Dark Canyon Wilderness Area and the Moon House Ruin on Cedar Mesa allow visitors to marvel at artistry and architecture that have withstood thousands of seasons in this harsh climate."

Because of this, two even tinier units are included in Trump's reduced monument: a little circle around Moon House, and a little circle around Doll House. Seriously. The Trump administration left those two specific archaeological sites in the monument, even though both are completely surrounded by non-monument land, simply because they appeared by name in the original monument proclamation.

Or, to put that another way, they utilized privileged information to pinpoint the exact locations of two extremely sensitive and important cultural resources on a map, and then shared that map with the public.

Isn't *that* an ARPA violation?

The monument reductions also accompanied the death knell for something called the Master Leasing Plans, which were nipped in the bud the moment the Trump administration assumed power. The MLPs were an inventive but short-lived BLM mechanism for managing resource conflicts on public lands that include or are adjacent to uniquely sensitive areas—e.g., those that are veritably overflowing with archaeological sites. The idea was to stave off lawsuits over leasing in sensitive areas by getting out in front of them. The MLPs were designed to do this by supplementing standard management plans for such areas with an added decision-making tool that included authoritative scientific and cultural data. Collection and synthesis of those data fell to CRM contractors.

Thus it was that I learned what now comprises the bulk of what I know about the Bears Ears area as a result of being hired by SWCA Environmental Consultants to help generate a predictive model and associated report (called a Class I or "existing litera-ture" report) for the Moab-area MLP. It was a lengthy and exhaus-tive process, as well as a fun one. I'd been researching the Bears Ears area for about ten years at that point, mostly on my own, and now I was being paid to gather and synthesize materials about it. Some of those materials required adventurous efforts to find and access, including a few reports that I needed special gloves to read.

All that effort, and all the taxpayer money that paid for it, was swept off the table and into the trash by the Trump administration. Not surprisingly, the lawsuits that were supposed to be headed off by the MLPs started flooding in again, explosively so once the leasing process ramped up in the reduced monument areas.

As soon as this all happened, the lawsuit on which I'd been asked to work—one of five, in fact: three for Bears Ears, and two for Grand Staircase-Escalante—also roared off the launch-pad. Trump's team just as immediately filed a motion to have the case moved to a Utah court. It was the first of two fully expected actions on the defendants' part, the other being a motion to dis-miss on the grounds that nobody is actually hurt by the actions identified by the plaintiffs. Both motions were soundly rejected.

Less than a year later, the so-called Midterm Blue Wave resulted in Raúl Grijalva replacing PLI architect Rob Bishop as chair of the House Natural Resources Committee. It also included the election of Alexandria Ocasio-Cortez, of whom I'm a bit of a fan, as well as the first Native American women ever elected to Congress: Sharice Davids of Kansas, and Deb Haaland of New Mexico.

Haaland had barely settled into her chair before she teamed up with Arizona congressman Ruben Gallego on proposed legis-lation to restore tribal consultation to Bears Ears National Mon-ument and return it to its *original* original size—all 1.9 million acres first proposed by the Inter-Tribal Coalition back in 2015. She and the rest of the committee also conducted a full hearing on Zinke's suspicious monument review process, with a partic-ular focus on how energy lobbyists and developers were given very attentive treatment while tribal representatives and *over two million comments* from the American public were completely ignored.

Because the reductions in both the Bears Ears and Grand Staircase-Escalante cases took the form of new national monument units created in place of the originals, the principle legal argument centers upon whether doing so was a violation of the legal intent of the Antiquities Act or not. Scholars of environmental and natural resource law almost unanimously contend that it was, since the act specifies *only* the creation of units of protection—not their reduction or elimination. Others disagree, pointing out how the smaller units that replaced both monuments are indeed new creations.

The first inkling of how federal judges may themselves feel about the issue appeared rather serendipitously in March of 2019. Four years earlier, then-President Obama had used the Outer Continental Shelf Lands Act (OCSLA) to withdraw portions of Alaska's Beaufort and Chukchi Seas and canyon areas from oil and gas leasing for NEPA review. Trump reversed that with an executive order in April of 2017, and was—of course—immediately sued for doing so by a group called the League of Conservation Voters. On March 29, 2019, the US District Court for the District of Alaska overturned the executive order.

Here's the kicker: the court, in their ruling, made specific reference to the similarities between OCSLA and the Antiquities Act, noting that "[n]either of these laws explicitly granted revocation authority to the President."

Meanwhile, back in the Bears Ears area, a lawsuit over blatant gerrymandering that gave the slight Indigenous majority in San Juan County only about one-third of its voting power finally got its own day in court in late 2017. The result was federally mandated redistricting that was, in sum, not so blatantly prejudiced. San Juan County's finest fought back, of course, and the case ended up in the United States Court of Appeals for the Tenth Circuit, which upheld the assertion that the county had violated the equal protection clause of the Fourteenth Amendment and Section 2 of the Voting Rights Act by gerrymandering all of its Native residents into just one of three districts.

The fairer and more accurate voting districts resulted in election of two Native American candidates, Kenneth Maryboy and Willie Grayeyes, to the three-person county commission. One of their first official acts was shutting down the county's pricey legal attacks on Bears Ears National Monument.

How pricey, you ask? Subsequent investigations by friend and fellow author Zak Podmore, conducted on behalf of the *Salt Lake Tribune*, revealed that San Juan County had spent about half a million taxpayer dollars hiring a Louisiana-based law firm to lobby for Trump's monument reduction. They also spent almost as much trying (and failing) to gain right-of-way through Recapture Canyon, a controversial case where the BLM dragged its feet a little too long in deciding whether or not unregulated ATV usage should continue in a place full of fragile resources. The county was also ordered to pay $2.6 million in plaintiff's fees to the Navajo Nation as a required provision of the Voting Rights Act, after the federal courts ruled that overtly prejudiced gerrymandering is a no-no.

The sum of all this casts considerable doubt on San Juan County's supposed reputation of looking out for the best interests of its mostly rural white citizens, who didn't vote for any of these costs but now have to shoulder them.

The forces that gerrymandered San Juan County in the first place are not relenting, though. Despite the good will toward Indigenous Utahns that Brigham Young initially preached to his followers, some of their descendants hold dim views of Lamanites having a two-thirds majority in local politics regardless of how accurately it reflects local demographics. Defeated in the Court of Appeals for the Tenth Circuit, new strategies to reassert colonial dominance boil out of the mire almost daily. Don't ask me who's paying for them.

If the national monument controversy is ever totally resolved, I don't know if I'll still be alive to see it. I'm not even sure how long it will matter, given how global climate conditions—both literal and political—appear at times to be tilting. But it certainly matters now. In the hundred-plus years between passage of the Antiquities Act and today, Bears Ears is the only national monument created primarily as a result of efforts by Indigenous peoples. Its very existence is symbolic of their feelings about how special places need to be treated.

Its fate is symbolic of how everyone else feels about that.

Special places engender special amalgamations. That's a bit of a theme in areas like Bears Ears.

Thus it was that I, a native of New York—by way of New Orleans, Montana, Alaska, New Mexico, Texas, Vermont, Oregon, Arizona, and some other places I've forgotten—lugged a heavy backpack along the bottom of the deep and sinuous defile that is Grand Gulch, crown jewel of Cedar Mesa in the heart of Bears Ears, about a decade and a half ago. Crowds were thin, at the time, although thickening by the year.

Less than a decade later, the presence of those crowds would contribute heavily toward the rationale behind designation of a contentious national monument, one of a handful of rallying cries among the allies of people who first moved to have the place protected for very different reasons. I would be involved in that process, albeit in a tiny way; and, in a slightly larger way, I would also be involved in the battle to defend it.

All of which would have astounded the greenhorn grown-up Goth kid stumbling around the place for a blissful week, all those years ago, before heading back to his job as a bartender in Flagstaff.

The Bears Ears area is one of overlapping frontiers. Cultural juxtaposition and hybridization so thoroughly saturate the human history of the place that my own presence and involvement there is not a novelty so much as just another iteration of an ageless tradition. People gathered there from all over the western portion of the continent during the earliest-known era of human occupation. They did it again during the early Holocene, merging lifeways from the opposite poles of the Colorado Plateau into something uniquely local. Ancestral Pueblo and Fremont farmers, both of whom are ancestral to a great number of Bears

Ears-affiliated tribes, met up and exchanged seemingly everything but ceramics. They did so at least once more during Chaco's
monumental expansion. The rise and fall of Chaco engendered
yet more cultural coalescence as a result of still poorly understood relationships between the San Juan and Kayenta subregions
of the Pueblo world. It happened again when Ute, Paiute, and
Diné groups intermingled under unifying leaders like Posey and
K'aayélii against increasing numbers of common threats. And yet
again during the historic period of Euro-American occupation,
with religious and ribald elements creating the sort of dynamic
tension that inspires ballads.

And it happens still. I wrapped up my draft of this book while
attending and volunteering at the fifth annual Bears Ears Summer Inter-Tribal Gathering atop Elk Ridge. Utah Diné Bikéyah
organized the event, as they always do. Local conservation group
Friends of Cedar Mesa provided volunteer labor and facilitated
trash removal. Cowboys (real ones, riding real horses) wrangled
cattle in the meadow just to the south. The Skull Valley Goshute
Tribe donated enough bison for an enormous roast—served, of
course, with Four Corners potatoes. Dancers from tribes all across
the region came dressed in their respective regalia to show their
stuff. An artist and storyteller from Acoma named Waya'aisiwa
(aka Gary Keene) told the assembled crowd some of the greatest Coyote and Macaw stories I've ever heard. Kevin Madalena, a
jovial geologist and paleontologist from the Pueblo of Jemez, gave
a lecture on the articulation between geology, paleontology, and
traditional cultural knowledge. I answered questions about my
own research and the stuff I know about local history, although
mostly I listened.

On the last day, representatives from every one of these
groups took part in either a 5k or a 10k race. I overheard Catua
and Umtua mentioned a few times.

This type of community is a scary idea to some people. It's
often the basis of what we nowadays call *identity politics*, where
people vote or otherwise get political in sole accordance with
perceptions of their own and/or their favored candidates' cultural identity, and it's almost always a defensive reaction against

manufactured illusions of invasion. At best, that's how you get segregation. At worst: fascism and genocide.

The thing is, being members a community doesn't require a whole lot of sacrifice, and it certainly doesn't require sacrificing one's own cultural identity. On the contrary, a diverse array of individual and cultural contributions is exactly what makes a community great in the first place. The alternative is like a stew with just one ingredient.

Back in upstate New York, two of the schoolmates that I befriended just before taking off for New Orleans were of Peruvian descent, and they were fiercely proud of it. It was from them that I learned rapper Tupac Shakur's middle name was Amaru, honoring the famously rebellious last ruler of the Inca. My friends and their mother spoke Spanish at home, cooked a lot of Peruvian food, flew to Peru from time to time, and generally mixed Peruvian things into their otherwise fairly typical suburban American activities. But that never stopped them from being active and engaged participants in the same local community as the Irish-American family that lived on one side of them or the African-American family that lived on the other side—or, for that matter, my own Italo-English family a little ways off in the sticks.

In that sense, I suppose, the United States of America is itself the backwoods of everywhere. The borderlands phenomenon writ large. Far removed from the geopolitical capitals of England, Peru, Ireland, Africa, Italy, Spain…a community built from episodes of cultural collision and coalescence, like those of Bears Ears, with pizza for dinner and *Theobroma cacao* for dessert.

Nor has Bears Ears ceased contributing to the history and development of Southwest archaeology as a field of study.

The rich tapestry that is its human history has donated much to the growth of that study, which describes its own culture-phase sequence in a manner not entirely unlike that used by Kidder at Pecos—the Imperialist period, the Overtly Racist period, the

Compulsory Consultation period, etc. What comprises much of current archaeology in the United States as a whole is demonstrative of the Enthusiastic Consultation period, with researchers and CRM professionals engaging with Native American tribes because they want to rather than (or in addition to) being compelled to do so by law.

For archaeologists, Bears Ears represents a step beyond even that. The place and its legacy are all about healing, according to the Inter-Tribal Coalition, and I have found this to be very much the case. I certainly did a lot of healing there! But the sort of healing they're talking about transcends the individual. As their mission statement proclaims, it involves "healing of the land…where the traumas of the past can be alleviated." Archaeology can help with that process, but the sort that was practiced there in the past.

I'm not a bartender, anymore. At least not for pay. But I'd also be hard-pressed to call what I do "archaeology," these days—at least not in the classic American sense. "Conservation science" or "environmental regulatory compliance" comes closer to the mark. Helping to prevent the rich material history of places like Bears Ears from being wantonly destroyed by forces too ignorant, disinterested, or malicious to minimize impacts on their own. This is where I think people like me, wily pilgrims with sturdy backpacks and open weekends who geek out on the beauty of really old stuff, can do the greatest good on its behalf.

As for interpretation of what that really old stuff *means* to its creators and their descendants, that's a task better suited to them. The deep history of Bears Ears is mostly Indigenous, after all, so the future of its archaeology should be mostly Indigenous as well. As I pointed out in the Introduction, even the most scientifically factual information about Indigenous history and culture is not an endpoint of understanding—it's a starting point. Seeking the endpoint, like seeking the center place, involves journeying together.

If a symbolic correlate for that conceptual endpoint exists anywhere in the physical world, it's Bears Ears. A place where Western and Indigenous ways of knowing have the unique opportunity to converge in a dance of reciprocity, continuing a storied history of traditions and practices from different peoples blending into intricate patterns seen nowhere else in the world.

That's the real essence of the place, and has been since time began.

Afterword

I first met Ralph Burrillo in a setting that may be familiar for many archaeologists, a dark, dingy bar in downtown Flagstaff, Arizona, that I and other coworkers frequented when our days in the field were done. It so happened that Ralph was the bartender on the afternoon I walked in and eased into a barstool. I had recently finished my graduate studies at Northern Arizona University and was working as an archaeologist with the National Park Service around the Flagstaff region and other Southwestern locales. Armed with a freshly earned master's degree and a few years of field experience, I was eager to embark on the career path I had chosen: to be a "guardian of Hopi cultural history," or some other lofty ideal I had at that early stage of my career (I was in my mid-twenties).

As Ralph slid my beer across the bar top, I caught sight of a tattoo he had on his forearm. I recognized it as an ancestral Hopi pottery design. "Hmm, what's the story behind this Pahanna (whiteman)?" I thought to myself. My youthful eagerness to flex some cultural muscle as well as validate my new academic credentials sometimes led to instances where I felt the need to educate the world about Hopi culture. In addition, as a Hopi person, I had learned to be cautious about non-Indigenous people who seemed to want to delve into our Indigenous cultures, often with their own personal gain as priority. Let me explain.

The suspicious mind of the Hopi people is a result of over four hundred years of human rights abuses by foreign cultures, including genocide, prohibition of traditional language and traditions, and policies such as Manifest Destiny. The aura of doubt in the Hopi mindset would later be tested as academics and other curious minds showed up on our doorsteps wishing to study us (based on nineteenth-century assumptions of the "Vanishing Indian"). If you were an outsider wishing to come to Hopi and do research, you were sure to be met by a highly apprehensive Hopi people, perhaps even a slammed door in your face. As my uncle Leigh Kuwanwisiwma, the former director of the Hopi Cultural Preservation Office, once wrote, "Intruders are not welcome, especially if they come dressed as anthropologists!" Indeed, proving your sincerity amongst Hopi people does not come easy, and definitely not over a couple rounds at the pub.

Ralph and I talked a bit more and I left that brief encounter never expecting to hear from or talk with him ever again. Or so I thought.

Fast-forward a decade or so and I continued to work in archaeology, adding the role of river guide working on the San Juan River in Southeastern Utah. It was exciting for me, as a Hopi archaeologist, being introduced to this landscape as I explored the area. Every now and then an old-timer river guide would offer a clue like, "maybe you oughta go poke around 'such-and-such' canyon," which is how I first encountered the Procession Panel and other sites.

At this time social media was taking off and I was slowly drawn into that world, where I found a myriad of archaeology groups. As it turned out, Ralph and I happened to be members in one of these groups and one day, out of the blue, he sent me a message, although I did not remember his name and only vaguely remembered our encounter a decade prior. As we got reacquainted, I learned that Ralph also pursued his dream of a career in archaeology and was in the midst of his graduate studies, with his research focused in the Bears Ears region.

As I learned more of Ralph's studies, and that of his colleagues, many of whom I now work alongside, I began to see how their knowledge and expertise could assist the Hopi Tribe in some of our endeavors. I decided then I needed to keep talking to this guy. Thus began the odyssey that would draw us all together into a shared goal: that of preserving the culturally and archaeologically important landscape of the Bears Ears.

The advocacy work centered around Bears Ears National Monument (BENM) involves many different perspectives and histories. None more critical than the collaborative work ongoing between Indigenous nations and archaeologists. So how did it come to be that two groups, Indigenous and scientists, would be able to overcome a troubled past and find common ground?

For starters, that past is never forgotten. As Indigenous people we are reminded daily of the historical traumas that we have endured. We also accept that it is our responsibility to work to resolve and overcome these issues. We do so with the hopes that future generations can move forward without shouldering these burdens. When BENM was initially proposed, I viewed this as an opportunity to right some of the wrongs of the past. I am a firm believer that while we must acknowledge the negatives of history, we must also be proactive in establishing and maintaining new ways of cultural preservation. This includes advocating for the protection of our ancestral lands, no matter if they lie outside our modern reservation boundaries.

Among the difficulties to overcome and address is the stigma that is a result of historical interaction between Indigenous peoples and the scientific community. There are still lingering doubts by Indigenous people towards academic research. Especially if the process and goals appear to only benefit the researcher, with little to no attention placed on what Indigenous people are interested in learning about or preserving. With the work involving Bears Ears, Indigenous people are wholly expecting that traditional values and knowledge will be presented and considered as equal to that of scientific inquiry.

Just how are we accomplishing that? Currently in BENM you will find tribal members working alongside scientists documenting not just the archaeological record, but a wide spectrum of flora, fauna, geology, hydrology, and paleontology. In some cases, Indigenous people are the scientists, bringing with them their own cultural teachings, allowing scientific research to be analyzed and interpreted through an Indigenous lens. There are now

Indigenous archaeologists, paleontologists, botanists, and many other areas of expertise working to document and protect their cultural history in BENM. As Diné/Hopi documentarian Angelo Baca states, "The time of the Indian Expert is over. It's time for the Expert Indians!"

Although I cannot speak directly for the other tribal groups involved in this issue, I can offer some insight from the Hopi perspective about how this collaborative work enriches the understanding of our ancestral history in the BENM. One question I am always asked is how are modern Hopi people, whose current reservation lands are two hundred miles south of Bears Ears, connected to this landscape? To answer that question requires an in-depth understanding and explanation of both Hopi cultural knowledge and archaeological research of the region. Unfortunately, there isn't enough space here to delve into the full spectrum of these sets of knowledge.

The short version of Hopi oral histories states our ancestors once inhabited a wide geographic region of the Southwest, including the Bears Ears. The proof of our ancestral presence is found in the archaeological record in the form of ancestral villages ("ruins"), rock art, ceramics, textiles, lithics, burials, shrines and many other "artifacts." In the Hopi perspective, all of these are viewed as "footprints of the ancestors," left in place to one day prove our previous occupations in these areas. In doing so, these landscapes become holy ground where ancestors dwell.

Placing these traditional perspectives into a context that can be appreciated by those who are not Hopi or Indigenous can be daunting to say the least. Yet this is exactly what we hope to achieve through the respectful sharing of traditional perspectives with our non-Indigenous counterparts. This work is also a reminder of a strong precedent set by Indigenous collaborators. That is, any scientific research involving the culture and lifeways of our ancestors must include the participation of their modern descendants.

A formal proclamation issued by the Hopi Tribe, in support of the monument's establishment, echoes these sentiments:

The Hopi Tribe is pleased to see that the President's

Proclamation calls for direct tribal involvement with the long-term management of the monument. This co-management will ensure that Hopi concerns, traditional knowledge and use of the area is maintained and respected. The Hopi Tribe is dedicated to ensure that there will be a continuation of the unprecedented collaborative efforts that lead to this positive step in public lands conservation ("Hopi Tribe Celebrates Bears Ears National Monument Proclamation," December 29, 2016).

The number of Hopi people involved in this effort has also increased and our presence extends beyond the political and legal realms. In the fall of 2018, a group of Hopi representatives conducted the first official field visit to cultural sites in the Bears Ears region. These individuals represent an official group known as the Cultural Resource Advisory Task Team (CRATT), and the members represent all three Hopi mesas, the twelve villages, and various religious societies and clans. They provide direct Hopi perspectives and knowledge to a wide range of issues involving archaeology, repatriation, language preservation, ethnography, and land management, to name a few. They are officially sanctioned by the Hopi Cultural Preservation Office and Hopi Tribal Government.

For many of the CRATT members, this was their first time to experience this landscape in person, though they had knowledge of it passed through Hopi oral traditions. During this excursion, which some of us viewed as a "return migration," we toured a handful of selected archaeological sites and discussed Hopi history of the area and our perspectives of how we feel these sites should be managed. We document these discussions so that we may share this information with our non-Indigenous counterparts. We emphasize that this process requires a two-way dialogue.

Since then, additional field visits to the Bears Ears region by Hopi representatives have occurred, each one being greatly assisted through past and present efforts of researchers, conservation groups, and volunteers. The scientific data and other information collected by their work helps the tribes understand the linear progression of cultural development in the area. Other tribes are now conducting their own field visits, working to expand their cultural understandings in the area. We continue to walk in the footsteps of our ancestors.

As expected, this work is, and has not been, easy. There are issues that need to be continually addressed including blatant racism, political gerrymandering, and attempts to minimize tribal involvement in development of land management policy. We realize there will be disagreement as to how these landscapes should be best managed. We can agree to disagree on some points.

We have no romanticized, utopian ideal in mind, but a realistic endeavor to work together as equals and present a balanced story of Bears Ears. With any luck, those who come after us will learn and benefit from the work we do now. In order for that to happen, the integrity of collaboration must be maintained. We must communicate honestly. We must listen to one another with open hearts and minds. We owe it to this landscape to speak up and defend it with unified purpose.

I am thankful that many individuals and organizations have stepped up to assist the tribes in this endeavor. I am grateful for their counsel, their willingness to share information and listen to our concerns. Above all, I have gratitude for the respectful relationships that have developed as a result of our mutual efforts. To all of my friends and colleagues involved in this effort, I say Kwah-kway! (Thank you!)

Lyle Balenquah

Selected References and Recommended Reading

For reasons of readability, I chose to forego the academic practices of in-text, footnote, and endnote citations on the ground that this is a work of public scholarship in which those things act like speed bumps. However, when you chop out the narrative elements, direct quotes from individuals, and everything that I researched on my own, the information contained in this book adds up to a concise but comprehensive literature review. What follows is a selection of what I consider the most useful source materials.

Abbey, Edward (1984) *Beyond the Wall: Essays from the Outside.* Macmillan

--- (1985) *The Monkey Wrench Gang.* Dream Garden Press

Atkins, Victoria M., and Lisa McClanahan. (1990) Anasazi Basketmaker: Papers from the 1990 Wetherill-Grand Gulch *Symposium.* Bureau of Land Management

Beck, C., & Jones, G. T. (1997) The terminal Pleistocene/early Holocene archaeology of the Great Basin. *Journal of World Prehistory*, 11(2): 161-236

Blackburn, Fred M. and Ryan A. Williamson (1997) *Cowboys and Cave Dwellers: Basketmaker Archaeology in Utah's Grand Gulch.* School for American Research Press

Brinkley, Douglas (2009) *The Wilderness Warrior: Theodore Roosevelt and the Crusade for America.* Harper Collins

Bryson, Bill (1998) *A Walk in the Woods: Rediscovering America on the Appalachian Trail.* Random House

Burrillo, R. E. and Benjamin A. Bellorado, eds. (2017) Sacred and Threatened: Cultural Landscapes of Greater Bears Ears. *Archaeology Southwest Magazine*, 31(4) and 32(1)

Byers, David A. and Andrew Ugan (2005) Should We Expect Large Game Specialization in the Late Pleistocene? An Optimal Foraging Perspective. *Journal of Archaeological Science* 32(2): 1624-1640

Cameron, Catherine M. (2009) *Chaco and after in the northern San Juan: Excavations at the Bluff Great House.* University of Arizona Press

Childs, Craig (2007) *House of Rain: Tracking a Vanished Civilization across the American Southwest.* Little, Brown

Coe, Sophie D. and Michael D. Coe (2013) *The True History of Chocolate.* Thames & Hudson

Crown, Patricia (2016) Just Macaws: A Review for the US Southwest/Mexican Northwest. *Kiva*, 82(4): 331-363

Cordell, Linda S. (1984) *Prehistory of the Southwest.* Academic Press

Cuch, Forrest S. (2000) *History of Utah's American Indians.* University Press of Colorado

Dongoske, Kurt E.; Michael Yeatts, Roger Anyan, and Thomas J. Ferguson (1997) Archaeological cultures and cultural affiliation: Hopi and Zuni perspectives in the American Southwest. *American Antiquity*, 62(4): 600-608

Earle, Rebecca (2012) *The Body of the Conquistador: Food, Race and the Colonial Experience in Spanish America, 1492–1700.* Cambridge University Press

Erdoes, Richard and Alfonso Ortiz, eds. (1984) *American Indian Myths and Legends.* Pantheon

Frison, George (1978) *Prehistoric Hunters of the High Plains.* Academic Press

Geib, Phil R. (2000). Sandal types and Archaic prehistory on the Colorado Plateau. *American Antiquity* 65(3): 509-524

--- (1996) *Glen Canyon Revisited.* University of Utah Anthropological Papers No. 119

Geib, Phil R. and Dale Davidson (1994) Anasazi origins: A perspective from preliminary work at Old Man Cave. *Kiva*, 60(2): 191-202

Glowacki, Donna M. (2015) *Living and Leaving: A Social History of Regional Depopulation in Thirteenth-century Mesa Verde.* University of Arizona Press

Gulliford, Andrew (2011) The 1892 Illustrated American Exploring Expedition. *Utah Adventure Journal*, November 13

--- (2009) How One "Girl Ranger" Helped Save the Southwest. *High Country News*, April 14

Huckell, Bruce B. (1996) The Archaic Prehistory of the North American Southwest. *Journal of World Prehistory*, 10(3): 305-373

Hurst, Winston (2016) "Not on Board with the Bears Ears Crusade." The Bill Lane Center for the American West, Stanford University Website

--- (2011) A Tale of Two Villages: Basketmaker III Communities in San Juan County, Utah. *Blue Mountain Shadows: The Magazine of San Juan County History*, Volume 44: 7-18

--- (2011) Collecting This, Collecting That: Confessions of a Former, Small-Time Pothunter. *Blue Mountain Shadows: The*

Magazine of San Juan County History, Volume 44: 46-18

Hurst, Winston and Jay Willian (2011) Ute and Navajo Archaeology in the Comb Ridge Area. *Blue Mountain Shadows: The Magazine of San Juan County History*, Volume 44: 46-18

Jennings, Jesse D. (1966) *Glen Canyon: A Summary.* University of Utah Press

Johnson, George (2008) "Vanished: A Pueblo Mystery." *The New York Times*, April 8.

Johnston, Barbara Rose, ed. (2007) *Half-Lives and Half-Truths: Confronting the Legacies of the Cold War.* School for Advanced Research, Resident Scholar Book

Judd, Neil M. (1968) *Men Met Along the Trail: Adventures in Archaeology.* University of Oklahoma Press

Kantner, John (2004) *Ancient Puebloan Southwest.* Cambridge University Press

Kidder, A. V. (1927) Southwestern Archaeological Conference. *Science* New Series 66(1716): 489-91

King, Thomas F. (2013) *Cultural Resource Laws and Practice.* Rowman & Littlefield

--- (2002) *Thinking about Cultural Resource Management: Essays from the Edge.* Rowman Altamira

Knipmeyer, James H. (2006). *In Search of a Lost Race: The Illustrated American Exploring Expedition of 1892.* Xlibris

Leake, Harvey (2018) The Gentleman Explorer: Charles Bernheimer and his Canyon Country Expeditions... *The Canyon Country Zephyr*, August 1

Lekson, Stephen H. (2018) *A Study of Southwestern Archaeology.* University of Utah Press

--- (2009) *A History of the Ancient Southwest.* School for American Research Press

--- (1999) *The Chaco meridian: Centers of Political Power in the Ancient Southwest.* Rowman Altamira

Lipe, William D. and Donald J. Rommes (2013) *Cliff Dwellers of Cedar Mesa - The Culture, Sites, and Exodus of the Ancestral Puebloans.* Canyonlands Natural History Association

Lipe, William D., ed. (2014) Tortuous and Fantastic: Cultural and Natural Wonders of Greater Cedar Mesa. *Archaeology Southwest Magazine*, 28(3-4)

--- (1989) Social Scale of Mesa Verde Kivas. In *The Architecture of Social Integration in Prehistoric Pueblos*, edited by William D. Lipe and Michelle Hegmon. Occasional Papers of the Crow Canyon Archaeological Center, No. 1: 53-71

Lipe, William D.; Mark Varien and Richard H. Wilshusen, eds. (1999). *Colorado prehistory: A Context for the Southern Colorado River basin*. Colorado Council of Professional Archaeologists

Louderback, Lisbeth A. (2014) The Ecology of Human Diets during the Holocene at North Creek Shelter, Utah. Unpublished Doctoral Dissertation, University of Washington Department of Anthropology

Madsen, David B. (1989) *Exploring the Fremont*. University of Utah Occasional Papers No. 8. Utah Museum of Natural History

Madsen, David B. and Steven R. Simms (1998) The Fremont Complex: A Behavioral Perspective. *Journal of World Prehistory* 12(3): 255–336

Mann, Charles C. (2005) *1491: New Revelations of the Americas Before Columbus*. Alfred a Knopf Incorporated

Matson, R.G. and Brian Chisholm (1991) Basketmaker II subsistence: Carbon isotopes and other dietary indicators from Cedar Mesa, Utah. *American Antiquity* 56(3): 444-459

Matson, R.G. (2016) The Origins of Southwestern Agriculture. University of Arizona Press

Martin, Paul S. (1973) The Discovery of America. *Science* 179: 969-974

McManamon, Francis P., ed. (2017) *New Perspectives in Cultural Resource Management*. Routledge

McNitt, Frank (1990) *Navajo Wars: Miltary Campaigns, Salve Raids, and Reprisals*. University of New Mexico Press

--- (1966) *Richard Wetherill: Anasazi*. University of New Mexico Press

McPherson, Robert S. (2009) *Comb Ridge: The Ethnohistory of a*

Rock. Utah State University Press

--- (2001) *The Northern Navajo Frontier 1860-1900: Expansion through Adversity.* Utah State University Press

--- (1995) *A History of San Juan County: In the Palm of Time.* Utah Centennial County History Series, Utah State Historical Society

Meltzer, David J. (2010) *First Peoples in a New World: Colonizing Ice Age America.* University of California Press

Moseley, Michael E.; Donna J. Nash, Patrick Ryan Williams, Susan D. DeFrance, Ana Miranda, and Mario Ruales (2005) Burning down the brewery: Establishing and evacuating an ancient imperial colony at Cerro Baúl, Peru. *Proceedings of the National Academy of Sciences* 102(48): 17264-17271

Piper, Matthew (2016) "Before a packed meeting, Interior Secretary Jewell sees harm visitors are causing at proposed Bears Ears monument." *The Salt Lake Tribune,* July 18

Podmore, Zak (2020) "Sutherland Institute's campaign against Bears Ears was relentless, effective and mostly funded by a tight circle of activists." *The Salt Lake Tribune,* January 12

--- (2019) "San Juan County Commission to pay $2.6 million in plaintiff fees for voting rights case." *The Salt Lake Tribune,* September 24

Prudden, T. Mitchell (1903) The Prehistoric Ruins of the San Juan Watershed in Utah, Arizona, Colorado, and New Mexico. *American Anthropologist* 5(2): 224-288

Reed, Paul F. (2008) *Chaco's Northern Prodigies: Salmon, Aztec, and the ascendancy of the Middle San Juan region after AD, 1100.* University of Utah Press

--- (2000) *Foundations of Anasazi Culture: The Basketmaker-Pueblo Tradition.* University of Utah Press

Reed, Paul F., ed. (2018) Chacoan Archaeology in the 21st Century. *Archaeology Southwest Magazine* 32 (2&3)

Richardson, Elmo R. (1965) Federal Park Policy in Utah: The Escalante National Monument Controversy of 1935-1940. *Utah Historical Quarterly* 33(2): 109-133

Roberts, David (2008) *The Pueblo Revolt: The Secret Rebellion that drove the Spaniards out of the Southwest.* Simon and Schuster

--- (1997) *In Search of the Old Ones: Exploring the Anasazi World of the Southwest.* Simon and Schuster

Rosen, Jeffrey (2010) "The Web Means the End of Forgetting." *The New York Times,* July 21

Sherman, Sean and Beth Dooley (2017) *The Sioux Chef's Indigenous Kitchen.* University of Minnesota Press

Simms, Steven R. (2016) *Ancient Peoples of the Great Basin and Colorado Plateau.* Routledge

Sjogren, Morgan (2019) Writing on the Wall. *The Gulch,* Issue 10

--- (2018) *The Best Bears Ears National Monument Hikes.* Colorado Mountain Club

Smith, Christopher (1994) "Cows are Evicted from Utah." *High Country News,* January 24

Spangler, Jerry L.; Andrew T. Yentsch, and Rachelle Green (2010) *Farming and Foraging on the Southwestern Frontier: An Overview of Previous Research of the Archaeological and Historical Resources of the Greater Cedar Mesa Area.* Antiquities Section Selected Papers, Vol. IX, No. 18. Utah Division of State History, Salt Lake City

Speth, John D.; Khori Newlander, Andrew A. White, Ashley K. Lemke, and Lars E. Anderson (2013) Early Paleoindian Big-Game Hunting in North America: Provisioning or Politics? *Quaternary International* 285: 111 – 139

Sucec, Rosemary (2019) Indigenous Landscapes of the Grand Staircase-Escalante National Monument. *Archaeology Southwest Magazine,* 33(1&2): 18-21

--- (2006) *Fulfilling Destinies, Sustaining Lives: The Landscape of Waterpocket Fold: An Ethnographic Overview and Assessment of American Indian Histories and Resource Uses Within Capitol Reef National Park, Utah, and on Lands Surrounding it.* US National Park Service

Topping, Gary (1997) *Glen Canyon and the San Juan Country.* University of Idaho Press

Trigger, Bruce G. (1989) *A History of Archaeological Thought.*

Cambridge University Press

Turner, Allen C. and Robert C. Euler (1983) A Brief History of the San Juan Paiute Indians of Northern Arizona. *Journal of California and Great Basin Anthropology* 5(1/2): 199-207

Warner, Ted J., ed. (1995) *The Domínguez-Escalante Journal: Their Expedition Through Colorado, Utah, Arizona, and New Mexico in 1776.* Translated by Fray Angelico Chavez. University of Utah Press

Watson, Adam S.; Stephen Plog, Brendan J. Culleton, Patricia A. Gilman, Steven A. LeBlanc, Peter M. Whiteley, Santiago Claramunt, and Douglas J. Kennett (2015) Early procurement of scarlet macaws and the emergence of social complexity in Chaco Canyon, NM. *Proceedings of the National Academy of Sciences* 112(27): 8238-8243

Wilkerson, Charles F. (1996) Home Dance, the Hopi, and Black Mesa Coal: Conquest and Endurance in the American Southwest. *Brigham Young University Law Review*, 449

Willey, Gordon R. and Phillip Phillips (1958) *Method and Theory in American Archaeology.* University of Chicago Press

Wilshusen, Richard H.; Gregson Schachner, and James R. Allison (2012) *Crucible of Pueblos: The Early Pueblo Period in the Northern Southwest.* Cotsten Institute of Archaeology Press, Monograph 71, University of California Press

Wilshusen, Richard H.; William D. Lipe, and Mark Varien (1999) *Colorado Prehistory: A Context for the Southern Colorado River Basin.* Colorado Council of Professional Archaeologists

Windes, Tom (2006) Chacoan Ecology and Economy. In *The Archaeology of Chaco Canyon: An Eleventh-Century Pueblo Regional Center*, edited by Steve Lekson. School for Advanced Research, Advanced Seminar Series

Woodbury, Richard B. (1979) Zuni Prehistory and History to 1850. In *Handbook of the North American Indians*, edited by Alfonso Ortiz, pp. 467-473. Handbook of North American Indians, Vol. 9, William C. Sturtevant, general editor. Smithsonian Institution, Washington, D.C.

Worley-Hood, Graham and Gavin Noyes (2013) Land and Resource Use of the Utah Navajo. Ethnographic Literature Review, MS on file with Monticello, Utah Bureau of Land Management

Zwinger, Ann (1986) *Wind in the Rock: The Canyonlands of Southeastern Utah.* University of Arizona Press

About the Author

R. E. BURRILLO is an archaeologist, author, and conservation advocate. His writing has appeared in *Archaeology Southwest, Colorado Plateau Advocate, The Salt Lake Tribune, Blue Mountain Shadows, The Moab Times, The Navajo-Hopi Observer, The Archaeological Record, Southwestern Lore, Flag Live, The San Juan Record*, and *Kiva*. He splits his time between Salt Lake City, Utah, and Flagstaff, Arizona.

This book was made possible by a grant from Patagonia and a generous gift from the Sam and Diane Stewart Family Foundation. Torrey House Press is supported by Back of Beyond Books, the King's English Bookshop, Jeff Adams and Heather Adams, the Jeffrey S. and Helen H. Cardon Foundation, Diana Allison, Jerome Cooney and Laura Storjohann, Robert Aagard and Camille Bailey Aagard, Heidi Dexter and David Gens, Kirtly Parker Jones, the Utah Division of Arts & Museums, Utah Humanities, the National Endowment for the Humanities, the National Endowment for the Arts, and Salt Lake County Zoo, Arts & Parks. Our thanks to individual donors, subscribers, and the Torrey House Press board of directors for their valued support.

Printed in the USA
CPSIA information can be obtained
at www.ICGtesting.com
JSHW021736110923
48263JS00005B/12